Economic Evolution, Learning, and Complexity

Uwe Cantner · Horst Hanusch
Steven Klepper (Eds.)

Economic Evolution, Learning, and Complexity

With 85 Figures
and 35 Tables

Springer-Verlag Berlin Heidelberg GmbH

PD Dr. Uwe Cantner
Prof. Dr. Horst Hanusch
WISO-Fakultät
University of Augsburg
Universitätsstrasse 16
86135 Augsburg
Germany

Prof. Dr. Steven Klepper
Department of Social and Decision Sciences
Carnegie Mellon University
Porter Hall 208
Pittsburgh, PA 15213-3890
USA

Some of the contributions have been published in
"Journal of Evolutionary Economics, Vol. 9, No. 1, 1999."

ISBN 978-3-642-63323-2

Library of Congress Cataloging-in-Publication Data
Economic evolution, learning, and complexity / Uwe Cantner, Horst Hanusch, Steven Klepper, eds.
p. cm.
ISBN 978-3-642-63323-2 ISBN 978-3-642-57646-1 (eBook)
DOI 10.1007/978-3-642-57646-1
1. Evolutionary economics. I. Cantner, Uwe. II. Hanusch, Horst. III. Klepper, Steven.
HB97.3.E257 2000
330–dc21

Originally published by Physica-Verlag Heidelberg in 2002
Softcover reprint of the hardcover 1st edition 2002

Cover design: Erich Kirchner, Heidelberg

SPIN 10755398 88/2202-5 4 3 2 1 0 – Printed on acid-free paper

Contents

Introduction

The twelve papers in this collection grew out of the workshop on "Economic Evolution, Learning, and Complexity" held at the *University of Augsburg*, Augsburg, Germany on May 23-25, 1997. The Augsburg workshop was the second of two events in the Euroconference Series on Evolutionary Economics, the first of which was held in Athens, Greece in September 1993. A special issue of the *Journal of Evolutionary Economics* (1993(4)) edited by *Yannis Katsoulacos* on "Evolutionary and Neoclassical Perspectives on Market Structure and Economic Growth" contains selected papers from the Athens conference. The Athens conference explored neoclassical and evolutionary perspectives on technological competition and increasing returns. It helped to identify the distinguishing features of evolutionary scholarship. The Augsburg workshop was more oriented toward exploring methodological issues in evolutionary and related scholarship. A number of the papers employed new methods, such as genetic programming and experimental analysis, some developed new econometric techniques or raised new empirical issues in evolutionary economics, and some relied on simulation techniques. Twelve papers covering a range of areas were selected for this collection.

The papers address central issues in evolutionary and Schumpeterian accounts of industrial competition, learning, and innovation. The processes studied include:

- how individuals and firms with limited computational ability and information learn and innovate
- the way market structure and stockholder valuation of firms evolve as new industries develop
- the role of academic scientists in the startup of new commercial ventures
- the interaction between innovation and competition
- the identification of structural change in diffusion processes following a logistic growth pattern
- the measurement of variety and technological evolution
- the relationship between national income growth and technological change
- the microeconomic forces of innovation and investment fostering macroeconomic growth

- the role and effects of technology policy in evolutionary environments.

Reflecting the diversity of work in evolutionary scholarship, a range of methodologies are employed in the papers, including simulation, experiments, and econometric analysis. Three of the twelve papers bring new data to bear on the questions analyzed, four analyze patterns of complex economic systems from computer simulation runs, three introduce new empirical methodologies suitable to evolutionary economics, one is an experimental study on learning behavior, and another is one of the first attempts to test basic evolutionary dynamics. Some of the papers use well established models to tackle new questions and problems. Others introduce entirely new approaches, which the authors indicate are still in a state of infancy and await further development. Each paper is briefly described below. We divided them into studies concerned with: *Oligopoly and Learning*; *Industry Studies*; *Econometric and Empirical Techniques*; *Growth, Human Capital and Innovation*; and *Governmental Learning and Policy.*

I Oligopoly and Learning

The first group of papers focuses on learning in oligopolistic markets. They explore mechanisms of learning in situations involving heterogeneous actors with imperfect knowledge and limited capabilities.

In chapter 1, *Giovanni Dosi*, *Luigi Marengo*, *Andrea Bassanini*, and *Marco Valente* consider how behavioral norms can emerge from simple, rule-based behavior. They consider the evolution of firm pricing in an oligopoly model in which industry demand and firm costs vary stochastically and firm market shares evolve based on relative firm prices. Firms set prices by choosing among simple pricing rules according to their past profitability. Using genetic programming, they show that if new rules emerge from mutation and agents stochastically change their rules over time, then pricing patterns emerge that resemble well-known norms such as markup pricing and tit-for-tat. These patterns reflect little of the strategic interaction among oligopolists that shapes game-theoretic predictions of oligopolistic pricing. Dosi et al. find that the more complex the market, the greater the tendency for the simulated pricing patterns to reflect simple norms. To the extent that popular norms can be given a secure foundation in human decision making, they can provide a useful alternative characterization of behavior to traditional optimizing models that abstract from the limited knowledge and capabilities of decision makers.

In chapter 2, *Rosemarie Nagel* and *Nick Vriend* probe experimentally the kinds of rules and learning procedures that lie at the heart of the norms analyzed by Dosi et al. The oligopoly model they consider shares a number of features with the setting which Dosi et al. simulate. Most importantly, it is difficult for decision makers to understand their environment because they are not informed about the choices of their rivals nor about how their choices and those of their rivals affect the demand for their output. They can, however, make inferences about both the process governing demand and the behavior of their rivals from how they fare in repeated plays of the game. Nagel and Vriend explore how well choices over time can be explained by a simple model in which players adjust their choices toward ones that worked best or could have worked better (if calculable) in recent plays of the game. Although subjects display considerable heterogeneity in their actual adjustment strategies that appears to be related to their initial choices and their perceptions about the experimental setup, they find that such a model can explain average choices quite well. Consistent with the findings of Dosi et al., this suggests that simple behavioral rules can provide a useful characterization of aggregate patterns when the environment is challenging for decision makers to understand.

Chapter 3 by *Uwe Cantner*, *Horst Hanusch* and *Andreas Pyka* is concerned with technological spillovers and learning in oligopolistic markets composed of heterogeneous firms. The firms differ in terms of their capital-labor ratio and in the productivity of capital and labor. Investments in R&D yield stochastic improvements in the productivity of capital and labor. Some firms also conduct R&D to enhance their ability to learn from the successful innovative activities of their competitors. Industry evolution is simulated under different conditions. For firms that devote all their R&D to improving their own labor and capital productivity, the direction of technological progress in terms of whether it is relatively labor or capital saving is determined by stochastic factors. In contrast, when firms invest to learn from their rivals, an orderly process of technological change occurs as the technological choices of better performing firms are imitated. This results from an unintended collective process fed by cross-fertilization. In this case, lasting changes in the direction of progress occur only when firms use similar production techniques and cross-fertilization effects are negligible. Furthermore, when appropriability conditions are weaker, allowing for greater R&D spillovers, and oligopolistic competition is more intense, investing to learn from rivals yields a greater return and firms that engage in such investments eventually overtake those that do not. Thus, with technological heterogeneity and stochastic returns to R&D, a strategy of devoting some R&D to being able to learn from rivals may prove superior.

II Industry Studies

The second group of papers focuses on the evolution of specific industries in the United States and in Italy. The contributions in chapter 4 and 5 look at two major industries in the United States, automobiles and biotechnology, that are at very different stages in their evolution. Both started with a large number of competitors. While the biotechnology industry is still in its infancy and continues to be populated by a large number of firms, the U.S. automobile industry evolved to be a tight oligopoly dominated by three firms. Chapter 6 considers the evolution of the Italian steel industry in the period 1988-1996 when the industry was quite mature and composed of a substantial number of competitors.

In chapter 4, *Marianna Mazzucato* and *Willi Semmler* study the evolution in the U.S. automobile industry of firm market shares and stockholder valuation of firms using data they collected for publicly traded automobile firms on market share, stock price, earnings, and dividends. They probe the connection between the volatility of firm market shares and a phenomenon known as excess volatility, which is the tendency for stock prices to vary considerably more than dividends and earnings, a pattern inconsistent with modern finance theories. Schumpeterian life-cycle models of industry evolution predict a decline in the volatility of firm market shares over time, which they find occurred in automobiles. They also find a decline in excess volatility over time for most firms. This suggests that excess volatility may be fundamentally related to uncertainty about firm prospects, which declines over time as industries evolve through predictable stages. Thus, not only real but also financial patterns may be illuminated by Schumpeterian accounts of industry evolution.

Reflecting the early stage of evolution of the biotechnology industry, in chapter 5 *David Audretsch* and *Paula Stephan* focus on the factors influencing the startup of new firms. They also use a life-cycle perspective, applied to academic scientists, to explore the incentives for academic scientists to commercialize new knowledge through startup ventures. For all U.S. biotechnology IPOs between March 1990 and November 1992, they trace the career paths of founders with a Ph.D. or M.D., half of which came from academia. Life-cycle theories predict that academic scientists involved in startups will be older and have more cited publications than nonacademic scientific founders, reflecting greater incentives for academic than nonacademic scientists to establish their reputation at young ages through publications. Audretsch and Stephan find that this holds not only for academic versus non academic scientific founders but also for academic founders who maintain their academic positions versus those that work full time for their startup. These patterns suggest that the varying incentives and opportunities of scientists shape the kinds of arrangements biotechnology startups make with their scientific founders. No doubt this has facilitated the commercialization of academic knowledge that has played a prominent role in the early success of the U.S. biotechnology industry.

Chapter 6 by *Mario Calderini* and *Stan Metcalfe* explores evolutionary dynamics among firms in a subsector of the Italian steel industry between 1988 and 1996. An evolutionary model based on replicator dynamics is developed to account for industry unit cost changes over time. Firms are assumed to differ in terms of their unit costs at any given moment and to experience different unit cost changes over time from innovation. Market selection operates through replicator dynamics, which causes demand to shift over time to lower-priced firms, and by firms desiring to grow according to their price-cost margins. This yields an equation relating changes in industry unit cost to variation across firms in both their contemporaneous unit costs and to changes in their unit costs from innovation. Accounting data for larger Italian firms producing a similar set of steel products are used to test the model. Assuming that selection forces work comparably over time, the model accounts well for industry unit cost changes except for 1994 and 1995 when the Italian steel industry experienced intense merger and acquisition activity. Generalizing the model to allow for such changes by introducing entry and exit does not improve its explanatory power. Most importantly, the framework developed by Metcalfe and Calderini shows how firm data can be used to test models of industrial competition based on replicator dynamics.

III Econometrics and Empirical Techniques in Evolutionary Economics

The third group of papers uses novel statistical methodologies to address particular issues in evolutionary analysis. One set of methodologies is used to detect structural change in an evolutionary process. A second set of methodologies is used to measure how variety, a central element in evolutionary theories, changes over time as industries evolve.

In chapter 7, *John Foster* and *Philip Wild* develop a new econometric methodology to detect structural evolutionary change in a process following a logistic diffusion growth path. Diffusion processes are often well approximated by a logistic function, but if they are shaped primarily by evolutionary rather than equilibrating forces then they will display distinctive oscillatory behavior about a logistic path as they approach saturation. Foster and Wild show how moving spectral methods can be used to detect such a pattern in the residuals of a logistic diffusion model even when conventional econometric tests would fail to reveal it. They apply their methods to the penetration of Building Societies in the retail deposit market in Australia. The path in these deposits is well approximated by an augmented logistic diffusion model, which allows both the diffusion rate and capacity limit of the model to be influenced by exogenous forces. Although conventional residual tests are supportive of the model, the proposed moving window spectral techniques indicate a significantly different residual structure as the process nears saturation than during its early history. As expected, the later period is characterized by more prominent higher frequency oscillations and a greater residual variance, suggestive of structural evolutionary change. Thus, the proposed techniques provide a distinctive lens to explore the role of evolutionary forces in diffusion processes following a logistic growth path.

Brian Morgan and *John Foster* pursue an alternative approach to handle structural change in a logistic diffusion process in chapter 8. They assume that the logistic diffusion process is deterministic, but the parameters of the process may vary over time. They represent this system using fuzzy regression. This approach allows the coefficients of the regression to vary over observations according to joint distribution that is based on fuzzy set representations. After a brief introduction to fuzzy set theory and fuzzy regression models, they use fuzzy regression to estimate the logistic diffusion model as applied to the Australian retail deposit market in Chapter 7. Their estimates of the most likely values for each of the regression coefficients agree closely with conventional ordinary least-squares estimates of the coefficients. Local parameter corrections which reflect how each parameter varies over time indicate considerable initial parameter variation, which subsequently subsides but later rises sharply after bank deregulation in Australia. They interpret the nature of the variation of the parameters as reflective of self organization theory; initial turmoil associated with opportunity-taking and macroscopic growth gives way to greater rigidity during the saturation phase of the diffusion process, followed by micro-breakdowns in the diffusion process resulting from bank deregulation. The complementary perspectives provided by the fuzzy regression and spectral methods of Chapter 7 suggest the use of both approaches to detect evolutionary structural change.

The contribution in chapter 9 by *Koen Frenken*, *Paolo Saviotti*, and *Michel Trommetter* is also concerned with the measurement of evolutionary change. One of the key elements of evolutionary theories is the diversity of product offerings. Two complementary approaches to measuring diversity are considered. One approach is based on entropy methodology. It employs a measure that reflects both the number of distinct product classes and the dispersion of product offerings over the classes. The second approach is based on Weitzman's (1992) diversity measure. It employs a measure that reflects the distance between products based on their characteristics, and can be applied to both discrete and continuous product characteristics using different distance measures. The two approaches are applied to new product offerings in aircraft and helicopters to assess whether major innovations led to the emergence of dominant designs that reduced diversity, as conjectured in some theories of industrial evolution. Both approaches reflect similar patterns. In helicopters diversity did appear to decline after the introduction of the twin turboshaft design of Kaman in 1954. Diversity similarly declined in aircraft after the introduction of the famed DC-3 by Douglas in 1936, but it later increased after the development of the jet engine. The two approaches are also used to develop a more refined characterization of how diversity changed over time that provides further insight into the technological evolution of the two products.

IV Growth, Human Capital and Innovation

The fourth group of papers deals with macroeconomic growth. During the 1980s growth theory attracted renewed interest from many perspectives. In 1982, Richard Nelson and Sidney Winter presented an evolutionary model of competition and innovation to explain growth regularities. Further progress on the microfoundations of growth occurred in the 1980s with the emergence of the New Growth Theory (e.g., Romer (1986, 1990), Lucas (1988)) and later Schumpeterian Growth Theory (e.g., Dinopoulos (1994)). The contributions in this group explore the microfoundations of growth and probe the empirical basis for Schumpeterian growth theory.

In chapter 10, *Elias Dinopoulos* and *Peter Thompson* probe empirically the determinants of national income growth. They reevaluate the fit of the augmented Solow growth model, which relates the national level of income per capita to the common expected level of technology in all countries, the rate of population growth, and the shares of GNP devoted to physical and human capital investment. Mankiw, Romer, and Weil's (1992) estimates of the model using the secondary school rate as a measure of the human capital saving rate indicate that the model performs impressively, accounting for three-quarters of the international variation in income per capita and yielding plausible estimates of factor shares. Dinopoulos and Thompson reestimate the model treating the secondary school rate as a measure of the level (not the savings rate) of human capital and also use two alternative, more precise human capital measures in place of the secondary school rate. The new estimates using the secondary school rate reject the overidentifying restriction implied by the model, while the estimates corresponding to the new human capital measures imply implausible factor share estimates. An alternative, Schumpeterian growth model is estimated. While this model incorporates an exogenous rate of growth, in contrast to the Solow growth model it allows country technology levels to vary according to the endowment of human capital per effective worker. Using the new human capital measures, this model yields plausible parameter estimates, supporting the Schumpeterian characterization that technology differences are a key source of the large and persistent international variations in income per capita.

In chapter 11, *Gunnar Eliasson* and *Erol Taymaz* analyze the microeconomic determinants of national growth in an evolutionary, micro-based model of national growth. They exploit the MOSES framework, a simulation model composed of 11 sectors of heterogeneous firms that is calibrated for the Swedish economy. It was introduced by Eliasson in the late 1970s and further developed with a number of collaborators as the Knowledge Based Information Economy and the Experimentally Organized Economy. Three mechanisms of the model that affect the rate of growth are analyzed: entry, labor market reallocation, and exit. The extent to which these mechanisms are operative determines how flexibly the economy responds to unanticipated events. Eliasson and Taymaz analyze how each of the mechanisms affects national growth under two alternative regimes concerning unanticipated changes in foreign prices. Simulation experiments show that when the economy is subject to greater unanticipated changes in foreign prices, greater flexibility in terms of allowing for entry and faster exit promotes national growth, but faster labor market reallocation does not. Alternatively, when foreign prices are more stable, faster exit and labor market reallocation compromise national growth whereas allowing for entry promotes growth. Thus, modeling the microeconomic foundations of growth reveals that greater economic flexibility is not unequivocally advantageous, especially in more stable environments.

V Governmental Learning and Policy

In the last section, technology policy in an evolutionary context characterized by uncertainty, imperfect information, and nonequilibrium dynamics is tackled. The normative neoclassical account based on market failure analysis cannot accommodate these circumstances (Metcalfe (1995)). Policy needs to preserve technological diversity up to the point where enough information can be gathered to intervene in favor of a specific beneficial technology. Policy making thus becomes a matter of dynamic learning and managing innovations rather than correcting traditional market failures. Consequently, technological development and policy intervention become interrelated, opening the possibility of policy failure.

In chapter 12, *Gilbert Laffond*, *Jacques Lesourne*, and *Francois Moreau* analyze the ability of regulation to promote the use of environmentally friendly technologies when uncertainty about the environmental risks and relative costs of competing technologies changes over time. A simulation model in which the government regulates three competing technologies with different costs and environmental risks is analyzed. The technology with the least environmental risk is initially the most costly but due to learning and scale economies its relative costs fall over time if it captures a sufficiently large share of the market. In each period, the demand for the three technologies is based on their relative costs and random factors, and new, noisy information is generated each period about the environmental risks of the three technologies. Regulators can influence the competition among the technologies through taxation, which alters the relative costs and thus market shares of the technologies, and through prohibition of any of the technologies. Generally, the faster regulators assimilate new information about the environmental risks of the competing technologies then the greater the chance of the least environmentally risky technology dominating the market. However, if tax rates are high or if regulators are quick to prohibit technologies in response to (noisy) information about their environmental risks, then faster assimilation of new information can actually make it less likely that the least environmentally risky technology prevails. Thus, to promote the use of environmentally friendly technologies policy makers have to steer a careful course between responding rapidly to noisy information and responding stringently to the information.

Final Remarks

The twelve papers convey the excitement and promise of recent evolutionary and Schumpeterian scholarship in economics. A great deal of stimulating work is being done. Indeed, many other stimulating papers employing a wide range of methodologies were presented at the Augsburg workshop. We hope this collection raises even more interest in evolutionary economics, provides some suggestions for future research directions, and initiates a lively discussion on the issues raised in the 12 chapters.

Last, we want to thank the financial sponsors of the workshop for their support and a few individuals whose help was indispensable. The workshop was made possible by funding from the European Union's *Human Capital and Mobility Program* for the *Euroconference on Evolutionary Economics* and from local donors University of Augsburg, Albert Leimer Stiftung (Augsburg), Bayer AG (Leverkusen), BÖWE Systec AG (Augsburg), Daimler Benz AG (Stuttgart), Haindl Papier GmbH (Augsburg), Höchst AG (Gersthofen), Kreissparkasse Augsburg, Phoenix Pharmahandel GmbH (Augsburg), Stadtsparkasse Augsburg, Zeuna-Stärker GmbH (Augsburg). We also thank Monika Bredow, Gaby Kaiser, Jens Krüger, Andreas Pyka, and Jörg Sommer for efficient and friendly management of the workshop, without which this volume would not have been possible.

Uwe Cantner, Horst Hanusch, Steven Klepper
Augsburg and Pittsburgh, February 2000

References

Dinopoulos E (1994), Schumpeterian Growth Theory: An Overview, *Osaka City University Economic Review* 29, 1-21

Lucas RE (1988), On the Mechanics of Economic Development, *Journal of Monetary Economics* 22, 3-42

Mankiw NG, D Romer, DN Weill (1992), A Contribution to the Empirics of Economic Growth, *Quarterly Journal of Economics* 106, 407-37

Metcalfe S (1995), Technology Systems and Technology Policy in an Evolutionary Framework, *Cambridge Journal of Economics* 19(1), Special Issue on Technology and Innovation, 25-46

Nelson RR, S Winter (1982), *An Evolutionary Theory of Economic Change*, Cambridge, Mass.: Belknap Press of Harvard University Press

Romer PM (1990), Endogenous Technological Change, *Journal of Political Economy* 98, 71-102

Romer PM (1986), Increasing Returns and Long-Run Growth, *Journal of Political Economy* 94, 1002-37

Weitzman ML (1992), On Diversity, *Quarterly Journal of Economics* 107, 363-406

Norms as emergent properties of adaptive learning: The case of economic routines*

Giovanni Dosi[1,2], Luigi Marengo[3], Andrea Bassanini[4], Marco Valente[5]

[1] Scvola Superiore S. Anna, Pisa, Italy
[2] IIASA, Laxenburg, Austria
[3] Department of Economics, University of Trento, Via Inama 1, I-38100 Trento, Italy (e-mail: lmarengo@gelso.unitn.it)
[4] Faculty of Statistics, University "La Sapienza", Rome, Italy, and OECD, Paris, France
[5] Aalborg University, Aalborg, Denmark

Abstract. Interaction among autonomous decision-makers is usually modelled in economics in game-theoretic terms or within the framework of General Equilibrium. Game-theoretic and General Equilibrium models deal almost exclusively with the existence of equilibria and do not analyse the processes which might lead to them. Even when existence proofs can be given, two questions are still open. The first concerns the possibility of multiple equilibria, which game theory has shown to be the case even in very simple models and which makes the outcome of interaction unpredictable. The second relates to the computability and complexity of the decision procedures which agents should adopt and questions the possibility of reaching an equilibrium by means of an algorithmically implementable strategy. Some theorems have recently proved that in many economically relevant problems equilibria are not computable. A different approach to the problem of strategic interaction is a "constructivist" one. Such a perspective, instead of being based upon an axiomatic view of human behaviour grounded on the principle of optimisation, focuses on algorithmically implementable "satisfycing" decision procedures. Once the axiomatic approach has been abandoned, decision procedures cannot be deduced

* Support to the research at different stages has been provided by the International Institute of Applied Systems Analysis (IIASA), Laxenburg, Austria, the Italian Ministry of University and Research (Murst 40%), the Italian Research Council (CNR, Progetto Strategico "Cambiamento Tecnologico e Sviluppo Economico") and the Center for Research in Management, University of California, Berkeley. Comments by an anonymous referee and by the participants at seminars at the Cerisy Association (Cerisy, France), the Santa Fe Institute (Santa Fe, New Mexico), and in particular Kenneth Arrow, are gratefully acknowledged. This work was awarded the "International A. Kapp Prize" for 1994 by the European Association of Political and Evolutionary Economics.

from rationality assumptions, but must be the evolving outcome of a process of learning and adaptation to the particular environment in which the decision must be made. This paper considers one of the most recently proposed adaptive learning models: Genetic Programming and applies it to one the mostly studied and still controversial economic interaction environment, that of oligopolistic markets. Genetic Programming evolves decision procedures, represented by elements in the space of functions, balancing the exploitation of knowledge previously obtained with the search of more productive procedures. The results obtained are consistent with the evidence from the observation of the behaviour of real economic agents.

Key words: Computability – Genetic Programming – Oligopoly

JEL-classification: C63; D43; D83

1 Introduction

As Kenneth Arrow – himself one of the major contributors to rational decision theory – puts it, a system of literally maximizing norm-free agents "... would be the end of organized society as we know it" (Arrow, 1987, p. 233). And indeed one only rarely observes behaviours and decision processes which closely resemble the canonical view from decision theory as formalized by von Neumann, Morgenstern, Savage and Arrow.

What are then the characteristics of norm-guided behaviours? And where do norms come from? Can they be assumed to derive from some higher-level rational choice? Or can one show different kinds of processes accounting for their emergence?

In this work we shall discuss these issues and present an evolutionary view of the emergence of norm-guided behaviours (i.e. routines[1]) in economics.

We shall call *rules* all the procedures linking actions and some representation of the environment. In turn, representations are likely to involve relations between environmental states and variables and require the fulfilment of certain conditions (IF-THEN rules). It is a familiar definition in Artificial Intelligence and cognitive psychology (see Newell and Simon, 1972; Holland et al., 1986). Of course representations may encompass both environmental states and internal states of the actor; and the action part may equally be a behaviour in the environment or an internal state, such as a cognitive act.[2]

Further, we shall call *norms* that subset of rules which pertain to socially interactive behaviours and, in addition, have the following characteristics:

1) they are context-dependent (in ways that we shall specify below), and
2) given the context, they are, to varying degrees, event independent, in the sense that, within the boundaries of a recognised context, they yield

[1] For a general discussion on organizational routines and their role in economics see Nelson and Winter (1982) and Cohen et al. (1995).

[2] Clearly, this very general definition of rules includes as particular cases also the procedures for decision and action postulated by "rational" theories.

patterns of behaviour whose selection is not itself contingent on particular states of the world.[3]

This definition of norms is extremely broad in scope and encompasses also behavioural routines, social conventions and morally constrained behaviours.[4] Thus our definition includes the norm of not robbing banks, but excludes robbing or not robbing banks according to such criteria as expected utility maximization; it includes the "rules of the games" in game theoretical set-ups, but excludes the highly contingent strategies which rational players are supposed by that theory to engage in thereafter.

Our argument is divided into two parts. First, we ask what is the link between norms, so defined, and the "rational" decision model familiar in the economic literature. In particular we shall address the question whether, whenever one observes those types of norm-guided behaviours, they can be referred back to some kind of higher-level rational act of choice among alternative patterns of action. We shall claim that this is not generally the case. The empirical evidence, even in simple contexts, of systematic departures of judgements and actions from the predictions of the rationality model is now overwhelming.[5] Here however we are not going to discuss such evidence, rather we shall pursue a complementary line of enquiry and show that, with respect to an extremely broad set of problems, a 'rational' choice procedure cannot even be theoretically constructed, let alone adopted by empirical agents. Drawing from computation theory, it can be shown that many choice set-ups involve algorithmically insoluble problems: in other words, there is not and there cannot be a universal rational procedure of choice. An optimization procedure cannot be devised even in principle: this is the negative part of the argument.

But what do people do, then? We shall suggest precisely that agents employ problem-solving rules and interactive norms, which: 1) cannot be derived from any general optimization criterion and, 2) are "robust", in the sense that they apply to entire classes of events and problems (Dosi and Egidi, 1991).

The second part of this work considers the origin and nature of these rules. The cases we shall consider regard the emergence of corporate routines applied to the most familiar control variables in economics, i.e. prices and quantities. However, there appear to be no a priori reason to restrict the applicability of the argument to economic behaviours. In fact, a similar

---

[3] Note that this definition as such does not imply any restriction on the use of information by the norms themselves. Some might be extremely simple and parsimonious in their handling of information (like those we shall show emerging in the exercises below). Others might imply sophisticated information-processing (such as, e.g. accounting routines in a firm). Both types, however, share the property that the *behavioural patterns*, although not necessarily the single actions, once established, are rather invariant throughout the whole set of contingencies that might occur in that context.

[4] These finer categorization are quite familiar in political sciences: see for example the discussion in Koford and Miller (1991). On the contrary, the broader notion of norms adopted here includes both moral constraints and positive behavioural prescriptions (i.e. both "morality" and "ethics" in the sense of Hegel).

[5] Cf., for instance, Kahneman, Slovic and Tversky (1982), Kahneman and Tversky (1979), Herrnstein and Prelec (1991).

analytical approach could be applied to several other forms of patterned behaviour in social interactions.

Concerning the origin of behavioural norms, we develop a model broadly in the perspective outlined by Holland (1975) and Holland et al. (1986): various forms of inductive procedures generate, via adaptive learning and discovery, representations or "mental models" and, together, patterns of behaviour: "the study of induction, then, is the study of how knowledge is modified through its use" (Holland et al., 1986, p. 5). In our model, artificial computer-simulated agents progressively develop behavioural rules by building cognitive structures and patterns of action, on the grounds of initially randomly generated and progressively improved symbolic building blocks and no knowledge of the environment in which they are going to operate. The implementation technique is a modified version of Genetic Programming (c.f. Koza, 1992, 1993), in which agents (firms) are modelled by sets of symbolically represented decision procedures which undergo structural modifications in order to improve adaptation to the environment. Learning takes place in an evolutionary fashion, and is driven by a selection dynamics whereby markets reward or penalise agents according to their revealed performances.[6]

A major point in the analysis which follows is that representations of the world in which agents operate and behavioural patterns co-evolve through the interaction with the environment and the inductive exploratory efforts of agents to make sense of it.[7] Indeed, we show that, despite the complexity of the search space (technically, the space of λ-functions), relatively coherent behavioural procedures emerge. Of course, none of us would claim that empirical agents do learn and adapt in a way which is anything like Genetic Programming, or, for that matter, any other artificially implementable formalism (but, similarly, we trust that no supporter of more rationalist views of behaviour would claim that human beings choose their course of action by using fixed-point theorems, Bellman equations, etc.). We do however conjecture that there might be a sort of "weak isomorphism" between artificial procedures of induction and the ways actual agents adapt to their environment.

The final question that we address concerns the nature of the behavioural patterns that emerge through our process of learning and market selection. In particular, in the economic settings that we consider, are these patterns algorithmic approximation to the purported rational behaviours which the theory simply assumes? Or, do they have the features of relatively

[6] A similar exercise has been recently proposed by Curzon-Price (1997). Like us he considers firms which adaptively learn their price and/or quantity fixation strategies in monopolistic and oligopolistic industries. But this paper employs standard Genetic Algorithms: as Curzon-Price himself argues in his conclusions, Genetic Programming is a richer modelling tool, which offers a much more appealing analogue to decision-making routines implemented by real firms.

[7] On the evolution of representations, see also Margolis (1987). In economics, such a co-evolutionary perspective is held by a growing minority of practitioners. More on it can be found in Nelson and Winter (1982), Dosi et al. (1988), March (1988), Marengo (1996), Dosi and Marengo (1994), Arthur (1992).

invariant and context-specific norms (or routines) as defined earlier? It turns out that, in general, the latter appears to be the case: surviving agents display routines, like mark-up pricing or simple imitative behaviour (of the type "follow-the-leader") in all environments that we experimented, except the simplest and most stationary ones. Only in the latter do we see the emergence of behaviours not far from what supposedly rational agents would do (and, even then, cooperative behaviours are more likely to come out than what simple Nash equilibria would predict[8]). The context dependence of emerging routines can be given a rather rigorous meaning: the degrees of complexity of the environment and of the problem-solving tasks can be mapped into the characteristics of the emerging routines. Interestingly enough, it appears that the higher the complexity, the simpler behavioural norms tend to be and the more potentially relevant information tends to be neglected. In that sense, social norms seem to be the typical and most robust form of evolutionary adaptation to uncertainty and change.

In Section 2 we shall show that, in general, it is theoretically impossible to assume that the rationality of behaviours could be founded in some kind of general algorithmic ability of the agents to get the right representation of the environment and choose the right course of action. Section 3 presents a model of inductive learning where representations and actions co-evolve. Finally, in Section 4 we present some results showing the evolutionary emergence of behavioural routines, such as mark-up pricing.

2 Rational vs. norm-guided behaviour

Let us start from the familiar view of rational behaviour grounded on some sort of linear sequence leading from 1) representations to 2) judgement, 3) choice and, finally, 4) action. Clearly, that ideal sequence can apply to pure problem-solving (for example proving a theorem, discovering a new chemical compound with certain characteristics, etc.), as well as to interactive situations (how to deal with competitors, what to do if someone tries to mug you, etc.).

At least two assumptions are crucial to this 'rationalist' view, namely, first, that the linearity of the sequence strictly holds (for example one must rule out circumstances in which people act and then adapt their preferences and representations to what they have already done) and, second, that at each step of the process agents are able to build the appropriate algorithm in order to tackle the task at hand. Regarding the first issue, the literature in sociology and social psychology is rich of empirical counterexamples and alternative theories.[9] Indeed, in the next section of this work, we shall present a model whereby representations and actions co-evolve.

---

[8] This is of course in line with the findings of Axelrod (1984) and Miller(1988).

[9] In addition to the references from footnote 4, see for discussions, among the others, Sen (1977), Simon (1986), Hodgson (1988), Elster (1986), Luhmann (1979), and, closer to the spirit of this paper, Nelson and Winter (1982), March (1994) and Dosi and Metcalfe (1991). For a more general discussion of these issues, cf. Dosi, Marengo and Fagiolo (1996).

The second issue is even more at the heart of the 'constructivist' idea of rationality so widespread in economics, claiming that agents are at the very least procedurally rational.[10] In turn this implies that they could algorithmically solve every problem they had to face, if they were provided with the necessary information about the environment and the degrees of rationality of their possible opponents or partners. Conversely, the very notion of rational behaviour would turn out to be rather ambiguous if one could show that, *even in principle*, the appropriate algorithms cannot be constructed.

It happens in fact that computability theory provides quite a few impossibility theorems, i.e. theorems showing examples of algorithmically insoluble problems. Many of them bear direct implications also for the micro assumptions of economic theory and, particularly, for the possibility of 'naturally' assuming the algorithmic solvability of social and strategic interaction problems.[11] We can distinguish between two kinds of impossibility results. First, it is possible to show the existence of classes of problems which are not solvable by means of a general recursive procedure (c.f. Lewis, 1985a,b). This implies that economic agents who look for efficient procedures for the solution of specific problems cannot draw on general rules for the construction of algorithms, because such general rules do not and cannot exist (c.f., also, Dosi and Egidi, 1991). Broadly speaking, we can say that nobody may be assumed to be endowed with the meta-algorithm for the generation of every necessary algorithm.

Second, it is possible to prove the existence of single problems whose optimal solution cannot be implemented by means of *specific* algorithms. Hence one faces truly algorithmically insoluble problems: economic agents cannot have readily available algorithms designing optimal strategies to tackle such problems. Therefore, unless they have been told what the optimal solutions are by an omniscient entity, they have actually to find other criteria and procedures to solve them in a 'satisfactory' way. In fact, they need novel criteria to define what a satisfactory solution is and inductively discover new procedures to accomplish their tasks (see again Dosi and Egidi, 1991).

Let us briefly examine these two kinds of impossibility results.

Lewis (1985a, b) proves a general result about the uncomputability of rational choice functions. Let P(X) be the set of all subsets of a space of alternatives X where an asymmetric and transitive preference relation has been identified, we can roughly define a rational choice function as a set function

$C: P(X) \rightarrow P(X)$ such that, for every $A \in P(X)$, C(A) is the set of acceptable alternatives.[12]

[10] The central reference on the distinction between 'substantive' and 'procedural' rationality is of course Herbert Simon: see especially Simon (1976, 1981, 1986).

[11] See Lewis (1985a), Casti (1992) and Rustem and Velupillai (1990). Note that, loosely speaking, algorithmic solvability means that one is able to define a recursive procedure that will get you, say, to a Nash equilibrium. This turns out to be a question quite independent from proving a theorem which shows the existence of such an equilibrium.

[12] Given a preference relation > on a set of objects X and a non-empty set A belonging to X, the set of acceptable alternatives is defined as: $c(A, >) = \{x \in A: \text{there is no } y \in A \text{ such that } y > x\}$.

Lewis considers some compact, convex subset of $R^n \setminus \{0\}$ as the space X of alternatives. Among these alternatives he takes into account only the set of recursive real numbers in the sense of Kleene and Post, i.e. the set of real numbers which can be codified as natural numbers by means of a particular Gödel numbering (for more details see Lewis, 1985a). Moreover, one operates directly on the codified values (which are called R-indices). Given a preference relation defined only on the space of R-indices and numerically representable by a computable function and given some non-triviality conditions, Lewis does not only show that the related rational choice function is uncomputable but also that so is its restriction over the sole decidable subsets.[13] Even more important than the proposition on undecidable sets (since in this case it may seem that the uncomputability of the function necessarily derives from the undecidability of the subsets), the result concerning only its restriction to the decidable subsets of R^n is quite powerful. It means in fact that the functions are uncomputable even if their domains are computable.

Obviously this result does not imply that the optimal solution cannot be algorithmically determined for every $A \in P(X)$. Lewis' theorems actually prove only that no automatic procedure can generate uniformly optimal solutions over the whole family of optimization problems identified by the set of all recursive subsets of R-indices of elements of X. This would be true even if there existed some specific solution algorithm for every single problem of this family (see Lewis, 1985a, p. 67). This result shows actually that there exist small enough classes (i.e. not so broad to be meaningless from a decision-theoretic point of view) of well-structured choice problems whose solution cannot be obtained by means of a general recursive procedure.

In economic theory, environmental or social interactions are usually represented by using subsets of R^n as spaces of alternative strategies. Thus, Lewis' results can be naturally extended to prove the generic uncomputability of the class of General Economic Equilibria and, relatedly, of the class of Nash equilibria for games (see Lewis, 1987).

Concerning the second type of uncomputability results, examples can be found in game theory: Rabin (1957) and Lewis (1985a) show that there is at least one two-person, zero-sum game with perfect information whose optimal strategies are uncomputable.[14] On the same token, similar uncomputability results concerning Post systems (Post, 1943; Thrakhtenbrot, 1963) directly bear upon production theory as they show that there is no guarantee that optimal productive processes can be algorithmically identified (even, as economists would say, under exogenous technical progress). Therefore it is impossible to assume that economic agents make always use of optimal processes without giving a context-specific proof.

---

[13] Broadly speaking, we call a set decidable if there exist an algorithm which is always able to completely identify its elements, i.e. if the membership function which characterises the set is computable.

[14] This result has been proven for a particular class of Gale-Stewart games: such games have infinite Nash equilibria with at least one sub-game perfect among them, nevertheless they admit no computable winning strategy.

It is worth emphasising that these impossibility results entail quite disruptive implications not only for the 'constructivist' concept of rationality, but also for the so-called *as-if* hypothesis (see Friedman, 1953; discussion in Winter, 1986). In order to assume that agents behave as if they were rational maximizers, one needs to represent a thoroughly autonomous selection process which converges to an optimal strategy equilibrium, i.e. one must be able to formalise something like an automatic procedure which ends up with the elimination of every non-optimizing agent (or behaviour).

However, the first group of results mentioned above, implies that, for some classes of problems, we are not allowed to assume the existence of a general and algorithmically implementable selection mechanism leading in finite time to the exclusive survival of optimal behaviours. In addition, the second group of results provides examples where one can definitely rule out the existence of every such a selection mechanism.

Moreover, the minimal prerequisite one needs for a selection-based *as-if* hypothesis on behavioural rationality is the existence of some agents whose behaviour is consistent with optimization in the first place (cf. Winter, 1971). But, if the set of optimal strategies is undecidable, how can we be sure of having endowed some agent with one optimal strategy? An approximate easy answer could be that if we consider a sufficiently large population of differentiated agents, we can safely suppose that some of them play optimal strategies and will be eventually selected. But how big should our population be, given that we cannot have any idea about the size of the set of possible strategies?

Finally there is also a problem of complexity which arises in connection with rational behaviour (both under a "constructivist" view and under the *as-if* hypothesis). Broadly speaking, we can roughly define the complexity of a problem as the speed of the best computation processes we could theoretically use to solve it (c.f., e.g., Cutland, 1980). But then the speed of environmental change becomes a crucial issue: as Winter (1986) and Arthur (1992) pointed out, the *as-if* view is primarily connected with a situation without change. In fact, even when the only kind of change we allow is an exogenous one, a necessary, albeit by no means sufficient condition for the hypothesis to hold is that the speed of convergence be higher than the pace of change. However, it is easy to find many examples of games whose optimal strategies, while existing and being computable, require too much time to be effectively pursued even by a modern computer.[15]

Moreover, if the environment is not stationary, it is unlikely that behaviour consistent with optimization in one environmental state will be so also in another one, unless we assume that the agent is actually using the optimizing algorithm (but this amounts to denying the "as-if" thesis one wants to prove).

We do not want to make too much out of these impossibility results: one of the reasons is that generic uncomputability might tell us little on the

[15] Think for instance to the game of Chess or to the Rubik cube.

average complexity of any one particular problem.[16] However, in our view, they do establish a sort of upper bound to the algorithmic rationality with which we may innocently endow the empirical agents whose behaviour we want to describe. These impossibility proofs, together with more familiar results on the indeterminacy of learning processes even under quite restrictive cognitive assumptions (such as "rational expectation" and Bayesian learning) add to the importance of an explicit analysis of the *processes of formation of representations and behavioural rules*. This is what we shall do in the next section, by considering the emergence of rules of cognition/action in some familiar economic examples of decision and interaction.

3 Genetic programming as a model of procedural learning

With a lag of at least two decades after Herbert Simon's repeated invitations to tackle "bounded rationality", a few recent models have finally begun also in economics to represent agents who adaptively improve their representations of the environment in which they operate and their repertoire of actions.

Some of the most promising modelling techniques are based on John Holland's Genetic Algorithms (Holland, 1975) and Classifiers Systems (Holland et al., 1986). Despite their variety, what this class of "adaptive learning" models has in common is the assumption that agents, at least at the start, are characterized by some sort of competence gap, as Ronald Heiner has put it (cf. Heiner, 1983, 1988). That is, beyond imperfect information and uncertainty about the states of the world, they are less than perfectly able to interpret whatever information they have and to establish the appropriate courses of action conditional on that information.[17] Having said that, the different adaptive learning models which have been produced so far differ quite a lot in the nature of the "competence gap" that they allow, in the environments that they depict, and in the spirit of the whole exercise. At one extreme, models such as Arifovic (1994) attempt to show how adaptive learning based on Genetic Algorithms in quite simple environmental set-ups yield convergence to the "optimal" behaviour generally assumed by economic theory. Conversely, Lindgren (1991), Miller (1988) and Marengo (1996), among others, study the properties of emergent behaviours in more complex interactive environments (prisoner's dilemma and intra-firms coordination problems, respectively).

In any case, irrespectively of the modelling philosophy, all these adaptive learning models allow for some mechanism of search and recombina-

[16] We owe this observation to Kenneth Arrow, who pointed to us the example of linear programming and the difference between "normal" and maximum computational complexity of simplex methods as compared to other ones.

[17] This is what in Dosi and Egidi (1991) we have called *procedural uncertainty*. As illustrations, think of the exercises of proving a theorem or solving a Rubik cube. There is no "substantive uncertainty" (i.e. no unknown move of nature) and the information might well be perfect. Still, "procedural uncertainty" remains, regarding what to do with the information and how to achieve the desired result.

tion of the initial knowledge apt to reduce the competence gap of the agents and improve their performances in the decision tasks at hand. However, quite a few problems of cognition, within and outside the economic arena, regard the discovery of the purported structure of the environment, i.e. the functional relations among environmental variables (being them e.g. the possible correlation between stochastic trend in some fundamental variable; the effect of investment on income growth, etc.). And also many procedural problems of decision/action involve the discovery of specific functions (whether it is the identification of a function to maximize, its first order condition, or also stationary rules such as "invest a given percentage of sales in R&D"). But, then, can one model artificial agents which explore and learn in some *space of functions*? This is precisely what we shall do next, applying a modified version of Genetic Programming (cf. Koza, 1992, 1993). Genetic Programming – GP henceforth – is a computational model which simulates learning and adaptation through a search in the space of representations/procedures. Similarly to John Holland's Genetic Algorithms, Genetic Programming pursues learning and adaptation by processing in an evolutionary fashion a population of structures which are represented by fixed length binary strings in the case of Genetic Algorithms and by symbolic functions in the case of GP.

In GP, the learning system (an artificial learning agent) is endowed with a set of basic "primitive" operations (such as the four arithmetic operations, Boolean operators, if-then operators) and combine them in order to build complex procedures (functions) which map environmental variables into actions. Each artificial agent is represented by a set of such procedures and learns to adapt to the environment through an evolutionary process which involves both fitness-driven selection among existing procedures and generation of new ones through mutation and genetic recombination (crossover) of the old ones.

General features of this model are the following:

1. *Representations and rule behaviour*: A common feature to many computational models of learning, including the one presented here, is that of modeling the learning process not just as acquisition of information and probability updating, but as modification of representations and models of the world. But contrary to other similar models (such as genetic algorithms and classifiers systems), genetic programming models learning and adaptation as an explicit search in the space of procedures, i.e. functions in their symbolic representation, which define functional relations among environmental and decision variables.[18]
2. *Adaptive selection*: Each artificial agent stores in its memory a set of alternative procedures of representation/action and selects at each moment of time a preferred one according to its fitness, i.e. the payoff cumulated by each procedure in the past.

[18] A more general formal tool in the same spirit and which we intend to apply in the near future is presented in Fontana (1992) and Fontana and Buss (1994), applied in the domain of biology to self-reproducing systems.

3. *Generation of new rules*: Learning does not involve only adaptive selection of the most effective decision rules among the existing ones, but also generation of new ones. Learning and adaptation require a calibration of the complicated trade-off between exploitation and refinement of the available knowledge and exploration of new possibilities. GP uses genetic recombination to create new sequences of functions: sub-procedures of the existing most successful ones are re-combined with the cross-over operator in order to generate new and possibly more effective combinations.

In GP symbolic functions are represented by trees, whose nodes contain either operators or variables. Operators have connections (as many as the number of operands they need) to other operators and/or variables, if they are variables they do not have, of course, any further connection and constitute therefore the leaves of the tree.

Thus, every node can be chosen in a set of basic function (e.g. the arithmetic, Boolean, relation, if-then operators) plus some variables and constants:

$$BF = \{+, -, *, /, ..., \mathrm{OR}, \mathrm{AND}, \mathrm{NOT}, >, <, =, ...v_1, v_2, v_3, ...c_1, c_2, c_3, ...\}$$

But basic functions can be freely defined depending on the kind of problem which is being faced (see Koza, 1993, for a wide range of examples of applications in different problem domains).

The execution cycle of a GP system proceeds along the following steps:

0) An initial set of function/trees is randomly generated. Each tree is created by randomly selecting a basic function; if the latter needs parameters, other basic functions are randomly selected for each connection. The operation continues until variables (which can be considered as zero-parameter functions) close every branch of the tree.

1) Once a population of trees is so created, the relative strength of each function is determined by calculating its own fitness in the given environment.

2) A new generation of functions/trees is generated. Two mechanisms serve this purpose: selection and genetic operators. Selection consists in preserving the fittest rules and discarding the less fit ones. Genetic operators instead generate new rules by modifying and recombining the fittest among the existing ones. The generation of new (possibly better) functions/trees in GP is similar to the genetic operators proposed by Holland for the Genetic Algorithms and is mainly based on the cross-over operators.[19] Cross-over operates by selecting randomly two nodes in the parents' trees and swapping the sub-trees which have such nodes as roots.

Consider for example the two parents functions:

$$P_1 := X + (Y^*Z) - Z \quad \text{and} \quad P_2 := Z/(Y^*X) - A$$

---

[19] For a discussion of the power of cross-over as a device for boosting adaptation, see Holland (1975) and Goldberg (1989).

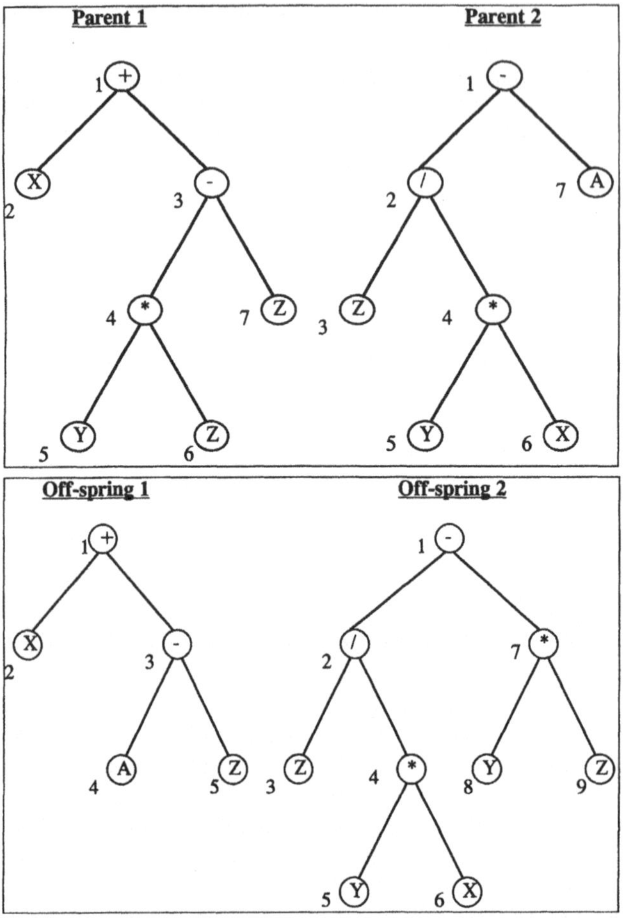

Fig. 1. Tree representation of the GP

which are depicted in Fig. 1 in their tree representation. Suppose that node 4 in the first function and node 7 in the second one are randomly selected: cross-over will generate two new 'off-spring' trees which correspond to the functions:

$$OS_1 := X + (A - Z) \quad \text{and} \quad OS_2 := Z/(Y*X) - (Y*Z)$$

Such off-spring substitute the weakest existing rules, so that the number of rules which are stored at every moment in time is kept constant.

3) Go back to 1).

4 Learning pricing procedures in oligopolistic markets

Here we shall consider one of the most typical problems of economic interaction, namely, an oligopolistic market.

Think of a small group of firms who sell their product (a homogeneous one, for simplicity) in a decentralized market where customers are imperfectly informed about the prices of other suppliers, there are search costs and/or customers exhibit some inertia (or "loyalty") in their purchasing behaviours.

In a full-fledged representation of such type of market interactions – indeed quite common in contemporary industrial economics – one would of course try to model "artificial markets" entailing the dynamics of search and purchases by multiple customers. However, here we want to focus primarily on the evolution of pricing rules by suppliers. Therefore, for the sake of simplicity, we accept the usual economists' convention of "black-boxing" the collective behaviour of customers into a downward-sloped industry demand curve, unknown to all suppliers, who have to set simultaneously their prices at discrete time intervals. To do so they can observe both the past values taken by the relevant market variables (quantity and prices) and the current value of such firm-specific variables as costs. However, they do not know either the parameters of the demand function or the prices competitors are about to set. Once all prices have been simultaneously set, the corresponding aggregate demand can be determined and individual market shares are updated according to relative prices.

This interactive set-up and the substantive uncertainty about both the exogenous environment (i.e. the demand function) and the competitors' behaviour require agents to perform a joint search in the space of representations and in the space of decision functions.

Let us examine more precisely the structure of the market we analyse in our simulations. There exist an exogenous linear demand function:

$$p = a - bq \qquad a,b > 0 \tag{1}$$

and n firms which compete in this market by choosing a price p_i. Firms are supposed to start up all with the same market share s_i:

$$s_i(0) = 1/n \qquad i = 1, ..., n$$

Price decisions are taken independently (no communication is possible between firms) and simultaneously at regular time intervals ($t = 1,2,.......$). Each firms is supposed to incur into a constant unitary cost c_i for each unit of production. Once all decisions have been taken, the aggregate market price can be computed as the average of individual prices:

$$p(t) = \Sigma_i s_i(t) p_i(t) \tag{2}$$

and the corresponding demanded quantity is thus determined. Such a quantity is divided up into individual shares which evolve according to a sort of replicator dynamics equation in discrete time:

$$s_i(t) = \eta[p(t)/p_i(t) - 1]s_i(t-1) \tag{3}$$

if $s_i(t) \geq 0.01$, otherwise the firm is declared "dead" and a new one enters with a 0.01 market share.

The parameter η is the reciprocal of the degree of inertia of the market.

Such a replicator-type dynamics of shares has to be taken as the simplest approximation to an imperfect adjustment of consumer behaviour to price differentials, in which customers stick to their previous suppliers or move to cheaper ones as a function of price differentials.[20]

Finally, individual profits are given by:

$$\Pi_i(t) = [p_i(t) - c_i(t)]\, s_i(t)q(t) - F_i \qquad (4)$$

where F_i are fixed costs, independent of the scale of production, but small enough to allow the firms to break-even for an excess of prices over variable costs, were they to pursue Bertrand-type competition.

We model these firms as artificial agents, each represented by an autonomous GP system, which, at each time step t, must select one pricing rule among those which it currently stores. Each artificial agent can observe at each moment of time t the following past (i.e. the values taken at time $t-1$) variables:

- average industry price $p(t-1)$,
- aggregate demanded quantity $q(t-1)$,
- individual prices of each agent $p_i(t-1)$, for $i = 1,2,\ldots n$
- own unitary cost $c_i(t-1)$
- own market share $s_i(t-1)$

moreover it can observe its current unitary cost $c_i(t)$.

Each agent is then endowed with a few basic "elementary" operations, i.e. the four arithmetic operations, if-then operators, Boolean operators and equality/inequality operators, in addition a few integers are given as constant to each GP system.

Each agent's decision rules are randomly generated at the outset, and a preferred one is chosen for action in a random way, with probabilities proportional the payoffs cumulated by each rule in the previous iterations. Periodically, new rules are generated through cross-over and replace the weaker ones.

In order to test the learning capabilities of an economic artificial agent represented by a GP, we started with a very simple model of a single agent in a monopolistic market. In such an environment, there is one and only one optimal behaviour for the agent, that is to set its price to the value which maximises its profit. As shown in Fig. 2, in this case with constant costs and stable demand curve, price rapidly converges to the optimal one. The optimal value can be computed from the available parameters of the

[20] Clearly, the stochastic version of eq. (3) form would be more adequate to describe the mechanism, but, for our purposes, the main property that we want to capture – namely, inertial adjustment of the market to price differential – is retained also by the simpler deterministic dynamics. Were agents to behave as in conventional Bertrand models, eq. (3) would still converge, in the limit, to canonical Bertrand equilibria. It must be also pointed out that our model is not concerned with the population dynamics of the industry but primarily with the evolution of pricing rules. Therefore we artificially set a minimum market share (1%) under which firms cannot shrink. According to the past performance record, firms may die, in which case they are replaced by a new agent which stochastically recombines some of the behavioural rules of the incumbents.

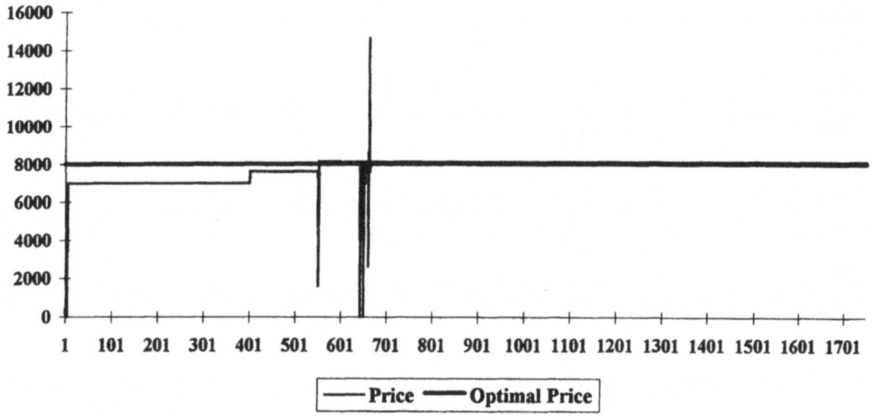

Fig. 2. Monopoly in a stationary environment

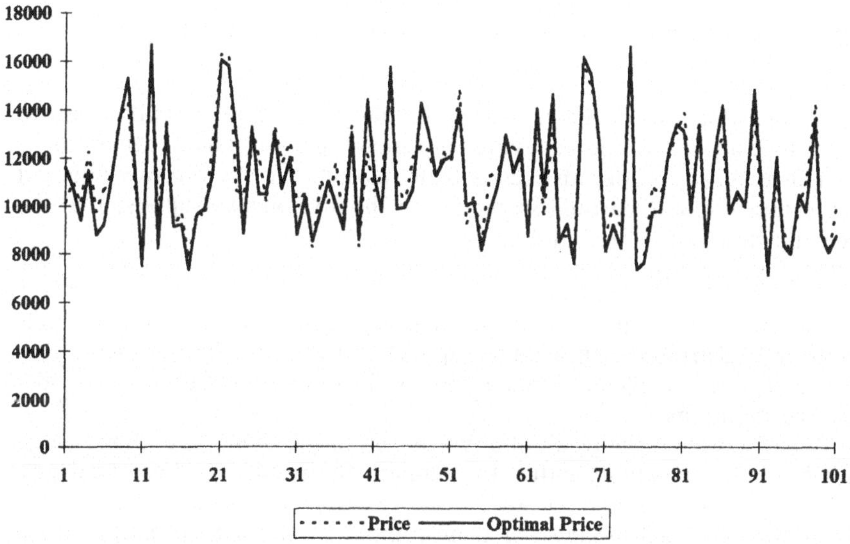

Fig. 3. Monopoly: random costs and demand

environment (demand curve) as the result of a maximisation process. But, this same result can be obtained by a wide variety of different functions. In Fig. 3 [21] the same monopolistic agent faces a more complex environment: both the parameters of the demand function and cost vary. Again, the selected procedures can be completely different from the "theoretical" optimal one in their functional forms but, their outcomes are hardly

[21] Since the pay-off of each function depends on random factors, we tested each function over 100 trials and the pay-off is the average of the values obtained. To show the level of performance, in the figure we plot only 100 iterations of the best emerging rule.

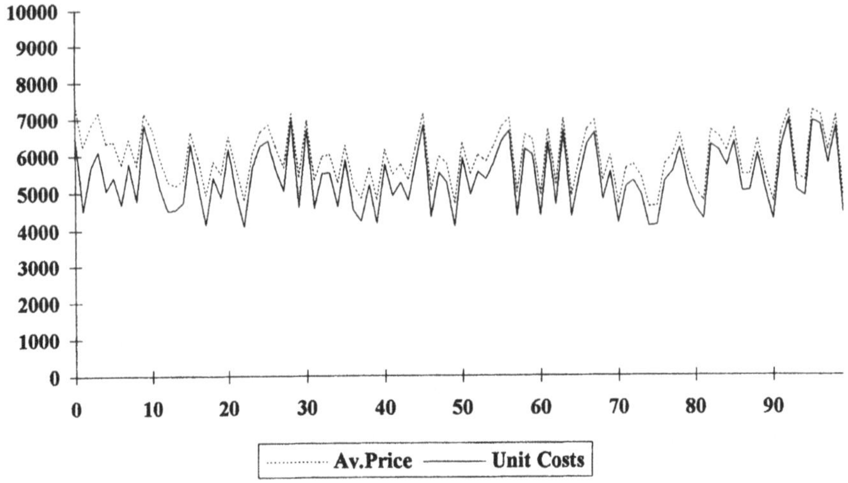

Fig. 4. Oligopoly: inertial learning case av. price and average unit costs

distinguishable. To conclude, these preliminary tests show that GP is able to reproduce an optimising behaviour in simple "non-strategic" situations.

Let us now consider an oligopolistic market. We explore two different environmental and learning scenarios. In the first one we suppose that the demand function is fixed and equal to:

$$p = 10\,000 - 10q$$

Moreover, unitary costs, identical for every agent, are a random variable uniformly distributed on a finite support. Finally, on the representation/action side, our artificial agents are allowed to experiment each set of rules for 100 iterations.

We will present the result of a typical run of the simulation. Since we do not have the possibility either to compare the results to theoretical predictions in this context (because none exist) or to explore formally the functions produced, because of their complexity, we did not carry over a formal statistical analysis about the robustness of our result. We systematically observed in different runs of the models that agents basically used behavioural rules which can be referred to two types.

In Fig. 4 we report the average price plotted against costs for an oligopolistic market with 9 firms. In Fig. 5a,b we report the price series for two typical firms: in Fig. 5a we observe a pricing strategy which strictly follows cost variations.

Although emerging rules are usually quite complex,[22] they behave "as if" they were simple mark-up rules. Another typical behaviour that we

[22] The complexity of the rules is at least partly due to the fact that our agents have to produce constants (such as mark-up coefficients) that they do not possess in their set of primitives and have therefore to be obtained by means of operations on variables (e.g. $(X + X)/X = 2$).

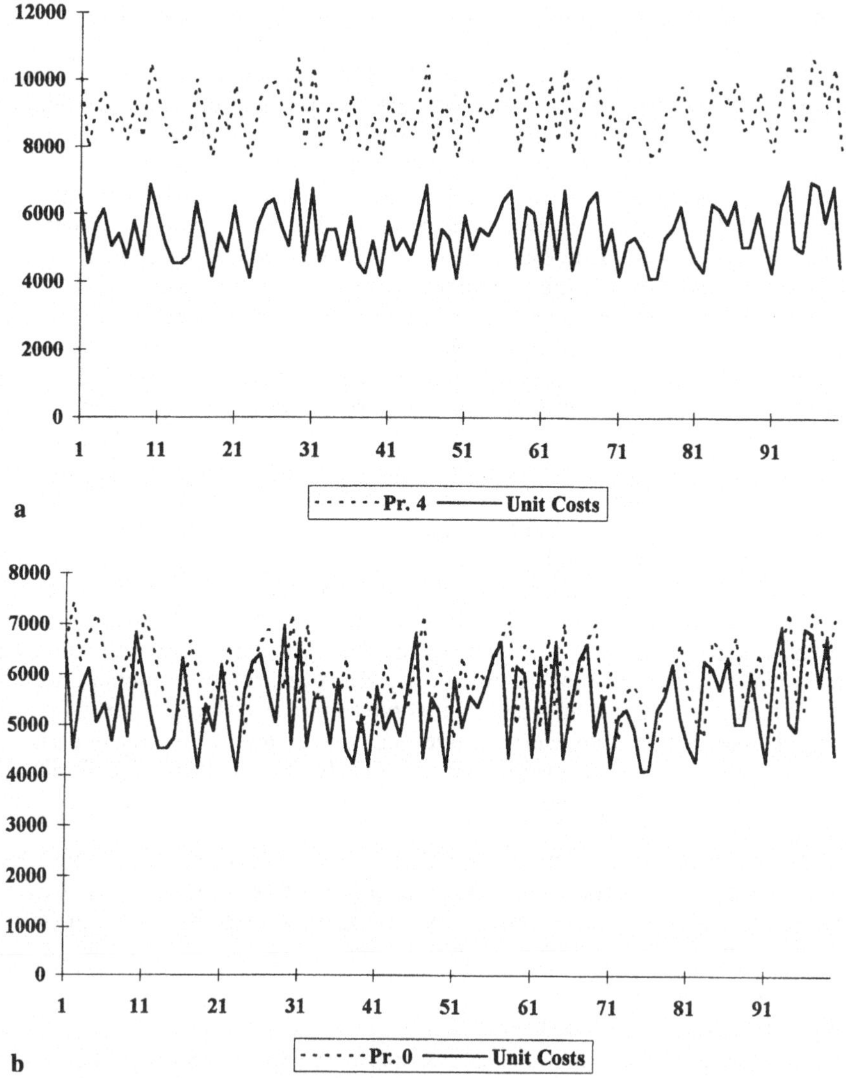

Fig. 5. a Oligopoly: costs and typical mark-up strategy. **b** Oligopoly: costs and typical follower strategy

observe is a follower type of pricing rule: in Fig. 5b, we present the plot of the pricing decisions of an agent using a typical follower strategy. Given the basic functions available to the agents, the follower strategy involves setting the price equal to the value of a past variable. The tree representing the function is a single node containing the name of the variable to follow. This strategy can produce low profits, but it is extremely persistent, since the cross-over cannot break such degenerate tree. Moreover, with a higher number of firms, the complexity of the coordination task increases and this, in turn, favours the emergence of simple imitative behaviour.[23]

Under a second scenario, the intercept of the demand function randomly fluctuates, drawing from a uniform distribution on the support [8000–12 000]. In addition, the individual unitary costs are given by the ratio between two variables: a component which is common to the entire industry and is represented by a random variable uniformly distributed over the interval [0;8000] and an individual productivity component, different for each firm, which is a random walk with a drift. Moreover, we allow agents to change stochastically their sequencies of rule at each period, i.e. to switch among the procedures of representation/action which they store. In this way, one forces behavioural variability (and, of course, this decreases predictability of each and every competitor). This extreme learning set-up prevents any rule from settling down and from proving its value in the long term, while facing rather stable behaviours of the competitors. Despite all this, the main conclusions reached under the former scenario hold: mark-up type policies still turn out to be the most frequent and most efficient response to environmental uncertainty.[24] Figures 6 and 7 illustrate costs and price dynamics for the industry

In other exercises, not shown here, we consider similar artificial agents whose control variables are quantities rather than prices. Again, as in the example presented above, a monopolist facing a stationary environment does discover the optimal quantity rule. However, under strategic interactions the agents do not appear to converge to the underlying Cournot-Nash equilibrium, but, rather, cooperative behaviours emerge. In particular, in the duopoly case, the decision rule has "Tit-for-tat" features (cf. Axelrod, 1984) and displays a pattern of the type "do at time t what your opponent did at time t−1".

It has been already mentioned that a straightforward "semantic" interpretation of the procedures which emerge is often impossible. However, their inspection – in the simplest cases – together with the examination of

---

[23] Econometric estimates of the form:

$$\ln p_t = \alpha + \beta \ln p_{t-1} + \cdots + \gamma_0 \ln_{ct} + \gamma_1 \ln_{ct-1} + \cdots$$

for the industry as a whole, always yield R^2 above 0.90 with significant coefficients for current costs and the first lag on prices only, and always insignificant lagged costs. Conversely, for the majority of the firms, no lagged variable significantly adds to the explanation: firms appear to follow a stationary rule of the simplest mark-up type, $p_i^t = m_i(c^t)$. However, for some firms (the "imitators") current prices seem to be set as a log-linear combination between costs and lagged average prices of the industry, or the lagged price of one of the competitors (as in the example presented in Fig. 5b).

[24] As may be expected, estimates of the form presented in footnote 23 yield somewhat lower R^2 as compared to the previous case – both for the industry aggregate and for the individual firms –, but still most often in the range between 0.6 and 0.8.
Also the other properties of individual pricing procedures stand, and in particular simple stationary rules characterize the most successful players, as assessed in terms of cumulated profits or average market shares. Finally, in analogy to the previous learning scenario, the adjustment dynamics in aggregate prices – where the first lag on prices themselves turns out to be significant – appear to be due primarily to an aggregation effect over most often stationary rules (for a general theoretical point on this issue, cf. Lippi, 1988).

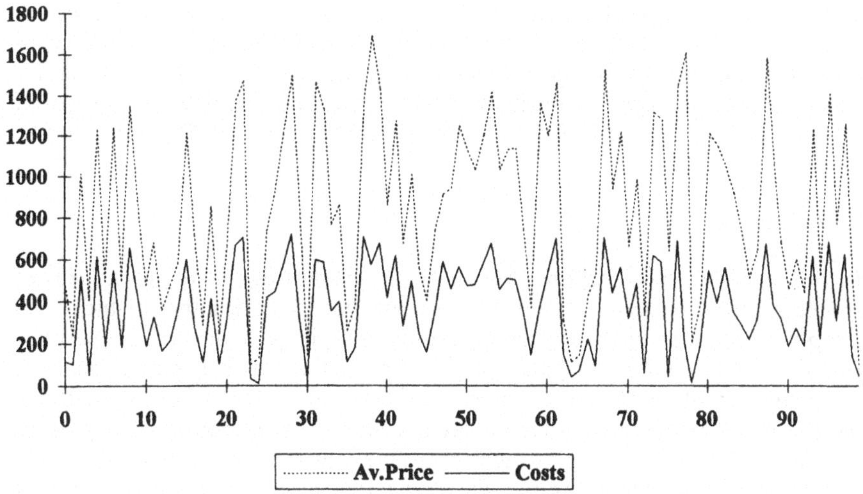

Fig. 6. Oligopoly: continuous adjustment case average costs and prices

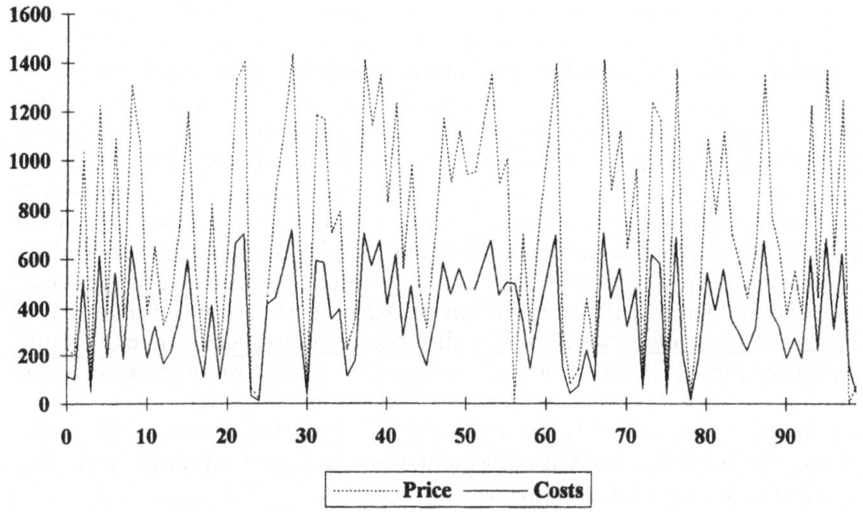

Fig. 7. Oligopoly: continuous adjustment case costs and prices of market leader

the behavioural patterns that they entail, allows an assessment of their nature. Some remarkable patterns appear. First, procedures which "look like" optimization rules emerge only in rather simple and stationary environments. Second, as the complexity of the representation/decision problem increases, rules evolve toward simpler ones, involving the neglect of notionally useful information and very little contingent behaviour. More precisely, the procedure which the evolutionary dynamics appear to select either neglect the strategic nature of the interactive set-up – thus transforming the decision problem into a game "against nature" – or develop very simple imitative behaviours. In all these circumstances the resulting collective outcomes of the interaction significantly depart from the equilibria prescribed by a theory of behaviour grounded on standard rationality assumptions (this applies both to the Cournot-Nash and to the Bertrand set-ups, corresponding to quantity-based and price-based decision rules).

5 Conclusions

In this work we have begun to explore the properties of the procedures of representation/decision which emerge in an evolutionary fashion via adaptive learning and stochastic exploration in a space of elementary functions. Following a negative argument on the general impossibility of endowing agents with some generic and natural optimization algorithms, we presented some preliminary exercises on the co-evolution of cognition and action rules. The results highlight the evolutionary robustness of procedures which – except for the simplest environments – have the characteristics of norms or routines, as defined earlier. Of course one can easily object that real agents indeed base their understanding of the world on a pre-existing cognitive structure much more sophisticated than the elementary functions we have assumed here, and that therefore our result might not bear any implication for the understanding of the actual evolution of norms. On the other hand, the problem solving tasks that empirical agents (and, even more so, real organizations) face are several orders of magnitude more complex than those depicted in this work. Indeed, we would like to consider the exercise presented in this work as a beginning of an answer to the challenge most often confronting the non-believers in (unbounded) rationality assumptions, namely, what do you substitute the latter with? How do you avoid *ad-hocery* and casual empiricism? There is indeed no claim of realism in the model we have presented: however, we suggest that some basic features of the evolution of the rules for cognition and action presented here might well hold in all those circumstances where a "representation gap" exists between the ability that agents pre-possess in interpreting their environment and the "true" structure of the latter. This is obviously a field of analysis where stylized modelling exercises on evolutionary learning can only complement more inductive inquiries from e.g. social psychology and organizational sciences.

References

Arifovic J (1994) Genetic algorithm learning and the cobweb model. Journal of Economic Dynamics and Control 18: 3–25

Arrow K (1987) Oral history: an interview. In: Feiwel GR (ed) Arrow and the ascent of modern economic theory. MacMillan, London

Arthur WB (1992) On learning and adaptation in the economy. Santa Fe NM, Santa Fe Institute, working paper 92-07-038

Axelrod R (1984) The evolution of cooperation. Basic Books, New York

Casti JL (1992) Reality rules. Wiley, New York

Cohen D (1987) Computability and logic. Ellis Horwood, Chichester

Cohen M, Burkhart R, Dosi G, Egidi M, Marengo L, Warglien M, Winter S, Coriat B (1995) Routines and other recurring action patterns of organizations: Contemporary Research Issues. Santa Fe, Santa Fe Institute, WP 95-11-101, Industrial and Corporate Change (forthcoming)
Cutland NJ (1980) Computability: an introduction to recursive function theory. Cambridge University Press, Cambridge
Curzon-Price T (1997) Using co-evolutionary programming to simulate strategic behaviour in markets. Journal of Evolutionary Economics 7: 219–254
Dosi G, Egidi M (1991) Substantive and procedural uncertainty. An exploration of economic behaviours in complex and changing environments. Journal of Evolutionary Economics 1: 145–168
Dosi G, Freeman C, Nelson R, Silverberg G, Soete L (eds) (1988) Technical change and economic theory. Pinter, London
Dosi G, Marengo L (1994) Some elements of an evolutionary theory of organizational competences. In England RW (ed) Evolutionary concepts in contemporary economics, pp 157–78. University of Michigan Press, Ann Arbor
Dosi G, Marengo L, Fagiolo G (1996) Learning in evolutionary environments. Laxenburg, Austria, International Institute for Applied Systems Analysis, Working Paper
Dosi G, Metcalfe JS (1991) On some notions of Irreversibility in Economics. In Saviotti PP, Metcalfe JS (eds) Evolutionary theories of economic and technological change. Harwood Academic Press, Chur
Elster J (1986) The multiple self. Cambridge University Press, Cambridge
Fontana W (1992) Algorithmic chemistry. In: Langton C, Farmer JD, Rasmussen S (eds) Artificial life. Addison Wesley, Redwood City, CA
Fontana W, Buss LW (1994) What would be conserved if "the tape were played twice"? Proceedings of the National Academy of Sciences USA, vol 91, pp 757–761
Friedman M (1953) Essays in positive economics. University of Chicago Press, Chicago
Goldberg DE (1989) Genetic algorithms in search. Optimization and learning. Addison Wesley, Reading, MA
Heiner RA (1983) The origin of predictable behavior. American Economic Review 73: 560–595
Heiner RA (1988) Imperfect decisions in organizations: toward a theory of internal structure. Journal of Economic Behavior and Organization 9: 25–44
Herrnstein RJ, Prelec D (1991) Melioration: a theory of distributed choice. Journal of Economic Perspectives 5: 137–156
Hodgson G (1988) Economics and institutions. Polity Press, London
Hogart RM, Reder MW (eds) (1986) Rational choice. Chicago University Press, Chicago
Holland JH (1975) Adaptation in natural and artificial systems. University of Michigan Press, Ann Arbor
Holland JH, Holyoak KJ, Nisbett RE, Thagard PR (1986) Induction: processes of inference, learning and discovery. MIT Press, Cambridge, MA
Kahneman D, Slovic P, Tversky A (eds) (1982) Judgment under uncertainty: heuristics and biases. Cambridge University Press, Cambridge, MA
Kahneman D, Tversky A (1979) Prospect theory: an analysis of decision under risk. Econometrica 47: 263–291
Koford KJ, Miller JB (eds) (1991) Social norms and economic institutions. University of Michigan Press, Ann Arbor
Koza JR (1992) The genetic programming paradigm: genetically breeding populations of computer programs to solve problems. In: Soucek B (ed) Dynamic, genetic and chaotic programming. Wiley, New York
Koza JR (1993) Genetic programming. MIT Press, Cambridge, MA
Lewis A (1985a) On effectively computable realization of choice functions. Mathematical Social Sciences 10: 43–80
Lewis A (1985b) The minimum degree of recursively representable choice functions. Mathematical Social Sciences 10: 179–188

Lewis A (1986) Structure and complexity. The use of recursion theory in the foundations of neoclassical mathematical economics and the theory of games. Cornell University, Department of Mathematics, Ithaca, mimeo

Lewis A (1987) On turing degrees of walrasian models and a general impossibility result in the theory of decision-making. Technical report n. 512, Institute for Mathematical Studies in the Social Sciences, Stanford University

Lindgren K (1991) Evolutionary phenomena in simple dynamics. In: Langton CG et al. (eds) Artificial life II. Addison Wesley, Redwood City, CA

Lippi M (1988) On the dynamics of aggregate macro equations: from simple micro behaviours to complex macro relationships. In: Dosi G et al. (eds) Technical change and economic theory, pp 170–196. Pinter, New York

Luhmann N (1979) Trust and power. Wiley, Chichester

March JG (1988) Decisions and organizations. Blackwell, Oxford

March JG (1994) A primer on decision making. Free Press, New York

Marengo L (1996) Structure, competences and learning in an adaptive model of the firm. In: Dosi G, Malerba F (eds) Organization and strategy in the evolution of the enterprise. MacMillan, London

Margolis H (1987) Patterns, thinking and cognition: A theory of judgement. Chicago University Press, Chicago

Miller JH (1988) The evolution of automata in the repeated prisoner's dilemma. Santa Fe Institute, working paper

Nelson RR, Winter SG (1982) An evolutionary theory of economic change. Harvard University Press, Cambridge MA

Newell A, Simon H (1972) Human problem solving. Prentice-Hall, Englewood Cliffs, NJ

Post E (1943) Formal reductions of the general combinatorial decision problem. American Journal of Mathematics 65: 197–215

Rabin MO (1957) Effective computability of winning strategies: contributions to the theory of games III. Annals of Mathematics Studies 39: 147–157

Rustem B, Velupillai K (1990) Rationality, computability and complexity. Journal of Economics Dynamics and Control 14: 419–432

Sen A (1977) Rational fools: a critique of the behavioral foundations of economic theory. Philosophy and Public Affairs 6: 317–344

Simon HA (1976) From substantive to procedural rationality. In: Latsis SJ (ed) Method and appraisal in economics, pp 129–148. Cambridge University Press, Cambridge

Simon HA (1981) The sciences of the artificial. MIT Press, Cambridge MA

Simon HA (1986) Rationality in psychology and economics. Journal of Business 59: supplement

Thrakhtenbrot DA (1963) Algorithms and automatic computing machines. Heath, Boston, MA

Winter SG (1971) Satisficing, selection and innovating remnant. Quarterly Journal of Economics 85: 237–261

Winter SG (1986) Adaptive behaviour and economic rationality: comments on Arrow and Lucas. Journal of Business 59: supplement

An experimental study of adaptive behavior in an oligopolistic market game*

Rosemarie Nagel[1], Nicolaas J. Vriend[2]

[1]Universitat Pompeu Fabra, Barcelona, Spain
[2]Department of Economics, Queen Mary and Westfield College, University of London, Mile End Road, London E1 4NS, UK (e-mail: n.vriend@qmw.ac.uk)

Abstract. We consider an oligopolistic market game, in which the players are competing firms in the same market of a homogeneous consumption good. The consumer side is represented by a fixed demand function. The firms decide how much to produce of a perishable consumption good, and they decide upon a number of information signals to be sent into the population in order to attract customers. Due to the minimal information provided, the players do not have a well-specified model of their environment. Our main objective is to characterize the adaptive behavior of the players in such a situation.

Key words: Market game – Oligopoly – Adaptive behavior – Learning

JEL-classification: C72; C91; D83

---

* We wish to thank Reinhard Selten for encouraging and discussing the experiments, and Klaus Abbink, Joachim Buchta, Cornelia Holthausen, Barbara Mathauschek, Michael Mitzkewitz, and especially Abdolkarim Sadrieh for their indispensable assistance in discussing and organizing the experiments. Steven Klepper helped us improving the paper a great deal by insisting with a number of pertinent questions and suggestions. We are grateful for comments and discussions concerning previous versions of this paper to Antoni Bosch, John Miller, Greg Pollock, Phil Reny, Al Roth, Arthur Schram, Ulrich Witt, and to seminar and conference participants in Pittsburgh, Ames, Long Beach, Barcelona, Augsburg, Trento, Amsterdam, Toulouse, Marseille, London, St. Louis, and Paris. The experiments were made possible by financial support from the Deutsche Forschungsgemeinschaft through Sonderforschungsbereich 303 at the University of Bonn. Stays at the University of Pittsburgh, and the Santa Fe Institute, and financial support through TMR grant ERBFMBICT950277 (NJV) from the Commission of the European Community are also gratefully acknowledged. The usual disclaimer applies.

1 Introduction

We consider an oligopolistic market game, in which the players are identical competitors in the same market. In each period, they decide how much to produce of a perishable and homogeneous consumption good, and they decide how many advertising signals to send into the population in order to attract customers. The firms know the parameters of the production and signaling technologies,[1] as well as the fixed price of the good. After every period, each firm observes only its *own market outcomes*. No further information about the environment is given.

Given the minimal information, even a rational player is not in a position to maximize his profits using standard optimization techniques. Following Savage's (1954) terminology, he is in a '*large world*', as opposed to the '*small world*' to which Subjective Expected Utility theory applies. In a large world, the agent's situation is ill-defined in the sense that he does not have a well-specified model of his environment. Hence, instead of *deducing* optimal actions from universal truths, he will need to employ *inductive* reasoning, i.e., proceeding from the actual situation he faces. In Savage's terminology, this is the '*cross that bridge when you meet it*' principle, which is also known as adaptive behavior.[2]

Studying this adaptive behavior in a large world is the main motivation for our simplified experimental setup. To create a large world in a relatively simple oligopoly game, we abstract from the process by which the price is determined, and from the determination of the market demand at that price level. This is perfectly compatible with a standard downward-sloping market demand curve. Notice also that there are many markets in which goods are sold at fixed prices (whether as a result of legislation, of vertically imposed restrictive practices, or of optimizing behavior of the sellers). While a *complete* economic analysis would explain such legislation, restrictive practices, or strategies, by which the prices are fixed, our analysis focuses instead on the learning and adaptive behavior of the firms, and thus applies equally to all the possible ways in which these prices may have been determined. Given the price level, competition can then take place along many dimensions,[3] for example through advertising, and it seems more than plausible that for some of these dimensions the information that an individual firm has about its competitors is far from complete. In our model, as we will show below, the only strategic variable to compete directly with the other firms is the signaling activity. Assuming that firms do not observe the

[1] Notice that we follow the common use of the word 'signaling', and not the more restrictive game-theoretic one related to signaling games.

[2] We would conjecture that many relevant economic problems, when considered at a moderately realistic level, are large-world problems (see, e.g., Arthur, 1992).

[3] Quantity and production capacity are obvious ones. Product differentiation is another one. The quality of a good depends upon many aspects, like, e.g., a warranty, add-ons like frequent flyer miles, or an after sale service. Firms also compete using entry deterring and other restrictive practices, by their choice of technology, location, or the timing of new product lines. Further competitive variables are the firms' R&D decision (including marketing research), and their efforts to build up a reputation.

level of their competitors' signaling activity in our simple model is a first approximation of this fact.[4]

What can be learned from large world experiments that cannot be learned from small-world experiments with fuller information? It is far from certain that you can learn the way in which people behave in large worlds by studying only small worlds. It might very well be that there is no substantial difference between the two as far as the behavior of the players is concerned, but we cannot know this in advance. The only way to check this is to study large-world experiments as well (see Page, 1994, for further arguments along this line). Related to this is the observation that it might be that many apparently small worlds are in fact large worlds as perceived by the players, due to the fact that the agents' rationality is bounded (see, e.g., Simon, 1959), or that their perception is limited (see also Vriend, 1996a). One of the key advantages of laboratory experiments is that one *controls* the players' environment. Hence, it might be true that due to bounded rationality and limited subjective perceptions, some players consider even a full information set-up as a large world, but we can make sure that it is a large world for *all* players by placing some explicit simple restrictions on the information provided to the players.[5]

Our main objective, then, is to characterize the adaptive behavior of the players in such a large world. First of all, we want to characterize the overall market outcomes that result from the interaction of the adaptive players. Second, we want to know whether we can use simple models of adaptive behavior to describe the actual behavior on average. Third, we will examine the distributions of actions and outcomes over the individual players underlying the market averages. As individual behavior is very heterogeneous, we will analyze the reasons for this heterogeneity, despite the market being symmetric.

In order to put the experimental data into perspective we use the following theoretical framework. First, to obtain a game-theoretical benchmark, we derive a stationary symmetric equilibrium, assuming complete information. The second way to put the experimental data into perspective is by using a simple 2-step model of adaptive behavior. Although we will show that this 2-step model is closely related to the game-theoretic analysis, it is very different in the sense that it is based exclusively on the minimal information that the players actually have, while making only minimal assumptions about the agents' reasoning processes. The 2-step model consists of two simple processes; learning direction theory, which has been successfully applied in various experiments (see e.g., Selten and Stoecker, 1986; or Nagel, 1995), and the well-known method of hill climbing, also known as the gradient method. As we will make clear below, these two steps share the following underlying principle. The players' own actions and outcomes in the most recent (two) period(s) give the player information

[4] For a more extensive justification of this type of oligopoly model we refer to Vriend (1996b), and the references cited therein.

[5] Some other 'large-world' experiments can be found in Atkinson and Suppes (1958), Sauermann and Selten (1959), Witt (1986), Malawski (1990), Stewing (1990), and Kampmann and Sterman (1995).

about the direction in which he may find better actions. We will also use this 2-step model to analyze the differences in actions and outcomes between the players.

We expected the players on average to adapt sufficiently to their environment to discover the underlying trading opportunities, and we hoped that the simple 2-step model of adaptive behavior would indeed be able to describe the typical behavior of the players in a satisfactory way. Although we expected to find some spread around the players' average actions and outcomes, we did not expect sharp differences between the players.

How does this study of adaptive behavior fit into more traditional analyses of evolutionary economics? Schumpeterian evolutionary analysis usually focuses on the long-run evolution of economic primitives such as technologies and preferences. In doing so, it tends to abstract from the short-run economic coordination problem by assuming a Walrasian perspective. However, if we are living in a large world, then also in the short-run agents need to be *entrepreneurs*, adaptively discovering and creating trading opportunities. We believe that the outcomes of these short-run evolutionary market processes must in one way or another have consequences for the developments in the longer run, certainly if one observes systematic differences in the players' perceptions of their short-run underlying opportunities such as in our experiment. A *complete* evolutionary economic theory should consider these short-run and long-run developments in a coherent analysis, but that is beyond the scope of the current paper.

The paper is organized as follows. In Section 2, we explain how a large world looks in a small experimental laboratory. In Section 3, we present the theoretical framework within which we will analyze the data. Section 4 contains an analysis of the data, and Section 5 concludes.

2 The experiment: model and design

We conducted two series of experiments in the computerized experimental laboratory at the University of Bonn, one with inexperienced, and one with experienced players. Before presenting the experimental design, we will first explain and discuss the oligopoly model used. Table 1 gives the notation used throughout. Superscripts will be used for the time index, and subscripts for the identity of a firm. In addition, Table 1 gives an overview of the parameter values. The last column indicates whether the parameter value was known to the players or not. As we will explain below, in addition to these parameter values, the players did not know the functional form of the demand they faced.

a) The oligopoly model

A fixed number of firms repeatedly interacts in an oligopolistic market. All firms are identical in the sense that they produce the same homogeneous

Table 1. Notation and parameter values

Symbol	Meaning	Value	Known
c	'*marginal*' cost production	0.25	yes
f	patronage rate satisfied consumers	0.56	no
g	price minus '*marginal*' cost production	0.75	yes
k	'*marginal*' cost signaling	0.08	yes
m	# firms	6	no
n	# consumers	712	no
N	total # agents	718	no
p	price of the commodity	1.00	yes
Π	profit	–	own
q	demand directed towards a firm	–	own
Q	aggregate demand	–	no
s	# signals sent by a firm	–	own
–	maximum value for s	4999	yes
S	aggregate # signals all firms	–	no
S_{-}	aggregate # signals other firms	–	no
V	value	–	no
x	sales	–	own
z	production	–	own
–	maximum value for z	4999	yes
–	# periods	±150	no

consumption good, using the same technology (see below). Time is divided into discrete periods. At the beginning of each period, each firm has to decide how many units of the perishable consumption good to produce. The production costs per unit are constant, and identical for all firms. The production decided upon at the beginning of the period is available for sale in that period. The firms also decide upon a number of information or advertising signals to be sent into the population, communicating the fact that they are a firm offering the commodity for sale in that period. Imagine the sending of letters to addresses picked randomly from the telephone directory. The costs per information signal sent to an individual agent are constant, and identical for all firms. The price of the commodity is fixed, invariant for all periods, and identical for all firms and consumers. The choice of the number of units to be produced, and the number of information signals to be sent, is restricted to a given interval.

Consumers in this economy are simulated by a computer program. In each period, when all firms have decided their production and signaling levels, consumers will be '*shopping*', with each consumer wanting to buy exactly one unit of the commodity per period. In fact, the consumer side is represented by the fixed, deterministic demand function given in equation [1].

$$q_i^t = \text{round}\left(\text{trunc}\left[f \cdot x_i^{t-1}\right] + \frac{s_i^t}{S^t} \cdot \left[1 - \exp\left(-\frac{S^t}{N}\right)\right] \cdot \left[n - \sum_{j=1}^{m} \text{trunc}\left(f \cdot x_j^{t-1}\right)\right]\right) \quad [1]$$

$$(\quad \text{I} \quad) + (\text{IIa}) \cdot (\qquad \text{IIb} \qquad) \cdot (\qquad \text{IIc} \qquad)$$

where

I = demand directed towards firm i by patronizing consumers
IIa = proportion of signals from firm i in aggregate signaling activity
IIb = proportion of individuals reached by one or more signals
IIc = number of 'free', i.e., non-patronizing, consumers
IIa · IIb · IIc = demand directed towards firm i as a result of current signaling

In each period, a fixed fraction of the number of customers satisfied by a given firm during the last period will *patronize* that firm [part I of eq. (1)].[6] The remaining consumers who received at least one signal (part IIc multiplied by IIb) are split between the firms, according to the firms' signaling activity relative to the aggregate signaling in the market (part IIa). Notice that when all firms signal very little, not all consumers will be reached by an information signal, implying that not all consumers will actually be present in the market. Hence, although all signaling has the form of informative advertising, and there is no persuasive signaling (see Stiglitz, 1993), one can distinguish two different effects: a business stealing effect, and an effect on the total demand in the market (see also Petr, 1997). In Vriend (1996b), in a closely related model, we consider explicitly a process of sending, receiving, and choosing individual signals, and show that this leads to a demand function faced by the individual firms that may be approximated by a Poisson distribution. The deterministic function given above equals the expected value of such a Poisson distribution. At the end of the period, all unsold units of the commodity perish. Notice that a firm cannot sell more than it has produced at the beginning of the period. Hence, a firm's profit in period t is given by:

$$\Pi_i^t = P \cdot x_i^t - c \cdot z_i^t - k \cdot s_i^t, \text{ where } x_i^t = \min[z_i^t, q_i^t] \qquad [2]$$

b) Information for the individual players

We now sketch the information available to the individual players, distinguishing technology, market, and experience factors. Appendix A presents the instructions given to the players, and Table 1 above summarizes which parameter values were known and which not.

The technology. The players know that they are identical firms, producing the same homogeneous consumption good, using the same technology. Both the production and signaling technology are common knowledge, and the same applies to the price of the commodity. As to the fact that the choice interval for production and signaling is limited, the players were told that "*this is due only to technological restrictions, and has no direct economic meaning*".
The market. The players were told that the consumers in this economy would be simulated by a computer program. They did *not* receive the

[6] See also Keser (1992) for duopoly experiments with demand inertia.

specification of the demand function [eq. (1)], and they did not know the number of competing firms,[7] the number of consumers, or the parameter value of the demand inertia. Instead they were given the following general picture of the consumption side. Each consumer wants one unit of the commodity in every period, and so a consumers has to find a firm offering the commodity for sale, and that firm should have at least one unit available at the moment he arrives. The participants were given two considerations concerning consumers' actions. First, a consumer who has received an information signal from a firm *knows* that this firm is offering the commodity for sale in that period, and second, consumers who visited a certain firm, but found only empty shelves, might find that firm's service unreliable. On the other hand, a consumer who succeeded in buying one unit from a firm might remember the good service, and might be more likely to come back. Participants were also told "*experience shows that, in general, the demand faced by an individual firm is below 1000*".[8]

Experience. At the end of the period, each firm observes only its own market outcomes, and never the actions and outcomes of the other players. Each firm knows the demand that was directed to it during the period, how much it actually sold, and its profits for that period. Sometimes the market outcomes are such that a firm makes a loss. A firm making cumulative losses is informed about these. Each firm faces a known upper limit for the total losses it may realize, and a firm exceeding this limit is declared bankrupt, with the participant removed from the session. This was known before the experiments started. The players did not know the number of periods to be played, but they knew that the playing time would be about 2½ hours. Given this minimal information, a player is not in a position to maximize his profits on the basis of a well-specified demand function. In other words, he finds himself in a 'large world', and must behave adaptively. During the instructions before the games, some players felt uncomfortable with so much 'mist', and many attempted to get more knowledge about the environment. The usual answer to those questions was 'you just don't know'.

c) The experiments

In the first series, we organized 13 sessions with inexperienced players. In each session, 6 firms were competing in one market, for a total of 78 players. In two of these sessions, the players faced an upper limit of 999 instead of 4999 for their production and signaling decision variables, but these two sessions are excluded from the analysis. The remaining 11 sessions are numbered 1 to 11 throughout this paper. In the second series, we organized 5 sessions with experienced players, with again 6 firms per session, for a total of 30 players. We asked all players to return for a very similar

[7] There were at most 12 players at the same time in the lab, but players did not know how many parallel sessions were going on.

[8] This was done to avoid players going bankrupt in one of the initial periods, without impeding them to choose levels above 1000.

oligopoly game with experienced players in order to test whether the players also learn over time to adjust the way in which they adapt to their circumstances.[9]

Most players came from various departments of the University of Bonn. Players sat in front of personal computers, and could not observe the screens of other players. Figure A.1 in appendix A presents an example of a computer screen viewed by a given player. In the sessions with inexperienced players, we played about 150 periods.[10] There was no time limit for the participants' decisions. Each player got a fixed '*show-up*' fee, and was paid according to the total profits realized by his firm. Losses realized were subtracted from the '*show-up*' fee. The total payoff for an individual player was given by: $\alpha + (\alpha/2000) \cdot$ (points realized).[11] Observe that bankrupt players had lost their '*show-up*' fee, and hence got nothing. Each session lasted about 2½ hours, and the average payment over the 66 players was DM 24.83 (≈ $16.36).

d) A closer look at the game

Besides the minimal information, there are two additional aspects of the structure of this game that are worth noting. First, there is a *positive feedback* mechanism. A fixed proportion f of a firm's satisfied customers will patronize the next period, and so firms having sold more in period t, will get more customers in period t+1. This positive feedback has two effects. First, it makes the game complicated from the individual player's point of view, and second, it may give rise to *lock-in* effects in both directions. For example, say each firm sends 927 signals, and receives 118 customers in a given period t. Of those 118 customers, $0.56 \cdot 118$ will come back in period t+1, $0.56^2 \cdot 118$ in period t+2, etc. In other words, the signals sent in a given period t lead to new customers arriving in the form of a wave, with a steep front that fades out gradually. As a result, in any period t, the demand faced by a firm is composed as follows: 52 customers are there because of a signal received in period t, $0.56 \cdot 52$ because they had reacted to a signal in period t−1, $0.56^2 \cdot 52$ because of a signal in period t−2, etc., up to 1 customer still coming back since period t−8.

The lock-in effect can be made visible as follows. For a given period, for a given firm, one can calculate for each possible (production, signaling)-pair the immediate profits that pair would realize, taking as given the signaling activity of the other firms and the sales of all firms in the preceding period.

[9] An analysis of the data of the sessions with the experienced players can be found in Nagel and Vriend (1999).

[10] The sessions with inexperienced players lasted 151 periods, except for the sessions 7 an 8 (131 periods), 10 (251 periods), and 11 (201 periods). These differences are mainly due to the fact that sessions 1 to 8 were organized with two sessions simultaneously, and that the next period could only start when all twelve players had made a decision.

[11] The value for α was DM 10 in sessions 1 and 2, 15 in sessions 3 to 6, and 20 in sessions 7 to 11, giving an average α of 16.4. The values for α were varied in advance in an effort to keep average payoffs at a level of about DM 15/h.

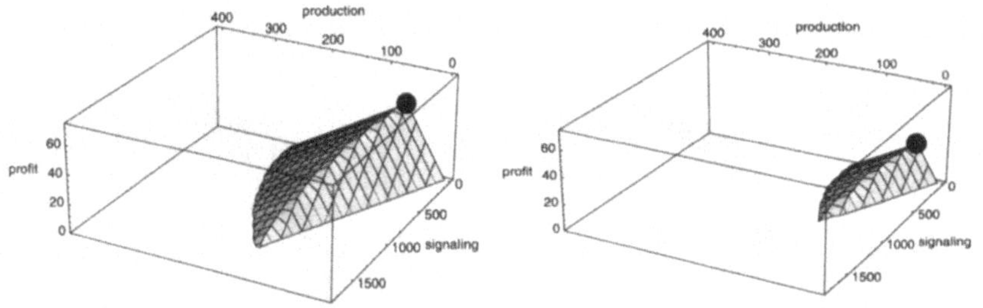

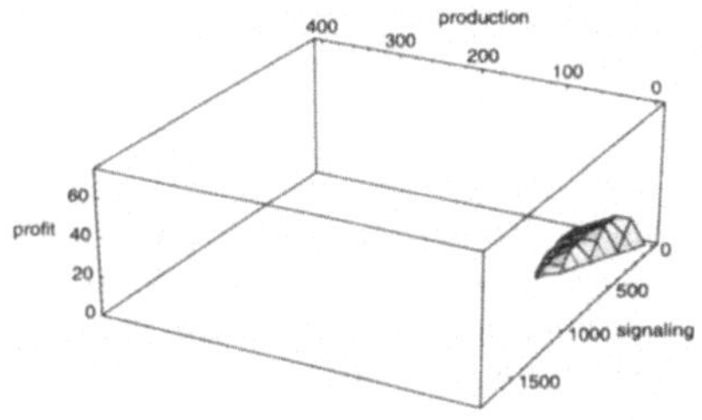

Fig. 1. Example immediate profit landscape: shrinking through immediate profit maximization (where • is action chosen)

Hence, we draw a 3-D '*immediate profit landscape*', showing all points that lead to positive immediate profits as an '*island*'. If, on the one hand, firms invest in order to build up a market, this island will grow. On the other hand, a firm's market may collapse if it does not signal enough. For example, it may be tempting for players to seek maximization of their immediate profits, i.e., to search for the peak in their immediate profit landscape. What would happen then? Analyzing every single instance in which an individual player had to make a decision in our experiments, it turns out that very often the global maximum of immediate profits is a corner solution with signaling at zero and production equal to the demand generated. This was the case 84% of the time in the first series of experiments. Hence, if a firm would try to maximize its immediate profits, its market will shrink away under its own eyes in most cases. An example of this effect is shown in Fig. 1, where the *dot* indicates the action chosen by the player considered, and where the other players each send 750 signals.

Figure 2 shows an example within the same environment of the opposite positive feedback effect, where a firm builds up its market by maximizing its sales subject to the condition that its immediate profits are positive.

A second aspect of this game that is worth stressing is the influence that each player's actions have on the outcomes of the other players. While one firm may try to walk up to a peak in its profit landscape, this landscape is deformed continuously by the other players who may be trying to reach their peaks. This coevolutionary process can be seen as a number of players walking simultaneously on one rubber mattress. Figure 3 shows an example, where the aggregate number of signals sent by each of the other players fluctuates from 750 to 1300 to 200. The interaction between the firms through the aggregate signaling activity shows up in the form of noise for an individual firm. If a firm has a larger immediate profit island, it will be

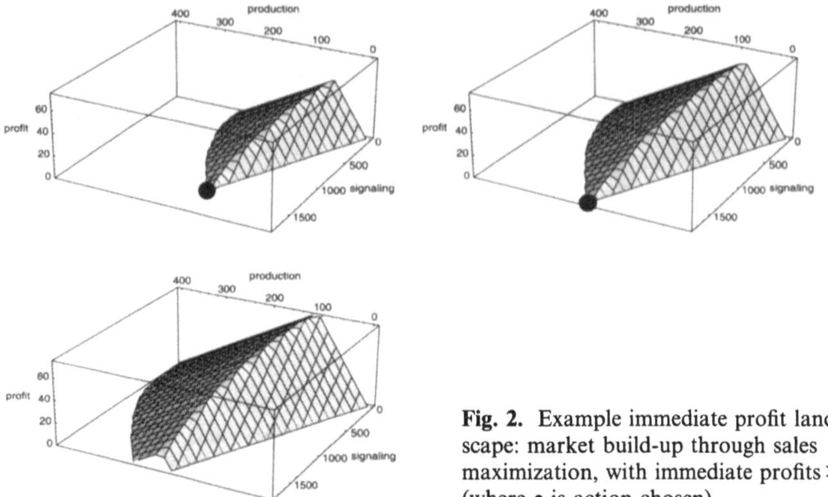

Fig. 2. Example immediate profit landscape: market build-up through sales maximization, with immediate profits > 0 (where • is action chosen)

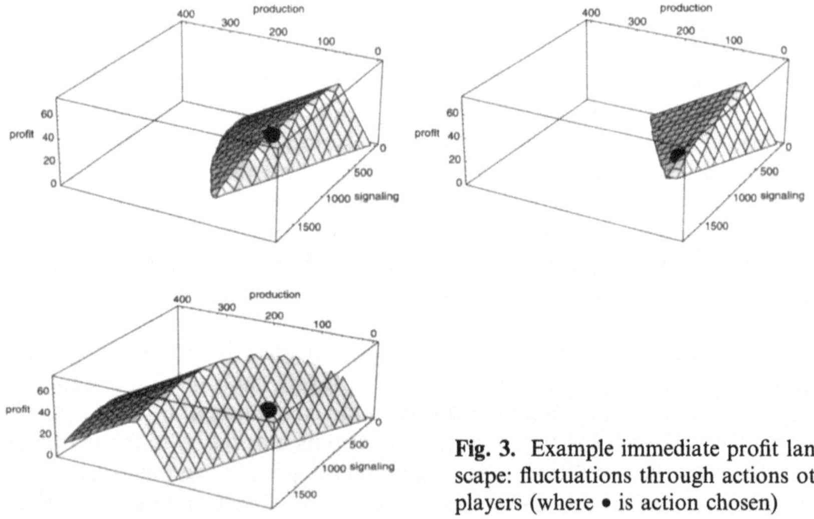

Fig. 3. Example immediate profit landscape: fluctuations through actions other players (where • is action chosen)

less vulnerable to this noise in the sense that it will lead less easily to negative profits. (This is because the firm's action can be farther away from the sea, and its island jumps up and down less than smaller islands.) As far as occasional negative profits induce firms to choose inactivity, this implies more positive feedback.

3 Theoretical framework

Our analysis of the experimental data will be structured through the following theoretical framework. In Section 3.a we present a game-theoretic analysis of the oligopoly game, and derive an equilibrium strategy. In Section 3.b we outline a simple 2-step model of adaptive behavior based on learning direction theory for the firm's production decisions, and hill climbing for its signaling decisions.

a) Game-theoretic analysis

In order to obtain a theoretical benchmark, we derive the symmetric stationary optimal policy for a given player for any given period, assuming complete information about the demand function.[12] Clearly, this cannot be a normative benchmark, but merely a yardstick. Of course, other theoretical yardsticks are possible, but the stationary symmetric equilibrium for the complete information game is particularly appealing in the sense that it is a simple and well-understood one.

Proposition 1. In the symmetric stationary equilibrium, the signaling level for an individual firm i in a given period t is given by:

$$s_i^t = \frac{g}{k} \cdot \left(\frac{m-1}{m^2}\right) \cdot n \qquad [3]$$

and the production is simply equal to the demand thus generated.

Proof. We derive the equilibrium signaling level in appendix B (see Table 1 for the notation used). Given this signaling level, the demand for an individual firm is given by equation (1). Since the demand function is deterministic, the optimal production level is simply equal to that demand.

The numerical values of this equilibrium implied by the parameters of the model are a production level of 118 and signaling level of 927.

---

[12] The symmetry feature is justified by the fact that the firms were identical. We do not consider the optimal strategy for the incomplete information game, because the literature on *monopolies* with uncertain, but linear, demand shows that it is often too complicated not only to determine the optimal pricing strategy (in order to maximize the discounted sum of profits) but also to establish convergence as such (see, e.g., Kiefer and Nyarko, 1989). Basically, the reason is that for each action there is a trade-off between the payoff a firm gets in the form of information which may lead to future profits, and the payoff in the form of immediate profits. As Kirman (1993) argues, trying to incorporate this problem into an oligopolistic model, in which there is also strategic interaction, seems unmanageable for the moment (see also, e.g., Green, 1983; or Kirman, 1983). Notice also that in the literature on double oral auctions with private information, it is the complete information outcome that is used as the theoretical benchmark (see Davis and Holt, 1992).

b) A simple model of adaptive behavior

Some recent models of adaptive learning and evolutionary dynamics in the economics literature are, for example, Ellison (1993), Kandori et al. (1993), and Young (1993). Marimon (1993) discusses the basic properties of such dynamic models. In the evolutionary dynamic models mentioned, adaptive behavior is basically a one-step error correction mechanism. The agents have a well-specified model of the game, they can reason what, given the actions of the other players, the optimal action would be, completely independent of any payoff actually experienced, and they play a best-response strategy against the frequency distribution of a given (sub-)population of other players (cf. fictitious play). The evolutionary dynamics consist of a coevolutionary adaptive process, players adapting to each others' adaptation to each other ..., plus experimentation in the form of trembling. In our game, the scope of such learning techniques is limited. The agents do not have a well-specified model of their environment, and they do not know what would be the best response. Hence, the very first task for our players, is to *learn* which actions would be good.

An important advance in the theoretical economics literature on learning involves models of Bayesian updating, in which the players optimize their actions based on present beliefs about the state of nature, the types of other players and the actions of other players, while updating these beliefs using Bayes' rule. McKelvey and Palfrey (1992), for example, explain the behavior in centipede games by a learning model in which players have a common belief about the existence of altruists in the population, and a common error rate about beliefs and actions which declines over time. While this kind of model requires a high amount of rationality, there is also a deeper problem: Bayesian updating applies only to small worlds, without surprises. It is mainly a dynamic consistency requirement. The real learning question is where the priors come from. In a small world they can be reasoned backwards using Bayes' rule, but clearly, this cannot apply in a world full of surprises (see also Binmore, 1991). Hence, we cannot apply such a model since a rational player would be unable to construct a plausible probability distribution of priors concerning his environment.

Adaptive behavior and learning have become important topics in experimental economics in the last decade. Learning in experimental economics is usually defined as a systematic change of behavior over time as a function of past information. Very few studies address, in this context, the question of which kind of adaptation is optimal.[13] Some papers have focused on comparing different learning models and finding which of these models describe best average behavior (see, e.g., Camerer and Ho, 1996; Stahl, 1996; Tang, 1996; or Nagel and Tang, 1998). Not surprisingly this turns out to depend on the game being played. This is supported by a recent debate in computer science and AI, about the alleged superiority of various search and learn algorithms. Macready and Wolpert (1995) prove a

[13] An important exception is Selten et al. (1997) who classify in great depth computer strategies submitted for Cournot supergames, and find that the best strategy against actual strategies is a simple measure-for-measure strategy.

so-called No Free Lunch theorem, which basically says that no such Holy Grail can exist, and that the success of an algorithm depends ultimately on the specifics of the search problems at hand.

Since searching for the ultimate learning model does not appear to be a promising strategy, some people began to search for simple models. In reinforcement learning models (see, e.g. Arthur, 1991; Roth and Erev, 1995), which are based on the psychological literature, no knowledge of the game or any beliefs of opponents' behavior is required, but only information on the actual payoffs experienced. Roth and Erev (1995) do not try to come up with the ultimate learning model, but instead take a simple model that has some plausibility, and start asking for what games does this model give a reasonably correct description of people's behavior *on average*. While Roth and Erev (1995) focus more on average behavior, Easley and Ledyard (1993) and Selten and Stoecker (1986) seek to make predictions for individual period-to-period choices based on the plausibility of some very weak qualitative assumptions concerning individual behavior. These models of adaptive behavior do not imply that the players are aware of the optimum, but only that they are continuously engaged in a process of adaptation in the direction of better actions (see also Holland, 1992). The fact that such models are based on some common general principles, and the plausibility of weak assumptions implies not only that they are parsimonious, but also that they are coarse, and that they avoid the problem of idiosyncracy. One would expect more specific learning models to share many of the qualitative conclusions of these simple models. The model of adaptive behavior that we will use fits into this approach.

As shown in the formal game-theoretic analysis, in case of complete information, the only choice variable for a firm is the number of signals to be sent, whereas production should be simply adjusted to the demand generated by these signals. This suggests a 2-step decision problem for the players in our experiment. The *first* step concerns the *number of signals* to be sent, while the *second* step adjusts the *production level* to the level of the demand generated. As we will see below, just as in the game-theoretic analysis, in this 2-step model the two-dimensional decision problem is basically reduced to one dimension, since production just tracks the observed demand. We will first analyze this second step.

Production: learning direction theory

Given the demand generated by a players' signals sent in the current and previous periods, the production level that would yield the highest profit would be equal to this demand. We conjecture that the players use a simple algorithm to achieve this. This is sometimes known in the experimental literature as '*learning direction theory*' (see, e.g., Selten and Stoecker, 1986; or Nagel, 1995). It is perhaps best illustrated by the following example given in Selten and Buchta (1994): "*(C)onsider the example of a marksman who tries to shoot an arrow at the trunk of a tree. If he misses the trunk to the right, he will shift the position of the bow to the left and if he misses to the left, he will shift the position of the bow to the right. The marksman looks at his experience from his last trial and adjusts his behavior according to a simple*

Table 2. Predictions learning direction theory

If		Then
(1)	$\text{production}_t < \text{demand}_t$	$\text{production}_{t+1} \geq \text{production}_t$
(2)	$\text{production}_t > \text{demand}_t$	$\text{production}_{t+1} \leq \text{production}_t$
(3)	$\text{production}_t = \text{demand}_t$	n.a.

qualitative picture of the causal relationship between the position of his bow and the path of the arrow." (p. 9). Given an action, and the corresponding feedback from his environment, it is assumed that the player has enough knowledge of the structure of the game and the payoff function to reason in which direction better actions could have been found (see also Selten, 1997). Notice that the feedback is not necessarily the specific value of the payoff generated. The player is supposed to move directly in his choice parameter space, but it is not necessary for learning direction theory to be applicable that a player knows exactly where the optimum is. Often only the direction is known. Therefore learning direction theory concerns only a qualitative learning mechanism.[14] Notice that although, on the one hand, the theory offers only a general qualitative prediction, it is, on the other hand, very precise in the sense that it predicts a player's action on the basis of his most recent action *alone*.

In our game, this direction learning mechanism can be applied as follows. If a firm faced more demand than it had produced, it *knows* that a higher production level would have led to higher profits. And if a firm faced less demand than it had produced, it *knows* that a lower production level would have led to higher profits. Therefore, in our model, learning direction theory would lead to the *predictions* given in Table 2. Notice that if production and demand were equal, the theory does not predict the direction of the change in production. Remember that, given the 2-step model (setting signals and adjusting production), these predictions are for a *given* demand level. Clearly, as we will analyze below, the demand depends upon the signaling level. Therefore, here we only consider those cases in which the players did not move in the opposite direction with their signaling level in order to induce a demand change.[15]

Under learning direction theory, the reasoning of the players is supposed to be boundedly rational in that it only considers what *would have been* a better action, that is, it considers actions *ex post*. In our formal analysis we explained that the demand was generated by a fixed deterministic demand function. Since this was not known to the players, there was subjective uncertainty. The problem for the players is not so much to maximize their

[14] Notice the similarity with supervised learning algorithms (see Vriend, 1994, for a discussion). With supervised learning it is not assumed that the player himself knows where the better actions are, but it is a supervisor who tells the player where the optimal action would have been. Also most supervised learning algorithms assume a gradual change in the right direction only.

[15] That is, if an increase in production is predicted there should be no decrease in signaling, and the other way round. This condition was satisfied in 63% of the cases.

ex post profits, but to maximize their expected *ex ante* profits. If demand is uncertain, and rationing is not all-or-nothing, some overproduction may be profitable, that is, the production that maximizes expected profits may be higher than the expected demand. Given the signaling level, the demand q faced by an individual firm is a stochastic function with p.d.f. f[q]. Hence expected profit E[Π] for a given output level z is: $E[\Pi(z)] = p \cdot \{\Sigma_{q=0}^{z} q \cdot f[q] + z \cdot \Sigma_{q=z}^{\infty} f[q]\} - c \cdot z - k \cdot s$. As can be easily shown: $\Delta E[\Pi(z)]/\Delta z = p \cdot (1 - F[z]) - c$. Hence, expected profit is maximized when $F[z] = 1 - c/p$. That is, if $c/p < 0.5$, as was the case, then we have $F[z] > 0.5$ at the optimal production level. In other words, the *ex ante* optimal production level is higher than the *ex post* average demand. We predict the players to recognize this in our experiment, and hence expect a bias towards 'overproduction' relative to the predictions of learning direction theory.

Signaling: hill climbing

As noted above, the adaptation of the production level is assumed to take place for a given demand level. Since this demand is generated eventually by the signals sent, it is time to turn to an analysis of the number of signals sent. Learning direction theory cannot predict much with respect to signaling. In the case where demand is higher than production, a firm knows that a lower signaling level would have given higher profits, but it does not know what the optimal signaling level would have been. However, in case production is higher than demand faced, a firm does not even know whether a higher signaling level would have led to higher profits. Perhaps even lower signaling levels would have given higher profits. Also, when the demand faced by a firm equals its production, it does not know in which direction to adjust its signaling. As we showed in Section 2, a player's opportunities could be depicted as a hill. The objective of a player is to find the top of the hill, but he does not know what the hill looks like, and the hill may be changing all the time. A simple way to deal with this problem would be to start walking in one direction, and if one gets a higher payoff, one continues from there; otherwise one goes back to try another direction. Eventually one should reach the top.[16] We conjecture that the players' adaptive behavior in signaling space can be described by such a *hill climbing*, or gradient, algorithm.[17]

In order to explain the essence of hill climbing, and the contrast with learning direction theory, let us continue the example of the marksman trying to hit the trunk of a tree. Now, assume that the marksman is blindfolded. After each trial the only feedback he gets from his environment is the level of enthusiasm with which the crowd of spectators reacts. The

[16] This might be a local top only. Simulated annealing is a more sophisticated variant of hill climbing in that it tries to avoid getting stuck at local optima. To achieve this, the algorithm accepts with some probability downhill moves, whereas uphill moves are always accepted. Since we do not have landscapes with local optima, we do not consider simulated annealing.

[17] See also Bloomfield (1994), Kirman (1993), Roberts (1995), and Merlo and Schotter (1994).

Table 3. Predictions hill climbing

If	Then
(1) $signaling_t < signaling_{t-1}$ and $payoff_t < payoff_{t-1}$	$signaling_{t+1} > signaling_t$
(2) $signaling_t < signaling_{t-1}$ and $payoff_t > payoff_{t-1}$	$signaling_{t+1} < signaling_{t-1}$
(3) $signaling_t > signaling_{t-1}$ and $payoff_t < payoff_{t-1}$	$signaling_{t+1} < signaling_t$
(4) $signaling_t > signaling_{t-1}$ and $payoff_t > payoff_{t-1}$	$signaling_{t+1} > signaling_{t-1}$
(5) $signaling_t = signaling_{t-1}$ or $payoff_t = payoff_{t-1}$	n.a.

closer he gets to the optimum, the louder they are expected to shout. Therefore, after two trials he can compare the levels of payoff, and shoot next time in the neighborhood in which the yelling was loudest. In other words, if an action leads to a worse outcome than the previous one, it is rejected as a new starting point. Hill climbers do not use any knowledge of the structure of the game, or of the payoff function. They are myopic local improvers, walking blindly in the direction of the experienced gradient in their payoff landscape. Hence, hill climbers rely completely upon the contours of the payoff landscape, whereas direction learning takes place directly in the space of actions. A deterministic variant of hill climbing would give the *predictions* presented in Table 3.

In our experiment there is one problem with hill climbing: as we showed in Section 2, the hills may change over time, even considering constant actions of the other players. Therefore, given the *dynamics* of the demand generated by the signals sent and the patronizing customers, a player should look further ahead than his immediate profits only. We showed that players could boost their immediate profits by signaling very little, i.e., by eating into their pool of customers. But future profits are adversely affected by this action. Of all the customers satisfied in a given period, some fraction will come back 'for free' in the next period, i.e., without the need to send them a signal. A firm can also forego some current profits by investing in the buildup of a pool of customers. The higher the current sales level, the better the firm's future profit opportunities, which was visualized by a larger island in Section 2. Hence, when considering the question of how well a firm performed in a given period, one should not only look at its immediate profits, but also at the change in its current sales level. The value of serving additional customers now (besides the immediate profits) is the profit that can be extracted from them in later periods.[18] Since patronizing customers come back 'for free' (without needing a signal), the profit margin for those customers will be the price minus the unit production costs of the commodity. Formally, the lookahead payoff in a given period is: $\Pi + \Delta x \cdot (p - c) \cdot \sum_{t=1}^{\infty} f^t$.

We will consider both the basic hill climbing variant, in which the players go myopically for their immediate profits only, and the variant in which the players climb hills, taking into account their lookahead payoff. If

[18] There is also an indirect effect related to a change in the player's sales level. It will change the number of 'free' consumers for which the player's signals compete with the other players' signals. This indirect effect will be relatively small because it is spread over the six firms (they compete for the same pool of free consumers), and will be ignored here.

there turns out to be myopic immediate profit hill climbers, we would expect to find them among the firms with low production levels, since they underestimate the value of keeping their sales levels up. Notice that since the players do not know the value of the patronage parameter f, nor the exact specification of the demand function, a priori they are not in a position to calculate explicitly the altitude of their lookahead hill. But during the game they can learn about the value of looking ahead. Hence, without specifying here the exact learning mechanism through which they may have learned this value, we will consider the question of how often the players behave '*as if*' they are hill climbing, having learned these lookahead payoff values correctly.

What kind of average time pattern would this 2-step model of adaptive behavior predict? We consider an unrefined numerical model, in which we use learning direction theory for the players' production decision, and hill climbing for their signaling decision. We start with all players choosing the average production and signaling levels observed during the experiments in the first period (see below), and restrict their choices to the same domain, i.e., 0 to 4999. Players follow the learning direction theory hypotheses for production as outlined above (see Table 2). The step size is equal to $|\varepsilon|$, with $\varepsilon \simeq N(0,5)$. If their production is equal to their demand, then they do not change their demand. And as explained above, the players do not change their production level if their signaling decision for that period points in the opposite direction. For hill climbing we use the lookahead variant explained above (see also Table 3). Comparing the payoffs realized in the preceding two periods, a player takes as the new starting value in the next period that signaling level that generated the highest payoff of the two. When the payoffs in the two preceding periods are equal, the new starting value is the average signaling level in those two periods. When the signaling level is unchanged during the two preceding periods, that value will again be the starting value for the next period. In order to generate the player's new signaling level, some noise is added, which is a draw from a truncated N(0, 10) distribution.[19] All players are modeled identically, but independently, which implies that their paths may diverge over time due to the stochastic factors. In Fig. 7 (in Section 4) we present the average behavior of 11 simulated sessions with 6 players, as well as the actual experimental data.

4 Data analysis

We will analyze the experimental data following the theoretical framework outlined above. In Section 4.a we will compare the experimental data with the game-theoretic benchmark presented in Section 3.a. In Section 4.b we will examine the data in comparison to the predictions of the simple 2-step model of adaptive behavior presented in Section 3.b, and the modifications thereof that take into account some specifics of the oligopoly game. As we will see below, perhaps the most striking feature of the data, given that the

[19] Here the truncation was determined each time such that the new signaling value stays at the correct side of the discarded signaling value that led to the lower payoff (see Table 3).

oligopoly game as such is symmetric, is the enormous differences between the individual players' actions and outcomes. Section 4.c will explain these differences.

a) Comparison experimental data to game-theoretic benchmark

Observation 1. The average actions actually chosen by the players are close to the symmetric optimal policy, but the differences between the players are considerable. The average actions chosen by the players get closer to the equilibrium policy as they play more periods, but the differences between the individual players increase, whereas the differences between the sessions decrease.

Figure C.1.a–c in Appendix C show the time series for the average signaling, production and profits of the 66 players for the periods 1 to 131 (with these variables at zero for bankrupt players),[20] and compare this with the symmetric stationary equilibrium. We observe a steep learning curve in the beginning, which leads to profits close to the equilibrium level early on. We see a lot of fluctuations during most of the history, and at the end we observe a movement towards the equilibrium levels. Table 4 presents some '*snapshots*' of this comparison between the symmetric stationary optimal policy and the actual average actions played in the game. The numbers in parentheses are the standard deviations. For each variable we calculate two standard deviations; one based on the averages for each of the 66 individual players, and the second based on the averages per session. Notice that the variance across sessions is small, and much smaller than across subjects, especially in the last 50 periods.

Given the minimal information about their environment available to the players, they are not in a position to specify the demand function. Hence, a player is not able to maximize his firm's profits directly with standard techniques. As their problem situation is ill-defined, they must learn and behave

Table 4. Comparison equilibrium, averages, and standard deviations (*subjects–sessions*)

	Sign.	(s.d.)	Prod.	(s.d.)	Profit	(s.d.)
Equilibrium	927	–	118	–	14.3	–
Period 1	864	(1016–480)	616	(443–205)	−107.6	(120.1–73.2)
Period 1–50	882	(867–163)	160	(121–13)	5.8	(23.3–11.3)
Period 81–130	938	(954–113)	133	(125–6)	8.1	(18.9–9.2)

[20] Throughout the paper, unless otherwise stated, we adhere to the following policy when computing averages. When the objective is to characterize the behavior of the individual players, or the differences between (categories of) individual players, we take the averages over the periods that a player was active, i.e., until the end of the session or until he went bankrupt, whichever came first. When we want to characterize the average actions and outcomes for one or more sessions as such, e.g., to compare it with the theoretical benchmarks computed, we average over all players, taking zero values for the actions and outcomes of bankrupt players.

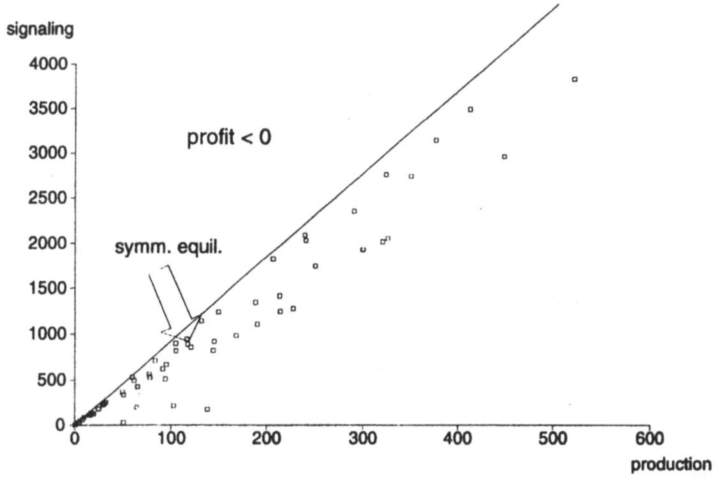

Fig. 4. Distribution actions, periods 81–130

adaptively. As we see, the players learn to choose actions that are on average close to a symmetric equilibrium, but there are large differences between these actions. Figure 4 shows the distribution of the individual players' signaling and production levels, averaged over the periods 81–130 (with zero values for bankrupt players). The arrow indicates the symmetric game-theoretic equilibrium given above. The straight line with slope $(p - c)/k$ serves as a benchmark. All combinations of production and signaling above it necessarily lead to negative profits. If every unit produced is actually sold, the net revenue is given by the price minus production costs per unit, multiplied by the production level: $(p - c) \cdot z$. Dividing that number by the cost of a signal (k) gives the number of signals beyond which profits can never be positive. We will return to these differences between the players in Section 4.c.

b) Comparison experimental data to simple model of adaptive behavior

We now turn to an analysis of the players' behavior using the 2-step model as a benchmark. We first examine the players' production decision in comparison with the predictions of learning direction theory, and then analyze their signaling decision in comparison with the hill climbing predictions.

Observation 2. The players change their production level in a direction that would be wrong according to learning direction theory in only 9% of the cases in which it makes a prediction. But there is an asymmetry in the success of learning direction theory between the cases in which production was too low, and those in which it was too high. This asymmetry seems related to the fact that the players are less boundedly rational than this theory assumes.

Figure 5 summarizes how far learning direction theory predicts correctly, distinguishing the cases of too high and too low production in the preceding period. If production was too low (1250 observations), learning

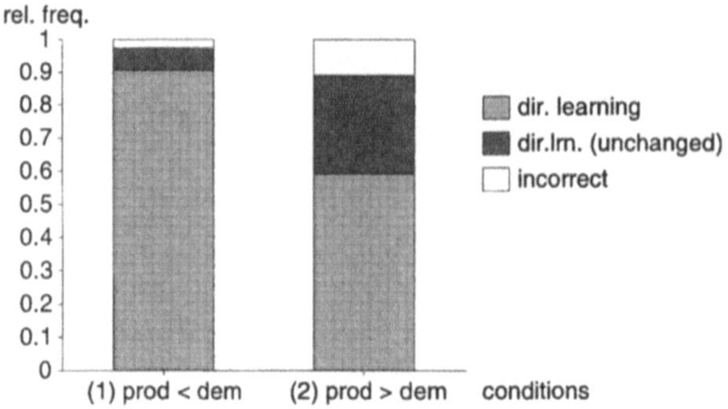

Fig. 5. Learning direction theory, with conditions as explained in Table 2

direction theory made a wrong prediction in only 3% of the cases. If production was too high (4571 observations), the relative frequency of wrong predictions was 11%. The weighted average of these two gives the 9% mentioned in observation 2. Production was equal to demand in only 8% of the cases (510 observations).[21]

Figure 5 clearly shows the asymmetry between these cases. As explained above, it seems that the players are more reluctant to decrease their production level when it is too high, because they understand that production should be higher than average demand; the players are less boundedly rational than learning direction theory assumes. Checking the players one by one, we find that 58 out of 66 subjects more often follow the learning direction theory hypothesis in the case in which production is less than demand, than in the case in which production is higher than demand. Also it turns out that *all* players, without any exception, on average overproduce; with the overall average production 1.20 times average demand.

Observation 3. Players adjust their signaling level in a way that is *wrong* according to the hypothesis of hill climbing in about a quarter of the cases. This applies equally to myopic (27%) and lookahead (25%) hill climbing. Further, the players seem only slightly inclined to looking ahead.

Figure 6a,b give the percentages of correct and wrong predictions by the hill climbing hypothesis for myopic and lookahead climbing.[22] As we see, Figures 6a, b are very similar. A first explanation is as follows. Analyzing all cases in which a player had changed his signaling level, it turns out that in 71% of the cases the payoff gradient happens to be in the same direction for myopic and lookahead hill climbing. That is, the player's immediate profits

[21] If we neglect the condition that signaling did not move in the opposite direction, considering all players together, the percentages of incorrect predictions would be 5 for the case in which production was less than demand, and 23 for the case in which production was greater than demand.

[22] Notice that if a player had not changed his signaling level during the last two periods, or if his payoff had not changed, there is no gradient, and hill climbing cannot be applied. This is condition (5) in Table 3, and it occurred in 33% of the cases. The absolute frequencies for the cases (1) to (4) in Fig. 6a are 560, 2311, 2997, and 810. In Fig. 6b these frequencies are 1305, 1583, 2121, and 1710.

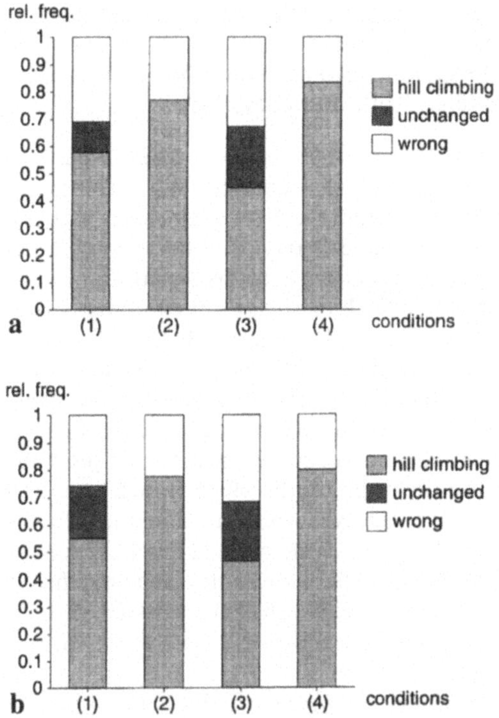

Fig. 6. **a** Myopic hill climbing, with conditions as explained in Table 3. **b** Lookahead hill climbing, with conditions as explained in Table 3

as well as his lookahead payoff (taking into account also the future profits related to his current sales level) had increased, or both had decreased. When we consider only the other 29% cases of opposite gradients, the cases in which myopic hill climbing and lookahead hill climbing predict a different change in signaling, we find that on average the players are inclined only slightly towards looking ahead; in 53.2% of those cases they follow the prediction of lookahead hill climbing, and in 48.8 the prediction of myopic hill climbing.

The numbers in parentheses on the horizontal axis denote the 'if ...' conditions as given in Table 3. The light shaded bars give the frequencies when the hill climbing prediction was strictly correct. The dark shaded bars give the frequencies with which players choose signaling in period t + 1 equal to signaling in period t. Notice that for conditions (2) and (4), those cases are already included in the strictly correct predictions. For conditions (1) and (3), according to the hill climbing hypothesis, a player should reverse the direction of the change in his signaling level, whereas it would be strictly wrong to continue moving into the same direction that led to a decrease in payoffs. The inertia indicated in the figures by the dark shaded bars is not exactly predicted by the hill climbing hypothesis, but it is also not strictly wrong. Moreover, there might be good reasons for this inertia. First, players might keep their signaling level constant for a period, in order to adjust their production level according to the rules suggested by the learning direction theory. Second, given the noise caused by the other players, it may be wise not to put all the weight on the last period alone. This suggests that a further refinement of the modeling of the players' behavior could be obtained, by considering algorithms taking into account more periods, such as in reinforcement learning (see, e.g., Roth and Erev, 1995).

Observation 4. There is an asymmetry between the cases in which a player's payoff had increased and those in which it had decreased. When things are going well, a player will *not* easily *switch* into the wrong direction with his signaling. When, on the other hand, a player's payoff is decreasing, he is more likely to *continue* into the wrong direction with his signaling.

For convenience, we consider here only lookahead hill climbing. Compare in Figure 6a, b the relative frequencies of *wrong* predictions for cases (1) and (3) with cases (2) and (4). In cases (1) and (3), the player's payoff had gone down, and so continuing to change his signaling level in the same direction would be wrong (29% of the times this happened). In cases (2) and (4), the player's payoff had increased, and so going back to his previous signaling level and then moving into the opposite direction would be wrong (21% on average). We used a sign test to analyze whether individual players were more likely to go into a wrong direction in the cases (1) and (3) than in the cases (2) and (4). For 43 out of 66 subjects this was the case (significant at 1.0% level; 1-sided). We conjecture that the fact that unsuccessful courses of actions are more easily continued than are successful ones reversed, is a more general psychological feature.

We have seen that the 2-step model we proposed does not perfectly describe the behavior of the players. But at the same time, the attraction of the model is its simplicity. A question, then, is whether the time-pattern of the average behavior of the players in the experiments fits the pattern predicted by this simple model. In Fig. 7 we present the average behavior of 11 simulated sessions with 6 players, and the average signaling levels observed in the experiments. As we see, the average signaling level not only converges to the same level, but it also shows a similar initial dip.[23]

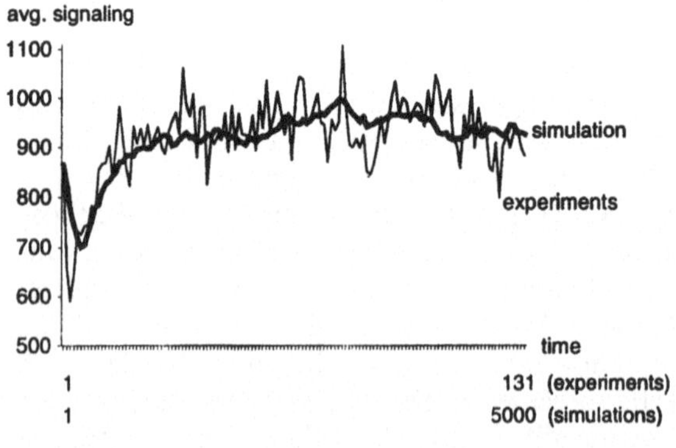

Fig. 7. Simulation 2-step model vs. experimental data

[23] It should be stressed that the two curves have a different time scale. Tinkering with the speed of adjustment of the players (e.g., adjusting the speed itself as well), would yield a better fit along this dimension, but that is not our objective. We use an identical and constant (but stochastic) low adjustment speed for all players.

c) Explaining the differences between the individual players

Although the average behavior of the players appears to fit rather well to the symmetric game-theoretic equilibrium, and also to the convergence level and time-pattern of the 2-step model, in Section 4.a we observed that underneath these averages there were strong differences between the players.[24] In this section we will analyze and explain these strong differences.

If we have a look at Fig. 4, showing the distribution of signaling and production levels of the individual players, a first question is how these differences in actions correspond to differences in performance; and a second is how we arrive at this distribution. In other words, in what sense does the behavior of some players differ from that of other players?

Observation 5. There are considerable differences in performance among the players. We can distinguish three categories. Category I: the successful players, Category II: the 'nil players', and Category III: the unsuccessful players. The category II players choose relatively low signaling and production levels, and realize profits close to zero. As for the category I players, category III players try higher signaling (and production) levels than category II players, but they are less successful than category I players.

A method to measure the difference in performance among the players is the Gini coefficient (see, e.g., Case and Fair, 1996), which measures the skewness in the wealth distribution of a population, using the Lorenz curve. If the poorest x% of a population has x% of the total wealth of that population for each $0 \leq x \leq 100$, we have an equal distribution, characterized by a Gini coefficient equal to 0. If the richest person in the population has 100% of the total wealth, the Gini coefficient will be 1. The Gini coefficient for the 66 players is 0.41.[25] Given this unequal performance, what does the distribution look like, and what is its relation to the actions chosen? In Figure 8a we order all 66 players in terms of their cumulative profit per period, and in Figure 8b we present for these same players their average signaling.[26] Although these categories can be identified easily visually, they can be derived formally as follows: Having ordered all players on their average profits, calculate average signaling for each player, consider any two possible boundaries yielding three categories, and take those

---

[24] This is similar to the findings by Keser and Gardner (1998) who observe that aggregate behavior in a common pool experiment is well explained by the subgame perfect equilibrium, although only 5% of the subjects play in accordance to the theory. See also Budd et al. (1993) and Midgley et al. (1996).

[25] In order to allow for a comparison between the different sessions, we consider the same number of periods played for each session, i.e., 131. The wealth for a player is the cumulative profits realized plus the initial 2000 points he could loose before going bankrupt. Hence, bankrupt players have an accumulated wealth of zero. The Gini coefficients per session are available upon request.

[26] These individual averages are taken over the periods in which a player was active, i.e. until he went bankrupt or until the end of the session, whichever came first. Adding production levels would yield little extra information since average production and signaling are almost perfectly correlated.

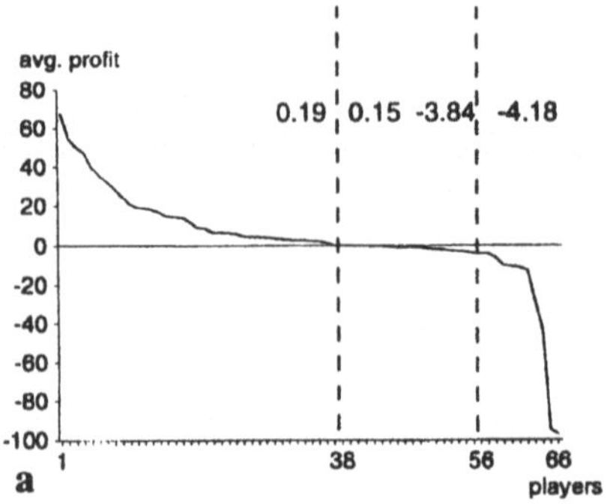

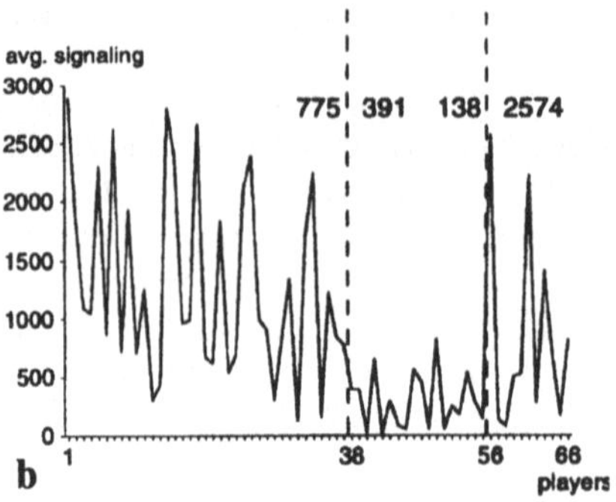

Fig. 8. **a** Average profit. **b** Average signaling

Table 5. Averages for the three categories

Players	#Players	Signaling	Production	Profits
all	66	951	160	4.0
cat. I	37	1301	194	16.6
cat. II	18	290	49	−1.4
cat. III	11	857	225	−29.5

boundaries for which the difference between the average signaling in the middle category and the other two categories combined is maximized.[27] We will use these three categories in our subsequent analysis, to see whether we can identify qualitative differences in the adaptive behavior between these three groups of players. The numbers in Fig. 8a, b give the values of profits and signaling respectively for the observations next to the boundaries.

Table 5 illustrates this categorization further by giving the average signaling, production, and profit levels per category as shown in Figure 8a, b. We use the Wilcoxon-Mann-Whitney test (Wilcoxon test from here on) to analyze whether the signaling levels of the individual players in the three categories are drawn from the same population. The alternative hypotheses are that the signaling level is stochastically higher for category I than for category II players (significant at 0.0% level), lower for category II than for category III players (significant at 2.6%), and different for category I and category III players (significant at 5.0%).

The question, then, is from where do these differences between the players' actions and outcomes arise?[28] We will offer three broad explanations. First, we will show how it is related to the dynamics of the oligopoly

[27] We imposed the additional restriction that there should be at least 3 players per category.

[28] The production and signaling technology are characterized by constant marginal costs. Hence, any firm size might seem efficient, and an unequal distribution of firm sizes would not be surprising. Notice, however, that the demand equation (1) implies that the marginal revenue of a signal sent is not constant, and depends upon the firm size.

game, and the players' perception thereof and success in dealing with it. Second, we will show how it is related to the players' initial choices, and the positive feedback inherent in the dynamics of the game. Third, we analyze the differences in the players' ambitions.

Observation 6. The observation (see Sect. 4b) that the players are less boundedly rational than learning direction theory assumes applies in particular to category I players.

Figure 9a,b summarize how far learning direction theory predicts correctly, distinguishing the cases of too high and too low production in the preceding period, and distinguishing the three categories of players. Comparing the frequencies of increasing production in those cases in which production was less than demand (Fig. 9a), players in category II increase their production less often than category I players (significant at 3.1% level with 1-sided Wilcoxon test). The difference between category II and category III players is not significant, and the fact that category III players increase their production less often than category I players is significant only at the 7.6% level. Looking instead at the frequencies of decreasing production in those cases in which production was higher than demand (Fig. 9b), players in category II decrease their production more often than category I players (significant at 1.0% level with 1-sided Wilcoxon test), and less often than category III players (significant at 1.1%). The difference between category I and category III players is not significant. Hence, it seems as though category I players understand best the desirability of overproduction, while category II players understand this least well, and as a result more easily become small players.

Observation 7. When hill climbing, category I players look ahead most often. Category II players do so least frequently.

Table 6 shows the frequencies with which the players go for immediate profits, and with which they look ahead in those cases in which the hill climbing hypothesis points to opposite directions. We observe that the differences in frequencies between the categories are not large. Category II players look ahead less frequently than category I players (significant at 0.9%; 1-sided Wilcoxon test), and also less frequently than category III

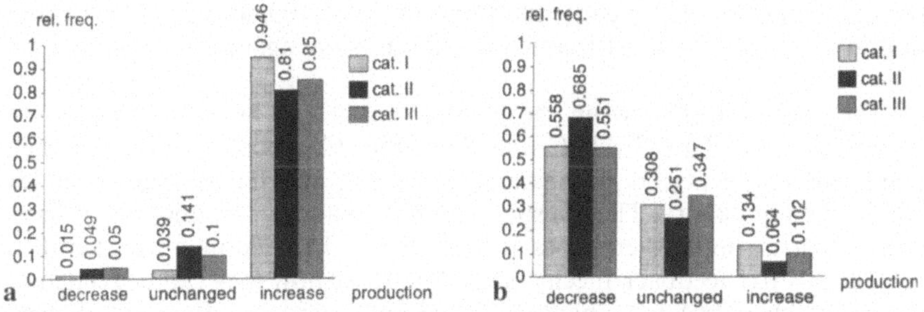

Fig. 9. **a** Direction learning after production < demand. **b** Direction learning after production > demand

Table 6. Frequencies myopic vs. lookahead hill climbing

Players	Absolute frequencies		Rel. frequencies (%)
	Myopic	Lookahead	Lookahead
all	1094	1243	53.2
cat. I	595	747	55.7
cat. II	383	364	48.8
cat. III	117	132	53.0

players (significant at 9%). There is no significant difference between category I and category III players. Hence, category II players are the most myopic, not putting enough resources into building their market, and this partly explains why they are small players.

A second explanation for the differences between the players is related to their choices in the initial periods, and, related to the dynamics of the game, the way in which these initial choices have prolonged effects on the players' behavior.

Observation 8. Both production and signaling levels in the first period are concentrated on focal points. Further, the individual players' sales in later periods are positively correlated with their sales in the initial periods. The correlation coefficient between the 66 individual players' average sales levels in the periods 1–10 and the periods 81–130 (taking zero values for bankrupt players) is 0.55 (significant at 0.0% level; 1-sided t-test).

In the first period, the players have very little information to guide their decisions. Nevertheless, these choices are far from uniformly randomly distributed over the relevant choice domain. First, we look at production. The choice domain ranges from 0 to 4999, but the players was told that the demand faced by an individual firm would in general be below 1000. Only 6 players (9%) chose production levels greater than 1000. 61 out of 66 players (92%) chose a multiple of 50, and 53 (80%) picked production levels that are multiples of 100. The favorite multiple of 100 is 500, chosen by 13 players (20%), followed by 800 (7 players, or 11%), and 1000 (6 players, or 9%). Thus, as observed in many other experiments, the midpoint is a focal point (see, e.g., Ochs, 1994 on coordination games). Next, we look at signaling 61 players (92%) chose multiples of 50 or 100, and 55 (83%) chose multiples of 100, the most frequently chosen being again 500 (8 players, or 12%).

The correlations between the players' initial and later experiences are further illustrated by Table C.1 in Appendix C, where we give for each player his initial period actions and outcomes, and his averages over his whole playing history. The question one has to address is, once we observe such a correlation, where does it stem from? In Section 2 we identified various positive feedback mechanisms. Let us see how they can be related to these positive correlations between initial and later sales. First, we showed the temptation to maximize immediate profits by choosing signaling equal to zero, with production greater than zero. In that way, a firm's costs would

Table 7. Shrinking customer pool by not signaling, with production > 0

Players	# Obs.	Shrinking	Rel. frequency
all	10174	391	3.8
cat. I	5877	107	1.8
cat. II	3078	156	5.1
cat. III	1219	128	10.5

be greatly reduced because there are no signaling costs, with the patronizing customers showing up 'for free', but a consequence would be the shrinking of its pool of customers, with negative effects on later sales and profitability. How often did the players follow this strategy? And are there differences between the categories?

Observation 9. Shrinking the customer pool by not signaling is done regularly by players in all three categories. But there are differences between the categories. Category III players are much more inclined to eat drastically into their customer pool than are category II players, who are in turn much more inclined to do so than are category I players.

Table 7 illustrates this. Notice that category III players do this in more than 10% of their decision periods, that this is almost 6 times as often as category I players, and more than twice as often as category II players. We use the Wilcoxon test to analyze whether these levels of the individual players in the three categories are drawn from the same population. The alternative hypotheses are that shrinking occurs less often for category I than for category II players (significant at 0.9% level), less often for category II than for category III players (significant at 4.0%), and less often for category I than for category III players (significant at 0.0%). Recall that category III players signal on average much more than category II players, that is, they counter the shrinking of their customer pool by extra signaling in the periods following it. This aggressive '*on-off*' signaling behavior might be one of the explanations for their low profits.[29]

A second positive feedback effect presented in Section 2 was related to the fact that small firms would more easily get negative profits. Players on small islands get wet feet easily. Clearly, positive and negative profits are only relative. However, when profits are negative, a player has always the option to play (0, 0) for (signaling, production). Since that leads to a sales level of zero, and no patronizing customers, it implies a strong negative lock-in effect.

Observation 10. Excluding bankruptcy cases, *switching* to inactivity is predominantly done by players after observing a loss in the preceding period. There are differences between the categories. Category II players are more

[29] It is not that players deliberately making themselves bankrupt increase these frequencies for category III players. In fact, leaving the bankrupt players out would give an even higher average frequency for shrinking for category III players (11.0%).

skeptical about their opportunities than the other two categories. They switch most easily to inactivity. Once voluntarily inactive, the probability to stay inactive the next period is much higher than the probability of returning to business (84% against 16%).

Table 8 illustrates the voluntary switching to inactivity. Considering the individual players, only 1 player out of 66 switches to inactivity less often after a loss than otherwise. Using the Wilcoxon test to analyze whether the switching-to-inactivity frequencies of the individual players in the three categories are drawn from the same population, we find that category II players switch to inactivity more often than category I players (significant at 0.0% level), and category II players switch to inactivity also more often than category III players (significant at 2.4%), whereas there is no significant difference between category I and category III players. Recall that category III players realized negative profits much more frequently than category II players, so they try hard to improve upon their payoffs by acting rather than staying out.

Up to this point we have discovered two main explanations for the differences between the players. A first factor explaining these differences is their perception of the dynamics of the game, and this is extensively documented in the analysis above. A second factor is that the players' choices and outcomes in the initial periods turned out to be an important explanatory factor for success, or lack thereof, in later periods. The players' actions and outcomes during the initial periods might be just a matter of good or bad luck, but it might also be related to their pre-game experience in real life – what they have learned outside the laboratory – or it might be related to other psychological factors. There is a third factor that might explain some of the differences between the three categories of players. This being the ambitions of the players. To consider this, in a previous paper (Nagel and Vriend, 1998) we carried out an aspiration level analysis. The basic idea of such an analysis is that agents, due to their bounded rationality, are not able to optimize, and therefore will settle for satisficing behavior. Which outcomes are satisficing for a certain agent depends upon his aspiration level, where those levels are a moving target based, for example, on the agent's direct experience, or on the outcomes of other agents. This is a qualitative theory of adaptive behavior, presuming that when an agent's targets are met, he will be satisfied, and hence not change his behavior, whereas if his targets are not met, he will try to improve upon his situation by changing his

Table 8. Relative frequency switching to voluntary inactivity

Players	# Observations		Rel. frequencies (%) inactivity	
	Profit < 0	Profit ≥ 0	After profit < 0	After profit ≥ 0
all	3434	6308	1.7	0.1
cat. I	1470	4334	0.5	0.0
cat. II	1349	1427	3.4	0.4
cat. III	615	547	1.1	0.4

actions.[30] The central question we studied there was whether there are differences between the three categories of players (the successful ones, the unsuccessful, and the 'nil' players). We found, among other things, that there are systematic differences between the players in the three categories as far as their reaction to satisfactory or unsatisfactory outcomes is concerned. In particular, category I players appear to be more ambitious than category II or III players, in the sense that they increase their production and signaling levels even when their aspiration level had been reached, whereas the latter two categories tend to keep production and signaling unchanged when their aspiration levels had been reached.

5 Conclusions

There are three main conclusions we can draw from this experimental study of adaptive behavior in an oligopolistic market game. The first is related to the average behavior of the players. Notwithstanding the minimal information the players were provided with, on average they learned to choose actions that were close to the symmetric stationary equilibrium for the complete information variant of the game. The second conclusion concerns the proposed a 2-step model, based on the game-theoretic analysis, in which the players use their signaling level as the basic strategic variable, whereas they adjust their production level towards the demand thus generated. It seems fair to conclude that learning direction theory, combined with the qualification concerning the *ex ante* optimality of overproduction, gives an accurate description of the players' behavior as far as their changes of production levels is concerned. The hill climbing hypothesis with respect to the players' signaling level was slightly less accurate, and made wrong predictions in about a quarter of the cases. In particular we detected an asymmetry in the players' behavior. When payoffs were increasing, players tend to continue their course of action. But when payoffs were decreasing and the players should have reversed the direction their signaling was moving into, they often continued walking downhill. We also showed that inertia in the players' behavior was important. This suggests that a further refinement of the modeling of the players' behavior could be obtained, by considering algorithms taking into account more periods than the most recent alone, e.g. reinforcement learning (see Roth and Erev, 1995).[31] Using the hill climbing hypothesis, we analyzed how far the players were inclined to go myopically for immediate profits: all players were only slightly more inclined to look ahead, and this was true above all for the successful players. A numerical exercise showed that the simple 2-step model seems to offer a reasonable explanation for the average market outcomes, both for the level and time-pattern of convergence.

---

[30] See Börgers and Sarin (1996) and Hart and Mas-Colell (1996) for two recent examples of aspiration level analyses.

[31] One of the first problems, then, is how to reduce the choice set of the players (see, e.g., Holland et al., 1986). Much more progress needs to be made here.

A third conclusion is that the players' behavior in this symmetric game is highly heterogeneous, much more so than expected. There are strong differences between the players, both with respect to their average actions and to their average payoffs. We showed that three categories of players could be distinguished: the successful ones, the 'nil players', and the unsuccessful players. The actions and outcomes in the initial period turned out to be important for the players' later performance. This could be due to good or to bad luck, but it also could be related to personality issues, both how daring they are in the first periods, and how they react to success or lack of it. We analyzed how this was related to some of the positive feedback mechanisms present in the market, and how the different categories of players dealt with these more or less successfully. In general, with help of the 2-step model, we showed that the players had different rates of success in adapting to their environment. An aspiration level analysis pointed to differences in the players' ambitions as an additional factor explaining their differences in performance.

Appendix A. Instructions, and computer screen

Table A.1 contains the English version of the instructions given to the players.

Table A.1. Instructions to the players

Actors:
* Each of you will be a firm in a market economy.
* The consumers in this economy are simulated by a computer program.

Each day:
* In the morning, firms decide:
  - Identical firms decide upon a number of units of a perishable consumption good (each firm the same good).
  - The production of each unit costs 0.25 point.
  - The production decided upon at the beginning of the day is available for sale on that day.
  - Experience shows that, in general, the demand faced by an individual firm is below 1000.
  - The firms also decide upon a number of information signals to be sent into the population, communicating the fact that they are a firm offering the commodity for sale on that day. Imagine the sending of letters to addresses picked randomly from the telephone book.
  - Sending one information signal to an individual agent always costs 0.08 point.
  - The price of the commodity is 1 point. The price of the commodity is given, it does not change over time, it is equal for all firms and consumers, and known to all agents.
  - It is not possible to enter values greater than 4999 for the number of units to be produced and the number of information signals to be sent. This is due only to technological restrictions, and has no direct economic meaning.

Table A1 (*Contd.*)

---

* During the day, consumers are '*shopping*':
  - When all firms have decided their actions, consumers will be '*shopping*'. Each day, each consumer wishes to buy exactly one unit of the commodity. Hence, consumers have to find a firm offering the commodity for sale, and such a firm should have at least one unit available at the moment they arrive.
  - We give you two considerations concerning the consumers' actions:

  a A consumer that has received an information signal from you knows that you are a firm offering the commodity for sale on that day.

  b Consumers who visited you, but arrived too late and found only empty shelves might find your service unreliable. On the other hand, a consumer who succeeded in buying one unit from you might remember the good service.
* At the end of the day, each consumer and each firm observes his own market outcomes:
  - Consumers turn home satisfied or not, i.e. with or without a unit of the commodity.
  - All unsold units of the commodity perish.
  - Each firm will know the demand that was directed to it during the day, how much it has actually sold (notice that it cannot sell more than it has produced at the beginning of the day), and its profits of that day.
  - It cannot be excluded that sometimes the market outcomes are such that a firm makes a loss. Each firm faces an upper limit of 2000 points for the total losses it may realize. A firm exceeding this limit will be declared bankrupt, implying that it will be forced to inactivity from then on.
  - A firm might have received some information signals sent to random addresses by other firms. These information signals will be listed (senders and numbers of signals), using fictitious names for the sending firms.

Time:

* There is no time limit for your daily decisions. From day 20 on, you will hear a warning sound when you are using more than one minute decision-time.
* The playing-time will be about 2½ hours.

Payment:

* Each player will be paid according to the total profits realized by its firm.
* Each player gets a '*show-up*' fee of DM 20.-.
* In addition, the payoff will be DM 10.- for each 1000 profit points realized.
* Note that losses realized will be subtracted from the DM 20.-.
* Bankrupt players have lost an amount of DM 20.-, and hence get nothing.

Anonymity:

* A player will never know the actions and outcomes of other players.

Keyboard:

* To confirm your choice: Enter [<]
* To delete: Backspace [<--]
* Please, before confirming your choices, always make sure that you did not make a typing-error.

Firm "X": RESULTS day 7

ACTIONS			OUTCOMES		
production	signaling		demand	sales	profits
123	450		114	114	47.25

The NEXT day is:

day 8

production =
signaling =

Firm "X", please enter your choices

price = 1.00; costs/unit produced = 0.25; costs/signal sent = 0.08

Fig. A.1. Computer screen firm 'X'

Figure A.1 shows the computer screen as viewed by a player acting as firm 'X' in a given period. At the beginning of day 1 the top part of the screen contained the following message: "Experience (from previous experiments) shows that, in general, the demand faced by an individual firm is below 1000". When a player had negative cumulative profits, he got a warning in the center of the screen saying: "WARNING! Your total losses are 192.25 (total losses greater than 2000.00 imply BANKRUPTCY!)".

Appendix B. Game-theoretic analysis

Proof of Proposition 1. First, we study the finite horizon case, and then obtain the stationary signaling policy as a limit. The profit function and demand function are given by: $\Pi_i^t = p \cdot x_i^t - c \cdot z_i^t - k \cdot s_i^t$, where: $x_i^t = \min[z_i^t, q_i^t]$, and: $q_i^t = \text{round}(\text{trunc}[f \cdot x_i^{t-1} + \frac{s_i^t}{S^t} \cdot [1 - \exp(-\frac{S^t}{N})] \cdot [n - \Sigma_{j=1}^m \text{trunc}(f \cdot x_j^{t-1})]])$. Since the demand function is deterministic, $z_i^t = q_i^t = x_i^t$. Hence, the only control variable is signaling. Assuming the game is played for T periods, the value V of an action in any period $T-t'-1$ equals the sum of the immediate profits Π in period $T-t'-1$ and the value V in period $T-t'$: $V_i^{T-t'-1} = \Pi_i^{T-t'-1} + V_i^{T-t'}$, which has to be maximized. The first-order condition is: $\partial V_i^{T-t'-1}/\partial s_i^{T-t'-1} = \partial \Pi_i^{T-t'-1}/\partial s_i^{T-t'-1} + \partial V_i^{T-t'}/\partial s_i^{T-t'-1} = 0$. We consider these two terms on the right hand side separately.[32]

Determination of the first term: The immediate profit in a given period is: $\Pi_i^t = g \cdot q_i^t - k \cdot s_i^t \Rightarrow \partial \Pi_i^t/\partial s_i^t = g \cdot \partial q_i^t/\partial s_i^t - k$. Neglecting the term

[32] Cf. Fudenberg and Tirole (1991) on equilibria in dynamic games.

$[1-\exp(-\frac{S^t}{N})]$, and the roundings and truncations, demand is given by: $q_i^t = f \cdot q_i^{t-1} + s_i^t/S^t \cdot (n - f \cdot Q^{t-1}) \Rightarrow \partial q_i^t/\partial s_i^t = S_{-i}^t/(S^t)^2 \cdot (n - f \cdot Q^{t-1})$, where S_{-i}^t is the aggregate signaling of the other players. Since all consumers visit a firm: $Q^{t-1} = n$. Hence, we get: $\partial \Pi_i^t/\partial s_i^t = g \cdot S_{-i}^t/(S^t)^2 \cdot n \cdot (1-f) - k$. We substitute $T - t' - 1$ for t.

Now we turn to the second term. We have to determine $V_i^{T-t'}$. We solve this first for the last period T, and then solve the game using backward induction. In the last period, period T, we have $\Pi_i^T = V_i^T$, and hence the first-order condition is: $\partial V_i^T/\partial s_i^T = \partial \Pi_i^T/\partial s_i^T = 0$. From above, we know $\partial \Pi_i^T/\partial s_i^T = g \cdot S_{-i}^T/(S^T)^2 \cdot (n - f \cdot Q^{T-1})$. Hence, we get: $\frac{k}{g} = S_{-i}^T/(S^T)^2 \cdot (n - f \cdot Q^{T-1})$. Since $S^T = m \cdot s_i^T$, and $Q^{T-1} = n$, we obtain: $s_i^T = g/k \cdot (m-1)/m^2 \cdot n \cdot (1-f)$, which is the optimal signaling level in the last period. Thus, the value V_i^T in the last period is

$$V_i^T = \Pi_i^T = g \cdot q_i^T - k \cdot s_i^T$$
$$= g \cdot [f \cdot q_i^{T-1} + \frac{1}{m} \cdot (n - f \cdot Q^{T-1})] - k \cdot [\frac{g}{k} \cdot (\frac{m-1}{m^2}) \cdot n \cdot (1-f)] \Rightarrow$$

$V_i^T = g \cdot [f \cdot q_i^{T-1} + \frac{n}{m^2} \cdot (1-f)]$. In other words, $V_i^T = g \cdot [A_0 \cdot q_i^{T-1} + B_0]$, or in general: $V_i^{T-t'} = g \cdot [A_{t'} \cdot q_i^{T-t'-1} + B_{t'}]$, where: $A_0 = f$, $B_0 = \frac{n}{m^2} \cdot (1-f)$ and: $A_{t'+1} = f + f \cdot A_{t'}$. Hence, $\partial V_i^{T-t'}/\partial s_i^{T-t'-1} = g \cdot A_{t'} \cdot \partial q_i^{T-t'-1}/\partial s_i^{T-t'-1} = g \cdot A_{t'} \cdot S_{-i}^T/(S^T)^2 \cdot n \cdot (1-f)$. Combining the two terms we get:

$$\frac{\partial V_i^{T-t'-1}}{\partial s_i^{T-t'-1}} = g \cdot \frac{S_i^{T-t'-1}}{(S_i^{T-t'-1})^2} \cdot n \cdot (1-f) - k]$$
$$+ [g \cdot A_{t'} \frac{S_{-i}^{T-t'-1}}{(S^{T-t'-1})^2} \cdot n \cdot (1-f)] = 0 \Rightarrow$$
$$g \cdot (1 + A_{t'}) \cdot \left(\frac{m-1}{m}\right) \cdot \frac{1}{S^{T-t'-1}} \cdot (1-f) \cdot n = k \Rightarrow$$

$s_i^{T-t'} = g/k \cdot (1 + A_{t'+1}) \cdot (m-1)/m^2 \cdot (1-f) \cdot n$. Now consider the difference equation $A_{t'+1} = f + f \cdot A_{t'}$, which can be solved as: $A_{t'+1} = [f - f/(1-f)] \cdot f^{t'+1} + f/(1-f)$, with $\lim_{t' \to \infty} A_{t'+1} = f/(1-f)$. Hence, for large enough t' the optimal action in a given period $T - t'$ in the steady state is: $s_i^{T-t'} = g/k \cdot [1 + f/(1-f)] \cdot [(m-1)/m^2] \cdot (1-f) \cdot n = g/k \cdot [(m-1)/m^2] \cdot n$. QED.[33]

[33] See also Stokey and Lucas (1989).

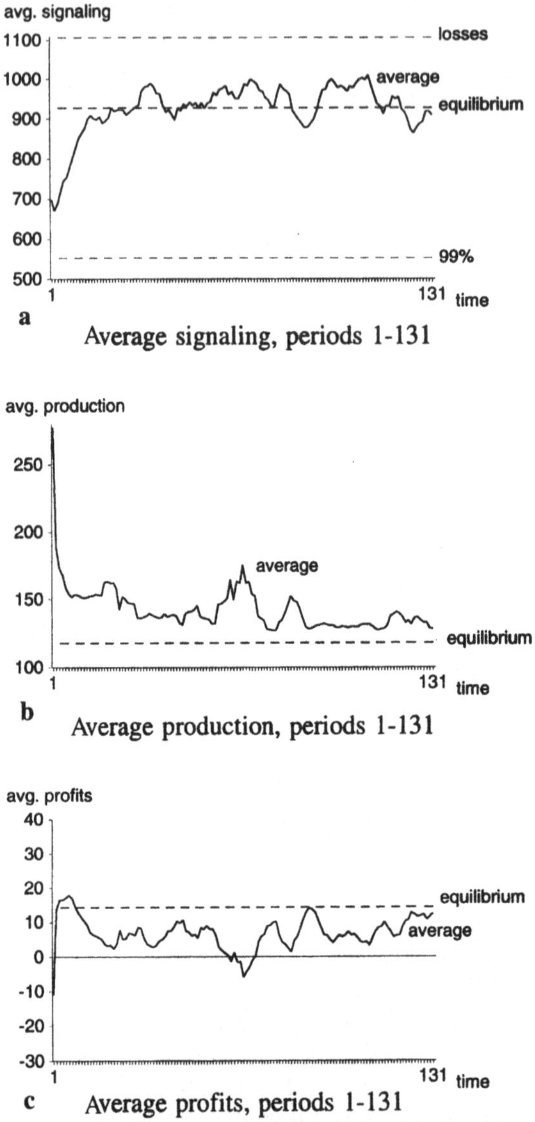

Fig. C.1. **a** Average signaling, periods 1–131. **b** Average production, periods 1–131. **c** Average profits, periods 1–131

Appendix C. Some additional data

Figure C.1.a, c present the time series for signaling, production, and profits for periods 1 to 131 averaged over the 66 players (with all variables at zero for bankrupt players). In all these graphs, we took a five period moving average for presentational reasons, and we added the equilibrium levels as a first benchmark. In the graph for signaling (C.1.a) we added two other benchmarks. The first one is called 'losses', and corresponds to the line drawn in Figure 4, as explained in Section 4. It is the signaling level beyond which positive profits are impossible, given the equilibrium production

Table C.1. Summary data individual players

Session	Player	Period 1			Avg. all periods			Profits	Number periods	Also session	Player
		Prod.	Sign.	Sales	Prod.	Sign.	Sales				
1	1	0	100	0	154	868	144	35.9	151	21	2
1	2	400	200	91	215	1096	192	50.4	151	21	1
1	3	500	500	228	197	1045	180	47.4	151	21	4
1	4	250	400	183	131	393	64	0	151	21	5
1	5	100	100	46	129	715	118	28.9	151	–	–
1	6	20	5	2	467	161	35	−94.9	22	–	–
2	1	1199	2199	522	362	2309	315	39.8	151	–	–
2	2	300	100	24	38	78	10	−6.1	151	–	–
2	3	200	0	0	207	1348	163	3.4	151	–	–
2	4	600	400	95	83	540	70	6.6	151	–	–
2	5	600	100	24	163	986	134	14	151	21	3
2	6	350	150	36	12	52	6	−1	151	21	6
3	1	1000	1500	113	138	827	99	−1.8	151	–	–
3	2	600	800	91	124	846	100	1.5	151	23	3
3	3	800	4800	216	9	54	5	−2	151	–	–
3	4	1200	2000	129	335	2574	286	−4.2	151	–	–
3	5	1000	800	91	36	170	20	−2.7	151	23	2
3	6	200	200	72	213	1699	192	2.6	151	–	–
4	1	500	1500	153	429	2893	406	67.8	151	23	1
4	2	1000	1000	124	439	820	78	−97	28	–	–
4	3	500	500	95	26	147	20	2.2	151	–	–
4	4	2000	2000	182	344	710	99	−44.2	68	–	–
4	5	900	400	89	50	298	40	4	151	–	–
4	6	100	50	69	202	1268	171	19.1	151	–	–
5	1	500	2000	285	356	2805	330	16.8	151	–	–
5	2	700	600	85	29	138	14	−3.8	151	–	–
5	3	500	600	85	86	505	52	−10.3	151	–	–
5	4	500	700	100	44	280	30	−3.3	151	24	6
5	5	500	500	71	229	1841	211	6.6	151	–	–
5	6	400	600	85	97	527	56	−10.8	151	24	4
6	1	1200	800	185	107	618	85	8.8	151	24	3
6	2	800	400	92	112	691	90	6.4	151	–	–
6	3	550	500	116	391	2627	340	32.3	151	24	2
6	4	400	300	69	6	20	3	−0.1	151	–	–
6	5	500	800	185	168	1228	142	2.2	151	24	5
6	6	234	234	54	113	272	37	−12.6	151	24	1
7	1	250	150	35	58	457	50	−1.1	131	–	–
7	2	600	900	207	138	991	118	4.4	131	25	3
7	3	400	400	92	274	2109	243	6.2	131	25	1
7	4	50	100	23	38	289	32	−0.5	131	–	–
7	5	2000	500	115	43	134	17	−4.3	131	–	–
7	6	800	1000	230	259	2230	232	−11.2	131	25	6
8	1	875	900	117	94	430	76	18.1	131	–	–
8	2	1000	100	13	173	962	135	14.5	131	–	–
8	3	500	500	65	77	299	62	18.8	131	–	–
8	4	400	500	65	350	1836	289	55	131	–	–
8	5	900	990	128	28	121	20	3.1	131	–	–
8	6	2255	2500	324	154	705	116	21	131	–	–
9	1	800	2000	334	95	540	64	−2.9	151	–	–

Table C.1 (*Contd.*)

Session	Player	Period 1			Avg. all periods			Profits	Number periods	Also session	Player
		Prod.	Sign.	Sales	Prod.	Sign.	Sales				
9	2	300	100	17	39	246	27	−2.3	151	–	–
9	3	200	600	100	269	2246	250	2.6	151	23	5
9	4	500	1000	167	295	2394	270	4.6	151	23	6
9	5	50	50	8	9	54	5	−1.2	151	–	–
9	6	750	500	84	103	775	88	0.2	151	23	4
10	1	800	400	55	16	84	10	−0.9	251	–	–
10	2	100	300	41	99	668	87	9.1	251	22	6
10	3	800	3000	414	265	1934	246	24.6	251	–	–
10	4	500	750	104	79	565	64	−1	251	–	–
10	5	350	400	55	354	2377	293	14.7	251	22	5
10	6	300	300	41	3	11	1	−0.4	251	–	–
11	1	800	1000	63	57	391	46	0.1	201	25	4
11	2	1000	3500	222	363	2667	316	11.9	201	25	5
11	3	500	450	28	255	1419	149	−28.4	84	–	–
11	4	500	4999	316	86	656	74	−0.2	201	–	–
11	5	1000	1000	63	117	912	107	4.3	201	25	2
11	6	300	300	19	101	842	96	3.6	201	–	–

Table C.2. Session averages

Session	Period 1			Avg. all periods			Profits	Number periods
	Prod.	Sign.	Sales	Prod.	Sign.	Sales		
1	212	218	92	149	690	117	25	151
2	542	492	117	144	886	116	9	151
3	800	1683	119	143	1028	117	−1	151
4	833	908	119	157	846	116	9	151
5	517	833	119	140	1016	116	−1	151
6	614	506	117	150	909	116	6	151
7	683	508	117	135	1035	115	−1	131
8	988	915	119	146	726	116	22	131
9	433	708	118	135	1043	117	0	151
10	475	858	118	136	940	117	8	251
11	683	1875	119	139	1010	117	1	201

level. The second additional benchmark is called '99%', and corresponds to the average signaling level needed to make sure that 99% of the consumer population receives at least one signal.

Table C.1 presents the individual averages and first period actions for the players. For each individual player, the averages are taken over the periods in which the player actually played. Table C.2 gives the session averages, where the averages are taken over the periods in which the session lasted (with production and signaling levels at zero for bankrupt players).

References

Arthur WB (1991) Learning and adaptive economic behavior. Designing economic agents that act like human agents: a behavioral approach to bounded rationality. American Economic Review 81: 353–359

Arthur WB (1992) On learning and adaptation in the economy. Working Paper 92-07-038, Santa Fe Institute

Atkinson RC, Suppes P (1958) An analysis of two-person game situations in terms of statistical learning theory. Journal of Experimental Psychology 55: 369–378

Binmore KG (1991) DeBayesing game theory. Mimeo, Lecture for the International Conference on Game Theory, Florence

Bloomfield R (1994) Learning a mixed strategy equilibrium in the laboratory. Journal of Economic Behavior and Organization 25: 411–436

Börgers T, Sarin R (1996) Naive reinforcement learning with endogenous aspirations. ELSE Working Paper, University College London

Budd C, Harris C, Vickers J (1993) A model of the evolution of duopoly: does the asymmetry between firms tend to increase or decrease? Review of Economic Studies 60: 543–573

Camerer C, Ho TH (1996) Experience-weighted attraction learning in games: A unifying approach. Mimeo

Case KE, Fair RC (1996) Principles of microeconomics, 4th edn. Prentice Hall, Upper Saddle River, NJ

Davis DD, Holt CA (1992) Experimental economics. Princeton University Press, Princeton, NJ

Easley D, Ledyard JO (1993) Theories of price formation and exchange in double oral auctions. In: Friedman D, Rust J (eds) The double auction market. Institutions, theories, and evidence. Addison-Wesley, Reading MA, pp 63–97

Ellison G (1993) Learning, local interaction, and coordination. Econometrica 61: 1047–1071

Fudenberg D, Tirole J (1991) Game theory. MIT Press, Cambridge, MA

Green JR (1983) Comment on "A. Kirman, On mistaken beliefs and resultant equilibria". In: Frydman R, Phelps ES (eds) Individual forecasting and aggregate outcomes: Rational expectations examined. Cambridge University Press, Cambridge

Hart S, Mas-Colell A (1996) A simple adaptive procedure leading to correlated equilibrium. Economics Working Paper 200, Universitat Pompeu Fabra

Holland JH (1992) Adaptation in natural and artificial systems. An introductory analysis with applications to biology, control, and artificial intelligence, 2nd edn. MIT Press, Cambridge, MA

Holland JH, Holyoak KJ, Nisbett RE, Thagard PR (1986) Induction: Processes of inference, learning, and discovery. MIT Press, Cambridge, MA

Kampmann C, Sterman JD (1995) Feedback complexity, bounded rationality, and market dynamics. Mimeo

Kandori M, Mailath GJ, Rob R (1993) Learning, mutation, and long run equilibria in games. Econometrica 61: 29–56

Keser C (1992) Experimental duopoly markets with demand inertia: Game-playing Experiments and the strategy method. Lecture Notes in Economics and Mathematical Systems 391. Springer, Berlin Heidelberg New York

Keser C, Gardner R (1998) Strategic behavior of experienced subjects in a common pool resource game. International Journal of Game Theory (forthcoming)

Kiefer NM, Nyarko Y (1989) Optimal control of an unknown linear process with learning. International Economic Review 30: 571–586

Kirman AP (1983) On mistaken beliefs and resultant equilibria. In: Frydman R, Phelps ES (eds) Individual forecasting and aggregate outcomes: Rational expectations examined. Cambridge University Press, Cambridge

Kirman AP (1993) Learning in oligopoly: Theory, simulation, and experimental evidence. In: Kirman AP, Salmon M (eds) Learning and rationality in economics. Blackwell, Oxford

Macready WG, Wolpert DH (1995) No free-lunch theorems for search. Working Paper 95-02-010, Santa Fe Institute

McKelvey R, Palfrey T (1992) An experimental study of the centipede game. Econometrica 60: 803–836

Malawski M (1990) Some learning processes in population games. ICS PAS Reports 678, Institute of Computer Science Polish Academy of Sciences, Warsaw

Marimon R (1993) Adaptive learning, evolutionary dynamics and equilibrium selection in games. European Economic Review 37: 603–611

Merlo A, Schotter A (1994) An experimental study of learning in one and two-person games. Economic Research Reports 94-17, CV Starr Center for Applied Economics, New York University

Midgley DF, Marks RE, Cooper LG (1996) Breeding competitive strategies. Management Science

Nagel R (1995) Unraveling in guessing games. An experimental study. American Economic Review 85: 1313–1326

Nagel R, Tang FF (1998) An experimental study on the centipede game in normal form–An investigation on learning. Journal of Mathematical Psychology (forthcoming)

Nagel R, Vriend NJ (1998) An experimental study of adaptive behavior in an oligopolistic market game. Working Paper No. 388, Queen Mary and Westfield College, University of London

Nagel R, Vriend NJ (1999) Do players really learn in an oligopolistic market game with minimal information? Industrial and Corporate Change (forthcoming)

Ochs J (1995) Coordination problem. In: Kagel J, Roth AE (eds) The handbook of experimental economics. Princeton University Press, Princeton, NJ, pp 195–252

Page SE (1994) Two measures of difficulty. Working Paper 94-12-063, Santa Fe Institute

Petr M (1997) A dynamic model of advertising competition: an empirical analysis of feedback strategies. Mimeo

Roberts M (1995) Active learning: Some experimental results. Mimeo

Roth AE, Erev I (1995) Learning in extensive-form games: Experimental data and simple dynamic models in the intermediate term. Games and Economic Behavior 8: 164–212

Sauermann H, Selten R (1959) Ein Oligopolexperiment. Zeitschrift für die gesamte Staatswissenschaft 115: 427–471

Savage LJ (1954) The foundations of statistics. Wiley, New York

Selten R (1997) Features of experimentally observed bounded rationality. Mimeo, Presidential Address of the 1997 Meetings of the European Economic Association, Toulouse

Selten R, Buchta J (1994) Experimental sealed bid first price auctions with directly observed bid functions. Discussion Paper No. B-270, University of Bonn

Selten R, Mitzkewitz M, Uhlich G (1997) Duopoly strategies programmed by experienced players. Econometrica 65: 517–555

Selten R, Stoecker R (1986) End behavior in sequences of finite prisoner's dilemma supergames. A learning theory approach. Journal of Economic Behavior and Organization 7: 47–70

Simon HA (1959) Theories of decision-making in economics and behavioral science. American Economic Review 49: 253–283

Stahl DO (1996) Boundedly rational rule learning in a guessing game. Games and Economic Behavior 16: 303–330

Stewing R (1990) Entwicklung, Programmierung und Durchführung eines Oligopolexperiments mit minimaler Information. Masters thesis, University of Bonn

Stiglitz JE (1993) Principles of microeconomics. Norton, New York

Stokey NL, Lucas RE, jr (1989) Recursive methods in economic dynamics. Harvard University Press, Cambridge, MA

Tang FF (1996) Anticipatory learning in two-person games: An experimental study. Part II. Learning. Discussion Paper No. B-363. University of Bonn
Vriend NJ (1994) Artificial intelligence and economic theory. In: Hillebrand E, Stender J (eds) Many-agent simulation and artificial life. IOS, Amsterdam, pp 31–47
Vriend NJ (1996a) Rational behavior and economic theory. Journal of Economic Behavior and Organization 29 (2): 263–285
Vriend NJ (1996b) A model of market-making (Economics Working Paper 184) Universitat Pompeu Fabra, Barcelona
Witt U (1986) How can complex economic behavior be investigated? The example of the ignorant monopolist revisited. Behavioral Science 31: 173–188
Young HP (1993) The evolution of conventions. Econometrica 61: 57–84

Horizontal heterogeneity, technological progress and sectoral development

Uwe Cantner[1], Horst Hanusch[1] and Andreas Pyka[1]

[1]University of Augsburg, Department of Economics, Universitaetsstr. 16, D-86135 Augsburg, e-mail: uwe.cantner@wiso.uni-augsburg.de

Abstract. This paper is concerned with the relationship between firm heterogeneity, different firm strategies, and technological spillovers and learning in an oligopolistic market. In a model of heterogeneous oligopoly firms are technologically different with respect to both the kind of production technique applied (as given by the capital-intensity) and the efficiency by which a specific technique is performed. In pursuing technological progress and building up appropriate technological know-how these firms may apply either a learning or absorptive strategy or contrariwise a conservative strategy that does not attempt to learn from competitors. Within this context the paper investigates the general direction of technological progress in the sense of labor or capital-saving. Applying simulation technique it is shown that the direction of progress changes purely stochastically in the case of conservative firms. Contrariwise, when firms follow the absorptive strategy a quite ordered pattern of development pursued by all firms is observed.

Key words: Absorptive capacity – Technological spillovers – Cross-fertilization – Direction of technological progress

JEL-classification: O3

Acknowledgements: We are grateful to two anonymous referees for helpful suggestions. Moreover we thank Steven Klepper, Paolo Saviotti, and Elias Dinopoulos for detailed comments on this paper. Previous versions benefited from the discussion with participants during workshops at Ancona, Athens, and Augsburg. All remaining errors are, of course, in our responsibility.

1 Introduction

The concept of heterogeneity is central to the population perspective within evolutionary theorizing. In the selection process, most often the fittest alternative – e.g. the firm with the lowest production costs – dominates (Metcalfe (1994a)). Besides this selection or competition effect, in social evolution and especially in economic and technological evolution, heterogeneity is considered as an additional source of progress. The formal or informal exchange of (technological) know-how (Pyka (1997)) leads to cross-fertilization effects, often increasing the probability of further success (Basalla (1988), Mokyr (1990), Sahal (1981), Kodama (1986)). Thus, heterogeneity and spillover effects are to be considered as core concepts within an evolutionary approach to techno-economic evolution (Cantner (1996)).

This paper deals with the concept of heterogeneity of firms, innovative activities understood as an collective evolutionary process, and resulting characteristic structural developments. As to the concept of heterogeneity, we focus on so-called *horizontal heterogeneity*, whereby firms apply quite different (local) production techniques, classified only as technologically different and not ranked as technologically superior or inferior. This heterogeneity in technology is caused and developed by successful individual research activities, the differences considered as additional sources of knowledge which – by the way of technology spillovers – promote further technological progress. For spillover effects to work we recognize that firms have to provide absorptive capacities which, in general, have to be built up by continuous learning and thus are resource-using. This behavior is called *absorptive strategy*. Contrariwise, firms not following this strategy are considered as *conservative*.

In other work (Cantner/Pyka (1998), Cantner/Hanusch/Pyka (1997)) – which is based on the so-called *realistic approach of evolutionary modeling* (Silverberg/Verspagen 1994) – we investigated the comparative performance of those strategies with respect to exploring and exploiting technological opportunities for process and product innovation. We found these strategies to differ considerably with respect to the timing, the intensity, the frequency of innovations, and the economic success of those endeavors. This paper takes up another issue and investigates the direction of research activities. We distinguish two main directions of R&D activities focusing on either labor-saving or on capital-saving innovations. We analyze how the direction of research a firm decides upon is affected by the performance of competitors and whether regularities can be detected for the firm and the group of firms (or industry). Doing this, the model enables us to detect structural developments and turbulences on the intra-industry level which are accompanied by rather ordered developments on a sectoral level.

In this paper we proceed as follows: Section 2 introduces the concept of heterogeneity and its importance to technological progress. A model of heterogeneous oligopoly is set up in section 3. Based on the work of Cantner/Pyka (1998) we modify this model with respect to horizontal heterogeneity. Simulation results are presented and discussed in section 4. A conclusion is given in section 5.

2 Heterogeneity and Technological Progress

Heterogeneity of agents within a population is a core concept within evolutionary theories in general and in *evolutionary economic approaches* in particular. In traditional neoclassical theory such heterogeneity is most often considered as analytically irrelevant, and any behavior or characteristic of a population under consideration can be explained and forecasted by referring to a representative agent or – just to represent some interaction – to a set of symmetric agents. Such analysis and modeling has a well-known tradition and even economists favoring evolutionary approaches consider it appropriate for rather stationary environments where all things have time to work out. Hence, the agents' behavior will converge and heterogeneity will vanish over time.

However, the economic sphere – as well as other social spheres – is in continuous flux, with changing speed and directions of change. Hence, *being different* and heterogeneous are central features of dynamic processes, and the population perspective appears to be the appropriate analytical stance. In this respect, the evolutionary approach is, on the one hand, interested in the forces driving and directing that change and in the forces creating novelty or sustaining the probability of the appearance of something new. On the other hand, everything responsible for the acceptance and the predominance of the new is of analytical interest. Thus, the degree of heterogeneity within a population depends on forces creating novelty (heterogeneity increases) and forces diffusing novelty (heterogeneity diminishes).

The economic theory of innovation and technological change is considered as a case proper for applying evolutionary concepts. As Joseph Alois Schumpeter (1912) forcefully stated, individuals intentionally attempt to create something new, and through this process they *create* and *reinforce* heterogeneity. Following this, market competition and imitative activities are both responsible for *reducing* this heterogeneity – both acting as a kind of selection process.

An interesting question is how the countervailing forces of creating heterogeneity and reducing heterogeneity interact. Of course, one may be forced to state that they are independent and thus a long-term balanced dynamic in this respect is rather casual. However, industrial sectors are quite often characterized by some regularity in the innovative behavior of firms, in market share dynamics, in technological development, etc. These regularities show up even though firms are assumed to follow individual routines, to rely on individual knowledge stocks and local experiences, etc. Thus, we observe a certain degree of heterogeneity among agents, on the one hand, and some coherent and rather regular but not necessarily steady common behaviour on the other. It seems plausible to argue that these phenomena are not casual events but are the result of an interaction between heterogeneity enhancing and heterogeneity reducing effects.

Investigating this relationship includes the *creation of novelty*, a process which is by no means well understood. Of course, innovations are often the outcome of the intentional behavior of agents, and one may ask, based on which circumstances will agents act in this way? It is well known that it is the combination of so-called aspiration levels and satisfycing behavior which can explain part of the story. Besides this, another question refers to the facts, circumstances and forces that enhance the probability of innovative success. There exists quite a large empirical literature which highlights R&D-expenditures, R&D capital stocks, several learning issues (learning-by-doing, learning-by-innovating, learning-by-interacting, ...), etc. Quite often these effects are intimately related to economic outcomes such as profits, market shares, cumulative output, etc. Thus, these forces are generated and shaped by the competitive success of agents – working as a positive feedback known as *success-breeds-success* (Phillips (1971)). Besides this, however, important non-market interactions, as found in *technological spillovers*, should also be taken into account.

Technological spillovers require heterogeneity because "in a world of symmetric firms it is impossible to conceive of knowledge spillovers. In such circumstances, knowledge is not additive, a firm's effective knowledge is its own knowledge, it cannot learn from any other identical firm." (Metcalfe (1994b, p.932)). Based on this, there exists rich empirical evidence and theoretical considerations supporting the fact that heterogeneity of agents, and thus just differences within a population, may prove to be an *additional source of progress*. Of course, the well-known innovator-imitator scheme highlights the fact that within a vertical relationship between a technologically superior and a lagging agent, the latter is able to learn from the former. We then observe a dynamics which is driven by catch-up processes.

Besides this, however, we often observe agents who cannot be distinguished as technologically superior or lagging: they are just different in their technological approach. This kind of heterogeneity may be labeled *horizontal heterogeneity* and gives rise to spillover effects that are often called *cross-fertilization effects*. In a first instance they do not lead to a technological catch-up but to a gradual adoption of production techniques and direction of innovative activities.

In both cases, whether spillovers arise from vertical or horizontal heterogeneity, in a world of local know-how, tacit competencies and latent public good characteristics of know-how, the usage of spillovers and the understanding of their information content often requires *absorptive capacities* (Cohen/Levinthal (1989)) or *receiver competencies* (Eliasson (1990)). Building up these competencies requires resources, and thus, they are to be considered as endogenous.

With this kind of horizontal heterogeneity (or variety) and spillover effects several questions can be posed:

(1) What are the relations between the rate of progress, the direction of progress, and the degree and change in heterogeneity?
(2) Which characteristic technological and economic development structures result from spillover effects and specific innovation strategies?
(3) What is the relationship between technological and economic performances with respect to the firms and the strategy chosen?

These questions will be analyzed within a modeling framework introduced below and which has already been used elsewhere (Cantner/Hanusch/Pyka (1998a, 1998b), Cantner/Pyka, (1998)). There, we focused on the question of how firms exploit endogenously generated vertical heterogeneity and exogenously given horizontal heterogeneity in order to introduce process and product innovations. On this basis, different innovation strategies and innovation routines have been *tested*, where the role and usage of cognitive capabilities to integrate external know-how have been a central point of concern.

In the following we apply this model, introduce endogenously generated horizontal heterogeneity, and restrict the analysis on the case of process innovations – the case of product innovations is neglected in order to keep the structure as simple as possible.[1] With respect to horizontal heterogeneity, we assume that firms not only attempt to influence the rate but also the *direction of progress*, understood as capital or labor-saving.

[1] For the discussion of product innovation see Cantner/Pyka (1998).

3 The Simulation Model

For our analysis we introduce a model suitable to deal with the heterogeneity of agents or firms. In particular, our model deals with the market competition of firms and their interaction as *users* and *producers* of technological spillovers. By this we distinguish heterogeneity on the product market combined with a certain degree of competition, and heterogeneity on the technology side related to the technology applied and technological progress. First, we turn to the product market.

Product market heterogeneity and competition

We assume that each of n firms produces a specific good. The goods of the firms are not perfect substitutes, and the degree of substitutability can be used as a measure of the degree of competition. This is given exogenously. Furthermore, we assume that firms compete in terms of prices only, and so there is no quality competition. Accordingly, we consider only price competition among *heterogeneous* firms. In order to keep the presentation of this part as simple as possible, we suggest a model of *heterogeneous oligopoly*[2] which by its very structure represents the kind of competitive relationships described.[3]

In a dynamic perspective, competition is mainly influenced by the competitors` innovative activities. Here, we consider only process innovations which improve the efficiency of production processes and so allow a firm to lower output prices. Depending on the degree of substitutability among goods, a successful innovator will be able to distract demand from his competitors. The substitution effects are induced by price changes, which are the result of the following actions and reactions:

- Process innovations allow the innovator to charge a lower price, attracting additional demand;
- as a reaction, non-innovators are forced to lower their prices in order to counteract against the loss of market shares.

One might argue here that a model of this type is an equilibrium model based on static optimization one not suitable for modeling evolutionary dynamics. However, we apply this model in a way that such equilibrium states will not be reached immediately. First, the reaction-functions are based on *past* prices (as the only available market information) so that, starting in a situation of disequilibrium the attainment of the

---

[2] See Kuenne (1992).

[3] The heterogeneous oligopoly setting is also applied in a simulation study by Meyer et al. (1996).

equilibrium state takes several periods.[4] Second, those tendencies are continuously disturbed and influenced by upcoming innovations. Thus, what we observe here is the interplay between *equilibrating and disequilibrating* forces.[5]

Within the proposed heterogeneous oligopoly every firm faces an individual linear demand function:

$$p_i^t = a - \eta \cdot q_i^t + \frac{h}{n-1}\sum_{j \neq i} p_j^{t-1} \text{, where} \tag{1}$$

a: = prohibitive price; η: = slope of demand;
h: = mutual market dependence; p_i^t: = price of firm i's product.

Supposing market behavior à la Bertrand and constant returns to scale in production, it is straightforward to calculate formally the firms' reaction functions

$$p_i^t = \frac{a + c_i^t}{2} + \frac{h}{2(n-1)}\sum_{j \neq i} p_j^{t-1} \text{, where} \tag{2}$$

c_i^t: = unit costs of firm i at time t;
and the corresponding output levels

$$q_i^t = \frac{a - c_i^t}{2\eta} + \frac{h}{2\eta(n-1)}\sum_{j \neq i} p_j^{t-1}. \tag{3}$$

This modeling strategy allows us to focus on the technology side of behavior, whereas the economic decisions of the competing firms are represented by a well understood oligopolistic setting. Moreover, we take account of the firms′ strategic behavior in the sense that firms react to the action of their competitors in the preceding period.[6] We do not deal with the formation of expectations and any resulting strategies.

Technological heterogeneity

The technological *heterogeneity* of firms is represented by the different production techniques applied. For characterizing the respective production techniques, we assume that in production each firm employs a firm-specific combination of labor and capital. Thus, production techniques

[4] For our model, simulation runs excluding any innovation processes show that, starting in a disequilibrium situation, it takes about 30 periods to achieve equilibrium.

[5] See Witt (1992, p. 42).

[6] This element is totally missing if, e.g. replicator dynamics are used. There, actors being less fit are selected out of the market without any reaction to this development.

are distinguished by their capital/labor-ratio (*k/l*). We also assume that there is no substitutability among production factors in the short run. A firm is supposed to change its technique and thus its capital/labor-ratio only by investing in research and development (R&D).

With respect to technological progress we distinguish several strategies firms apply to their R&D activities. As idealized strategies we distinguish a *conservative strategy* and an *absorptive strategy* (Cantner/Pyka (1998)). The former aims only at own R&D and does not care about the R&D projects of competitors. The absorptive strategy explicitly attempts to learn from the technology and the progress of competitors. In the following we formalize these two strategies and begin with the conservative one.

Technological progress and the conservative strategy

A firm which engages in research and development does so in order to have a chance to run production processes more efficiently. For our model we have to formalize the way in which a firm determines the level of R&D, how this probabilistically adds to the level of technological know-how, and how this translates into an improvement of production efficiency.

A firm which engages in research and development activities decides on the level of R&D expenditures for each period. Since innovative activities are characterized by genuine and strong uncertainty, firms do not know the density function of innovative success. Thus, R&D activities are not be performed optimally. In order to determine the level of R&D expenditures, firms are supposed to apply *routines* (Winter (1971), Nelson/Winter (1982)) drawing back on only *procedural rationality* (Simon (1976)). For the model here, we refer to a quite simple routine, where periodical R&D investment r_i^t is defined as a fixed percentage γ_i of sales. Thus the periodic profit π_i^t of a firm net of R&D expenditures reads as follows:

$$\pi_i^t = \left(p_i^t - c_i^t\right)q_i^t - r_i^t \tag{4a}$$

$$\pi_i^t = q_i^t \cdot \left[(1-\gamma_i)p_i^t - c_i^t\right]. \tag{4b}$$

With R&D, firms attempt either to improve labor efficiency by reducing the share of employed labor, or to enhance capital efficiency by reducing the capital required to produce one unit of output, or to provide for a combination of both. The routinized R&D decision rule for determining periodic R&D expenditures r_i^t, which are partly used in reducing capital input r_{ki}^t, and partly in lowering labor input r_{li}^t, reads as follows:

$$r_i^t = r_{ki}^t + r_{li}^t = \gamma_i (p_i^t \cdot q_i^t). \tag{5}$$

The total R&D budget r_i^t is split up on the two possible directions of research activities according to a variable ε_i^t, resp. $(1-\varepsilon_i^t)$. This share variable, however, is not a constant indicating a fixed rule, but varies stochastically from period to period:

$$r_{ki}^t = \varepsilon_i^t \cdot \gamma_i \left(p_i^t \cdot q_i^t\right), \tag{6a}$$

$$r_{li}^t = (1-\varepsilon_i^t) \cdot \gamma_i \left(p_i^t \cdot q_i^t\right), \tag{6b}$$

where ε_i^t is uniformly distributed between 0 and 1. Thus, in each period the R&D projects initiated aim either at more capital-reducing or at more labor-reducing innovations.

Any successful R&D project enhances a firm's stock of technological know-how. According to the two main directions of research we distinguish two R&D capital stocks, one with respect to labor-saving R&D R_{li}^t, and the other with respect to capital-saving R&D R_{ki}^t. These are accumulated just as physical capital – we assume a depreciation rate of 0.

In performing R&D projects, each firm attempts to exploit some given technological opportunities step by step. Given a certain level of technological know-how, the degree of innovative success in each project increases with the amount of R&D spent at a declining rate. The more the given technological opportunities become exploited, the lower will be the incremental innovative success of R&D expenditures.

In order to formalize the exploitation of technological opportunities, we define the accumulated innovative success of R&D projects, is_{ki}^t and is_{li}^t, where we again distinguish between capital and labor-saving opportunities.[7] The accumulated innovative success of a firm is related to the accumulated R&D expenditures or the R&D capital stocks. In equations (7a) and (7b), is_{ci}^t and is_{li}^t are defined in a way to represent the degree to which the respective technological opportunities for factor reduction have been exploited at time t:

$$is_{ki}^t = 1 - e^{-\alpha \cdot \kappa_i^t \cdot R_{ki}^t} \tag{7a}$$

$$is_{li}^t = 1 - e^{-\alpha \cdot \kappa_i^t \cdot R_{li}^t}. \tag{7b}$$

α: = parameter;
κ_i^t: = impact of external knowledge (introduced below, see eq.(15))

[7] is_{ki}^t and is_{li}^t can also be interpreted as the technological levels achieved at time t.

R&D activities do not necessarily lead to innovative success – innovative success is stochastic with the following properties. The probability of innovative success is assumed to depend on two factors or circumstances. First, the R&D success of firms is positively influenced by the firm's know-how (experience) accumulated during time. Second, the larger the degree of unexploited technological opportunities on the firm-specific technological trajectory (i.e. capital or labor-saving technologies), the more likely will be innovative success. Thus, as the opportunities on a single trajectory – due to physical, chemical laws etc. (see e.g. Sahal (1985)) – become increasingly exhausted, and technological constraints and bottlenecks become more tight, the likelihood of innovative success declines. According to these two influences, the likelihood of innovative success changes during the exploitation of certain technological opportunities – a feature the well-known paradigm/trajectory approach suggests to hold for entrepreneurs or firms which attempt to exploit some rather vaguely described technological opportunities.[8]

Innovative success translates into a reduction of labor, l_i, and/or capital, k_i. To avoid production with no inputs, we additionally introduce some fixed inputs, $\bar{l}$ and $\bar{k}$, necessary for the production of one unit of output. The capital and labor requirements per unit of output in period t are determined according to equations (8a) and (8b):

$$k_i^t = k_0 \cdot (1 - is_{ki}^t) + \bar{k} \tag{8a}$$

$$l_i^t = l_0 \cdot (1 - is_{li}^t) + \bar{l}\ . \tag{8b}$$

As a consequence, since factor prices are assumed to be constant, both kinds of innovation translate to unit cost reductions. Supposing constant wages, w, and capital costs, i, the unit costs c_i^t of output in period t amount to:

$$c_i^t = w \cdot l_i^t + i \cdot k_i^t\ . \tag{9}$$

Equations (1-9) fully describe the behavior of *conservative firms*. These firms only invest in direct R&D and neglect external developments initiated by competitors (hence, for those firms in (7a) and (7b) κ_i^t is equal to one). For firms following an absorptive strategy equations (1) to (9) hold too. In the following, we show how these firms attempt to apply knowledge generated elsewhere.

[8] Without an exploration of new extensive opportunities (Coombs (1988)) either by cross-fertilization of ex-ante different technologies or even by a paradigm shift, technological development would come to rest. During these phases uncertainty becomes more severe again.

Absorptive strategy and endogenous spillovers

Absorptive firms do not engage only in own R&D, but they invest a share σ_i of their periodical research expenditures in the building up of capabilities allowing them to understand and to apply external knowledge. By this, absorptive capacities have a twofold effect. First, they allow a firm to screen the technologies of the competitors and thus to get information about the direction into which further R&D activities should be initiated. Second, absorptive capacities enable a firm to use other firms' currently generated technological know-how so as to increase its probability of innovative success and its rate of technological improvement. We take up these issues in turn.

Absorptive capacities ac_i^t are considered as know-how stocks and are built up in the same cumulative way as R&D capital stocks. We assume that absorptive capacities and R&D capital stocks can be separated:

$$ac_i^t = \sigma_i \gamma_i \cdot \sum_t \left(p_i^t q_i^t\right), \tag{10}$$

where the share $(1\text{-}\sigma_i)$ is used to build up the R&D capital stocks.

Absorptive capacities allow a firm to look for promising *directions of research*. In the model, the direction of research activities is represented by the variable ε_i^t which divides the R&D budget into efforts devoted either to capital or labor reduction, as given in (6). Whereas conservative firms on average split their R&D efforts equally in both research directions ($E(\varepsilon_i^t) = 0.5$), an absorptive firm i watches its competitors j who are more profitable than itself ($\pi_j > \pi_i$, $i \neq j$). However, the absorptive firm i cannot imitate this competitor at once and perfectly, but attempts to gather some information about competitor j's superior technology . The magnitude of information is assumed to increase with the logarithmic distance of firm i's technology to the one of competitor j. The measure s_t^i is the sum of the distances between firm i and all more profitable competitors j. Thus, for $\pi_j > \pi_i$ $(i \neq j)$, it holds that

$$s_i^t = ac_i^t \cdot \sum_{\substack{j=1 \\ j \neq i}}^{n} [\ln(\frac{k_i^t}{l_i^t}) - \ln(\frac{k_j^t}{l_j^t})]. \tag{11}$$

The weight ac_i^t attached in (11) provides that only firms that have invested in absorptive capacities are able to gather information s_i^t. The sign of s_i^t indicates whether compared to firm i, more successful firms are on the average more capital-intensive ($s_i^t > 0$) *or* more labor-intensive ($s_i^t < 0$). This information will be used to direct firm i's R&D activities into more labor-reducing or capital-reducing process innovations. Additionally, we assume that firm i gathers information about competing technologies not only in a particular period but continuously over time. Therefore, the s_i^t accumulate to a stock s_{ci}^t:

$$s_{ci}^t = \sum_t s_i^t \ . \tag{12}$$

Thus, (a) only lasting changes in the competitors technologies have an influence on the sign of information s_{ci}^t, and (b) information s_i^t gathered with higher ac_i^t has a larger impact on s_{ci}^t.

The information measure s_{ci}^t determines the direction of research as follows. In the case of $s_{ci}^t>0$, economically more successful firms are on average more capital-intensive. Therefore, the respective firm attaches more importance to R&D activities aiming at a reduction of labor. In the other case of $s_{ci}^t<0$, more profitable technologies employ relatively more labor, so the respective firm aims at reducing labor inputs. Thus, the sign of s_{ci}^t determines a weight ε_i^t according to which absorptive firms split up their R&D endeavors:

$$\varepsilon_i^t = \omega, \begin{cases} \omega \in [0;0,5[& if\, s_{ci}^t > 0 \\ \omega = 0,5 & if\, s_{ci}^t = 0 \\ \omega \in]0,5;01] & if\, s_{ci}^t < 0 \end{cases} \tag{13}$$

ω: = equally distributed random variable in the respective interval.

The other effect of absorptive capacities concerns the capability of using technological spillovers for the firm´s own research activities. The potential spillover pool of firm i in period t is given by the aggregated R&D-success of all firms in period t that apply a technology with a capital/labor-ratio different to the one by i – because only different technologies contain helpful information. The periodic R&D success, Δis_{li}^t and Δis_{ki}^t respectively, is just the difference between the accumulated R&D success in t and the one of t-1, $\Delta is_{li}^t = is_{li}^t - is_{li}^{t-1}$ and $\Delta is_{ki}^t = is_{ki}^t - is_{ki}^{t-1}$. The respective innovative success of a competitor is divided by the distance of the respective technology – measured by the logarithm of the difference in capital/labor-ratios – in order to reflect the greater difficulty of learning from more distant technologies. Thus, the endogenous spillover pool SP_i^t of firm i is given by:

$$SP_i^t = \sum_{\substack{j \\ j \neq i}} \frac{\Delta is_{lj}^t + \Delta is_{kj}^t}{\left| \ln(\frac{k_i^t}{l_i^t}) - \ln(\frac{k_j^t}{l_j^t}) \right|}, \text{ for } \frac{k_i^t}{l_i^t} \neq \frac{k_j^t}{l_j^t}, \tag{14}$$

A positive constant ξ is added to these endogenous spillovers, reflecting additional exogenous effects such as feedback from science, etc. This total spillover pool supports the innovative endeavors of absorptive firms by determining a weight κ_i^t which has a positive influence on innovation success as given in (7a) and (7b):

$$\kappa_i^t = 1 + \frac{\xi + SP_i^t}{1 + e^{d_i^t - \alpha \cdot ac_i^t}}. \tag{15}$$

The effectiveness of the absorptive capacity ac_i^t on κ_i^t develops in a non-linear way. The respective threshold-effect of additional information is given by the denominator in (15). Here, the variable d_i^t reflects learning in building up absorptive capacity: On the one hand, there is experience with respect to the richness of different spillover sources and, on the other hand, an advantage in experience with the integration of external knowledge should be expected. Therefore, d_i^t describes the specific impact of the absorptive capacity effect, and is determined by a learning parameter θ and the absorptive capacity ac_i^t:

$$d_i^t = 1 - ac_i^t \cdot (1+\theta)^t. \tag{16}$$

Thus the higher is ac_i^t, the lower will be d_i^t, leading to higher κ_i^t and a higher chance for innovative success. With the above equations we have fully specified the behavior of absorptive and of conservative firms as well as technological and market relationships. We can now start analyzing the three questions raised in chapter 2.

4. Simulation Results

Our simulation runs deal with different scenarios in order to outline the basic structure and the role heterogeneity plays in technological development. In a first analysis, all firms apply the same strategy, either conservative or absorptive. These steps will show the general mechanisms of market competition and innovation processes. In a second step we investigate the comparative development of firms applying different strategies.

Before starting the simulations, some remarks with respect to the initial setting and also to the validity and robustness of results are necessary. All firms start with identical unit production costs and are confronted with the same degree of competition. Each simulation is run for 1,000 periods on an artificial time scale. As to the *direction of innovative endeavors*, due to the stochastic elements, we cannot claim strong robustness of results. In some cases the firms attempt to reduce capital per unit of output; in others, labor-saving innovations are their main objective.

However, with respect to technological and economic effects, there is no formal difference between these two. Thus, for market shares, periodic profits etc. sensitivity and robustness analyses can be provided.[9] For this reason, in the appendix, we state the corridor of values and the respective average result which are based on a *Monte-Carlo-Simulation*, i.e. several repetitions with different random numbers. Quite small fluctuations around the mean value suggest validity, at least with respect to qualitative results. Additionally, to give some intuition with respect to the role of the most crucial parameters, we discuss for a specific setting different scenarios by varying the degrees of appropriability and of competition.

In the following simulations, the firms under consideration exploit given technological opportunities for process innovations. We are interested in the kind, degree and intensity firms pursue this, depending on the strategy chosen and the technological and economic interdependencies assumed. Whenever all firms have exploited the given opportunities, they all end up technologically equal, and produce at equilibrium output and prices. Before, however, prices and quantities are never set at equilibrium, and any tendency to adjust to equilibrium will be steadily interrupted by the introduction of process innovations. Thus, the objective of our investigation is not the final equilibrium state but the way in which it is achieved.

The conservative strategy

In the first scenario we investigate the development of three conservative firms. Figure 1 clearly illustrates that, in this scenario, fluctuations at the beginning have important consequences: The most fortunate firms are able to occupy larger market shares for several periods. However, decreasing technological opportunities are responsible for converging market shares. At about period 300 the market shares of the three competitors are nearly identical.

A closer look at the capital/labor-ratios in figure 2 shows that capital/labor-ratios finally converge to a value of 0 (ln1) unique for all firms for the same reasons as market shares converge. However, variability of the individual development paths shows that conservative firms more or less proceed without following a specific direction of change. They continue in depleting their opportunity space by switching stochastically between labor and capital-saving progress.

[9] See Cantner/Pyka (1998) for a detailed sensitivity analysis.

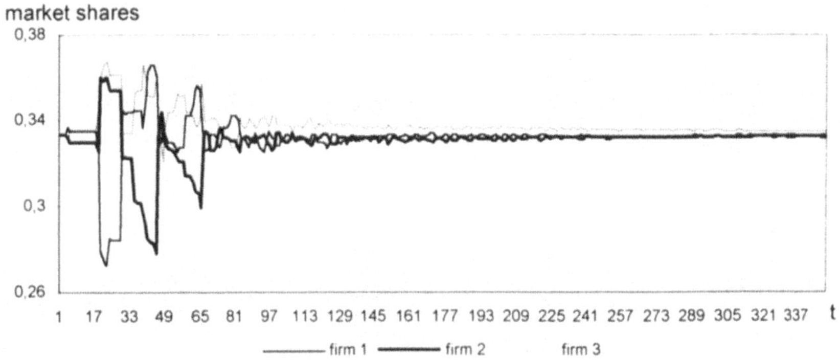

Fig. 1. Market shares in the conservative scenario

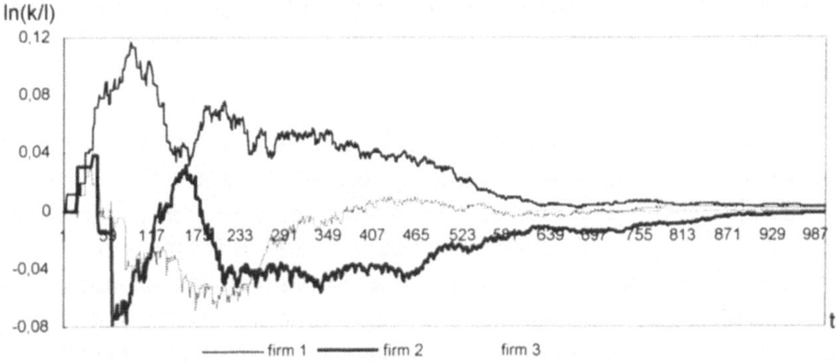

Fig. 2. Capital/labor-ratios in the conservative scenario

The absorptive strategy

In the next scenario, we investigate three firms applying the absorptive strategy. Assuming first that these firms build up absorptive capacity at the same intensity, $\sigma_i=\sigma$, we observe that, due to stochastic effects at the beginning, the firm in a leading position holds this position throughout. Thus, we find a rather stable development of market shares with a clear ranking of firms in this respect.

However, more interesting is the case in which firms differ in their intensity to invest in absorptive capacity, σ_i (figure 3). Market shares now follow a rather characteristic development. In early periods there are stochastic effects followed by an ordering of market shares in accordance with σ_i. Thus, the firm with the lowest (highest) σ_i will dominate (lag behind) first. With further progress, however, the backward firms catch-up in market shares and even overtake. Thus, we find a period where

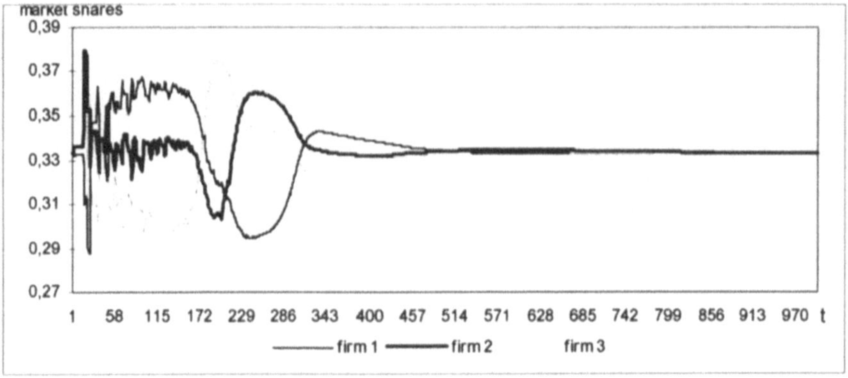

Fig. 3. Market shares in the absorptive scenario

turbulence in market shares and changing leaderships can be observed. Later on, when technological opportunities are increasingly depleted, market shares converge again.

Consider now the technological development represented by the development of the capital/labor-ratio (figure 4). Contrary to the case of conservative firms, the individual development paths show a common direction of progress. As shown in figure 4, all firms first move in the direction of labor-saving and then suddenly redirect into capital-saving. The individual paths also do not show an erratic movement, but rather a clear tendency in one direction for a longer period of time (interrupted only by unsuccessful attempts).

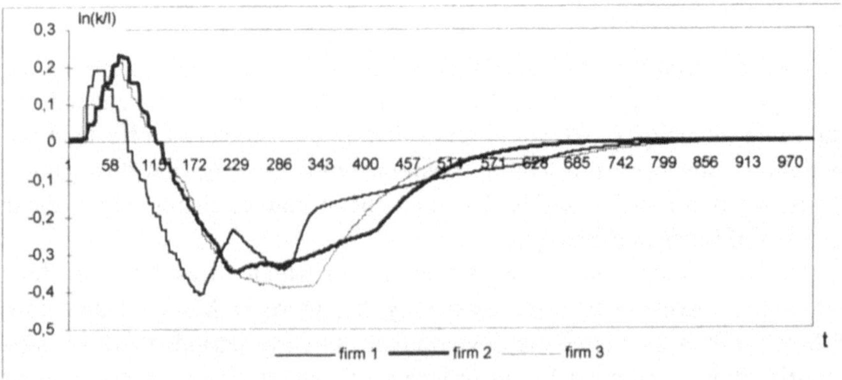

Fig. 4. Capital/labor-ratios in the absorptive scenario

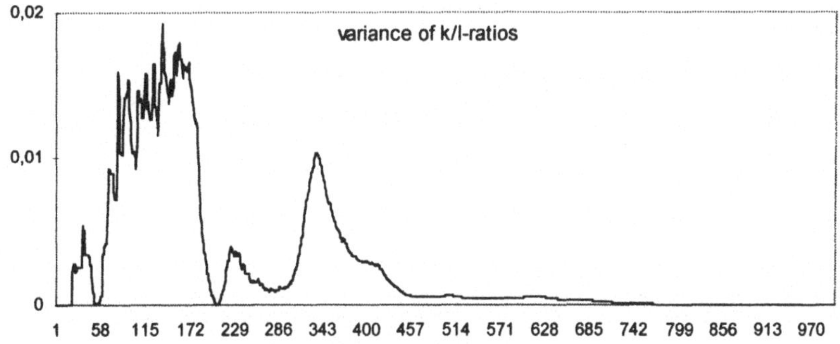

Fig. 5. Variance of k/l-ratios

The points of redirection are closely related to a low level of heterogeneity. Figure 5 shows the variance in capital/labor-ratios. At about period 60 and at about period 200, variance, and thus heterogeneity, is about 0. Around these periods redirection of research endeavors take place. Here, spillover effects do not *connect* the research endeavors of firms and each firm chooses stochastically a certain direction of further progress. Whenever one firm succeeds first and earns higher profits, other firms will tend to follow this direction of technical change. It can also be observed here that between t=200 and t=300 heterogeneity is quite low (and profit leadership changes more often), leading to a rather *uncoordinated* direction of technological development. With increasing heterogeneity, the ordering effects then become more powerful again.

The duopoly case

A third scenario looks at the comparative performance of the two innovation strategies. To simplify the presentation, we first investigate only one conservative and one absorptive firm. Considering market shares (figure 6), in the beginning of the simulation run the conservative firm dominates: It does not invest in absorptive capacity and compared, to the absorptive firm, it runs a higher level of direct R&D. The initially backward absorptive firm, however, will catch up later on: it builds up absorptive capacity, allowing it to use the spillover effects arising out of the different developments in k/l-ratios. The absorptive firm then is in a position to overtake the conservative firm with respect to market shares. This late advantage is due to the effect of *dynamic efficiency* of R&D efforts.[10]

[10] Thus, the causation here is quite different to the one of dynamic decreasing returns to scale which have to do with firm size. Here we analyze only firm strategies, the allocation of R&D expenditures and their dynamic efficiency effect.

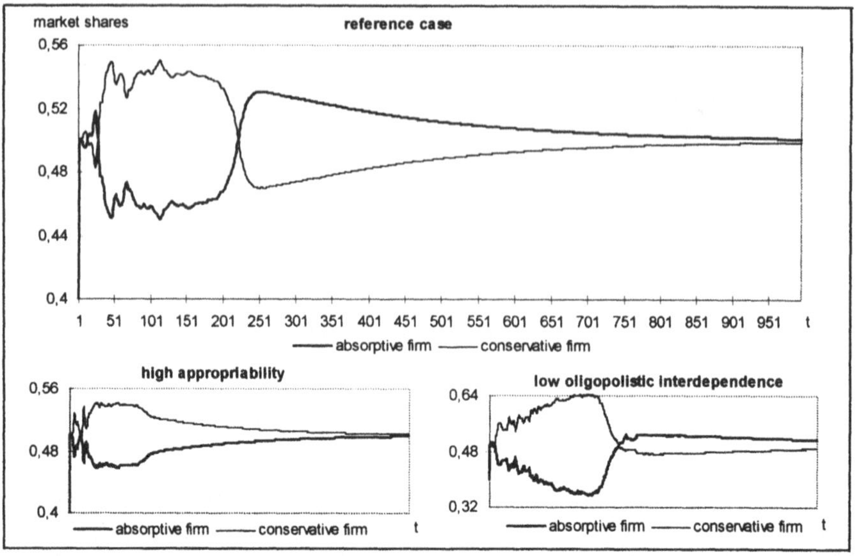

Fig. 6. Market shares in the duopoly case

With technological opportunities become more and more depleted, however, this advantage will finally vanish.

To give some intuition of the sensitivity of our model with respect to some crucial technological as well as economic parameters, we simulate two additional scenarios. In the first, appropriability conditions are increased significantly so that the absorptive firm is faced with a significantly lower access to the spillover pool. Although the absorptive capacity effect is still working here, compared to the reference scenario smaller gains in market shares are experienced. Accordingly, in this case the building up absorptive capacity is not sufficient to compensate for the voluntary „staying behind“ at the beginning of the simulation run. In the second scenario, the degree of oligopolistic competition is decreased, so that the two firms are able to act more in monopolistic isolation. Now, the conservative firm is able to increase market shares more extensively in early periods, because consumers are less able to substitute between both producers in this scenario. Despite all efforts to follow the decreasing prices charged by the conservative firm due to early innovative success, the absorptive firm cannot attract enough demand. Consequently, the market share of the absorptive firm is declining, leading to declining sales and consequently to lower R&D-budgets. Although the absorptive capacity effect still works, the market share of the absorptive firm is always lower than in the reference case.

The different technological developments of the two firms is shown in figure 7. As above, the conservative firm moves along a k/l-ratio relatively close to 1. By contrast, the absorptive firm shows a clear direction of progress, and switches after a while from labor to capital-saving. Until about period 240, these changes are due to the fact that the absorptive firm follows the more successful conservative firm. Later on, the absorptive firm is more profitable and accordingly ignores the performance of its competitor.

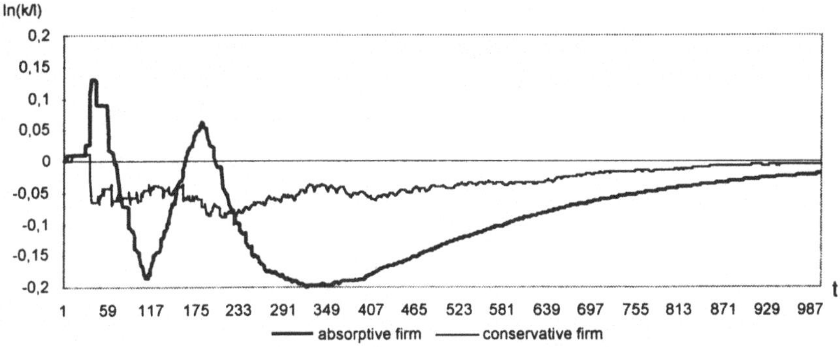

Fig. 7. Capital/labor-ratio in the duopoly case

The oligopoly case with different strategies

Finally, we consider an oligopoly case with 10 firms, five of which are conservative while the other five follow the absorptive strategy with different intensities σ_i . Looking at the development of market shares, we find variability with catch-up and taking-over effects. This is to be considered as an overlapping of the competitive and innovative effects we showed before. More interesting is whether increasing the number of firms *affects* the research orientation of firms. For this purpose, figure 8 shows the still erratic R&D efforts of a conservative firm investing in capital saving.

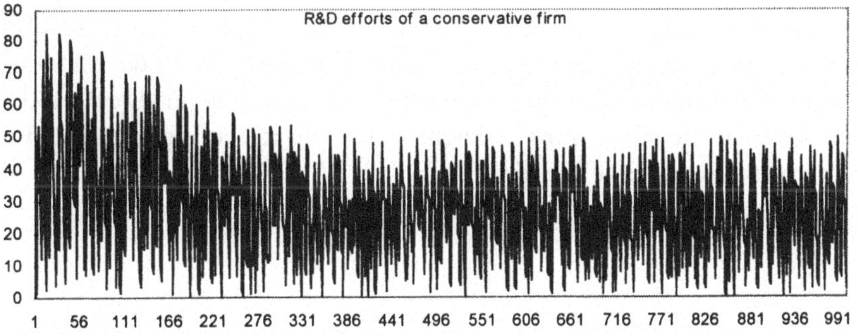

Fig. 8. R&D efforts of the conservative firms (reducing capital intensity)

Compared with this, absorptive firms deliver a rather ordered development, switching phases of intense capital saving and intense labor-saving (figure 9). During phases of low investment in capital-reducing technological progress, investment in labor-reducing investment is high, and vice versa. Thus, the ordering and structure-building feature of spillovers arising from horizontal heterogeneity still works with a larger number of firms. The duration of intense capital and labor-saving research tends to become longer with further progress. This is due to the fact that, in the beginning, the leadership in profits changes quite often, leading to a higher frequency of switching. In later periods, the absorptive firms become economically dominant, and so changes in profit ranking are less.

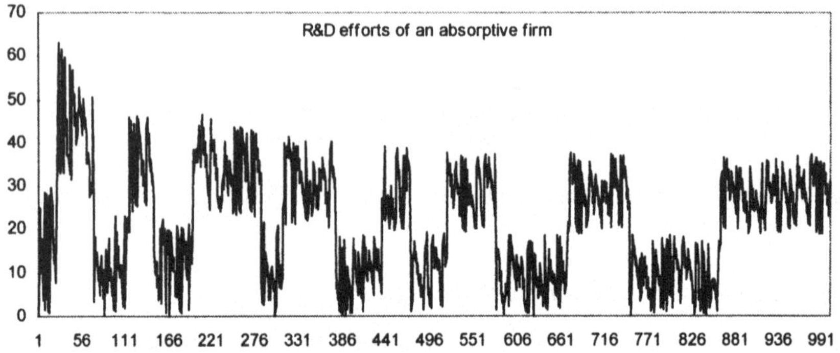

Fig. 9. R&D efforts of the absorptive firms (reducing capital intensity)

Finally, within this oligopolistic setting, it is interesting to get an idea about the long-run profitability of the different strategies under consideration. Does investment in R&D and the rather *coordinated* research behavior of absorptive firms pay in the longer run? Figure 10 shows the cumulated profits of each firm. Firms 6 to 10 are conservative and the differences in their profits are due to stochastic effects (augmented by success-breeds-success effects). Their average profit level is clearly below that of the absorptive firms (1-5). For the absorptive firms, we also observe stochastic variation in profit levels. However, due to the trade-off between investing in absorptive capacity and investing in direct R&D, there seems to be some most efficient σ_i leading to the highest accumulated profits. In this case it is firm 3.

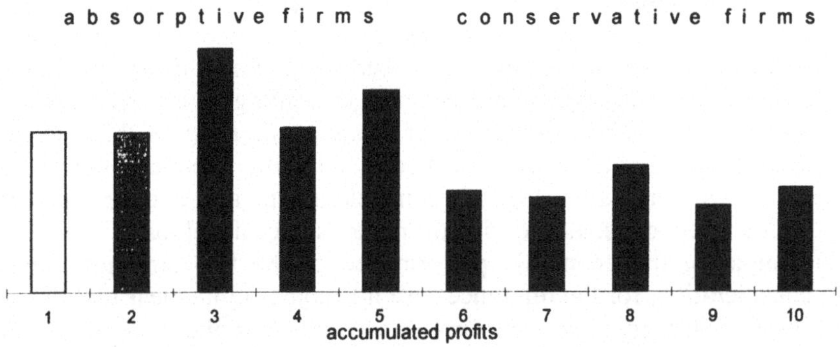

Fig. 10. Accumulated profits

5. Conclusions

In this paper we investigated the effects of horizontal technological heterogeneity among firms and their ability to absorb spillovers arising out of the heterogeneity in the direction of research. For this purpose we analyzed a model of heterogeneous oligopoly in which firms act on different markets but where nevertheless oligopolistic interdependencies provide for price competition. Firms are assumed to engage in R&D in order to improve production processes. In doing so, they differ with respect to the innovation strategies followed. Here, we distinguish between the absorptive strategy and the conservative strategy. Whereas the latter invests only in own R&D efforts, the former attempts to build up absorptive capacity allowing it to use technological spillovers from other firms. The spillover pool is modeled endogenously by relating it to the various production techniques in use, and thus, to technological heterogeneity. This heterogeneity diminishes by the degree to which spillovers are used. However, individual R&D-efforts then again provide for increasing heterogeneity.

Within this context, our analysis has shown the following results:

(1) Spillover effects and absorptive capacities are responsible for a quite ordered technological development of firms within a sector. They follow common directions of research, i.e. labor or capital-saving. This ordering effect depends directly on the heterogeneity among firms, and thus, the concept that *evolution consumes its own fuel* is at work here. The higher heterogeneity, the more ordered and coordinated is the development. With decreasing heterogeneity, switches in the research direction become more likely.

(2) For firms applying different strategies – either conservative versus absorptive, or absorptive strategies of different intensities – the market share development becomes quite turbulent. Early disadvantages of absorptive firms switch into advantages leading to an overtaking in market shares. Thus, the effects of *dynamic efficiency* of R&D expenditures comes into play. For firms following identical innovation strategies, early advantages become dominant and a clear structure with a rather constant ordering of market shares develops.
(3) Comparing the economic performance of the two strategies under consideration, for the reference case it becomes quite clear that the absorptive strategy allows the firm to accumulate higher profits than the conservative one. This result does not necessarily hold in the case of high appropriability of know-how or in the case of low oligopolistic interdependence. These results are dependent on a trade-off relationship between exploiting in-house knowledge and exploring external knowledge – this even applies for discussing absorptive strategies with different intensities σ_i.

Although our analysis is entirely theoretical, our results are important for empirical observations in industries in which competition could be described as oligopolistic. The automobile industry is just one example. There, different car models are produced which differ in price and quality, and so the competitive situation can be represented by the model of a heterogeneous oligopoly. There, each firm has its own market – which can be justified by a kind of consumers' brand loyalty – but where nevertheless oligopolistic interdependencies are at work. Thus, the respective markets are related. Looking at the development of market shares in those oligopolistic markets, quite often a development like the one found in the cases of turbulence above – e.g. the German automobile industry during 1981-1993 (Cantner (1999), Mazzucato (1998)) – can be found. It would be interesting to relate these empirical findings to the mechanism presented in this paper.

Appendix

Figure A1 shows the range of profits for an *absorptive firm* in a Monte-Carlo-Simulation, performed 25 times with different random numbers. As can been seen, the stochastic effects are only of major importance at the beginning of the simulation runs due to the contingencies of undepleted and new technological opportunities. Nevertheless, even there the resulting corridor of values is not so large that a qualitative change of our results could be expected.

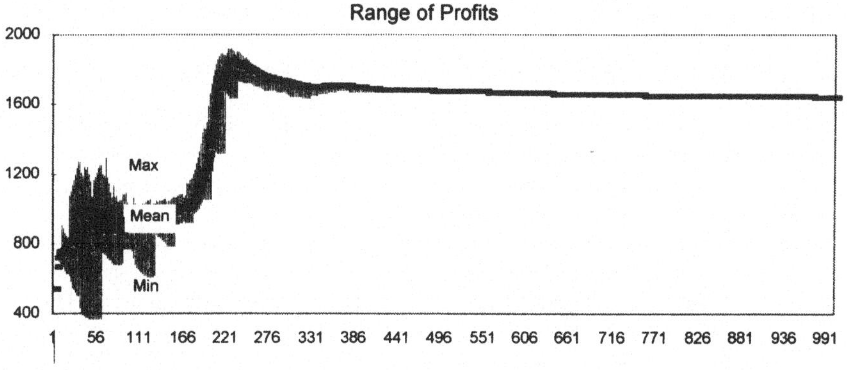

Fig. A1. Range of profits

In table A1a) and b) the initial values and parameter-values of our simulations are listed.

a) Parameter values:

bending of the innovation success	α	0.0002
inter-industry spillovers	ξ	1
learning-parameter	θ	0.005

b) Initial values:

price	$p_i(0)$	125
costs	c_0	100
impact of absorptive capacity	d_0	1
prohibitive price	a_0	50
output	$x_i(0)$	40

References

Basalla, G (1988), *The Evolution of Technology*, Cambridge: Cambridge University Press., 1988

Cantner, U (1996), *Heterogenität und Technologische Spillovers: Grundelemente einer ökonomischen Theorie des technologischen Fortschritts*, Habilitationsschrift, Universität Augsburg, 1996.

Cantner, U (1999), Heterogenität, Technologischer Fortschritt und Spillovers, forthcoming in: M Lehmann-Waffenschmidt, HW Lorenz (1999), *Studien zur Evolutorischen Ökonomik*.

Cantner, U, Hanusch, H, Pyka, A (1998a), Routinized Innovations, Dynamic Capabilities in a Simulation Approach, in: Eliasson G, Green C, McCann CR (eds), *Microfoundations of Economic Growth – A Schumpeterian Perspective*, Ann Arbor: University of Michigan Press, 1998, 131-55.

Cantner, U, Hanusch, H, Pyka, A (1998b), Pushing Technological Progress Forward: a Comparison of Firm Strategies, in: Lesourne J, Orlean A (eds), *Advances in Self-organization and Evolutionary Economics*, London, Paris, Genéve: Economica, 1998, 114-45.

Cantner, U, Pyka, A (1998), Absorbing Technological Spillovers, Simulations in an Evolutionary Framework, *Industrial and Corporate Change* 7(2), 1998, 369-97.

Chamberlin, EH(1931), The Theory of Monopolistic Competition, 6th edition, Harvard University Press, Cambridge, MA, 1948.

Cohen, WM, Levinthal D (1989), Innovation and Learning: The two Faces of R&D, *Economic Journal* 99, 1989, 569-596.

Coombs, R (1988), Technological Opportunities and Industrial Organization, in: Dosi, G, Freeman C, Nelson R., Silverberg G, Soete L (eds.), *Technical Change and Economic Theory*, London: Pinter Publishers, 1988, 295-308.

Eliasson, G (1990), The Firm as a Competent Team, *Journal of Economic Behavior and Organization* 19, 1990, 273-298.

Kodama, F (1986), Technology Fusion and the New R&D, *Harvard Business Review*, July-August, 1992, 70-78.

Kuenne, RE (1992), *The Economics of Oligopolistic Competition, Price and Nonprice Rivalry*, Oxford UK, Cambridge, USA: Blackwell, 1992.

Mazzucato, M (1998), A Computational Model of Economies of Scale and Market Share Instability, *Structural Change and Economic Dynamics* 9, 1998, 55-83

Metcalfe, JS (1994a), Competition, Fisher's Principle and Increasing Returns to Selection, *Journal of Evolutionary Economics* 4, 1994, 327-346.

Metcalfe, JS (1994b), Evolution Economics and Technology Policy, *Economic Journal* 104, 1994, 931-44.

Meyer, B, Vogt, C, Voßkamp, R (1996), Schumpeterian Competiton in Heterogeneous Oligopolies, *Journal of Evolutionary Economics* 6, 1996, 411-423.

Mokyr, J (1990), *The Lever of Riches*, New York: Oxford University Press, 1990.

Nelson, RR, Winter, SG (1982), *An Evolutionary Theory of Economic Change*, Cambridge, Mass.: Cambridge University Press, 1982.

Phillips, A (1971), *Technology and Market Structure*, Lexington, Mass.: D.C. Health, 1971.

Pyka, A (1997), Informal Networks, *Technovation* 17, 1997, 207-220.

Sahal, D (1981), *Patterns of Technological Innovation*, Reading, Mass: Addison Wesley, 1981.

Sahal, D (1985), Technological Guideposts and Innovation Avenues, *Research Policy* 14, 1985, 61-82.

Schumpeter, JA (1912), *Theorie der wirtschaftlichen Entwicklung*, Berlin: Duncker&Humblot, 8th edition, 1993.

Simon, HA (1976), From Substantive to Procedural Rationality, in: Latsis, SJ (ed.), *Method and Appraisal in Economics*, Cambridge, London et al.: Cambridge University Press, 1976.

Winter, SG (1971), Satisfycing, Selection, and the Innovating Remnant, *Quarterly Journal of Economics* 85, 1971, 237-261.

Witt, U (1992), Überlegungen zum gegenwärtigen Stand der evolutorischen Ökonomik, in: Bievert, B (Hrsg.), *Evolutorische Ökonomik: Neuerungen, Normen und Institutionen*, Frankfurt a.M.: Campus, 1992.

Market share instability and stock price volatility during the industry life-cycle: the US automobile industry*

Mariana Mazzucato[1,2], Willi Semmler[3,4]

[1]London Business School, Sussex Place, Regents Park, London, NW1 4SA, UK (e-mail: Mmazzucato@lbs.ac.uk)
[2]Department of Economics, University of Denver, CO 80208–2685, USA
[3]University of Bielefeld, D-33615 Bielefeld, Germany
[4]Graduate Faculty of the New School for Social Research, 65 Fifth Avenue, New York, NY 10003, USA (e-mail: SemmlerW@newschool.edu)

Abstract. Market share *instability*, during certain stages of the industry life-cycle, has become a stylized fact in the industrial organization literature. In the finance literature, volatility in the form of *excess volatility*, i.e. the much larger volatility of stock prices than dividends (although stock prices should in theory trace the present value of future dividends), has given rise to controversies regarding stock price determination (Campbell and Shiller, 1988; Shiller, 1989). Recent evolutionary models, both theoretical and empirical, have tied the presence of market share instability to industry specific variables, such as specific periods in the industry life-cycle and specific "technological regimes". The object of the paper is to explore whether there is a relationship between market share instability and stock price volatility and to what degree this relationship is connected to the concept of the industry life-cycle, and hence to industry specific factors. To do so, we explore the relationship in one particular industry, the US automobile industry. Since neither life-cycle nor finance theories attack this problem directly, we use insights from both approaches to build hypotheses which guide the data analysis. The empirical results confirm many of these hypotheses, suggesting that the degree of excess volatility is indeed partly affected by industry specific factors.

*We would like to thank Steven Klepper for his many valuable suggestions during the various stages of the paper's preparation. We also thank the anonymous referee and all the participants at the conference on "Economic Evolution, Learning and Complexity – Econometric, Experimental and Simulation Approaches", held on May 23–25, 1997 at the University of Augsburg, Germany. M. Mazzucato acknowledges research support from a TMR grant from the European Commission (ERBFMBICT 972263).

Key words: Market share dynamics – Industry life-cycle – Stock price volatility

JEL-classification: L11; 030; G12

I. Introduction

Market share instability, during certain stages of an industry's life-cycle, has become a "stylized fact" in the industrial organization literature, causing new indices of competition and new ideas regarding firm size distributions to emerge (Gort, 1963; Hymer and Pashigan, 1962; Ijiri and Simon, 1977). In the finance literature, volatility in the form of *excess volatility*, i.e. the much larger volatility of stock prices than dividends (although stock prices theoretically trace the present value of future dividends), has given rise to new ideas regarding stock price determination (Campbell and Shiller, 1988; Shiller, 1989). Both fields have gone through a similar set of reactions to the phenomenon of volatility, divided between those who try to interpret it with traditional theory and those who instead go to the opposite extreme, offering quasi-non economic explanations. An example of the latter is the use of stochastic processes (e.g. Gibrat's law) to reproduce firm size distributions, and the claim by Shiller (1989) that stock price volatility has more to do with investors' "over-reactions" (due to herd effects and fashions) than with strict movements in fundamentals.

Recent evolutionary models, both theoretical and empirical, have tied the presence of market share instability to industry specific variables. Empirical studies have found market share instability to be higher during the *early* stage of an industry's life-cycle (Klepper, 1996), in industries in which *small* firms are more innovative (Acs and Audretsch, 1990), and in industries characterized as "Schumpeter *Mark I*", i.e. industries with high entry, less persistence in firms' ability to innovate, and a more codifiable knowledge base (Malerba and Orsenigo, 1996). Evolutionary simulation models by Dosi et al. (1995) and Mazzucato (1998), which connect the emergence of different industrial structures to alternative types of "technological regimes", both find that the Mark I regime is characterized by more market share instability.

The object of our study is to explore whether there is a relationship between market share instability and stock price volatility and to what degree this relationship is connected with the concept of the industry life-cycle. Since neither life-cycle studies nor finance studies have studied the relationship between these two forms of market turbulence, we use insights from both fields to develop hypotheses concerning the possible relationship. We then compare such hypotheses to the empirical patterns in one particular industry, the US automobile industry, for which detailed data regarding market shares, earnings, and stock prices can be collected for most of its history. This is a particularly interesting industry to look at due to the many, sometimes contrasting, studies which have connected the evolution of its market structure (number of firms, instability, concentration) to underlying changes in competition, innovation and production. Given the industry specific nature of market share instability, an empirical relationship between market share instability and excess volatility could suggest that while over-reaction explains the *existence* of excess volatility, industry specific factors contribute to the *degree* of excess volatility.

The relationship between changes in market shares and changes in stock prices is particularly relevant to an evolutionary perspective since such changes represent two different types of *selection* mechanisms, one at the product market level and the other at the stock market level. Models in evolutionary economics often make a firm's market share a function of its relative fitness condition and formalize this "distance from mean" dynamic using replicator equations (Silverberg et al., 1988; Metcalfe, 1994). Stock prices, however, are less affected by current fitness than by *expected* future fitness. Hence in periods of high market share instability, during which there is less predictability of future firm growth patterns, it may be that a 10% increase in a firm's market share sends a very different signal to the stock market than the same 10% increase during a more stable period. The study considers these types of issues when developing hypotheses on the relationship between market share instability and stock market volatility.

The paper is organized as follows. Section II reviews the stylized facts regarding market share instability and stock price volatility in the US automobile industry and some associated measurement issues. The patterns observed here are decreasing market share instability as the industry gets older, a rising degree of market concentration, and the presence of excess volatility of stock prices. Section III contains some background history of the US automobile industry regarding changes in innovation, market shares and demand. Section IV reviews some possible explanations of the empirical regularities using ideas from life-cycle theories and from finance theory. Insights and implications from both approaches are used to develop hypotheses concerning the relationship between market share instability and excess volatility. Section V reports statistical results obtained from data on market shares, earnings and stock prices for the US automobile industry from 1921–1995. Both the firm level and industry level data are divided into sub-periods in order to evaluate whether there are distinct patterns of volatility in different phases of industry evolution.

II. The stylized facts regarding volatility

Before considering the possible relationship between market share instability and stock price volatility, we review the actual patterns, volatility measurement issues, and some traditional explanations.

Market share instability

The presence of intra-industry market share instability, i.e. periodic market share changes and "switching" between firms, has caused industrial economists to question (a) the use of traditional concentration ratios as adequate measures of competition[1] (Hymer and Pashigan, 1962; Gort, 1963; Grossack, 1965), and (b) the use of standard cost theory to account for the emergence of different types of market structures (Ijiri and Simon, 1977; Gersoski et al., 1997). Hymer and Pashigan (1962) use the early years of the US automobile industry as an example: large instability in market shares occurred with a relatively constant concentration ratio, making the latter a poor measure of quantitative and qualitative change. Others, such as Klein (1977), question whether such instability, found also in the early history of the semi-conductor and airframe industry, can be explained by the standard theory of economies of scale. Something more than static scale economies seems to underlie the instability. The lack of empirical support for the predictions which emerge from the traditional microeconomic theory of the firm ("optimal" firm size) have caused some economists to focus on an atheoretical approach to the subject, exploring the different types of statistical (random) processes which might lead to the skewed firm-size distributions observed in the data (Simon and Bonini, 1958; Ijiri and Simon, 1977). Gibrat's law, which states that firm growth rates are i.i.d. random variables independent of firm size, is the most commonly studied statistical process in this literature. It can be made consistent with traditional theory by making the optimal size of a firm a random variable itself, constantly changing due to firm specific shocks (Hart and Oulton, 1996).

The three graphs in Fig. 1 provide a visual image of market share instability in the US automobile industry. The market share data are taken from *Ward's Automotive Yearbooks* (1936-1995). Since we focus on the dynamics of US automobile producers only, we have adjusted firm market shares to represent the share of each firm in total US firms' production only. We look only at US firms for two reasons: (1) the S&P automobile stock price data, used in section V below, is based on only US firms, and (2) it is more convenient for our analysis to have a relatively steady group of firms to look at.

We see that from 1909 to the late 1930's there was a significant amount of change in firm market shares[2], followed by a more stable but still turbulent period between the mid-1940's and the late 1960's, with the most stable and concentrated period occurring in the last phase from the mid 1970's to the present. This general pattern of instability followed by stability and concentration corresponds with empirical regularities, or *stylized facts*, found in several industries (see French, 1990 for the tire industry; Phillips, 1971 for the airframe industry; Gruber, 1994 for the semiconductor industry; and Datta, 1971 for the television industry). To formally measure

---

[1] *"One of the chief objections to "concentration ratios" as description of market structure is that high ratios may be consistent with considerable instability in the market shares of individual firms. In judging the intensity of competition in an industry, the ability of leading firms to maintain their relative position in a market is probably more significant than the extent of concentration at a single point in time."* (Gort, 1963, p. 91)

[2] This period of instability is seen even more clearly in a graph provided by R.C. Epstein showing movement in the 28 leading automobile producers ranked according to size in production in Epstein, R.C., *The Auto Industry*, A.W. Shaw CO, 1928, Fig. 9, p. 206.

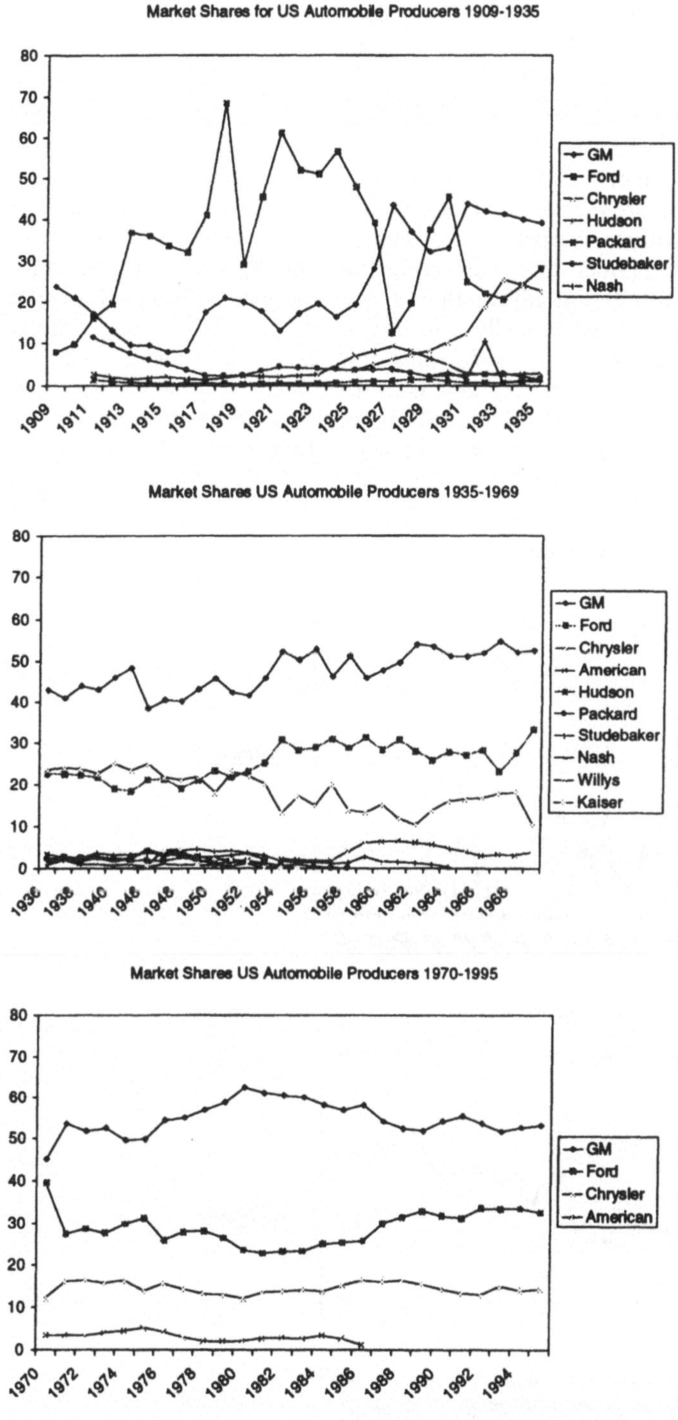

Fig. 1. Market shares of US automobile producers (% of US production only)

the degree of market share instability, we use an "Instability index" devised by Hymer and Pashigan (1962). The index is defined as:

$$I = \sum_{i=1}^{n} [|s_{it} - s_{i,t-1}|] \ , \tag{1}$$

where s_{it} = the market share of firm i at time t. The larger is the value of I, the more unstable are market shares in the industry. Such "change" can be interpreted to indicate the presence of competition, regardless of the concentration ratio (Hymer and Pashigan, 1962; Gort, 1963). Hymer and Pashigan have noted that although the index might be affected by the number of firms, it is empirically not very sensitive to it because: "*Small firms do not contribute greatly to the value of the index since they account for so small a share of the industry and since they tend to grow no faster on average than large firms*" (1962, p. 86). To measure concentration, we use the Herfindahl index $H = \sum_{i=1}^{n} s_i^2$, which is a function of the number of

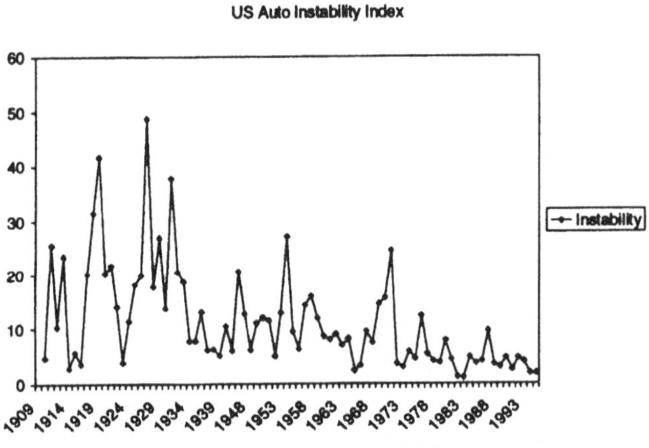

Fig. 2. Concentration and market share instability in the US automobile industry

firms and the variance of firm market shares. The two graphs in Fig. 2 use the Instability index and the Herfindahl index to illustrate the pattern of concentration and market share instability in the US automobile industry–increasing concentration and varying levels of market share instability, with a generally higher level of instability in the beginning of the life-cycle.

Excess volatility

Although stock prices should, according to the Efficient Market Theory, represent the present value of future dividends (the efficient discounting of new information), the actual variability in stock prices has been found to be much larger than that of fundamentals, causing many to question the validity of the theory. Shiller (1989) formalizes the concept of "excess volatility" through the analysis of variance inequalities. The EMM states that the real price is the expectation of discounted future dividends:

$$v_t = E_t v_t^* \;, \tag{2}$$

$$v_t^* = \sum_{k=0}^{\infty} D_{t+k} \prod_{j=0}^{k} t+j \;, \tag{3}$$

where v_t^* is the ex-post rational or perfect-foresight price, D_{t+k} is the dividend stream, γ_{t+j} is a real discount factor equal to $1/(1+r_{t+j})$, and r_{t+j} is the short (one-period) rate of discount at time $t+j$. If Eq. (2) holds, and if we assume for simplicity a constant discount rate r then since $v_t^* = v_t + u_t$ (where u_t is the error term), it can be shown that there is an *upper bound* to the variability of stock prices given by:

$$\sigma(\Delta v_t^*) \leq \sigma(D_t)/\sqrt{2r} \;, \tag{4}$$

where σ denotes standard deviation (for formal proof see Shiller, 1989, p.82). That is, the EMM predicts not only that changes in stock prices should reflect innovations in discounted dividends but also that the volatility of dividends (fundamentals) should be larger than the volatility of stock prices. The data instead show that it is exactly the opposite: stock prices are much more volatile than discounted dividends, causing many to question whether they reflect movements in dividends at all[3].

The concept of excess volatility can be illustrated graphically by manipulating stock price and dividend data as Shiller (1989) did for the S&P 500. The stock price and dividend time series data are first divided by the Consumer Price Index and then detrended using an exponential trend line to make sure that the series are stationary and hence their variances comparable. To calculate the series (v_t) generated by the EMM the following equation is used recursively:

[3] Even in the years around the Great Depression, dividends and earnings did not increase wildly when the stock market peaked around 1929, nor did they fall abruptly when the stock market fell dramatically in 1932 (Shiller, 1989).

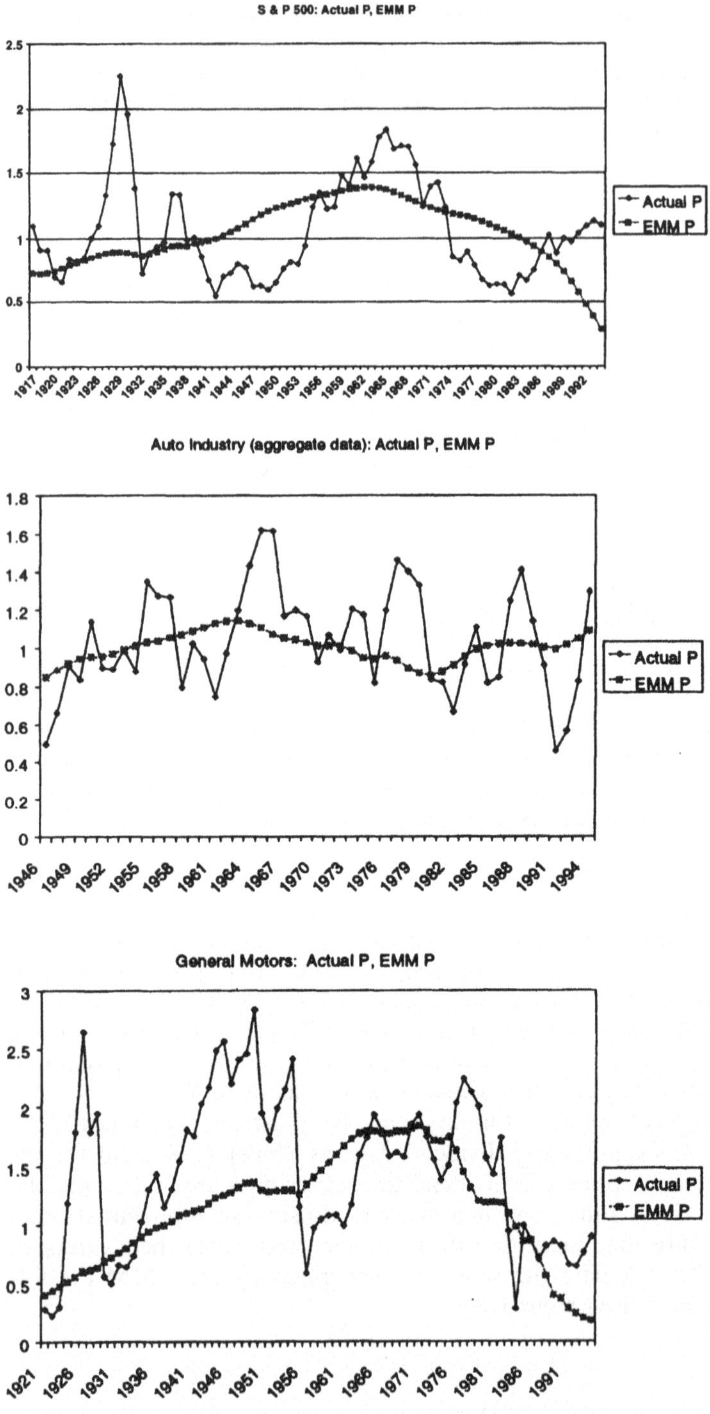

Fig. 3. Excess volatility

$$v_t = \frac{v_{t+1} + D_t}{(1+r)} , \qquad (5)$$

where r is the constant discount rate and D the dividend per share[4]. The calculations can also be made based on earnings/share since studies have shown this to not affect the result of excess volatility (Shiller, 1989). Given the lag in Eq. (5), it is not possible to calculate the EMM for the last period. If there are 100 periods, the value for the EMM at $t = 99$ is calculated by using the actual stock price at $t = 100$ in place of v_{t+1} in Eq. (5). Then for each other value from $t = 1$ to $t = 98$, Eq. (5) is used. In Fig. 3 below, we document the results that emerge from this procedure for three sets of data: the S&P 500 index data (the data used by Shiller, 1989), the aggregate US automobile data, and the data for one particular firm, General Motors. The per share stock price and dividend data for the S&P 500 and for the automobile industry are taken from *Standard & Poor's Analyst Handbook*, while that for General Motors is taken from the annual editions (1924–1997) of *Moody's Manual of Investments*. To adjust for the effect of macroeconomic factors, the industry level and firm level data are first divided by the corresponding S&P 500 data. Since average dividend data for the automobile industry are only available from 1946 onwards, in Fig. 3 we illustrate the EMM price from 1946–1995. The stock price and dividend data for General Motors have been adjusted for stock splits with information on splits obtained from *Moody's*. In each of the three cases, we observe excess volatility: the line tracing the actual detrended stock price is much more volatile than the line tracing the EMM.

The sections below will not study the *origin* of excess volatility in the automobile industry, but the forces which contribute to the *degree* of excess volatility over time.

III. Brief historical background of the US automobile industry

The US automobile industry began around 1894 with a total of 4 producers in the industry. By 1909 that number had reached 275!

This first stage, which approximately covers the period 1894–1909, was a pioneering one in which product design was not standardized and demand was not stable. Many different designs, technologies and propulsion systems were tried. The trial and error stage led to much oscillation in market shares. In his ranking of the 28 most successful cars produced between 1903 and 1924, Epstein (1928) shows the large instability in market shares

---

[4] Shiller's studies (1989) have shown the result of excess volatility to be insensitive to the particular discount rate chosen. He also experiments with time varying discount rates, where the variation is approximated by changes in real consumption data. He finds that such variation does not alter the results on excess volatility (Shiller, 1989, p. 115). The only way that the stock prices generated from the EMM can be made to be as volatile as real stock prices is to make the discount rate vary greatly at each point in time, a highly unrealistic assumption. To conclude, he states: "*The movements in expected real interest rates that would justify the variability in stock prices are very large – much larger than the movements in nominal interest rates over the sample period.*" (Shiller, 1989, pp. 124–125).

which occurred: market shares in 1903 were not good predictors of market shares in the 1920's. Of the ten leaders in 1924, only 3 were in business prior to 1908. On the consumer side, cars were more of a hobby than a necessity.

The advent of Ford's Model T in 1909 marks the beginning of a new stage in the US automobile industry. The high innovation and flexibility of Ford in its early years allowed it to take advantage of the opportunity which the 1910's and 1920's offered; rising incomes and a rising demand for cars. The mass production system used to make the Model T caused throughput time to fall from 21 days to 4 days and cut labor hours by 60% (Abernathy and Wayne, 1974). In 1909, when Ford's cost reduction program began, it only had a market share of 10% (GM 23%) while in 1916 Ford had 40% and in 1921 almost 60%. This second stage of the industry, which approximately covers the period 1909–1927 during which the Model T dominated production and sales, marks a distinct period. The new standardized product and stable demand allowed Ford to reap large economies of scale and remain the market leader for two decades. Economies of scale contributed to the strong shakeout (of smaller producers) which occurred in the beginning of the period: by 1930 there were only a dozen firms left. Figure 4 illustrates that the steady decline in the number of automobile producers (the beginning of the "shakeout") started to occur precisely in the year that the Model T was introduced.

A third stage, covering the period 1927–1940, marks the great change in market shares which occurred when Ford lost its first place position to General Motors (GM). As we will see in Section IV(A) below, some economists have attributed this fall to Ford's large size and concentration on mass production which prevented it from (flexibly) foreseeing the changing nature of demand. GM quickly responded to the new demand for a heavier closed body and more comfortable car, while Ford was overcome

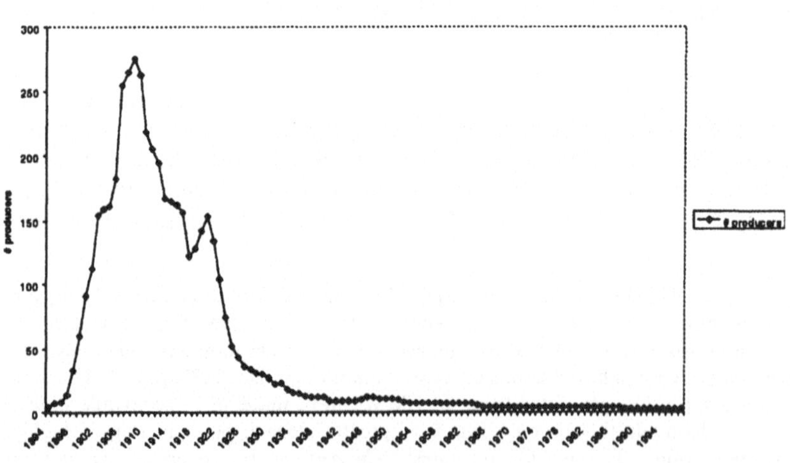

Fig. 4. Number of car producers in the US automobile industry (source: Ward's Automotive Yearbook)

with inertia. Others have attributed Ford's loss of leadership to the idiosyncratic nature of Henry Ford's personality. Nevertheless, from 1926 to 1940, GM increased its market share from 20% to 50% while Ford fell from 50% to 20%. After this time, GM never lost its lead among US producers. Market shares became much more *predictable* than in the period 1900–1930.

In the 1950's small cars began to enter the US market, but only with the energy crisis of the 1970's did foreign imports of small cars seriously affect US producers' market shares. The market shares of US producers (as a percentage of US production only) since the 1970's have not changed much, with most of the change in market shares occurring between US vs. foreign made cars.

IV. Theoretical insights: life-cycle and finance theory

Having reviewed in Section II the way that the characteristic patterns of market share instability and stock price volatility apply to the US automobile industry, and in Section III the underlying historical events in that industry, we now ask how such patterns might be related to one another.

To do so, we first review different life-cycle perspectives on market share instability. We then ask what implications these perspectives may have for the evolution of stock price volatility. We are interested in life-cycle analysis due to its emphasis on how industry patterns *evolve* over time. Since there is no life-cycle literature which explicitly connects market share instability and stock price volatility, we turn to some ideas in finance theory regarding uncertainty and stock price determination to provide more insight on the possible connection. At the end of this section, some informal hypotheses are drawn based on insights from both the life-cycle and finance literature. These hypotheses are used to interpret the data in Section V.

A. Market share instability: life-cycle and technological regimes

The industry life-cycle literature, as well as the Schumpetarian literature on technological regimes, has drawn links between industry evolution and market share instability. Gort and Klepper (1982) found the following stylized facts to hold across 46 products: during the early stage of an industry's evolution, there is high entry with many small firms and the product price is relatively high. This phase is characterized by market share instability and relatively low concentration. As entry and total output increase, the product price falls. At some point, the number of producers reaches a peak, after which it falls steadily (a "shakeout"), although total industry output continues to rise. This stage is characterized by more market share stability and greater market concentration. Life-cycle models have attempted to provide explanations, both formal and informal, of the dynamics underlying these regularities.

One group of life-cycle ideas claims that changes in market share patterns result from a "switch" in regime. Klein (1977), for example, claims that it is switch from "dynamic" to "static" efficiency which caused market share instability to decline in the US automobile industry. He defines static efficiency as decision making "along a given production possibilities frontier" and dynamic efficiency as the "extension of the frontier". While in the former the lack of uncertainty allows decisions to be based on initial conditions, in the latter the existence of uncertainty prevents optimal tradeoffs to be known beforehand, rendering decisions based on "perfect knowledge" irrational. He claims that market share instability is more typical of periods in which firms compete based on dynamic efficiency, while market share stability is more typical of periods in which firms compete based on static efficiency. This view is similar to Abernathy and Wayne (1974), who claim that the changing nature of market patterns in the US auto industry resulted from the changing nature of demand and technology, which no longer made the learning curve (based on economies of scale) a good strategy to pursue. In explaining the changes in market shares that resulted from Ford's failure to adapt to changing demand conditions, they state:

"..the highly specialized production process lacked the balance to handle the new product ... management needs to recognize that conditions stimulating innovation are different from those favoring efficient, high-volume, established operations." (Abernathy and Wayne, 1974, pp. 116 and 118).

In this view, the strong economies of scale from 1909–1924 resulted in market share stability, while the changing nature of demand at the end of the 1920's (which required more flexible and explorative strategies to be used) led to more market share instability. When demand and technology became stable again, so did market shares (the above quote refers specifically to the changes that occurred at the end of the 1920's). Aoki (1986) too has claimed that when the environment surrounding a firm is stable, then economies of specialization are important and the hierarchical structure of (large) firms is better suited for the "exploitation" of such economies. If instead the environment is turbulent, and the adjustment to changing consumer tastes becomes crucial, decentralized information processing (more typical of small flexible firms) might be better for "exploration" and adaptation (Aoki, 1986).

Recent contributions in the Schumpeterian literature connecting market structure and technological regimes have made similar arguments (Malerba and Orsenigo, 1996). The technological regime called Schumpeter Mark I refers to those industries, or periods during the industry life-cycle, which are characterized by high rates of entry, less persistence in firms' abilities to innovate, and a more codifiable knowledge base. Under these conditions of "creative destruction", it is more common for innovators to be small firms. Mark II is instead characterized by strong economies of scale, more persistence in innovation, and a tacit knowledge base, causing a "success breeds success" dynamic. Under these conditions it is more common to find that typical innovators are large firms. The distinction between Mark I and Mark II can take place both between different periods in an industry's life-cycle (the early period is characterized more by Mark I while the mature period by Mark II), as well as between different industries or sectors. For example, Malerba and Orsenigo (1996) find that the chemical sector falls more into Mark II while the mechanical engineering sector falls more into Mark I. Likewise, the shampoo industry is currently more characterized by Mark I while automobiles by Mark II. Empirical studies by Malerba and Orsenigo (1996) have found market share instability to be higher in Mark I industries and concentration to be higher in Mark II industries. In an evolutionary simulation model which explores the types of market structures which emerge from these different types of technological regimes, Dosi et al. (1995) find that the former are characterized by more market share instability than the latter. Similarly, in a simulation model by Mazzucato (1998), in which Mark I (II) is defined as the negative (positive) effect of size on the rate of cost reduction, market share instability is also found to be more characteristic of the Mark I period.

Another life-cycle approach is that found in Klepper (1996). In this view, it is not "switches" in regime that cause different types of market instability and concentration to emerge. There is always *positive* feedback between size and innovation but this does not lead to a monotonic increase in concentration due to the effect of randomly distributed innovation capabilities and timing of entry, which cause the early stage of the industry to be characterized by more market share instability. Market share instability later declines as a few firms get ahead and price-cost margins fall, reducing firm incentives to grow and to change their market shares given the related costs of adjustment. The role of chance events in the evolution of industry structure is also emphasized:

"*...chance events and exogenous factors that influence the number of potential entrants to the industry, the growth rate of incumbent firms, and the ease of imitation of the industry leaders will influence the ultimate number and size distribution of firms in the industry.*" (Klepper and Graddy, 1990, p. 27)

This is similar to Brian Arthur's emphasis on the effect of random events on positive feedbacks in the economy:

"*...small fortuitous events – unexpected orders, chance meetings with buyers, managerial whims – to determine which ones achieve early sales and, over time, which firms dominate*" (Arthur 1994, p. 5).

Having reviewed different life-cycle theories' interpretation of market share instability, we now review some ideas in finance theory to gain insight into the possible co-evolution of market share instability and stock price volatility.

B. Stock price volatility: insights from finance theory

How might the market share patterns described above affect stock price changes? Basing their work on the stylized facts found in Gort and Klepper (1982), Jovanovic and MacDonald (1994) make some predictions concerning the evolution of the average industry stock price around the "shakeout" period of the industry life-cycle. Focusing on the US tire industry, they build a model which assumes that an industry is born as a result of a basic invention and that the shakeout occurs as a result of one major refinement to that invention[5]. They predict that just before the shakeout occurs the average stock price will fall because the new innovation precipitates a fall in product price which is bad news for incumbents. Later,

> "*...as some firms establish themselves as early winners in the innovation race, the index rises sharply, reflecting those firms' enormous increase in both market share and value. Finally the index declines as the innovation diffuses, dissipating the rents earned by early innovators.*" (Jovanovic and MacDonald, 1994, pp. 344 and 345)

Although Jovanovic and MacDonald (1994) is one of the few papers which directly connects the industry life-cycle to the evolution of stock prices, it does so at the industry level (and only during one specific period of the life-cycle), so that inter-firm variations are not accounted for, and it is only the *level* of stock prices, not stock price *volatility* over time, that is the focus. Our analysis attempts to add to both these dimensions.

Indeed, the possible co-evolution of market share instability and stock price volatility is rooted in the mechanism by which market share instability affects "uncertainty" and how uncertainty affects stock prices. Market share instability creates the type of "uncertainty" which Frank Knight distinguished from "risk"[6]:

> *"The practical difference between the two categories, risk and uncertainty, is that in the former the distribution of the outcome in a group of instances is known (either from calculation a priori or from statistics of past experience). While in the case of uncertainty that is not true, the reason being in general that it is impossible to form a group of instances, because the situation dealt with is in a high degree unique..."* (Knight, 1964, pp. 232–233)

It is "uncertainty" which Klein (1977) describes when reporting the market share instability in the early phase of the US auto industry's life-cycle which made market shares in the 1930's completely unpredictable based on market shares in the early 1900's. What is the impact of the uncertainty arising from market share instability on the speculative evaluation of firms? One might postulate that in periods of higher market share instability (e.g. Mark I), investors are less willing to use current market share as a signal of future performance and hence base the firm's market value less on its market share. This would suggest a period in which there is less correlation between a firm's market share and its stock price. At the same time, there may be more excess volatility during this period due to the constant corrections which investors must make to their previous predictions. We consider such hypotheses below after reviewing some basic concepts in finance theory.

---

[5] They admit that this is a strong assumption but motivate it through the fact that a single shakeout is typical in the Gort and Klepper (1982) data and that particularly in the US tire industry there seems to have been one major invention, the Banbury mixer in 1916, which caused the shakeout to occur (Jovanovic and MacDonald, 1994, pp. 324–325).

[6] Quoted in Shiller (1989, p. 13).

In standard finance models, the stock price is taken to be the present value of future dividends or earnings. Letting P stand for the price of a share, D the (annual) dividend per share in the previous year, r the appropriate rate of discount, and g the expected growth in dividends, we have (provided $g < r$, otherwise the price is infinite):

$$P = \sum_{i=1}^{\infty} D \frac{(1+g)^i}{(1+r)^i} \quad . \tag{6}$$

In Eq. (6), both r and g could be made time-varying. The same equation can be expressed in terms of the price-earnings ratio. Dividing each side by earnings per share, E, and summing, we obtain an expression for the price-earnings ratio:

$$\frac{P}{E} = \frac{D}{E} \frac{(1+g)}{(r-g)} \quad . \tag{7}$$

The price-earnings ratio is thus a function of the dividend payout ratio and the expected long-term growth rate of the dividend stream (both equations are developed in Malkiel and Cragg, 1970)[7].

Under uncertainty it is the *expected* dividends or earnings (and their future growth rate) that are relevant. The presence of *risk* can be incorporated into Eq. (7) with a term representing the (expected) variance of the future returns stream from each stock. Since the horizon over which growth can be forecasted is a function of the variability of returns (the higher variance then the less predictability), the P/E should be negatively related to the variance term (Malkiel and Cragg, 1970)[8]. An important measure of risk called the Beta index, used in the context of the CAPM model, looks at the covariance between the returns of each individual security and that of a composite market index (the higher the covariance the higher the risk). Covariances are assumed to emerge due to the fact that all individual (firm) returns partially depend on the returns in the whole market (such as the S&P index), or on the returns of a particular industry (Beaver and Morse, 1978). Ceteris paribus, a stock whose movements are not highly correlated with the market (a low Beta) will tend to reduce the variability and thus risk of the portfolio, causing the price-earnings of the stock to increase (Malkiel and Cragg, 1970). Yet the fact that the covariances and variances that are being valued in the market are those *perceived* by investors, not some "true" set, means that this relationship is not so predictable. For example, a higher dividend payout should theoretically, in Eq. (3) cause the P/E to increase,

---

[7] The firm earnings/share figures used in Section V to calculate price-earnings are those reported in *Moody's Manual of Investment*. These are earnings *net of interest paid to bondholders*. This is important since earnings/share will otherwise be affected by the finance structure of firms (e.g. their debt/equity ratio).

[8] Malkiel and Cragg (1970) explain: "*....the horizon, N, over which firm growth prospects can be forecasted is itself a function of the variance of the returns stream. Hence investors would project extraordinary earnings growth over only a very limited horizon for companies where the anticipated variance of the earnings stream is large. Since it can be shown that* $\delta(P/E v \delta N) > 0$, *it follows that price-earnings should be negatively related to the variance term*". (1970, p. 602).

yet if the high dividend payout is interpreted to mean low future growth (due to low reinvested earnings), then it could actually cause the P/E to fall.

Shiller's (1989) theoretical and empirical studies have contributed to this analysis of market evaluation by emphasizing the role of "social" factors. He has shown that the Efficient Markets hypothesis faces serious problems due to the much larger volatility of stock prices than dividends. He has suggested that the reason for this "over-reaction" might lie in the way that investors interact with each other and the degree to which popular models (driven by intuition, the diffusion of opinions, herd effects, and social movements) affect investment behavior (i.e. affect future expectations).

We ask how all the above factors, i.e. dividend payouts, the expected growth of earnings, the expected risk, and the social psychology of investors, might be related to the market share patterns discussed in Section II, and to the processes underlying such patterns discussed in the life-cycle theories in Section IV(A) above. The connection can be posited principally through the effect of market share instability on investors' abilities to place market values on firms.

As regards the effect of market share instability on investors' anticipation of firm *growth*, various studies, including Ryals (1985) and Beaver and Morse (1978), have found that the P/E ratios are strongly affected by investors' attitude, confidence and mood (Keynesian "animal spirits"). Beaver and Morse (1978) have attempted to measure such emotional anticipation of future events with detailed data reflecting how security companies make their predictions. They find growth anticipations to have less to do with the statistical patterns of *past* growth (the traditional way that economists have incorporated anticipated growth into models) than with more subtle ways in which expectations are formed[9]. Thus in a period of high market share instability, since investors have less information regarding firm growth prospects (and hence future market shares as illustrated in Klein, 1977), they might be less "confident" to give a high price to a firm which experiences a sudden increase in market share than they would be in a more stable period. It is especially in such unstable periods that investors will be more likely to be influenced by the speculation of other investors, leading to herd effects and the type of over-reactions emphasized by Shiller (1989).

Although in periods of market share instability each firm individually has a stronger prospect for growth than in a more stable period, such growth prospects might be counteracted in the investor's mind by his/her inability to make predictions. The higher risk characteristic of the early phase of the industry life-cycle should cause the P/E ratio to be relatively lower in this period due to the reasons outlined above.

---

[9] They stress, for example, Keynes' idea of the "beauty contest" where the rational contestant would not pick those girls that he himself found prettiest, but those that he anticipated the other contestants would believe the *average* opinion would consider prettiest: "*We conclude that if one wants to explain returns over a one-year horizon it is far more important to know what the market will think the growth rate of earnings will be next year rather than to know the realized long term growth rate*" (Malkiel and Cragg, 1970, p. 616).

Kester (1984) offers an alternative view in his emphasis on the need for investors to balance considerations from net present value analysis and those from *expected future* growth analysis. While the former is better for simple growth options (from routine cost reduction, replacement projects, etc.), the latter is better for "compound growth options" (from research and development, entry into a new market, etc.). Although his study is focused on the evaluation of investment projects, the analysis is useful for understanding the role of risk on stock prices. He states that it is often the smaller firms that have the highest growth opportunities (almost entirely based on future growth potential rather than on current cash flow). As an example, he cites an executive of a major consumer products company:

"*If you know everything there is to know about a [new] product, it's not going to be a good business. There have to be some major uncertainties to be resolved. This is the only way to get a product with a major profit opportunity.*" (Kester, 1984, p. 157).

Hence in this alternative view, strong instability of market shares and earnings might represent the type of uncertainty signaling growth *opportunities*, causing the firm's price-earnings ratio to be higher. Interestingly, Kester ends his article with a very similar question to that posed in the present study: "*What influence do industry structure and competitive interaction have on growth option value*?" He states that the answer will vary from one situation and industry to another.

Lastly, in terms of the variance of stock prices *across* firms, the above analysis might also prove useful. If periods of market share instability (signaling future growth opportunities for firms which are not currently leading) cause investors to have less confidence to bet too strongly with the firms who currently have attractive cash flows, the dispersion of stock prices (and price-earnings) between firms would be expected to be lower in the unstable period than in the more stable period.

C. Hypotheses: co-evolution of market share instability and stock price volatility

Having reviewed the evolution of market share instability over the industry life-cycle and the possible effect of market share instability on stock prices, we now state some possible hypotheses that emerge from that discussion. The hypotheses are stated informally due to the fact that there is no commonly accepted theory of stock price determination, and furthermore that market share and stock price volatility have not been connected in either the industrial organization or finance literatures. The main contribution of the life-cycle literature is to provide insight into the industry specific factors which affect the evolution of market share instability over time and/or among industries. If there is a relationship between market share instability and stock price volatility, then there are reasons to believe that the degree of excess volatility may also be affected by industry specific factors. The hypotheses stimulate the questions asked in the empirical analysis in Section V, which address each of these hypotheses.

1. Evolution of firm numbers, output and stock price over the life-cycle

Based on case studies, life-cycle theory predicts that at the beginning of most industries' history there is a rapid entry of firms, then a mass exit ("shakeout") and finally a stabilization in the number of firms. As stated above, Jovanovic and MacDonald (1994) relate the shakeout to changes in the stock price index: just before the shakeout the index falls due to the bad news of the innovation for incumbents, then as some firms establish themselves as winners of the innovation race, the index rises (reflecting those firms' increase in value), and finally the index falls as the innovation diffuses and dissipates the rents by early innovators. However, there is no clear reason why market share *instability* should affect the stock price level, while instead there are reasons to believe that it might affect excess volatility, the level of price-earnings, and inter-firm variance of stock prices and price-earnings.

2. Market share instability and stock price volatility

Market share instability is higher in the first phase of an industry's life-cycle due to the effect of entry, changing demand, and changing technology. The uncertainty which results from such market share instability might cause stock prices to fluctuate more than in stable periods due to the uncertain profit opportunities.

3. Excess volatility

In the phase characterized by market share instability, the degree to which stock prices are more volatile than fundamentals should be higher than in more stable periods due to the greater difficulty in predicting firms' growth potentials. In this phase, since current performance is not a good predictor of future performance, even if a firm has strong earnings or dividends, its stock price may be abnormally high or low depending on the particular expectations regarding that firm's future growth. Expectation formation is likely to be dependent on the type of social interactions and "over-reactions" described by Shiller (1989) *more* in unstable periods than in more stable periods (during which investors can rely more on past information as an indicator for the future).

4. Level of price-earnings

The level of price-earnings is related to the concept of excess volatility since it captures the difference between expected performance (stock price, P) and real performance (earnings, E). But whereas excess volatility refers to the changes in stock prices, which indeed should be more volatile during unstable periods due to the over-reactions and constant corrections referred to above, the level of price-earnings captures the absolute difference between actual and speculated performance and is hence less clearly affected by unstable periods. Its level during unstable periods will depend on the particular interpretation of uncertainty by investors; on the one hand, greater variance in firm growth prospects causes the horizon for which growth can be forecasted to fall and hence the price-earnings to fall (Malkiel and Cragg, 1970). On the other hand, the fact that uncertainty is often associated with greater profit opportunity for individual firms might cause the price-earnings to rise (Kester, 1984).

5. Variance

The variance *across* firm stock prices might be higher in the more stable (mature) phase of the industry life-cycle because it is easier for investors to make predictions on future winners and losers (Klein, 1977). This gives them more confidence to give a higher than average stock price to a firm with a currently high market share, as opposed to an unstable phase where it is not so clear that high market share today means high market share tomorrow. This should cause the inter-firm variance to be lower in the unstable period due to the more cautious speculation.

V. Empirical analysis: the US automobile industry

We now turn to the data. We look at the following variables in the US automobile industry from 1921–1995: market shares, stock prices, and earnings. We ask to what degree the volatility in market shares is correlated with the volatility of stock prices and with the price-earnings level. The data are divided into firm level annual data and industry annual level data.
Firm level data: The firm level annual market share data were taken from *Ward's Automotive Yearbook* and adjusted to include only the fraction of each firm's production in total US production[10]. For each firm, the average yearly stock price was taken from the *New York Times* quotation which occurred usually around January 3 or 4 of the following year. The earnings/share data were taken from *Moody's Industrial Manual*. Each variable was adjusted for stock splits based on information from *Moody's Industrial Manual*. The firm level price-earnings ratios were calculated by dividing each firm's stock price by the firm's earnings per share (each adjusted by their S&P counterpart). The statistical results from the firm level data are reported in Table 1.
Which firms were included: We collected data for the majority of US automobile firms which were quoted in the stock market. The full list, obtained from *Standard & Poor's Analyst Handbook*, includes (dates in parentheses refer to the date that the firm started being quoted): Chrysler (12-18-25), Ford Motor (8-29-56), General Motors (1-2-18), American Motors (5-5-54 to 8-5-87), Auburn Automobile (12-31-25 to 5-4-38), Chandler-Cleveland (1-2-18 to 12-28-25), Hudson Motor Car (12-31-25 to 4-28-54), Hupp Motor Car (1-2-18 to 1-17-40), Nash-Kelvinator Corp. (12-31-25 to 4-28-54), Packard Motor Car (1-7-20 to 9-29-54), Pierce-Arrow (1-2-18 to 12-28-25), Reo Motor Car (12-31-25 to 1-17-40), Studebaker Corp. (10-6-54 to 4-22-64)[11], White Motor (1-2-18 to 11-2-32), and Willy's

[10] We provided a justification for this in Section II above.

[11] Formerly Studebaker-Packard.

Overland (1-2-18 to 3-29-33). Of these, we did *not* include in our analysis Auburn, Chandler, Pierce, Reo and White, either because of the unavailability of data for these firms or due to the extremely short time period during which their shares were traded. Although Ford only began to be publicly traded in 1956, we included it in the sample due to its importance in the US auto industry. We did not adjust for mergers. The only adjustment made was for stock splits. For example, after General Motors merged with American Motors (in 1987), the stock price data for General Motors includes that of American Motors, but an adjustment was made for the 2:1 stock split which followed the merger.

Industry level data: Average annual stock price data from 1921–1995 are from *Standard and Poor's Analyst Handbook*. The firms included by *Standard & Poor's* to calculate the industry average are those listed in the paragraph above. Since the corresponding average dividend/share and earnings/share data are not available from *Standard & Poor's* for the whole time period (only from 1946 onwards), we derive the average dividend/share and earnings/share data from 1921–1995 by averaging across firms using the firm level data we collected.

Detrending: Stock prices, price-earnings ratios and dividends for US automobile firms, as well as for the industry as a whole (aggregate data), are divided by their S&P 500 composite counterpart to isolate the dynamics of the automobile industry from the dynamics of the economy as a whole. Furthermore, when computing correlations and standard deviations, the variables (including market shares) are detrended by an *exponential* trend line. This insures that the series are stationary and hence comparable (as in Shiller, 1989)[12]. The results from the industry level analysis are found in Tables 2 and 3.

Sub-periods: To capture the life-cycle concept we analyze the co-evolution of financial and industrial dynamics in two distinct periods. The total time span comprising both periods was chosen to coincide with the years in which *both* financial (stock prices, dividends) and industrial (market share, earnings) data were available. So although the Ford Motor Company was established in 1903, since it only went public in 1956, we start the analysis of Ford in 1956 when both sets of data are available. Having chosen the total time period, we then divide this period into two to look at the first half of the firm's history compared to its second half. Data for the entire period are also included. This procedure makes the dating of the two phases different across firms depend on the firm's founding date, the date at which the firm

[12] Different detrending procedures, such as dividing by a linear, moving average or a lognormal trendline, could have been used. Campbell and Shiller (1988) detrend stock prices by dividing them by a long moving average of lagged dividends. Since these long moving averages are fairly smooth and trendlike, dividing price by such a moving average is a method of detrending or of removing low-frequency components. Mankiw, Romer and Shapiro (1985) instead detrend by using a proportional-to-divident rule for price. We did not consider using any type of *constant* trend, such as the last mentioned or the linear trend, since real divident series are not smooth at all (linear lines bias the results if there is non-stationarity in levels). We found that detrending with a moving average trendline or an exponential trendline did not produce different qualitative results.

went public, and the date at which the firm ceased to exist (either due to a merger or to exit).

The same division is performed for the industry level data. The resulting three periods are 1921–1958, 1959–1995, and 1921–1995. The two phases at the firm level will thus not necessarily coincide with the dating of the phases for the industry life-cycle (early stage of the life-cycle, mature phase of the life-cycle). Yet the phases are divided in this way to avoid an arbitrary choice of years to include and also to include as many years as possible for each firm. *These qualifications suggest that perhaps the two most interesting firms to look at when interpreting the firm-level data are General Motors and Chrysler precisely because their early founding date and the early date at which their shares went public make the division of their particular life-cycle coincide with that of the aggregate industry life-cycle.* For these same reasons, we will de-emphasize the results that pertain to Kaiser (due to the few years for which data were available) and to Ford (due to the very late date at which it went public). It was in fact tempting to report only the results for General Motors and Chrysler but given the fact that data were collected for other firms as well, we thought that illustrating the patterns for other firms could only add to the insight gained from the exercise.

Analysis of results

Below we report the results from the data analysis and compare them to the hypotheses listed in section IV(C) (with the same numbering).

1. Evolution of firm numbers, industry output and stock price

Figure 4 above documents the evolution of the number of automobile producers from 1904 1995: a steady rise until 1909 and then a steady fall (except for a short period in the late 1920's) until the present day. Figure 5 below shows that (a) during this time, the average industry stock price first rose (from 1921 to the early 1970's) and then fell (from the late 1970's to the present); and (b) that the total number (actual units) of automobiles sold/year rose steadily but at a decreasing rate.

The relationship between the industry shakeout and the fall in the stock price predicted by Jovanovic and MacDonald (1994) is hard to detect in the data since the shakeout in this industry occurred between 1909 and 1926 and our average stock price index data only begin in 1918 (in 1918 the number of producers was already half of what it was in 1909). Figure 5 indicates that a long-term fall in stock price started around 1960, but Jovanovic and MacDonald (1994) do not address changes over such a long period. The large bump in stock price between 1926 and 1932, does however, coincide with the change in technology from the Model T to the new "heavier, closed body more comfortable car" and the associated change in market leadership referred to in Section III (Abernathy and Wayne, 1974). Future research can perhaps look at this particular period more closely to draw an association with the dynamics described by Jovanovic and MacDonald (1994). Nevertheless, as stated in Section IV, there is no apriori reason to believe that

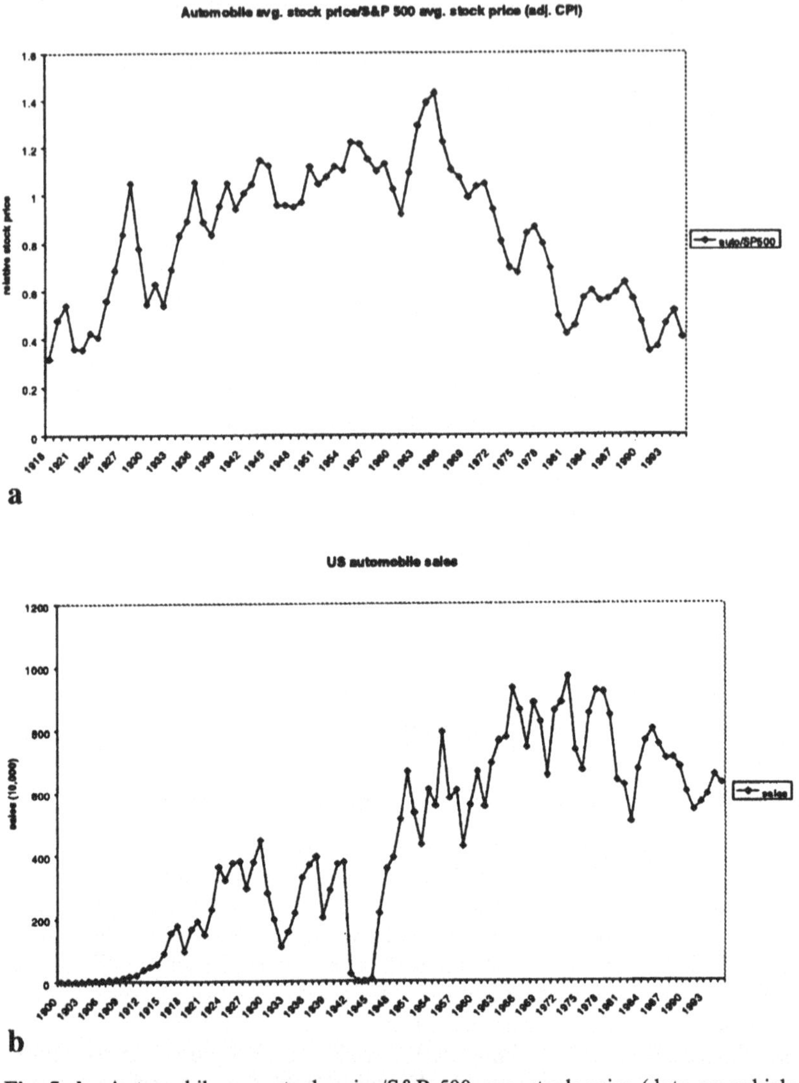

Fig. 5a,b. Automobile avg. stock price/S&P 500 avg. stock price (data on vehicle sales from Ward's Automotive Yearbook, 1996, p. 19)

market share instability should affect the average level of stock price. There are, however, reasons to believe that it can affect excess volatility, the level of price-earnings and inter-firm variance of firm stock prices and price-earnings.

2. Market share instability and stock price volatility

Firm level data. Columns 2, 3, 5, 6 and 8 in Table 1 below analyze the volatility of (detrended) variables by analyzing the standard deviation of their values over time.

Table 1. Firm level data

1	2 stdev ms	3 stdev p/e	4 avg p/e	5 stdevP	6 stdev EMM	7 exc. volat.	8 stdvms stdvsp
GM							
1921–58	0.2263	0.5602	0.6508	0.7563	0.3159	0.4403	−0.53
1959–95	0.1067	0.6784	1.324	0.5062	0.5687	−0.0625	−0.3995
1921–95	0.1768	0.6277	0.9829	0.6445	0.4734	0.1711	−0.4677
FORD							
1958–76	0.1147	0.7667	1.128	0.2128	0.2083	0.0044	−0.0981
1977–95	0.133	0.7427	0.9442	0.492	0.3474	0.1146	−0.359
1956–95	0.1243	0.7481	1.043	0.373	0.2846	0.0884	−0.2487
CHRYSLER							
1925–56	0.4417	0.7185	2.18	0.7756	0.3697	0.4058	−0.3339
1957–95	0.1133	0.4151	0.3355	0.3963	0.2097	0.1866	−0.2831
1925–95	0.3366	0.6346	1.271	0.6729	0.3136	0.3592	−0.3363
AMERICAN							
1955–70	0.4314	2	0.6188	0.3888	0.1589	0.2299	0.0426
1971–86	0.3259	1.058	0.9758	0.2616	0.3235	−0.0619	0.0643
1955–86	0.3767	1.594	0.809	0.3278	0.2562	0.0716	0.0489
NASH							
1927–37	1.29	0.9235	0.9113	1.864	0.348	1.5166	−0.574
1938–52	0.3256	0.4696	0.453	0.1462	0.2914	−0.1452	0.1794
1927–52	0.9237	0.7446	0.6821	1.4501	0.3073	1.1428	−0.5264
HUDSON							
1952–37	0.3382	1.095	0.7686	0.6565	0.7202	−0.0636	−0.3183
1938–53	0.3278	0.4412	0.4125	0.5632	2.678	−2.114	−0.2354
1925–53	0.3313	0.887	0.6054	0.6057	3.131	−2.52	−0.2744
PACKARD							
1922–35	0.3216	1.4227	1.303	1.1	0.1749	0.9258	−0.7784
1936–53	0.4941	0.6046	1.308	0.3806	0.2562	0.1244	0.1135
1922–53	0.4311	1.0759	1.306	0.8092	0.2164	0.5927	−0.3781
STUDBAKER							
1922–40	0.2254	1.3124	0.668	0.8552	0.209	0.6461	−0.6298
1941–64	0.1621	3.9301	0.9884	0.7971	0.2236	0.5735	−0.635
1922–64	0.2393	2.9614	0.8371	0.8151	0.2198	0.5953	−0.5758
WILLY'S							
1936–46	0.5753	1.422	0.4196	1.2798			−7045
1947–52	0.3686	0.9624	0.2281	1.5314			−1.1628
1936–52	0.4732	1.1926	0.3239	1.3893			−0.9161
KAISER							
1948–51	0.6095	0.4006	0.0718	0.2353			0.3742
1952–54	1.239	2.0699	0.05	0.2059			1.0331
1948–54	0.846	1.3216	0.0625	0.215			0.831

Column 1: three phases: 1st half, 2nd half, and total # of years during which firm was quoted
Column 2: standard deviation of detrended market shares
Column 3: standard deviation of detrended price-earnings
Column 4: average level of price-earnings
Column 5: standard deviation of detrended stock price
Column 6: standard deviation of detrended market value derived from EMM
Column 7: difference between 5 and 6 = excess volatility
Column 8: difference between stdev. of market shares (2) and stdev. of actual stock price (5)

Table 2. Industry level data

	1	2	3	4	5	6	7
	MS ins	avg. P/E	avg. SP	stdev P/E	stdev SP	SP ins	P/E ins
1921–58	14.082	1.879	0.9805	1.4198	0.1594	6.1659	1.1567
1959–95	6.3447	0.83	0.8719	0.9658	0.1996	0.2334	1.424
1921–95	10.324	1.3622	0.9277	1.3192	0.1869	3.2844	1.2885

Column 1: market share Instability index
Column 2: average price-earnings
Column 3: average stock price
Column 4: standard deviation of detrended price-earnings
Column 5: standard deviation of detrended stock price
Column 6: stock price Instability index (relative)
Column 7: price-earnings Instability index (relative)

The value of 0.5602 for GM in column 3 means that between 1921 and 1958 the standard deviation of GM's annual price-earnings ratio was 0.5602. In columns 2, 3, and 5 we see that the standard deviation of market shares, price-earnings, and stock prices for most firms are higher in the first half of the firms' histories. The notable exception is Studebaker, which has a much higher standard deviation of price-earnings in the second phase. The other exceptions either have a minimal difference between the two phases, or else pertain to the two firms which we are de-emphasizing (Ford and Kaiser). Hence the overall level of volatility seems to be higher in the early phase of each firm's life-cycle.

Industry level data. Column 1 in Table 2 below indicates that market share instability (calculated via Eq. (1)) is higher in the first phase (14.082) compared to the second phase (6.344), a result also shown graphically in Fig. 2. The Instability index for stock prices and price-earnings is also calculated using Eq. (1) except that instead of market shares it is the *relative* values of stock prices and price-earnings (e.g. each firm's stock price divided by the *industry* average stock price) that are used. The use of relative stock prices and price-earnings captures the changes *among* firms independent of the change experienced on average by all firms, and allows direct comparison with the Instability index of market shares which are *relative* by nature.

In columns 4 and 5 of Table 2 we see that the average price-earnings ratio has a higher standard deviation in the first phase (1.4198 vs. 0.9658) while the average stock price has a higher standard deviation in the second phase (0.1996 vs. 0.1594). While column 5 indicates that the second period is characterized by greater variation of stock prices experienced by *all* firms, column 6 indicates that there is more variation *among* firms in the first period. The fact that the Instability index of stock prices is much higher in the first phase is, as postulated in Section IV(C), probably connected to the greater degree of market share instability in that phase. In the case of price-earnings, the exact opposite holds: while the first phase is characterized by a higher standard deviation of average price-earnings, the second stage is characterized by a higher Instability index of price-earnings. This suggests that the period characterized by relative stability in market shares causes price-earnings differences among firms to be more unstable. One reason for this might be that investors react more strongly to changes in firm earnings in the period in which market shares are relatively stable due to the greater confidence they have in those performance measures as indicators of future performance. This would cause changes in earnings to be accompanied, perhaps with a lag, by changes in stock prices *more* in the stable period than in the unstable period. The fact that such changes in prices and earnings will not necessarily be proportional to each other, nor constant over time, will only add to the instability of price-earnings. Hence even if the Instability index of stock prices is higher in the more unstable period, the particular way in which stock prices react to changes in earnings could make the Instability index of price-earnings higher in the period in which market shares are more stable.

3. Excess volatility

To measure excess volatility we compare the standard deviation of actual stock prices to the standard deviation of the EMM price. As in Shiller (1989), it is the *detrended* values of both stock prices and the EMM price that we analyze. The EMM price is calculated using Eq. (5) in Section II. We use earnings/share instead of dividends/share due to their greater availability, but as already mentioned in Section II, Shiller's (1989) studies have found that this does not make a difference on the degree of excess volatility. While we use a discount rate of 0.05, the qualitative results are insensitive to the particular rate used (see also footnote 4 above).

We first look at the *existence* of excess volatility in the US automobile industry and then look at the *degree* of excess volatility in different sub-periods. At the firm level, the presence of excess volatility is seen in Table 1, column 7 where the difference between the standard deviation of the actual price and the standard deviation of the EMM price is calculated. For each firm except Hudson the difference for the overall period is positive, meaning that on average stock prices are more volatile than the EMM price, i.e. excess volatility exists.

As regards the different sub-periods, column 7 indicates that the difference between the standard deviation of the actual price and the standard deviation of the EMM price is higher for all firms in the first phase except Ford and Hudson. In the case of Ford this result is not terribly informative since its first phase occurs relatively late in its history. Hence in general, excess volatility is larger in the first phase of each firm's history. We provided a possible reason for this in point 3 of Section IV(C).

Another aspect of excess volatility can be captured by comparing the variance in market shares to the variance in stock prices. Column 8 calculates the difference between the standard deviation of (detrended) market shares and the standard deviation of (detrended) stock prices. For almost every firm (except American and Kaiser), the standard

Table 3. Variance among firms (with standard deviations in parentheses)

	1 avg var MS	2 avg var P/E	3 avg var SP
1921–58	.294 (.16)	.0351 (.1803)	.0237 (.1440)
1959–95	.463 (.21)	.0579 (.2198)	.0313 (.1666)
1921–95	.378 (.19)	.047 (.2008)	.0274 (.1550)

Column 1: average of inter-firm market share variance
Column 2: average of inter-frm (relative) P/E variance
Column 3: average of inter-firm (relative) stock price variance

deviation of market shares is much smaller than the standard deviation of stock prices (indicated by the negative sign). The degree to which stock prices are more volatile than market shares is higher in the first phase of the life-cycle for most (relevant) firms. Using an evolutionary simulation model, Mazzucato and Semmler (1997) show that this result is exactly the opposite of the result which emerges from the Efficient Market Model[13].

All these results indicate that in the period in which market shares are more unstable, stock prices are more volatile than real performance measures (earnings, dividends, and market shares).

4. Average price-earnings

In Table 1, column 4, the average level of the price-earnings ratio is higher for some firms in the first half of their history (Ford, Chrysler, Nash, Hudson, Willys), while it is larger for other firms in the second half (GM, American, Studebaker). In column 2 of Table 2 we see that the average price-earnings for the whole industry was quite a bit higher in the first phase (1.979) than in the second phase (0.83). A higher price-earnings in a period characterized by market instability (uncertainty) runs counter to arguments in finance theory that predict the price-earnings ratio to be lower during more uncertain periods due to the reduced ability of investors to predict

[13] Mazzucato and Semmler (1997) build a simulation model which a) reproduces empirical regularities in market share patterns by exploring different Schumpetarian scenarios connecting the evolution of market shares to firms' rates of cost reduction (innovation), and b) embodies assumptions from the EMM to make predictions regarding the differences between market share instability and stock price volatility. The EMM is used as a benchmark case as in Shiller (1989). In relating market shares to innovation, the model embodies arguments found in Abrenathy and Wayne (1974) and Klein (1977) by assuming that in the first stage of the life-cycle there is negative feedback (as market share rises the rate of cost reduction falls) while in the later stage there is positive feedback. While the model generates market share patterns resembling the actual ones observed, the EMM fails to generate the empirical patterns resembling the actual ones observed, the EMM fails to generate the empirical patterns of market values; the model predicts market shares and profits (a proxy for dividends) to be more volatile than market values and the difference to be higher in the first phase of the industry. The results above indicate the opposite to be true. For a copy of the paper please contact the authors directly.

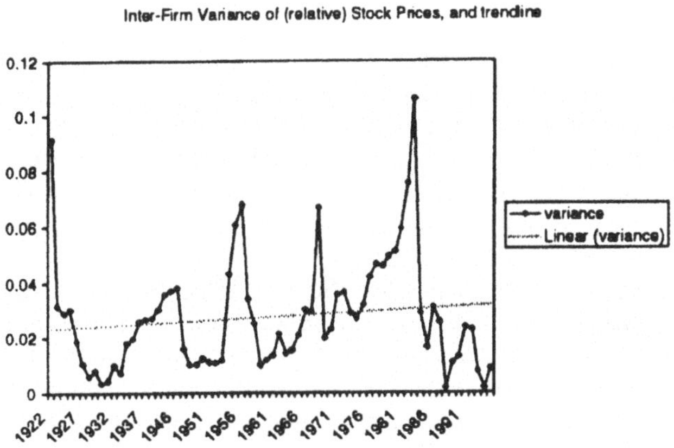

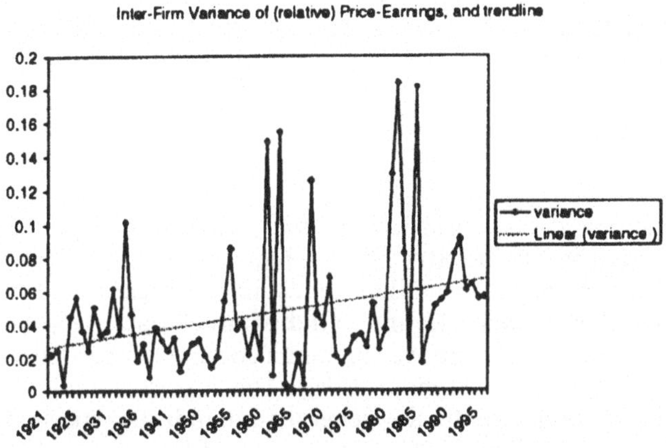

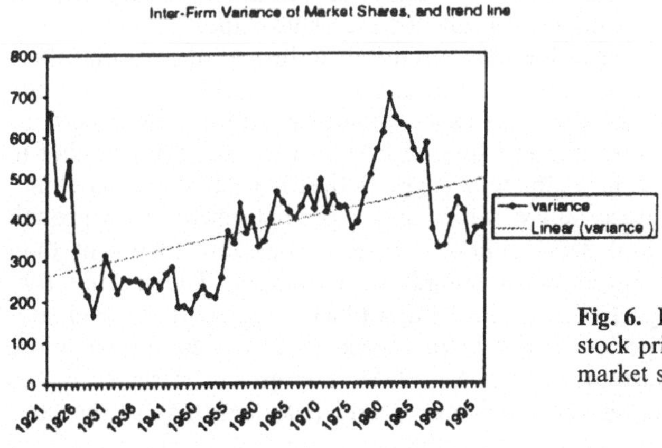

Fig. 6. Inter-firm variance of stock prices, price-earnings and market shares

growth prospects of firms (Malkiel and Cragg, 1970). On the other hand, this result accords with Kester's (1984) view that price-earnings ratios should be highest in periods of uncertainty due to the greater growth prospects which such periods offer.

5. Variance in firm stock prices

Columns 1–3 in Table 3 show still another type of volatility: the variance *across* firms in market shares, stock prices and price-earnings[14]. The focus here is on the differences across firms at any point in time and the evolution of those differences over time. Variances are computed annually and then averaged over each of the three periods. Columns 1–3 in Table 3 indicate that the average dispersion of market shares, stock prices and price-earnings was lower in 1921–1958 than 1959–1995.

This result was predicted in hypothesis 5 of Section IV(C) where it was argued that in the later period of industry evolution when market shares are more stable and market concentration is higher (supported by different life-cycle theories), investors have more reason to use current market share as an indicator of future performance and hence to give a consistently higher market value to firms which are current leaders. This causes the dispersion of market values to increase in the later stage of an industry's evolution. We show the result graphically in Fig. 6 where we see a rising trend (the dotted line represents a linear trend).

VI. Conclusion

Empirical studies have linked market share instability to industry specific factors, such as the period in the industry life-cycle and the type of "technological regime". Market share instability tends to be higher in the beginning stage of the industry life-cycle, and in industries characterized by high entry, the lack of persistence in innovation and a codifiable knowledge base (Klepper, 1996; Malerba and Orsenigo, 1996). The "excess volatility" of stock prices has been connected to the general (not industry specific) "over-reaction" of investors (Shiller, 1989). We focused on the relationship between market share instability and stock price volatility to study whether industry specific factors might also affect "excess volatility".

The empirical analysis of the US automobile industry suggests that there are distinct patterns in the evolution of stock price volatility over the life-cycle, and hence that the *degree* of excess volatility might be influenced by industry specific phenomena. The finding that excess volatility is higher in the first phase of each firm's history suggests that market share instability produces a form of "uncertainty" which makes predictions of future growth rates more difficult and hence market values to be more turbulent than actual performance measures (dividends or earnings). The finding that average price-earnings are higher in the first phase suggests that the greater uncertainty of this period might have caused investors to foresee more general growth opportunities (Kester, 1984). The greater variance *across* firms in their market shares, stock prices and price-earnings in the later phase of the life-cycle suggests that in the phase in which market shares are more stable, investors are more willing to make strong bets for/against

[14] The same general patterns were found using the standard deviation instead of the variance.

specific firms due to their greater confidence in being able to predict the future performance of these firms.

Although the results are rough and pertain to only one industry, we hope that they will stimulate new stylized facts regarding the financial side of the life-cycle to be added to the ones we already know concerning the "real" side (Gort and Klepper, 1982; Klepper, 1996; Jovanovic, 1998). The Schumpetarian literature that identifies and categorizes the differences in technological patterns and "regimes" in particular industries over time, as well as across industries during specific periods in time, can provide a useful framework for such future research.

References

Abernathy WJ, Wayne K (1974) Limits to the learning curve. Harvard Business Review 52: 109–120

Ackert LF, Smith BF (1993) Stock price volatility, ordinary dividends, and other cash flows to Shareholders. Journal of Finance 48 (4): 1147–1160

Acs ZJ, Audretsch DB (1987) Innovation, market structure and firm size. Review of Economics and Statistics LXIX (4): 567–574

Aoki M (1986) Horizontal vs. vertical information structure of the firm. American Economic Review 76: 971–83

Arthur B (1994) Increasing returns and path dependence in the economy. University of Michigan Press, Ann Arbor, MI

Beaver W, Morse D (1978) What determines price-earnings ratios. Financial Analysts Journal July: 65–76

Campbell J, Shiller R (1988) The dividend-price ratio and expectations of future dividends and discount factors. Review of Financial Studies 14: 195–228

Datta Y (1971) Competitive strategies and performance of firms in the US Television Set Industry, 1950–60. PhD Dissertation, SUNY, Buffalo, Business Administration Department

Dosi G (1988) Sources, procedures and microeconomic effects of innovation. Journal of Economic Literature 26: 126–171

Dosi G, Marsili O, Orsenigo L, Salvatore R (1995) Learning, market selection and the evolution of industrial structures. Small Business Economics 7: 411–436

Cochrane JH (1991) Volatility tests and efficient markets. Journal of Monetary Economics 27 (3): 463–485

Comanor WS (1967) Market structure, product differentiation, and industrial research. Quarterly Journal of Economics 85: 524–531

Epstein R (1928) The automobile industry; its economic and commercial development. Arno Press, New York

French MJ (1991) The US tire industry. Twayne, Boston

Gort M (1963) Analysis of stability and change in market shares. Journal of Political Economy 71: 51–63

Gort M, Klepper S (1982) Time paths in the diffusion of product innovations. Economic Journal 92: 630–653

Grossack I (1965) Towards an integration of static and dynamic measures of industry concentration. The Review of Economics and Statistics 47: 301–308

Gruber H (1994) Learning and strategic product innovation; theory and evidence for the semiconductor industry. North-Holland, Amsterdam

Hart P, Oulton N (1996) Growth and size of firms. Economic Journal 106: 1242–1252

Hymer S, Pashigan P (1962) Turnover of firms as a measure of market behavior. Review of Economics and Statistics 44: 82–87

Ijiri Y, Simon H (1977) Skew distributions and sizes of business firms. North Holland, Amsterdam
Jovanovic B, MacDonald G (1994b) The life-cycle of a competitive industry. Journal of Political Economy 102 (2): 322–347
Jovanovic B (1998) Michael Gort's contribution to economics. Review of Economic Dynamics 1: 327–337
Kester CW (1984) Today's options for tomorrow's growth. Harvard Business Review 62(2): 153–160
Klein BH (1977) Dynamic economics. Harvard University Press, Cambridge, MA
Klepper S, Graddy E (1990) The evolution of new industries and the determinants of market structure. Rand Journal of Economics 21: 24–44
Klepper S (1996) Entry, exit, growth, and innovation over the product life cycle. American Economic Review 86 (3): 562–583
Knight F (1964) Risk, uncertainty and profit. Kelley, Clifton
Malerba F, Orsenigo L (1996) The dynamics and evolution of industries. Industrial and Corporate Change 5(1): 51–88
Malkiel BG, Cragg JG (1970) Expectations and the structure of share prices. American Economic Review 60(4): 601–617
Mankiw G, Romer D, Shapiro M (1985) An unbiased reexamination of stock market volatility. Journal of Finance 40: 677–687
Mazzucato M (1998) A computational model of economies of scale and market share instability. Structural Change and Economic Dynamics 9: 55–83
Mazzucato M, Semmler W (1997) Market share instability and stock price volatility over the industry life-cycle: a simulation model. Economics Department, New School for Social Research, Mimeo
Metcalfe JS (1994) Competition, Fisher's principle and increasing returns in the selection process. Journal of Evolutionary Economics 4 (4): 327–346
Moody's Industrial Manuals (1927–1995) Moody's Investor Services, New York
Phillips A (1971) Technology and market structure: a study of the aircraft industry. Heath Lexington Books, Lexington
Ryals SD (1985) Secular and cyclical trends in price-earnings ratios. Business Economics 20(2): 19–23
Seltzer LH (1973) A financial history of the american automobile industry, 1st edn. Kelley, Clifton
Shiller RJ (1989) Market volatility. MIT Press, Cambridge, MA
Silverberg G, Dosi G, Orsenigo L (1988) Innovation, diversity and diffusion: a self-organizing model. Economic Journal 98(393): 1032–1054
Simon HA, Bonini CP (1958) The size distribution of business firms. American Economic Review 48(4): 607–617
Wards Automotive Yearbook (1936–1995) Ward's Communications, Detroit

Knowledge spillovers in biotechnology: sources and incentives

David B. Audretsch[1], Paula E. Stephan[2]

[1] Indiana University, Institute for Development Strategies, SPEA, Bloomington, IN 47405-2100, USA (e-mail: daudrets@indiana.edu)
[2] School of Policy Studies, Georgia State University, Atlanta, 6A 30303, USA

The late twentieth century has witnessed a scientific gold rush of astonishing proportions; the headlong and furious haste to commercialize genetic engineering. This enterprise has proceeded so rapidly – with so little outside commentary – that its dimensions and implications are hardly understood at all.

Michael Crichtron. Introduction to **Jurassic Park**

Abstract. This paper sheds light on the questions, *Why does knowledge spill over*? and *How does knowledge spill over*? The answer to these questions we suggest lies in the incentives confronting scientists to appropriate the expected value of their knowledge considered in the context of their path-dependent career trajectories. In particular, we focus on the ability of scientists to appropriate the value of knowledge embedded in their human capital along with the incentive structure influencing if and how scientists choose to commercialize their knowledge. We conclude that the spillover of knowledge from the source creating it, such as a university, research institute, or industrial corporation, to a new-firm startup facilitates the appropriation of knowledge for the individual scientist(s) but not necessarily for the organization creating that new knowledge in the first place.

Key words: Biotechnology – Knowledge spillovers – Science – Entrepreneurship – Startups

JEL-classification: LO; O1; O3

1 Introduction

A recent wave of empirical studies has confirmed the validity of the knowledge production function, which links knowledge inputs to innovative output. However, the exact unit of observation at which the knowledge production function exists is less certain, due to the presence of knowledge spillovers, which obscure the links between knowledge sources and innovative output. The answers to where knowledge comes from, and how and why it spills over are thus often elusive. This has moved Paul Krugman (1991a, p. 53) to argue that economists should abandon any attempts at measuring knowledge spillovers because "...knowledge flows are invisible, they leave no paper trail by which they may be marked and tracked."

While Krugman's (1991a) observation is undeniably true, the creation of a new firm, especially in a high-technology, science-based industry, such as biotechnology, produces an event that leaves traces for studying the knowledge production function. One of the most striking features of firms making Initial Public Offerings (IPOs) in biotechnology is that they are typically able to raise millions of dollars in the absence of having a viable product at the time when they go public. Indeed, new firms are founded and receive financing on the prospects of transforming technological knowledge created at another source into economic knowledge at a new firm through the development and introduction of an innovative product.

The purpose of this paper is to shed some light on the questions, *Why does knowledge spill over*? and *How does knowledge spill over*? We suggest that the answer to these questions lies in the incentives confronting scientists to appropriate the expected value of their knowledge considered in the context of their path-dependent career trajectories. In the metaphor provided by Albert O. Hirschman (1970), if voice proves to be ineffective within incumbent organizations, and loyalty is sufficiently weak, scientists will resort to exit from a corporation or university to form a new biotechnology company.

The plan of this paper is as follows. Section 2 focuses on the production of new economic knowledge and problems encountered in estimating the knowledge production function due to the presence of spillovers. The ability of scientists to appropriate the value of knowledge embedded in their human capital is also examined as well as the incentive structure influencing if and how scientists choose to commercialize their knowledge. Section 3 describes the data base. The links between knowledge sources and flows are examined in Section 4, and the incentives confronting scientists are examined in Section 5. A conclusion and summary are presented in Section 6.

2 New economic knowledge

2.1 Production

The starting point for most theories of innovation is the firm.[1] In such theories the firm is assumed to be exogenous and its performance in generating technological change is endogenous.[2] For example, in the most prevalent model found in the literature of technological change, the *knowledge production function*, formalized by Zvi Griliches (1979), the firm exists exogenously and then engages in the pursuit of new knowledge as an input into the process of generating innovative activity. As Cohen and Klepper (1992a,b) conclude, the most important source of new knowledge

[1] For reviews of this literature see Baldwin and Scott (1987).

[2] For examples see Scherer (1992), Cohen and Klepper (1992a,b) and Arrow (1962).

is generally considered to be R&D. Certainly a large body of empirical work has found a strong and positive relationship between knowledge inputs, such as R&D, and innovative outputs.

The knowledge production function has been found to hold most strongly at broader levels of aggregation. For example, the most innovative countries are those with the greatest investments in R&D. Little innovative output is associated with less developed countries, which are characterized by a paucity of production of new knowledge. Similarly, the most innovative industries also tend to be characterized by considerable investments in R&D and new knowledge. Not only are industries such as computers, pharmaceuticals and instruments high in R&D inputs that generate new economic knowledge, but also in terms of measured innovative outputs (Audretsch, 1995). By contrast, industries with little R&D, such as wood products, textiles and paper, also tend to produce only a negligible amount of innovative output. Thus, the model of the knowledge production function linking knowledge generating inputs to outputs certainly holds at aggregated levels of economic activity.

The relationship becomes less compelling, however, at the disaggregated microeconomic level of enterprise, establishment, or even line of business. For example, with Acs and Audretsch (1990) found that the simple correlation between R&D inputs and innovative output was 0.84 for four-digit standard industrial classification (SIC) manufacturing industries in the United States, it was only about half, 0.40, among the largest U.S. corporations.

The model of the knowledge production function becomes even less compelling in view of the recent wave of studies revealing that small enterprises serve as the engine of innovative activity in certain industries. These results are startling, because as Scherer (1992) observes, the bulk of industrial R&D is undertaken in the largest corporations; small enterprises account for only a minor share of R&D inputs. Thus, the model of the knowledge production function seemingly implies that, as the *Schumpeterian Hypothesis* predicts, innovative activity favors those organizations with access to knowledge-producing inputs – the large incumbent organization. The more recent evidence identifying the sources of innovative activity raises the question, *Where do new and small firms get the innovation producing inputs, that is the knowledge*?

One answer, proposed by Audretsch (1995), is that although the model of the knowledge production function may certainly be valid, the implicitly assumed unit of observation – at the level of the establishment or firm – may be less valid. The reason why the model of the knowledge production function holds more closely for more aggregated degrees of observation may be that investment in R&D and other sources of new knowledge spills over for economic exploitation by third-party firms.

This view is supported by theoretical models which have focused on the role that spillovers of economic knowledge across firms play in generating increasing returns and ultimately economic growth (Romer, 1986; Krugman; 1991a,b; Grossman and Helpman, 1991). These theories have been supported by the emergence of a wave of recent studies that have identified the existence of knowledge spillovers (Jaffe, 1989; Jaffe et al.,

1993; Audretsch and Feldman, 1996; Feldman, 1994a,b). Stephan (1996) identifies three distinct lines of inquiry which establish that such a relationship is present.

What happens within the black box of the knowledge production function, however, is vague and ambiguous at best. The exact links between knowledge sources and the resulting innovative output remain invisible and unknown. In many instances external knowledge is absorbed and used by existing firms. In other cases, however, the development of new knowledge provides an incentive for the establishment of new firms. Sometimes these firms are established by individuals who have played a central role in the creation of the new knowledge; in other instances the firms are established by individuals who grasp the opportunity that the new knowledge may provide. Thus, the establishment of a new firm in a knowledge-based industry provides an opportunity for examining properties of the knowledge production function. At the same time it should be recognized that this reveals only a particular aspect of knowledge flows occurring within the framework of the knowledge production function.

2.2. Appropriability and incentives

A large literature has emerged focusing on what has become known as the appropriability problem.[3] The underlying issue revolves around how firms which invest in the creation of new knowledge can best appropriate the economic returns from that knowledge (Arrow, 1962). Audretsch (1995) proposes shifting the unit of observation away from exogenously assumed firms to individuals – agents with endowments of new economic knowledge. As J. de V. Graaf observed nearly four decades ago, "When we try to construct a transformation function for society as a whole from those facing the individual firms comprising it, a fundamental difficulty confronts us. There is, from a welfare point of view, nothing special about the firms actually existing in an economy at a given moment of time. The firm is in no sense a 'natural unit'. Only the individual members of the economy can lay claim to that distinction. All are potential entrepreneurs. It seems, therefore, that the natural thing to do is to build up from the transformation function of men, rather than the firms, constituting an economy. If we are interested in eventual empirical determination, this is extremely inconvenient. But it has conceptual advantages. The ultimate repositories of technological knowledge in any society are the men comprising it, and it is just this knowledge which is effectively summarized in the form of a transformation function. In itself a firm possesses no knowledge. That which is available to it belongs to the men associated with it. Its production function is really built up in exactly the same way, and from the same basic ingredients, as society's."

When the lens is shifted away from the firm to the individual as the relevant unit of observation, the appropriability issue remains, but the question becomes, *How can economic agents with a given endowment of new*

---

[3] See Baldwin and Scott (1987).

knowledge best appropriate the returns from that knowledge? Different work contexts have different incentive structures. The academic sector encourages and rewards the production of new scientific knowledge. Thus the goal of the scientist in the university context is to establish priority. This is done most efficiently through publication in scientific journals (Stephan, 1996). By contrast, in the industrial sector, scientists are rewarded for the production of new economic knowledge but not necessarily new scientific knowledge *per se*. In fact, scientists working in industry are often discouraged from sharing knowledge externally with the scientific community through publication. As a result of these differential incentive structures, industrial and academic scientists develop distinct career trajectories.[4]

The appropriability question confronting academic scientists can be considered in the context of the human capital model. Life-cycle models of scientists suggest that early in their careers scientists invest heavily in human capital in order to build a reputation (Levin and Stephan, 1991). In later stages of their career, scientists trade or *cash in* this reputation for economic return. Thus, early in their careers, scientists invest in the creation of knowledge in order to establish a reputation that signals the value of that knowledge to the scientific community. With maturity, scientists seek ways to appropriate the economic value of the new knowledge. But how should a scientist best appropriate the value of her/his human capital? Alternatives abound, such as working full-time or part time with an incumbent firm, licensing the knowledge to an incumbent firm, or starting or joining a new firm.

Scientists working in the private sector are arguably more fully compensated for the economic value of their knowledge. This will not be the case for academic scientists unless they *cash out*, in terms of Dasgupta and David (1994) by selling their knowledge to a private firm. This suggests that academic scientists seek affiliation with a commercial venture in a life-cycle context. By contrast, industrial scientists consider leaving the incumbent firm when a disparity arises between the firm and the individual concerning the expected value of their knowledge. In the former situation, age is a good predictor of when the scientist establishes ties with industry. In the latter case, factors other than age are expected to play a more important role in determining when the scientist leaves the incumbent firm.

Once a scientist has decided to commercialize his knowledge, why should (s)he choose to do this by starting a new firm? In fact, in a model of perfect information with no agency costs, any positive economies of scale or scope will ensure that the appropriability problems of the firm and individual converge. If a scientist has an idea for doing something differently than is currently being practiced by the incumbent enterprises, that idea can be sold to an incumbent enterprise. Because of the assumption of perfect knowledge, both the firm and the scientist would agree upon the expected

[4] One must not overstate the effect that institutional affiliation has on the willingness and ability of scientists to share information. Some firms make the results of their research public. Some academics engage in practices that lead to the privatization of knowledge (Stephan, 1996).

value of the innovation.[5] The incumbent firm and the inventor of the idea would be expected to reach a bargain splitting the value added to the firm contributed by the (potential) innovation. The payment to the scientist, either in terms of a higher wage or some other means of remuneration, would be bounded between the expected value of the innovation if it is implemented by the incumbent enterprise on the upper end, and by the return that the agent could expect to earn if (s)he used it to launch a new enterprise on the lower end.[6]

3 Measurement

This paper uses a new database drawn from the prospectuses of 60 firms that made an initial public offering (IPO) in biotechnology during the period March 1990 to November 1992 to study the sources and incentives for commercializing new knowledge (Audretsch and Stephan, 1996). Prospectuses for the offerings were carefully read in order to identify the scientific founders of the new firms. In cases where it proved difficult to identify founders from the prospectuses, telephone calls were made to the firm. In addition, firm histories were checked and confirmed in *BioScan*. Founders having a Ph.D. or an M.D. were coded as scientific founders for the purposes of this research. In addition, several individuals who did not have a doctorate but were engaged in research were included as scientific founders. All told, we were able to identify 101 scientific founders for 52 firms making an initial public offering during this period.

Biographical information was also collected from the prospectuses and was supplemented by entries from standard references works such as *American Men and Women of Science*. Four types of job experience were identified – academic experience (which includes positions at hospitals, research foundations and the government); experience with pharmaceutical companies; training experiences (as a student, post-doc, or resident), and "other" experience. This information was used to distinguish among five distinct career trajectories followed prior to the founding of the company:

1. The *academic trajectory* describes scientists who had spent all of their time since completing their training employed in the academic research sector;

[5] In his 1911 treatise, Schumpeter argued that the gap between those firms creating knowledge and those appropriating it triggered a process of creative destruction. However, by 1942, Schumpeter had modified his theory, arguing instead that, "Innovation itself is being reduced to a routine. Technological progress is increasingly becoming the business of teams of trained specialists who turn out what is required to make it work in predictable ways" (p. 132).

[6] As Frank Knight (1921, p. 273) observed more than seventy years ago. "The laborer asks what he thinks the entrepreneur will be able to pay, and in any case will not accept less than he can get from some other entrepreneur, or by turning entrepreneur himself. In the same way the entrepreneur offers to any laborer what he thinks he must in order to secure his services, and in any case not more than he thinks the laborer will actually be worth to him, keeping in mind what he can get by turning laborer himself."

2. The *pharmaceutical trajectory* describes those scientists whose careers subsequent to receiving training had been entirely spent working in the drug industry;
3. The *mixed trajectory* describes scientists who had worked in both the pharmaceutical industry and the academic research sector;
4. The *student trajectory* describes individuals who went directly from a training position to founding a biotechnology firm; and
5. The "other trajectory", which includes scientists who have been employed by non-pharmaceutical firms.

Additional biographical information coded was ascertained concerning date of birth and educational background. Citation counts to first-authored published scientific articles were measured using the 1991 *Science Citation Index* produced by ISI and are used here as an indicator of scientific reputation.

4 Knowledge sources and flows

Summary data, presented in Table 1, show that fifty percent of the scientific founders' careers followed an academic trajectory; slightly more than 25 percent a pharmaceutical trajectory. Half of this latter group had established their careers exclusively with large pharmaceutical companies such as SmithKline and Beckman; half had come from smaller pharmaceutical firms, some of which, like Amgen, were first generation biotech firm. Table 1 also indicates that approximately an eighth of the founders had a mixed career in the sense that prior to founding the firm they had held positions in both a pharmaceutical company as well as a university or non-profit research organization. A handful of founders moved directly from a training position such as a residency or post-doctorate appointment to the startup firm, thereby short-circuiting the traditional trajectories from pharmaceutical firms and/or academe. The career trajectory of the

Table 1. The age and citation record of founders

	Birth date				Citations		
	N	M	SD	N_{known}	M	SD	N_{known}
All scientific founders	101	1943.18	10.20	96	92.13	171.05	99
All academic founders	50	1940.55	10.06	49	149.32	226.51	49
Part time	35	1938.79	10.29	34	172.71	259.03	35
Full time	15	1945.06	8.54	15	72.21	78.70	15
All drug founders	28	1945.61	9.20	28	29.71	46.28	28
Small	14	1945.93	9.84	14	30.30	57.40	14
Big	12	1947.00	7.67	12	34.00	34.41	14
Mixed career	13	1943.80	8.76	13	62.69	57.56	13
Student career	6	1957.00	3.54	5	58.17	83.72	6
All full time	57	1945.64	9.61	57	46.59	60.69	57
All part time	40	1939.42	10.03	37	159.30	245.52	37

remaining scientists was either indeterminate or followed another type of path.

The employment status of the founders with the biotechnology company was also determined. We find that 59 of the 101 scientific founders were working full time with the new firm at the time of the public offering; 41 were working part time, and almost all (35) of these had followed an academic trajectory. This means that 70 percent of the academic founders maintain full-time employment with their academic institutions, serving as consultants or members of the Scientific Advisory Boards to the startup firms. Only 15 of the academic founders had moved to full-time employment with the firm by the time the IPO was made. By contrast, all 28 scientists whose careers had been exclusively in the pharmaceutical sector held full-time positions with the firm at the time of the IPO; 9 of the 13 whose careers followed a mixed trajectory were full time.

5 Incentives

The evidence from Table 1 supports the hypothesis that the incentive structure varies considerably between the pharmaceutical founders and the academic founders. Those founders coming from universities and non-profit research organizations have the option of eating their cake and having it too, by maintaining formal contacts with their previous employer, often in a full-time position. Even those from the academic sector who are full time with the new firm are often able to maintain some connection with the non-profit sector as adjunct or clinical faculty. By contrast, those who have a career path in pharmaceuticals take full-time positions with the company, at least by the time that the company goes public.

There are other differences between those coming from an academic trajectory and those coming from a pharmaceutical trajectory. The most notable is the difference in age at the time the public offering was made. On average, those coming from academe were born approximately five years earlier than those coming from the pharmaceutical sector, a difference which is statistically significant at the 95 percent level of confidence. As would be expected, we also find that those following the academic trajectory have significantly more citations than those coming from a pharmaceutical trajectory. Of perhaps even greater interest are the differences between the part-time academics and the full-time academics. Academic founders who remain full-time with their institution, working but part-time for the new firm, were, for example, born more than six years earlier than academic founders who leave their institution to go full time with the firm. The part-timers are not only older; they are also more eminent, have significantly more cations than academics who go full time with the firm. This suggests that eminence gives these scientists the luxury of hedging their bets; both the firm and their research institution welcome a chance to claim them as affiliates. And, although we did not measure the incidence, such individuals often serve as directors and members of Scientific Advisory Boards of *additional* start-up firms. The full-timers, by contrast, have developed sufficient human capital to be recognized as experts but lack the luster to hold "dual" citizenship. In terms of both citation counts and date of birth they are remarkably similar to their fellow founders who followed a pharmaceutical trajectory.

The above discussion suggests that the incentive structure depends crucially upon the career trajectory that the scientists has followed as well as upon whether the scientist has established sufficient eminence to be able to sustain multiple roles. Scientists working in incumbent pharmaceutical firms face the well known problem, described in the appropriability literature, of deciding whether to remain with the firm or start a new firm. Furthermore, the goal of industry to capture their economic knowledge seldom permits them to establish reputations based solely on publication. Instead, their scientific reputations are often established in terms of the products they helped to develop and are known primarily to "insiders" in the industry. Scientists in academe, however, face a different incentive structure. They live in a world where publications are essential for the establishment of reputation. Early in their careers they invest heavily in human capital in order to build a reputation. In the later stages of their career, scientists may trade or cash in on this reputation for economic returns. A variety of avenues are available to do this, including the establishment of a new firm.

The data suggest that this *cashing out* pattern is determined in part by eminence. As noted, a number of academic founders have established sufficiently strong reputations to eat their cake and have it too. They maintain their full-time jobs in academe, while seeking part-time opportunities to gain economically from their knowledge and scientific reputation. The economic returns are tied to the shares they own in the startup companies. A subset of academic scientists, however, go full time with the firm. They, too, hold stock in the firm. But, their rewards are more immediate in terms of the salaries paid to executives in the companies.[7] And, while they have established solid reputations, they are considerably less cited than those academic founders who maintain full-time positions in academe. Although this may be a result of age (they are, after all, about five years younger), it is more likely a characteristic that age cannot alter. Science, as numerous researchers have established, is noteworthy for persistent inequality which age merely amplifies.[8]

Conclusions

This paper has attempted to penetrate the black box of the knowledge production function. In addressing the questions how and why knowledge spills over, an assumption implicit to the model of the knowledge production function is challenged – that firms exist *exogenously* and then

[7] Note that our data do not permit us to compare the *full-timers* and *part-timers* to university-based scientists who *do not* found firms. One would expect that this group is younger, and less eminent than either of the other groups.

[8] Scientific productivity is not only characterized by extreme inequality at a point in time (Lotka, 1926); it is also characterized by increasing inequality over the career of a cohort of scientists (Weiss and Lillard, 1982; Stephan, 1996).

endogenously seek out and apply knowledge inputs to generate innovative output. Although this may be valid some, if not most of the time, the evidence from the biotechnology suggests that, at least in some cases, it is the knowledge in the possession of economic agents that is *exogenous*. In an effort to appropriate the returns from that knowledge, the scientist *endogenously* creates a new firm. Thus, the spillover of knowledge from the source creating it, such as a university, research institute, or industrial corporation, to a new-firm startup facilitates the appropriation of knowledge for the individual scientist(s) but not necessarily for the organization creating that new knowledge in the first place.

This paper also has shed some light on questions which has plagued economists for decades, *Where do new industries, like biotechnology, come from*? The answer appears to have something to do with new knowledge created with perhaps one purpose in mind, but is, in fact, valuable in a very different context. We observe that the participants in the biotechnology industry come from a broad range of diverse backgrounds. Because no biotechnology industry has traditionally existed, no set career paths have been established. Rather, the participants in an emerging industry choose to leave what otherwise would be established career trajectories in more traditional industries. Through the flow of scientists into this new industry, knowledge which was generated with a more traditional context in mind becomes applied in the process of creating a new industry.

References

Acs ZJ, Audretsch DB (1990) Innovation and small firms. MIT Press, Cambridge

Arrow K (1962) Economic welfare and the allocation of resources for invention. In: Nelson R (ed) The rate and direction of inventive activity. Princeton University Press, Princeton, NJ, pp 609–626

Audretsch DB (1995) Innovation and industry evolution. MIT Press, Cambridge

Audretsch DB, Feldman MP (1996) R&D spillovers and the geography of innovation and production. American Economic Review 86(3): 630–640

Audretsch DB, Stephan PE (1996) Company-scientist locational links: the case of biotechnology. American Economic Review 86(3): 641–652

Baldwin WL, Scott JT (1987) Market structure and technological change. Harwood Academic Publishers, New York

Cohen WM, Klepper S (1992a) The tradeoff between firm size and diversity in the pursuit of technological progress. Small Business Economics 4(1): 1–14

Cohen WM, Klepper S (1992b) The anatomy of industry R&D intensity distributions. American Economic Review 82(4): 773–799

Dasgupta P, David PA (1994) Toward a new economics of science. Research Policy 23(5): 487–521

Feldman MP (1994a) The geography of innovation. Kluwer, Boston

Feldman MP (1994b) Knowledge complementarity and innovation. Small Business Economics 6(5): 363–372

Graf J, de V (1957) Theoretical welfare economics. Cambridge University Press, Cambridge

Griliches Z (1979) Issues in assessing the contribution of R&D to productivity growth. Bell Journal of Economics 10(10): 92–116

Grossman G, Helpman E (1991) Innovation and growth in the global economy. MIT Press, Cambridge

Hirschman AO (1970) Exit, voice, and loyalty. Harvard University Press, Cambridge
Jaffe AB (1989) Real effects of academic research. American Economic Review 79(5): 957–970
Jaffe AB, Trajtenberg M, Henderson R (1993) Geographic localization of knowledge spillovers as evidenced by patent citations. Quarterly Journal of Economics 63(3): 577–598
Knight FH (1921) Risk, uncertainty and profit. Houghton Mifflin, New York
Krugman PA (1991a) Geography and trade. MIT Press, Cambridge
Krugman PA (1991b) Increasing returns and economic geography. Journal of Political Economy 99(3): 483–499
Levin SG, Stephan PE (1991) Research productivity over the life cycle: evidence for academic scientists. American Economic Review 81(4): 114–132
Lotka AJ (1926) The frequency distribution of scientific productivity. Journal Washington Academy Science 16(12): 317–323
Romer P (1986) Increasing returns and long-run economic growth. Journal of Political Economy 94(5): 1002–1037
Scherer FM (1992) Schumpeter and plausible capitalism. Journal of Economic Literature 30(3): 1416–1433
Schumpeter JA (1911) Theorie der wirtschaftlichen Entwicklung: Eine Untersuchung über Unternehmergewinn, Kapital, Kredit, Zins und den Konjunkturzyklus. Duncker und Humblot, Berlin
Schumpeter JA (1942) Capitalism, socialism and democracy. Harper and Row, New York
Stephan PE (1996) The economics of science. Journal of Economic Literature 34(3): 1199–1235
Stephan PE, Levin SG (1992) Striking the mother lode in science. Oxford University Press, New York
Weiss Y, Lillard LA (1982) Output variability, academic labour contracts, and waiting times for promotion. In: Ehrenberg RG (ed) Research in labor economics, vol 5, pp 157–188

Chance, necessity and competitive dynamics in the Italian Steel Industry

John S. Metcalfe[1] and Mario Calderini[2]

[1]The University of Manchester, CRIC, Dept. Of Economics, Dover Street Building, Oxford Road, Manchester M13 9PL, UK
[2]DSPEA, Politecnico di Torino, Corso Deca degli Abruzzi, 24, Torino 10129, Italy

Abstract. This paper reports on the first stages of an empirical investigation into the evolutionary dynamics of the competitive process in the Italian Steel Industry. Central to this investigation is that the mode and tempo of change within well-defined populations of firms are driven by the evolutionary competitive processes of development and selection. The purpose of the paper is to assess the relative importance of these different evolutionary processes to the pattern of change in the Italian Steel Industry. To provide for this, first, a discrete time selection model is introduced. Second, this model is confronted with the empirical data. It is shown that in a mature sector – as the Italian Steel industry – the development term is the major factor driving the decrease in the average unit costs in the population, whilst the selection factor seems to play a major role.

Key words: evolution and competition – replicator dynamics – steel industry

JEL-classification: O30, L61

1 Introduction

Since the publication of Nelson and Winter's deeply influential work on economic evolutionary processes (1982), there has been a flowering of theoretical development in relation to the economics of selection. Many of the models developed in this literature are based on the assumption that firms differ in only one dimension of their behaviour, typically unit costs. From a more general point of view this is problematic, in that we expect the competitive process to reflect a multiplicity of firms' characteristics of which unit cost is only one. Because of this, one expects that in practice economic evolution will be very noisy. When firms differ in more than one dimension, one cannot be certain that the more efficient firms, in a narrow sense of those with a lower unit cost, will grow at the expense of less efficient rivals. However, there have been few attempts empirically to work through the relative contribution of different causal factors in the evolutionary process. This is not surprising, the data demands of such an exercise are formidable and very few data sets are available to mount a proper investigation of competition and selection. This paper reports the first stages of one preliminary empirical investigation into the evolutionary dynamics of the competitive process in the Italian Steel Industry. This is a well-established sector in which there have been relatively few technological breakthrough in the recent years. It is one of several studies we are carrying out using different data sets to unravel the forces working in favour of economic change at industry level. The central theme of these studies is that the mode and tempo of change within well-defined populations of firms are driven by evolutionary competitive processes which reflect two specific classes of event: namely, changes in those characteristics of the firms which give rise to competitive advantage; and, changes in the relative economic significance of those firms in terms of their comparative market shares. We shall call the first of these classes development and the second we shall call selection. Selection in turn involves three logically distinct but economically interdependent processes. The entry of new firms, the exit of existing firms and the competitive dynamic of changing market shares in relation to the surviving firms. Our principal purpose in this paper is to assess the relative contributions of these different evolutionary processes to the pattern of change in our case study industry. The structure of the paper is as follows. In section two we provide a very brief sketch of the evolutionary dynamic in a given population of firms, focusing upon the way in which the population distribution of behaviours changes over time. The core of this approach lies in what is called Fisher's Principle which we have developed in a discrete time context. In section three we enrich our model by explicitly taking into account entry and exit. In section four we briefly describe the data set which we intend to use in order to gain a rough cut empirical insight into the selection dynamics of a population. The preliminary results of this exercise are reported in section 5. We emphasise here, that the time period is too short to reach definitive conclusions, we are simply indicating the various steps through which one needs to proceed to "test" evolutionary models of competition.

2 Competitive Processes and Selection Dynamics: Fisher's Principle and the Cumulant Theorem

Let us begin by considering an abstract industry, defined in terms of a population of competing firms producing an identical product but employing different constant returns to scale production methods. The behaviour of the firms is defined in terms of sets of rules which link the increase on their output to their economic profits above some minimum (normal!) rate. Each firm is selling into a market composed of a group of customers who choose their suppliers on the basis of how its price compares with the prices set by other firms and switch at a given rate, not necessarily constant. Over time the overall demand for the product is growing at a given rate. Add to this picture two behaviour rules and we have all the elements to define an evolutionary competitive dynamic. The first is that each firm sets its price to keep a balanced relation between the growth of output and the growth of demand, provided growth of demand is positive. Secondly, any firm which breaks even is not increasing its output and any firm making losses shuts down production. We shall comment further on these two rules below but for the moment they suffice as a minimalist statement of what is needed to make the industry evolve. We now work out the competitive dynamic in discrete time.

Let time be divided into periods of unit length such that period t denotes the time lapse between dates (t) and $(t-1)$. Denote the market share of firm i in period t as $s_i(t)$. If $g_i(t)$ denotes the growth rate of the firm between period (t) and period $(t-1)$ it follows arithmetically that

$$s_i(t) = s_i(t-1)\left\{\frac{1+g_i(t)}{1+g(t)}\right\} \tag{1}$$

where $g(t) = \Sigma s_i(t-1)g_i(t)$, is the aggregate growth rate of the market. Notice that $g(t)$ must be defined using the market share weights of the previous period if (1) is to be valid.

Relationship (1) is the clearest possible statement of a replicator dynamic, relating divergence in growth rates about their average to the corresponding changes in the structure of the industry.

Each firm is defined by a relationship between its current profitability and the growth rate of its output, such that firms which just cover their costs are stationary while profitable firms grow and conversely.

$$g_i(t) = f_i(p_i(t-1) - h_i(t-1)) \tag{2}$$

where p_i and h_i are the price set by and the unit cost defining firm i. There is a one-period lag between the current growth rate and the unit profit margin of the firm. In general, f, the propensity to grow of the firm will differ between the rivals but as our starting point we assume that its value is common to all the firms in the industry.

On the demand side, the growth of each firm's market is given by

$$g_i(t) = g_D(t) + \delta\left[\bar{p}_s(t-1)p_i(t-1)\right] \tag{3}$$

where $g_D(t)$ is the aggregate growth of market demand and $\bar{p}_s(t-1) = \Sigma s_i(t-1)p_i(t-1)$ is the average price set by firms in the industry.

On combining (2) and (3) we find that

$$g_i(t) = g_D(t) + \psi\left[\bar{h}_s(t-1) - h_i(t-1)\right] \tag{4}$$

where $\psi = \dfrac{f\delta}{f+\delta}$ is the market selection coefficient for the industry and $\bar{h}_s(t-1) = \Sigma s_i(t-1)h_i(t-1)$ is average practice unit cost in the industry.

Now (4) provides us with the replicator dynamic for the industry. Firms grow or decline relative to the market average as their unit costs $h_i(t-1)$ are less than or greater than the industry average; and they do so at a rate which depends on the market selection coefficient ψ. In turn ψ depends on the growth propensity parameter f and the market imperfection coefficient δ. When the market is perfect, $\delta = \infty$, and all firms are required to set a common price p if they are to sell anything at all. At the other extreme, $\delta = 0$, corresponds to a world of individual monopolies in which the selection process does not operate.

The picture of structural change which emerges from this replicator process is naturally complicated and so it is sensible to enquire as to the movement of average behaviour in the population of firms. Indeed, this is a natural component of an evolutionary analysis which relates to changes in the moments of the population distribution of firm behaviours. How then does average unit cost change in this population? By definition

$$\Delta\bar{h}(t) = \Sigma s_i(t)h_i(t) - \Sigma s_i(t-1)h_i(t-1) \tag{5}$$

so that the change depends on the evolution of the market shares and any development, $d_i(t)$, in the unit cost structures of the individual firms. Development relates to any factor which changes the unit costs of the firm in question. Let,

$$h_i(t) = h_i(t-1) + d_i(t)$$

define the degree of development of the individual firm. Substituting this expression into (5) and taking account of (1) gives

$$\Delta \bar{h}_s(t) = \Sigma s_i(t-1)\left\{\frac{1+g_i(t)}{1+g(t)}\right\}[h_i(t-1)+d_i(t)] + \Sigma s_i(t-1)h_i(t-1)$$

$$= \frac{1}{1+g}\{\Sigma s_i(t-1)h_i(t-1)[g_i(t)-g(t)] + \Sigma s_i(t-1)d_i(t) + \Sigma s_i(t-1)g_i d_i\}$$

However, by taking account of the replicator process (5) we can eliminate the endogenous firm growth rates to give the final expression for the rate of change of average unit cost, thus,

$$\Delta \bar{h}_s = \bar{d}_s - \frac{\psi}{1+g}\{V_s[h(t-1)] + V_s(d) + C_s[h(t-1),d]\} \tag{6}$$

where these terms are defined as follows

$$\bar{d}_s = \Sigma s_i(t-1)d_i(t),$$

$$V_s[h(t)] = \Sigma s_i(t-1)[h_i(t) - \bar{h}_s(t)]^2,$$

$$V_s(d) = \Sigma s_i(t-1)[d_i(t) - \bar{d}_s(t)]^2, \qquad \textit{and},$$

$$C_s[h(t-1),d] = \Sigma s_i(t-1)[d_i(t) - \bar{d}_s(t)][h_i(t-1) - \bar{h}_s(t-1)]$$

The difference between the total change in average unit cost and that due to the average development of the individual firms is the amount of change which is due to the forces of selection including the interaction between those forces and the development of the individual firms. If there is no selection then the change in the average unit costs is equal to $\bar{d}_s$. Conversely, if all the d_i values are zero then

$$\Delta \bar{h}_s = -\frac{\psi}{1+g}V_s(h) \tag{7}$$

which corresponds to Fisher's Fundamental Theorem of competitive selection. In the special case in which development takes place but is randomly associated with previous cost levels then

$$\Delta \bar{h}_s = \bar{d}_s - \frac{\psi}{1+g}\{V_s(h) + V_s(d)\} \tag{8}$$

Notice carefully that these results depend upon a particular moment of market coordination; if that coordination process changes so will the relationships reported in (6), (7), (8).

In general we expect $\bar{d}_s$ to be negative, and since the variance terms are positive, development and selection jointly work to reduce average practice unit costs.

Relations (6) to (8) provide us with a framework to explore empirically the relative effects of selection and development in the competitive process. Before we do this our basic framework needs to be extended to incorporate the other dimensions of the selection process.

3 Entry, Exit and Mergers

The previous section has sketched a pure economics of selection and development which remains, however, only a partial picture of the dynamic of industrial change. In any practical situation we have also to contend with entry of new firms, the exit of existing firms, and the combination of existing firms to form merged business units. Each of these has the potential to modify considerably the working of the evolutionary mechanism.

To deal first with entry and exit we can follow the analysis in Metcalfe (1998) to see how relations (6) to (8) must be modified. To do this we consider the aggregate industry output in period 't' as the sum of three elements: the output of those firms that operate at (t) and ($t-1$), the survivors, plus the output of the new entrants within the period to (t), less the output of the firms which exit within the same period. Let, 'n', denote the ratio of the output of entrants to total output in period (t), $X(t)$, and let, 'e', denote the fraction of output $X(t-1)$ which is attributable to firms which exit the industry between ($t-1$) and (t). Then

$$X(t) = X(t-1)[(1-e)(1+g_s)] + X(t-1)e(1+g_e) + nX(t)$$

The first term is the contribution to $X(t)$ of the survivors whose aggregate growth rate is g_s. The second term is the output of the exiting firms contribute to total output during period 't' and their average growth rate over the period is g_e. The final term is the output in period 't' associated with the new entrants. It simplifies matters greatly to assume that all exits occur at the beginning of the period, whence $g_e = -1$. Notice carefully that the magnitude of entry and exit are not measured by the changes in the number of firms but rather by the consequential contributions to the output of the industry.

Let g be the aggregate growth of output, defined by $X(t) = X(t-1)(1+g)$ and it follows that the various growth rates and the entry and exit rates are related by

$$\frac{1+g_s}{1+g} = \frac{1-n}{1-e} \tag{9}$$

The growth rate of the surviving firms, g_s, exceeds or falls short of the aggregate growth rate of the whole industry, g, as the exit rate exceeds, e, exceeds or falls short of the entry rate, n.

One consequence of entry and exit is that we must be careful how we measure the change in market share of the firms which survive between $(t-1)$ and (t).

Consider then a survivor, for which

$$s_k(t) = s_k(t-1)\left\{\frac{1+g_k}{(1-e)(1+g_s)+n(1+g)}\right\}$$

and while $\Sigma s_k(k-1) = 1$ this is not true for $\Sigma s_k(t)$ unless $e = n$. Indeed,

$$s_k(t) = s_k(t-1)\left[\frac{1+g_k}{1+g}\right] \tag{10}$$

where g the total growth rate of output is not equal to g_s as indicated by (9).

Thus when calculating the change in average practice unit costs we must now use (10) rather than (1) as the basis for deriving the relation between growth rates and market shares for the surviving firms. The second consequence of entry and exit follows when calculating the change in average unit costs in the whole population of firms.

Of the firms existing at date $(t-1)$, k in number survive to time (t), j in number exit before (t) and to the survivors must be added entrants with aggregate market share n. Then average unit cost at time (t), for the i firms operating at (t), is given by

$$h(t)=\sum_i s_i(t)h_i(t)=(1-e)\sum_k s_k(t-1)h_k(t)\left\{\frac{1+g_k}{1+g}\right\}$$
$$-e\sum_j s_j(t-1)h_j(t)\left\{\frac{1+g_j}{1+g}\right\}+n\bar{h}_n(t)$$

when, $\bar{h}_n$ is average unit cost of the entrants in period (t). Maintaining the condition that $g_j=-1$ for all the exiting firms and taking account of (9) it follows that

$$h(t)=(1-n)\sum_k s_k(t-1)h_k(t)\left\{\frac{1+g_k}{1+g_s}\right\}+n\bar{h}_n=(1-n)\bar{h}_s(t)+n\bar{h}_n$$

Similarly,

$$h(t-1)=\sum_k s_k(t-1)h_k(t-1)+\sum_j s_j(t-1)h_j(t-1)$$
$$=(1-e)\sum_k s_k(t-1)h_k(t-1)+e\bar{h}_e$$

where $\bar{h}_e(t-1)$ is the average cost in period '$t-1$' for the firms which exit in period 't'.

From this we can derive the analogue to (6) which is

$$\Delta\bar{h}(t)=\left[(1-n)\bar{h}_s(t)-(1-e)\bar{h}_e(t-1)\right]+n\bar{h}_n(t)-e\bar{h}_e(t-1)$$

with the term in the square bracket referring to those 'k' firms operating throughout both periods. Further calculations reduce this to

$$\Delta h(t)=\sum_k s_k(t-1)\left[\frac{g_k-g_s}{1+g_s}\right]-n\sum_k s_k(t-1)h_k(t-1)\left[\frac{1+g_k}{1+g_s}\right]$$
$$+(1-n)\Sigma s_k(t-1)d_k(t)\left[\frac{1+g_k}{1+g_s}\right]+n\bar{h}_n-e\bar{h}_e$$

To eliminate the growth rates g_k we proceed as before but taking into account the fact that the market for the surviving firms has been reduced by the entry rate and enhanced by the exit rate. Thus, for any surviving firm

$$g_k = g'_D + \psi\left[\bar{h}_s(t-1) - h_i(t-1)\right]$$

with

$$g'_D = \frac{(1+g_D)(1-n)-(1-e)}{(1-e)} = g_s$$

Substituting these expressions into the formula for $\Delta\bar{h}(t)$ we obtain after much simplification

$$\Delta h(t) = -\frac{\psi(1-e)}{1+g_D}\left[V_s[h(t-1)] + V_s(d(t)) + C_s[h(t-1)d(t)]\right] + (1-n)\bar{d}_k(t) + n\bar{h}_n - e\bar{h}_e(t-1) \quad (11)$$

where $\bar{d}_k(t)$ is the average rate of development for the surviving firms.

The relationship with (6) will be readily apparent. The term in the square bracket, which applies only to those surviving firms, is identical to the equivalent expression in (6), and reduces to this when $n = e = 0$. However, the coefficient of selection has been reduced by the factor, $(1-e)$. Similarly, the development rate $\bar{d}_k$ has been reduced by the factor $(1-n)$. The remaining terms in (11) are new and reflect the direct impact on average costs of entry and exit.

Having derived a form of the selection equation consistent with entry and exit processes we can turn more readily to the final complication which is that of merger. Here matters are more straightforward, for we treat the unit costs of the combined entity as the weighted average of the unit costs of the individual firms, with any deviation from this being picked up in the associated development term for the combined entity. No further adjustment is required for our measurement formulae.

4 A case study: fitting data from the steel industry.

In this section we provide a brief description of the data set and of the population that we are studying. The data set that we are constructing in order to empirically test our theoretical findings describes the evolution of a sub-sector of Italy's steel industry over the years 1988-1996, derived from the Mediobanca's accounting data report (Mediobanca, 1988-1996). Firms included in our data set report annual revenues greater than a threshold of 25,000 millions lira. As far as price indexes, market shares and aggregate sectoral trends are concerned, our data set has been integrated by the information provided by the annual reports from Federacciai (1989-1996) and Assofond (1988-1996).

It is out of the scope of this paper to review the recent history of Italy's steel sector. It will suffice to clarify that the time span that we intend to examine is characterised by important changes and turmoil, starting with the creation of the giant Ilva replacing the former Finsider and Italsider, through the deep crisis of the years 1991-1992 and ending with the complete privatisation of the formerly state-owned Ilva in 1994.

According to the Mediobanca's annual publication, the iron and steel sector as a whole includes, over the ten years, 228 firms. This figure includes both firms surviving through the whole period and firms which either disappear or start-up during the period. Since the model that we have specified in the previous section is based on the assumption of product homogeneity, we have limited the analysis to a very specific subsector. This latter consists of the firms producing raw pig-iron and steel, iron and steel ingots and billets, rolled iron and steel strip, iron and steel rods, bars, sections, rolled steel girders, piling steel. The criteria used for inclusion in the sample are based on the classification scheme used in the Kompass repertory of Italian firms: we selected firms listed under the

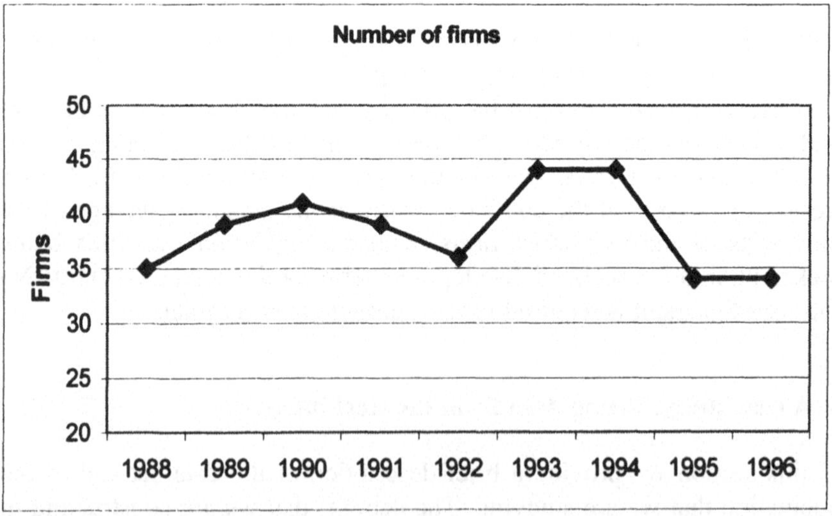

Fig. 1. Number of business units in the population over the years 1988-1996.

codes 34-01.0, 34-05.0, 34-07.0. 34-09.0, 34-12.0, 34-14.0. The ratio that guided us in the definition of the sample was to exploit the trade-off between having enough product homogeneity and preserving a sufficient size of the sample. This case study is based, on aggregate, on a population of 62 business units, which operated at some point during the period 1988-1996. Figure 1 shows the variation in the total number of operating firms over the period.

As with many industrial sectors, there is a considerable degree of turnover, in terms of entry and exit. Given the nature of our data set, a new entry in the population can be either a new start-up or more simply a firm that has grown bigger than the critical threshold for inclusion in the data set. Similarly, when a firm exits the population, this can be due to either bankruptcy or to the fact that it is not any longer eligible for inclusion according to the threshold criteria. This means that our sample is likely to be showing a much greater turbulence than the actual population. Moreover, it has to be specified that the period considered has been characterised by a remarkable number of mergers and acquisitions. We have tried, as far as possible, to accurately trace the history of single firms, although a small number of controversial events is yet to be clarified[1].

As far as the number of employees is concerned, figure 2 shows that the average remains fairly stable, with a peak in 1992. Since our interest is in understanding the evolution of variety in the population over the years, in figure 2 we have also plotted the trend of the variance, which is shown on the right axis. In 1992, the variance in the number of employees shows a remarkable increase, remaining constant for the rest of the period. This is due to the fact that in 1992 we observe intense merger activity, which involves mainly medium firms. The size of the firms in the population becomes more spread out and the number of small and medium firms decreases with respect to the number of larger firms.

Finally, we provide a description of the evolution of our data set in terms of market shares. For the sake of brevity we will report the histograms of market share (Figure 3) at the beginning and at the end of the period. This allows the reader to notice that the distribution has been relatively stable over the years, exception made for the emergence of a

[1] Among the most important Nuova Sirma splits in Nuova Sirma Parma and Nuova Sirma Venezia in 1989, in 1991 ICMI acquires Industrie e Cantieri Metallurgici Italiani, in 1991 Siderpotenza is acquired by Lucchini Siderurgica, in 1994 Dalmine Tubi Industriali acquires Dalmine Tubi speciali, Aluteck acquires Getti Speciali and ILVA splits into Acciai speciali Terni and Ilva laminati piani. Finally in 1996 Gruppo Riva controls Ilva laminati piani, Lavezzari, Ilvaform, Silpa Tubi, Ilva lamiere e tubi, Riva prodotti siderurigici, Acciaierie del Tanaro, Acciaierie di Caronno, Officine Galtarossa, Eurosider, Silca, ICMI.

Fig. 2. Number of employees (average and variance)

few large firms, which have consolidated relatively consistent market shares. On the contrary, a considerable number of firms has reduced its market shares to quotes of about 1% of the market, generating a more spread out distribution.

Finally, we want to make it very clear that our data set suffers of major limitations. First, the fact that our data set is drawn from the accounting reports of individual firms, which, as it is well known, not always coincide with actual cost figures of the business units. Second, although our population is made of firms manufacturing nearly homogeneous products, it is almost impossible to define a common unit of production. Therefore, when we deal with unit production costs we will refer to cost per unit of revenue, as measured by the ratio between total costs and total revenues. We argue that in our sample, where the prices of output is relatively invariant among the firms, this can be considered an efficient proxy of unit costs.

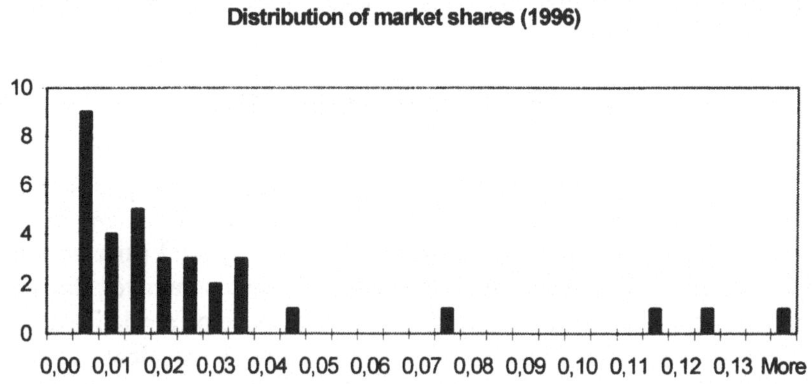

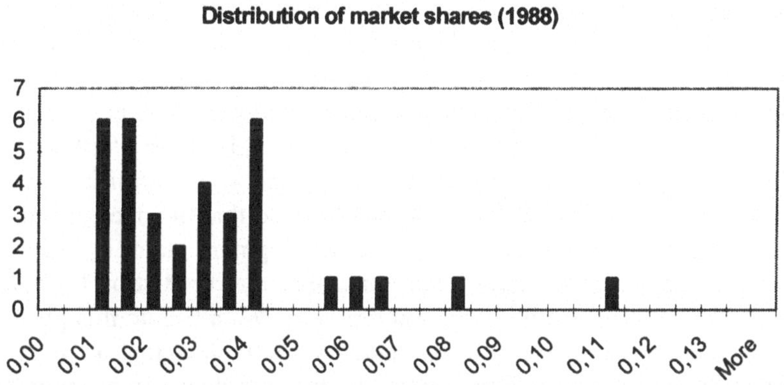

Fig. 3. Distribution of market shares (1988 and 1996)

Third, many observations in our data set derive from accounting reports of multiplant business units. Therefore, in some cases we have not been able to isolate the costs that are strictly associated to our set of products from the aggregate cost figure.

The data that we dispose of per single firm are: total revenues, market shares, number of employees, labour costs, energy costs and materials costs.

5 The Fisher principle at work: empirical evidence

The theoretical arguments developed in Section 2 are formalised in equation (6). This equation shows how the difference between the total change in average unit costs and that due to the average development of the individual firms is the amount of change which is due to the forces of selection including the interaction between those forces and the development of the individual firms.

$$\Delta\bar{h}_s = \bar{d}_s - \frac{\psi}{1+g}\{V_s[h(t-1)] + V_s(d) + C_s[h(t-1)d]\} \tag{6}$$

We will try to investigate how the data available in our population fit in equation (6), in order to empirically support our argument that the forces of selection in the population are governed by the Fisher principle. In equation (6) we have virtually a single unknown parameter, the selection coefficient ψ. Unfortunately, since we dispose of a relatively short time series, we will not be able to carry out a proper statistical estimation of the coefficient.

As we have previously stated our data set includes observation over a nine years period, from 1988 to 1996. Given the structure of our model we lose the first observation thus reducing the time series to eight observations. Per each of the nine years we have calculated the terms which appear in equation (6). Figure 4 and Table 1 show the results.

It is evident that the model fits data very well between 1989 and 1993, whilst the predictions of equation (6) become very unreliable in years 1994 and 1995. In particular it can be observed that the decrease in average unit costs is well explained by the development factor d_s until 1994. On that year the model gives a very unsatisfactory prediction for both the development term and the selection term (ψ). We attribute this phenomenon to the relative maturity of the industry. We believe that in years 1994 and 1995 our data set suffers greatly by the turbulence in accounting reports generated by the privatisation of ILVA in 1994. In 1996, the development term seems again to be able to predict the decrease in unit costs.

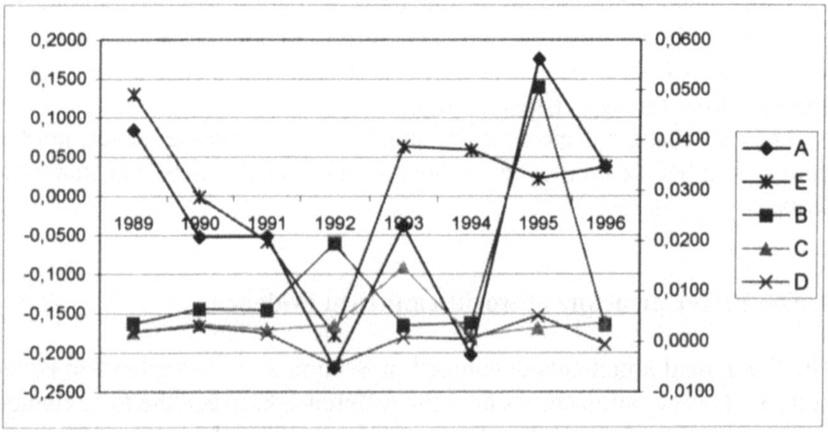

Fig. 4. The single terms in equation (6)

Table 1. Single terms in equation (6)

	1989	1990	1991	1992	1993	1994	1995	1996	
A	0,0840	-0,0522	-0,0517	-0,2189	-0,0376	-0,2030	0,1757	0,0380	□$h_s(t)$
B	0,0035	0,0064	0,0062	0,0195	0,0032	0,0036	0,0506	0,0032	$V_s[h(t-1)]$
C	0,0019	0,0034	0,0023	0,0032	0,0147	0,0011	0,0027	0,0036	$V_s[d]$
D	0,0018	0,0030	0,0016	-0,0047	0,0008	0,0005	0,0051	-0,0005	$C_s[h(t-1),d]$
E	0,1300	-0,0012	-0,0577	-0,1774	0,0630	0,0585	0,0220	0,0371	d_s

In order to isolate the contribution of the selection term in equation (6), in Figure (5) we have plotted our calculation of the coefficient ψ per year of operation, obtained through the relation:

$$\psi = -\frac{\Delta\bar{h}_s - \bar{d}_s}{\{V_s[h(t-1)] + V_s[\bar{d}\,] + C_s[h(t-1),d]\}} \cdot (1+g)$$

Once again it can be noticed that the calculation of the selection term gives fairly stable results all through the period but in years 1994 and 1995. The coefficient is positive as expected in every period but one and it is nearly zero in two.

Since we elaborated a richer version of the model in section three, we tried to fit our data in equation (11), which accounts for entry and exit, in order to be able to obtain a more accurate calculation of the selection term (ψ). Unfortunately, results have been poorer than expected.

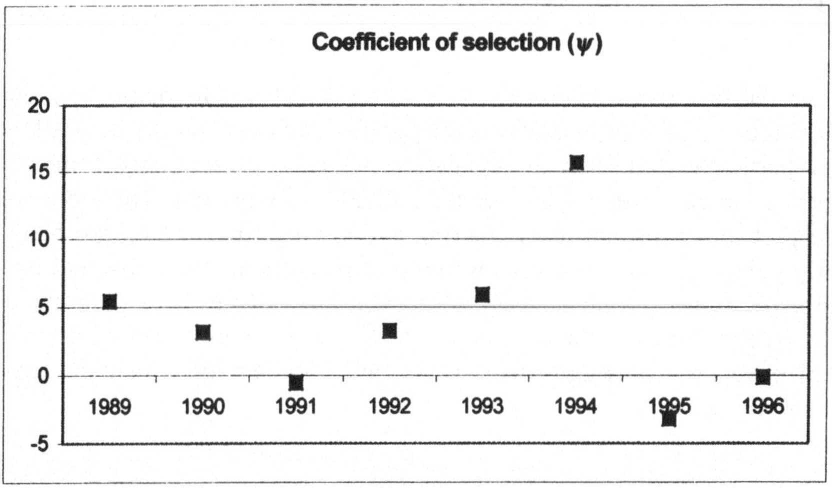

Fig. 5. Coefficient of selection in equation (6)

$$\Delta h(t) = -\frac{\psi(1-e)}{1+g_D}\left[V_s[h(t-1)] + V_s(d(t)) + C_s[h(t-1)d(t)]\right] + (1-n)\bar{d}_k(t) + n\bar{h}_n - e\bar{h}_e(t-1) \quad (11)$$

We have already discussed how the structure of (11) is identical to the one of (6), but the effect of the selection term is reduced by a coefficient (1-e). In order to estimate the coefficient of selection in (11) we have calculated the single terms of the equation in order to qualitatively assess the single contributions of the different factors. The results are illustrated in Figure 6. The reader is referred to the following Table 2 for the legend of figure 6.

Table 2. Terms in equation (11)

	1989	1990	1991	1992	1993	1994	1995	1996	
A	0,972	1,088		0,701	0,769	0,775	0,930		h_i (exit)
B	1,088	1,078	1,028		0,703	0,855			h_i (entry)
C	1,026	1,025	0,952	0,725	0,786	0,839	0,848	0,896	h_i (surviving)
D	0,003	0,005	0,006	0,004	0,003	0,003	0,008	0,003	V[h_i] surviving)
E	0,002	0,003	0,001	0,000	0,000	0,000	0,002	-0,002	Covar(h,d) (surviving)
F	0,019	0,003	0,005	0,017	0,002	0,004	0,007	0,005	V[d] (surviving)
G	0,129	-0,003	-0,054	-0,211	0,040	0,047	0,071	0,050	d_k (surviving)
H	0,084	-0,052	-0,052	-0,219	-0,038	-0,203	0,176	0,038	Δh
I	0,122	0,033	0,006	0,130	0,312	0,764	0,176	-0,158	g_D
L	0,043	0,061	0,000	0,241	0,129	0,347	0,130	0,000	e
M	0,008	0,012	0,159	0,000	0,038	0,224	0,000	0,000	n

In the first part of Figure 6, it is well evident that in years 1994 and 1995 the rate of entry and exit in the population in unnaturally boosted by our particular definition of population, which considers only firms reporting annual revenues greater than 25,000 millions lira. Therefore we are probably considering as entering and exiting firms which are really only going up and down the threshold. This explains the noise that disturbs our results on those years. Moreover, this justifies the counterintuitive results shown in the second part of figure 6, where it can be noticed that unit costs of exiting firms in years 1992-1994 are lower than the ones of surviving firms.

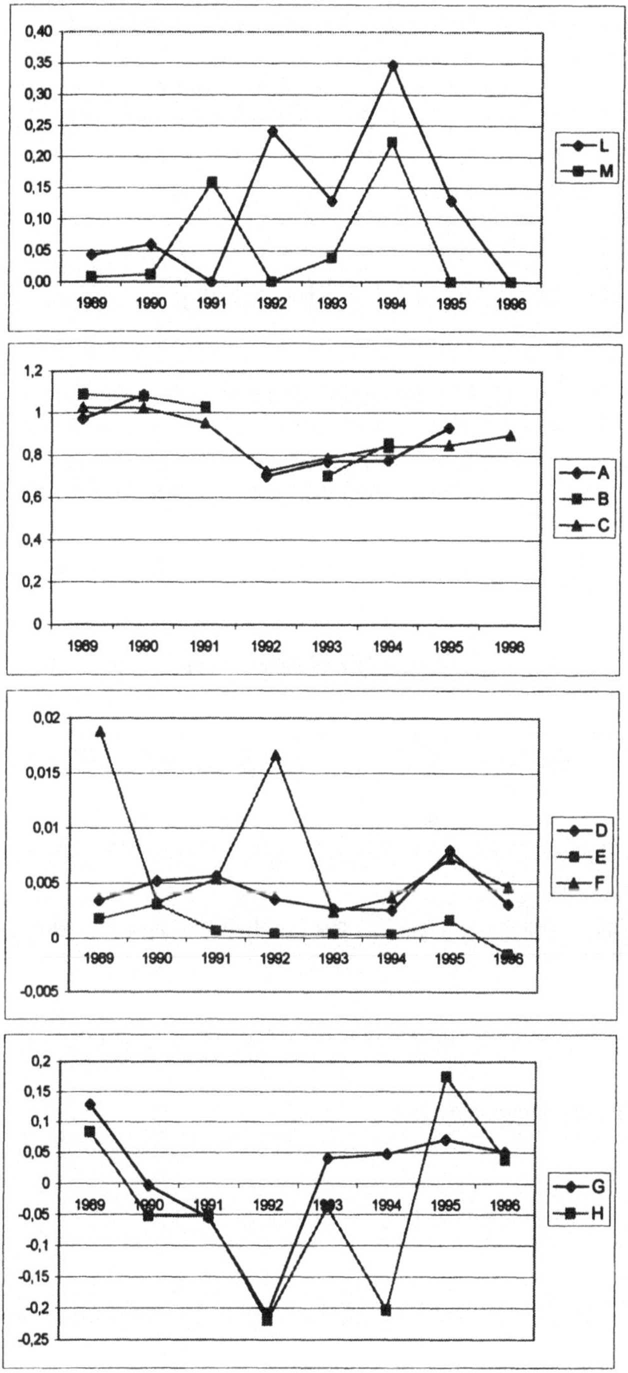

Fig. 6. Terms in equation (11)

Once again, it can be noticed that the model provides good fitting only for the years of relative stability of the industry (1989-1993 and 1996). On those years the development term plays a major role in explaining the variation of unit costs, whilst the selection term seems to be relatively unimportant. Nevertheless, we have tried to assess the contribution of the selection term, by calculating:

$$\psi = -\frac{\Delta\bar{h}(t) - (1-n)\bar{d}_k - n \cdot h_n + e\bar{h}_e(t-1)}{\{V_s[h(t-1)] + V_s[\bar{d}\,] + C_s[h(t-1), d]\}} \cdot (1 + g_D)$$

as derived by equation (11). The results are plotted in Figure 7.

The estimation of the coefficient gives results that are generally comparable to the ones obtained for equation (6), even though taking account of entry and exit seems to introduce greater turbulence in the model, which we explain with the aforementioned problems about the definition of the population.

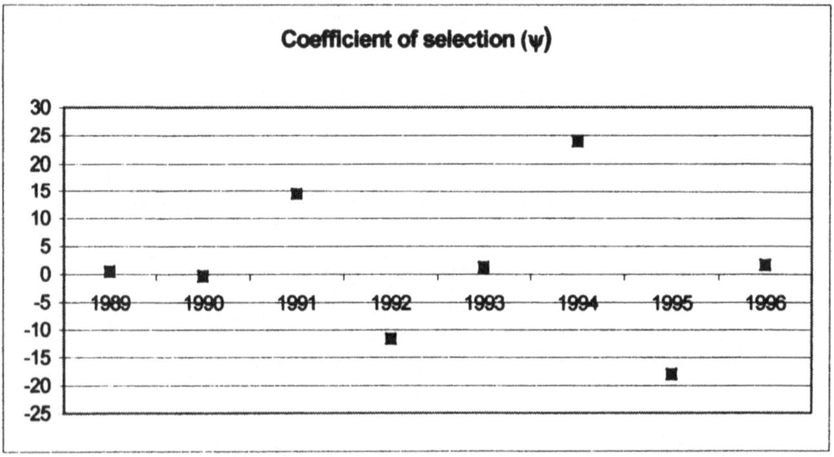

Fig. 7. Coefficient of selection

Conclusions

This paper makes two contributions: first, we have written a discrete time selection model with entry and exit; second we show how demanding it is to confront this with data. The model shows how the decrease in weighted average unit costs in a population of firms is a complex function where two main components can be identified: a development term and a selection term. The model has been developed in a simpler form, without taking into account entry and exit and in a more sophisticated form, where we allow for entry and exit in the population. We believe that the model should be confronted with a solid empirical test, which is extremely demanding given the nature of the data required: having a complete set of unit costs in a population of firms manufacturing homogeneous products is a very ambitious task, which at the present state of our research we are still far from achieving. Nevertheless, since we are convinced of the validity of our modelisation of the competitive dynamics, we have attempted a provisional data fitting exercise presented in the paper in order to illustrate what should be done in the direction of obtaining a proper validation of the model. We are well aware of the major limitations in our data, which can be summarised in the fact that we have used accounting data, derived from multiplant business units, in a time period which was characterised by a very intense merger and acqusition activity that we have only partially been able to trace back. Nevertheless, the results that we have obtained allow us to understand that in a mature sector, the development term is the major factor driving the decrease in the average unit costs in the population, whilst the selection factor seems to play a minor role. The calculation of this latter provides fairly stable results over the first years, whilst it becomes extremely unstable in years 1994-95. Oddly enough, the simpler model seems to provide a more accurate representation of the phenomena, probably due to the fact that in our sample we have a distorted notion of entry an exit.

Besides this qualitative results, the results of this exercise leave us with the strong belief that the arduous task of organising a more appropriate data set for a consistent estimation of the selection term in our model is well worth the effort. For this reason this is the next time on our research agenda.

References

Mediobanca, "Le principali Società Italiane", Annual Report, 1988-1997.

Nelson, R., Winter, S., 1984, *An Evolutionary Theory of Economic Change*, Harvard University Press, Cambridge.

Metcalfe, S., 1998, Evolutionary Economics and Creative Destruction, Routledge, London.

Detecting self-organisational change in economic processes exhibiting logistic growth*

John Foster,[1] Phillip Wild[2]

[1]Department of Economics, University of Queensland, Brisbane QLD 4072, Australia
[2]The School of Economic Studies, University of Manchester, Manchester M13 9PL, UK

Abstract. This paper offers an econometric methodology for the detection of self-organisational change (defined in terms of the presence of time irreversibility, structural change and fundamental uncertainty) in economic processes that follow logistic diffusion growth paths in historical time. The approach we adopted is built upon recent developments in 'moving window' spectral methods which are applied to the scaled residuals generated by estimated logistic diffusion models. We illustrate the use of such methods by examining the case of a financial instrument, namely, the Australian Building Society Deposit, which experienced logistic growth in its market share until bank deregulation was enacted in the 1980s. We show that there is clear evidence that self-organisational change is present over the historical period considered.

Key words: Discontinuity – Evolution – Logistic diffusion – Non-linearity – Non-stationarity – Self-organisation – Spectral methods

JEL-classification: C4; C5; N1; N2

* We would like to thank the Maison des Sciences de L'Homme for their financial support. Special thanks are due to Maurice Aymard for all his assistance during visits to France. We are grateful to Brian Lovell (UQ Electrical Engineering), Melvin Hinich for helping us to apply moving window spectral methods correctly. Drafts of this paper were presented as seminars at the CEPREMAP Research Institute in Paris, the Department of Applied Economics at the University of Cambridge and the School of Economics at the University of Manchester. Thanks are due to all participants who made comments. We are particularly indebted to David Anthony, Robert Delorme, Pierre Garouste, Brian Henry, Michel Juillard, Brian Morgan, Pradeep Philip and Alessandro Vercelli for their detailed comments. However, all responsibility for errors and omissions remains with the authors.

1 Introduction

Over the past decade, there has been a significant rise in interest in evolutionary perspectives on economic behaviour. This is witnessed in the large body of literature recently reviewed by, for example, Hodgson (1993), Andersen (1994), Nelson (1995) and Vromen (1995). A variety of approaches now exist which, in the main, deal with technological, institutional and organisational change in the economic system. In the spirit of evolutionary biology, much of the literature is concerned with the underlying processes of selection and adaptation which give rise to such change, following the lead of, for example, Alchian (1950), Boulding (1980) and Nelson and Winter (1982).

Although modern evolutionary economics has provided many fascinating insights, difficulty has arisen in offering theoretical representations of evolutionary processes from which hypotheses can be drawn and tested using aggregated historical data. Some economists, such as Richard Day, have undertaken pioneering attempts to provide theoretical representations of growth trajectories, which are presumed to overlay processes of evolutionary change. These involve the application of dynamic mathematics to generate nonlinear paths, which do not tend towards fixed point equilibria but, rather, multiple equilibria, equilibrium curves and equilibrium regions. However, given the deterministic character of mathematics, we cannot conclude that such an approach can offer complete representations of the growth dynamics which overlay evolutionary processes in historical contexts. Evolutionary change must contain non-deterministic elements (see Foster and Wild, 1996) and these cannot be captured directly in dynamic mathematical formulations.

However, through the astute selection of appropriate combinations of discrete intervals and complex nonlinear feedback mechanisms, it has been possible to capture non-deterministic elements in an indirect and *ex post* way and to generate simulations of fluctuating growth paths which mimic those observed in past history. Thus, although the 'true' evolutionary features of the growth process have not been captured, those who have devised such models have made important *theoretical* contributions in demonstrating the serious limitations of linear, equilibrium theorising in contexts where significant evolutionary change is occurring.

Unsurprisingly, theorising which has attempted to deal with nonlinear complexity has had a minimal impact upon econometric modelling. The conventional approach of viewing time series data as series of disequilibrium points between static equilibrium states, suggested by economic theory, remains central. Correspondingly, the cointegration and associated 'equilibrium-correction' approaches to modelling time series data remain the most favoured. The difficulties of addressing complex, nonlinear theory with econometric methods are acknowledged (see Granger, 1993) but no alternative modelling strategies have come to prominence. The absence of an appropriate alternative means that evolutionary economists are restricted in their ability to provide econometric support for their theoretical propositions concerning the impact of evolutionary change on the historical paths of key economic variables.

In this paper we attempt to rectify this situation, not by proposing more complex nonlinear dynamic mathematical forms to subject to complex econometric and statistical procedures, but by suggesting a much simpler methodology which recognises, explicitly, the fact that historical growth trajectories contain both deterministic and non-deterministic components. In so doing, we approach evolutionary economic change from the perspective of the self-organisational approach in which the deterministic component of a process of structural change is nonlinear and the non-deterministic component is non-stochastic. We apply statistical tests which can indicate whether self-organisational change is present. In this regard, a process of self-organisational change is viewed as possessing three interconnected characteristics: a degree of time irreversibility in structure; ongoing structural change, because time irreversibility must imply reactions to stimuli which involve structural adaptation; a degree of true uncertainty, since structural change is not a predictable process.

The remainder of the paper is organised as follows. In Section 2, we show how an augmented logistic diffusion model can capture the deterministic, nonlinear component of a growth trajectory and we explain how moving window spectral methods can be applied to discover if the non-deterministic component of such a trajectory (i.e. the unexplained residuals) behaves in a manner consistent with the presence of underlying self-organisational change. In Section 3, we introduce the illustrative example used in Foster and Wild (1998), namely the retail deposit market penetration of Building Societies in postwar Australia, and re-estimate an augmented logistic diffusion model using monthly, rather than quarterly data. In Section 4 we apply time-varying spectral methods to the scaled residuals of our estimated model and provide a detailed evaluation of the results. In Section 5 we offer some conclusions.

2 An econometric methodology

In Foster and Wild (1998), it is argued that historical data concerning the growth of a variable that is the product of an underlying process of structural development will conform to the well-known logistic diffusion equation popularised by Griliches (1957). Logistic diffusion models have, in the main, been viewed as providing evidence of disequilibrium, rather than non-equilibrium, processes [see Dixon (1994) for a review]. Foster and Wild (1998) explain why the logistic diffusion equation can be viewed as an abstraction derived from an endogenous 'theory of historical process'. Such a theory is embedded in the self-organisation approach to system dynamics, which views 'dissipative structures' as capable of structural development, through parallel increases in organisation and complexity towards a capacity limit.[1] An augmented logistic diffusion model (ALDM) that allows the diffusion rate and the capacity limit to be subject to exogenous and interactive effects, is developed.

[1] See Foster (1992, 1993, 1994) for an assessment of the applicability of the self-organisation approach in economic contexts.

An ALDM can be based on several alternative logistic equations. The Mansfield variant, expressed in terms of a growth rate, is chosen because of its convenient properties:[2]

$$\ln X_t - \ln X_{t-1} = b_1[1 - \{X_{t-1}/K(\ldots)\} - a(\ldots)] + b_2(\ldots) + c\{\ln X_t - \ln X_{t-1}\}_{t-1} + e_t \qquad (1)$$

where b_1 is the underlying density dependent, or diffusion, coefficient (after allowing for deterioration rates, death rates, etc); $K(\ldots)$ represents a carrying capacity which can vary because of exogenous external factors; $a(\ldots)$ contains competitive factors due to the presence of other systems in the same 'niche', altering the effective capacity limit that can be attained; $b_2(\ldots)$ contains exogenous influences which cause the net diffusion rate to vary. The lagged dependent variable is included to capture 'momentum' effects, which cushion the impact of exogenous shocks.

Eq. (1) is an endogenous growth specification, which can be applied in historical episodes when structural development is taking place. As it stands, many might interpret it as the specification of a disequilibrium process, following a jump in a 'long run equilibrium' K, given that ongoing structural change is homogenised into a growth measure. However, in the presence of structural change which is self-organisational in character we cannot accept this interpretation because dissipative structures which structurally develop and, thus, grow towards a capacity limit are not in disequilibrium. If we rely upon self-organisation theory, we can predict that, as the growth of such systems tends towards zero they do not approach a stable equilibrium but, rather, a state of structural instability.

In general, processes, which involve endogenous structural change are not deterministic and cannot tend, asymptotically, to stable long-run equilibrium outcomes. However, this does not mean that the conventional notion of equilibration is inapplicable. A self-organisational process can still be viewed as a moving temporary equilibrium which tends, asymptotically, to K. Homoeostatic mechanisms operate to return the process to its logistic path when external shocks are experienced. If a growth process is perceived in this way, then structural instability relates to the extent to which the basin of attraction around such moving equilibria changes over time. If the logistic growth path is viewed as capturing the deterministic component of the process of structural development, then variation in the basin of attraction can be seen as reflecting its non-deterministic component. Self-organisation theory suggests that there will be a tendency for the basin to narrow as the system in question moves up the logistic growth curve, increasing the likelihood that it will be exceeded to such an extent that structural discontinuity of some type will occur.

Typically, students of technological diffusion draw families of logistic curves over time with gaps, or overlaps, between them stressing the uniqueness of each diffusion process with the gaps confirming the existence of structural discontinuities. Thus, there is implicit acceptance in such

[2] The time subscripts in eq.(1) do not denote behavioural discreteness but rather the observational intervals which are present in time series data.

studies that a tendency towards saturation in a technological diffusion process is not a tendency towards a stable equilibrium. Foster and Wild (1998) show that the particular ALDM growth trajectory that they study is not mean reverting, but neither is it a random walk, with or without drift. The level of the variable under investigation and the (moving) capacity limit are not linearly co-integrated. Thus, in the case considered, it is difficult to argue that the observed ALDM provides evidence in support of an equilibrium/disequilibrium process, either from the standpoint of deterministic or stochastic trends in time series data.

The absence of linear cointegration between time series is an indication to the conventional modeller that s/he should not proceed. However, the relationship may be a nonlinear logistic one between a variable and a limit which, when specified as an ALDM, can be estimated, provided linear cointegration exists between $\ln X_t - \ln X_{t-1}$ and $X_{t-1}/K(\ldots)$ in eq. (1). The conventional modeller might well respond that such evidence is consistent with a nonlinear equilibrium relationship between $X, K(\ldots)$ and $a(\ldots)$ which is not due to an underlying process of self-organisational change. As pointed out above, we do not reject the notion that a logistic equation captures a nonlinear equilibrium path. Instead, we argue that it is the behaviour of the basin of attraction, which is crucial. In Foster and Wild (1998) for example, a significant discontinuity occurs in the near stationary saturation phase of the logistic trajectory, indicating, *ex post*, that structural instability must have been present, rather than a stable equilibrium state.

However, relying on *ex post* discontinuities is not very satisfactory. First of all, it is possible that a strong exogenous influence was excluded from an ALDM, which, if included, would have yielded stable equilibrium properties. Secondly, we need to be able to show *ex ante* that structural instability was present. In this regard, evidence in support of an ALDM is necessary, but not sufficient, to establish that structural change of a self-organisational type is present. As we have stressed, the ALDM must constitute the deterministic component of a growth process – the non-deterministic component relates to the topography of the basin of attraction.

Whether the basin of attraction is, on average, constant or narrowing over time is decisive in establishing the presence of self-organisational change. Proponents of the self-organisation approach argue that the likelihood of structural discontinuity will increase significantly as a logistic diffusion process moves into its saturation phase. By definition, a deterministic equation cannot deal directly with manifestations of structural change. It is well known that the discrete interval version of the logistic equation and the continuous interactive version can both generate bifurcations for threshold parameter values. However, these both remain deterministic representations of deducible bifurcation properties which are internal to the chosen closed mathematical form. Despite their capacity to mimic the effect of a structural discontinuity on growth, they remain tenuously related to the open, endogenous process of structure building in self-organising systems.

Clearly, we cannot know which of many such mathematical forms, with their array of equilibrium points, sets, curves and regions, is relevant *ex ante*, thus, deducibility bears little relation to predictability. Equation (1) is an abstract mathematical description which recognises the smoothness of self-organisational change in a phase of structural development. Its deterministic content allows us to parameterise the growth process, but we also know that it cannot embrace the non-deterministic features of structural change which culminate in structural instability. We cannot deduce from our deterministic model a bifurcation point because the sources of structural instability lie outside the estimated model, in what has not been explained, and it is necessary to introduce other statistical methods to discover what these features are.

In assessing whether or not a time series can be seen as having a tendency to return, asymptotically, to a long run path, it is necessary to render it stationary and then to examine whether or not the power spectrum representation of the variance structure conforms with this requirement. This involves, in the first instance, confirming that the power spectrum has the properties conventionally associated with I(0) processes. Does the power spectrum have an associated power density function which is non-zero but bounded by the zero frequency, as required in Engle and Granger (1987, p. 252)? However, Foster and Wild (1995) point out that it is also necessary to examine whether this property is time invariant through the application of moving window (or evolutionary) spectra. In cointegration studies, the requirement of co-variance stationary residuals involves the same property. Again, an examination of the evolutionary spectra is necessary before time invariance (co-variance stationarity) can be said to be present.

On the other hand, if the time series in question overlays a process of self-organisational development and displays a tendency towards emerging structural instability as a stationary state is approached, then this should also be detectable in the evolutionary spectra. Often, because of insufficiency of data, or simply statistical ignorance, the evolutionary spectral evidence is not examined. However, this not only constitutes omission of an essential step in establishing whether some notion of an asymptotic long-run equilibrium can be supported, but can also miss an opportunity to establish whether the growth of the variable under investigation is driven by a process of self-organisational change.

To establish whether an ALDM is self-organisational in character, its saturation phase should exhibit some type of emergent critical features if discontinuous structural transition is to eventuate. Such behaviour should be associated, statistically, with variation, which is not explained by the ALDM, i.e., the residuals. A process which is subject to self-organisational change and, thus, has a moving equilibrium with a changing basin of attraction, should display a finite residual variance which has both a changing structure (spectral decomposition) and a changing magnitude.[3] Adopting the conventional definition of power spectrum (based on second-order moments), a changing spectral decomposition can provide direct evidence of the presence of both non-stationarity and time-irreversibility, which are both features of a self-organisational process.[4]

---

[3] The possibility of a changing spectral decomposition is closely linked to the fact that evolutionary systems are non-autonomous (time-dependent).

[4] For example, consult Subba Rao and Gabr (1984, p. 10).

Furthermore, in the context of economic time series, evidence of falling residual variance and a steadily changing spectral decomposition over time, giving increasingly greater prominence to higher frequency components, can be viewed as reflecting a narrowing basin of attraction and an associated increasing likelihood of structural discontinuity. This is because the tendency for the basin of attraction to narrow will induce higher frequency oscillation accompanied by a falling residual variance. However, the observed decline in the residual variance should reverse in the critical stage of saturation – increasing numbers of basin 'spillovers' will cause the residual variance to rise as a structural discontinuity is approached.

The discovery of such patterns can provide support for the presence of on-going structural change of a self-organisational type. Furthermore, because the domination of high frequency oscillation signals a rise in the likelihood of structural discontinuity, we can argue that true uncertainty also increases, particularly when residual variance begins to increase in saturation. Thus, time-varying spectral methods offer a way of testing whether or not an estimated ALDM exhibits the three characteristics of a self-organisational process which have been identified.

In the initial, emergent phase of an ALDM, growth is approximately exponential because the effect of K, the capacity limit, is still small. We would expect the oscillatory behaviour of the residuals in this phase to be dominated by low frequency components, indicating relative structural stability.[5] In the saturation phase, where growth is approximately parabolic, because of the strength of K, the picture should be quite different if self-organisational change is present. High frequency components should dominate if structural instability and associated uncertainty are present. Thus, we would expect to observe significant time dependence of a particular type in the (unconditional) variance/covariance structure, if self-organisational change is present.

The most appropriate spectral methods for application in such circumstances are based upon frequency domain techniques which have been employed extensively in engineering and signal processing but not, to our knowledge, in economic applications. These frequency domain concepts are associated with time-varying spectral methods, which would appear to be most appropriate for dealing with the non-autonomous (time-dependent) character of self-organisational change.[6] These methods can generate a continuously changing spectrum, displaying the property of time-dependence (Priestley, 1988, p. 141). Although it is not possible to estimate a time-dependent spectrum for a particular instant of time, if the spectrum changes smoothly over time, then it is possible, using local

[5] Consult Granger (1966). This type of spectral decomposition would indicate the prominence of longer run factors in stimulating growth in the system. The existence of prominent low frequency components would also suggest that the long run "growth" factors are dominating shorter run transitory factors, thus indicating that the system is still robust or insulated against the effects of noise and other exogenous shocks.

[6] This approach, in emphasising a time-varying methodology, can be clearly contrasted with the conventional methods which incorporate mathematical descriptions based largely upon autonomous differential or difference equation systems.

functions of the data, to estimate some form of average spectrum of the process in any neighbourhood of a particular time instant (Cohen, 1989, p. 964).

Two main methods for computing time-varying spectra have been identified in the literature (see Foster and Wild, 1995).[7] In this paper, we adopt the so-called frequency modulated approach, commonly employed in engineering applications, which underpins the 'moving window' method of spectral analysis – often termed the spectrogram. With regard to estimation, this method is based on the short-time Fourier transform (STFT).[8] The approach we adopt is closely related to that of Rao and Shapiro (1970), who employed the concept of evolutionary spectra, determined by computing "...successive spectra of overlapping portions of the time series..." in order to view "...the series through a moving time window of fixed length" (Rao and Shapiro, 1970, p. 210).

With regard to economic applications of STFT, the key building block is the notion of the short-time autocorrelation (or, equivalently, the autocovariance function).[9] This approach generates average estimates in the vicinity of a specific time t through the use of a short-time observation window centred about t. Moreover, by employing a sliding (fixed length) observation window centred consecutively on each time period in the observation horizon, it is possible to obtain a short-time spectral estimate as a function of time (Hammond, Harrison, Tsao, and Lee, 1993, p. 359).

The computation of the power spectrum $g^e(w)$ is based upon conventional formulae:

$$g^e(w) = \frac{1}{2\pi}\left[C(0) + 2\sum_{s=1}^{m-1}\alpha(s)C(s)\cos ws\right] \tag{2}$$

where $\alpha(s) = 1 - (s/m)$, m is the number of lags used in the computation of the auto-covariance function $C(s)$, and $\alpha(s)$ is termed a lag window.[10] The autocovariance function $C(s)$ is estimated by:

$$C(s) = \frac{1}{n}\sum_{t=1}^{n-s}(x_t - x^{\mathrm{m}})(x_{t+s} - x^{\mathrm{m}}) \tag{3}$$

with x^{m} depicting the estimated mean of the process, and is given by

[7] See Priestley (1965, 1966) and Loynes (1968) for seminal contributions in this field.

[8] Cohen (1989, p. 963); Lovell (1991, pp. 1–2). A key property of this approach is that its focus is on the estimation of a "broad" range of frequencies. This is consistent with the spectral theory of evolutionary processes which is essentially based upon an assessment of the relative importance of low and high frequency components.

[9] See Flanagan (1972, p. 155); Rabiner and Schafer (1978, pp. 141–149, 162–164), and Schafer and Rabiner (1973). A general theoretical discussion of the link between the autocorrelation/autocovariance function and spectral density function can be found in Priestley (1981, pp. 210–215).

[10] Consult Granger and Hatanaka (1964, pp. 59–60), Granger and Engle (1983), Jenkins and Watts (1968, pp. 258–260), Kay (1988, Ch. 5), Koopmans (1983), Nerlove (1964), and Priestley (1981, pp. 433–434).

$$x^{\mathrm{m}} = \frac{1}{n}\sum_{t=1}^{n} x_t \tag{4}$$

In the context of short-time analysis, $g^e(w)$ is taken to represent the short-time Fourier transform of the autocovariance function $C(s)$ which is, in turn, calculated from a fixed partition of the original time series $X(t)$.[11] The lag window $\alpha(s)$ introduces the smoothing required to obtain a consistent estimate of the power spectrum. In general, $g^e(w)$ becomes a function of time as the fixed partition of $X(t)$ is translated through time. In this latter context, $g^e(w)$ represents the local behaviour of $X(t)$ as viewed through a sliding window.

In numeric simulations, the Parzen window is employed (Priestley 1981, pp. 443–444). This is given by:

$$\alpha_P(s) = 1 - 6(e)^2(1 - e), \quad \text{for } 0 < s \leq m/2 \tag{5}$$

$$\alpha_P(s) = 2(1 - e)^3, \quad \text{for } m/2 \leq s < m \tag{6}$$

where $e = s/m$

Two conventional methods of applying time-varying spectral methods have been employed to investigate patterns of non-stationarity and related properties, such as time-irreversibility.

The first method is based upon the employment of confidence bounds in order to establish the statistical *bona fides* of observed spectral patterns. This is implemented by taking, for example, the first and last one hundred (non-overlapping) observations of the process and using confidence intervals to establish whether observed spectral patterns are robust. If this can be established then, to the extent that observed spectral patterns are significantly different, evidence of second-order non-stationarity and time-irreversibility will immediately follow. It is possible to compute confidence intervals for the power spectrum – provided non-overlapping data segments are employed – with the details dependent on the particular lag window adopted in the estimation of the spectrum. Specifically, the quantity $\sigma g^e(w)/g(w)$ is, approximately, a Chi^2 distribution with σ degrees of freedom with $\sigma = 3.71^*(n/m)$ for the Parzen window.[12] It is possible to derive the 100(1–β)% confidence interval for $g(w)$, which can be activated as:

$$\log g^e(w) + \log\left[\frac{\alpha}{\mathrm{Chi}^2_{(\alpha)}(1 - \beta/2)}\right] \tag{7}$$

and

$$\log g^e(w) + \log\left[\frac{\alpha}{\mathrm{Chi}^2_{(\alpha)}(\beta/2)}\right] \tag{8}$$

To estimate the statistical significance of shifts in spectral decomposition we can apply the homogeneity test developed in Wild (1996). In this test,

[11] See Allen and Rabiner (1977, p. 1558), Flanagan (1972, pp. 142–144), and Portnoff (1980, pp. 57–58).

[12] Consult Jenkins and Watts (1968, pp. 252, 255) and Priestley (1981, pp. 467–468).

heterogeneity encompasses both shifts in the variance and autocovariance structure of the residuals.

The second method often follows application of the first and involves a systematic reduction in the size of data partitions in order to estimate non-stationary patterns more rigorously. This entails the use of overlapping data partitions, so the employment of confidence intervals is not strictly valid. However, some indication of the qualitative validity of the resulting spectral pattern, often plotted as a function of time, is discernible from the first method. The lowest permissible bound for the size of the data partitions is also crucially dependent upon whether high or low frequency components are prominent. If high frequency components are prominent, then smaller data partition sizes can be employed. However, in general, there are no generic rules or an established distribution theory associated with this latter method.

3 The estimation of a logistic diffusion model

In order to demonstrate how these methods can be applied to detect self-organisational change, we chose the same example as in Foster and Wild (1998), namely, the determination of Australian Building Society Deposits (ABSD). This example was chosen because it provides a very clear example of a diffusion process, with self-organisational features, which culminated in a phase of saturation in the early 1980s (see Fig. 1). It was necessary to re-estimate the model using monthly data over a longer period in order to generate the number of observations required for a spectral investigation. The data series generated from our estimated ALDM, for input into time-varying spectral methods, is the set of time-indexed scaled residuals. The scaling is accomplished by dividing the one-step residuals by the overall standard error of the estimated relationships.[13] The practice of employing scaled residuals to test for nonlinear serial dependence and forms of non-stationarity has become widespread in econometrics.[14] Given our hypothesis that the underlying evolutionary generating mechanism will have non-stationary and non-linear tendencies, it seems natural to test this hypothesis against the null hypothesis (and key restriction) in econometrics relating to a postulated residual structure, which has the properties of stationarity and Gaussianity. Indeed, this rationale has underpinned the construction of many of the well-known specifications tests such as tests for ARCH, serial correlation, and normality.

Some controversy has emerged over whether one needs to apply tests for non-linearity and non-stationarity to the original source time series, or if it is necessary to first identify and fit a (stationary) linear model for the time series in question. One important result associated with the application of bispectral linearity test statistics to (stationary) nonlinear processes is that they are invariant to the linear filtering of the data.[15] In this particular case,

[13] See Doornik and Hendry (1994, p. 127).

[14] See Ashley, Patterson, and Hinich (1986) and Brock, Hsieh, and Le Baron (1991, p. 19).

[15] See Ashley, Patterson, and Hinich (1986) and Stokes (1991, pp. 198–200).

it does not matter if the test is applied to the source series or residuals of the best linear fitted model. This implies, in turn, that:

"If the mechanism that generates the data is nonlinear and the data is fitted using a linear (e.g. ARMA) model, the nonlinearity will be swept into the residuals." (Ashley, Patterson, and Hinich, 1986, p. 165).

Our approach involves the replacement of a statistical time series model (such as an ARMA model) with an explicitly theoretical representation of a self-organisational process. From this, we can deduce that the scaled residuals must contain additional information concerning the structural integrity of the system in question. In order to avoid possible complications relating to spurious regression, eq. (1) is chosen as a linear transformation of the logistic diffusion model, ensuring that, across the entire sample, the residuals are stationary, in the conventional sense. In so doing, we can purge the smooth, parametric dimension of the process from the data, leaving any non-stationary and non-linear properties of the process in the residual structure.[16]

An ALDM, as specified in eq. (1), was adopted to model the determination of ABSD. As in Foster and Wild (1998), niche competition in $a(\ldots)$ was represented by the level of the building society to bank deposit interest ratio. Net diffusion rate competitive effects in $b_2(\ldots)$ were captured by the rate of change of this relative interest rate ratio. The capacity K for ABSD was taken to be a linear function of broad money, $M4$ (ie $kM4$), which is taken to be the total pool of available deposits.[17] The chosen specification also includes the rate of change of $M4$ to allow for the fact that ABSD grows in nominal terms. As such, this specification represents an unrestricted mix of the two restricted specifications estimated in Foster and Wild (1998):[18]

$$\begin{aligned}\ln(B)_t - \ln(B)_{t-1} = {} & b_1[1 - (B/M4_{t-1}/k)] - b_1 a\left[\ln(R_b/R_a)_t \cdots \ln(R_b/R_a)_{t-n}\right] \\ & + b_2\left[\{\ln(R_b/R_a)_t - \ln(R_b/R_a)_{t-1}\} \ldots \{\ln(R_b/R_a)_{t-n}\right. \\ & \left. - \ln(R_b/R_a)_{t-n-1}\}\right] + c\left[\ln(B)_t - \ln(B)_{t-1}\right]_{t-1} \\ & + m\left[\ln(M4)_t - \ln(M4)_{t-1}\right] + \mathrm{e}_t \qquad (9)\end{aligned}$$

Because of the presence of some seasonal patterns in the monthly ABSD data used, seasonal dummies were included in this ALDM and retained if statistically significant.[19] Estimation was conducted, using Pc-Give 8, by

[16] It should be noted that, in dividing the one-step residuals by the (constant) standard error of the fitted relation, the properties of non-linearity and non-stationarity will be invariant to the scaling employed.

[17] Cointegration tests were conducted on the levels of ABSD and M4 for the periods 1967(11)–1985(5) and 1967(11)–1988(8). In both cases, the residuals were found to be I(1) by both the Dicky Fuller (DF) and Augmented Dicky Fuller (ADF) Tests in Pc-Give 8. Thus, the presence of a non-equilibrium relationship between the two variables was supported (these results are available from the authors by request).

[18] The spectral evidence for the two restricted specifications is qualitatively similar to that reported below.

[19] The monthly dummies were retained purely on the basis of statistical significance, irrespective of sign. Two types of dummy were used: one set that becomes operative from 1976(7) and another for the entire sample period. This allows for a change in the seasonal characteristics of the ABSD data employed.

Table 1. OLS estimates of Eq. (9) for 1967(11) to 1988(8)

Variable	Coefficient	Std.error	t-value
Constant	0.016534	0.0020292	8.148
$B/M4_{t-1}$	−0.087599	0.011287	−7.761
$d\ln(R_b/R_a)_t$	0.023656	0.0093019	2.543
$d\ln(R_b/R_a)_{t-3}$	0.017400	0.0092186	1.888
$d\ln(R_b/R_a)_{t-7}$	0.016857	0.0095484	1.765
$d\ln(R_b/R_a)_{t-9}$	0.021391	0.0093088	2.298
$d\ln(R_b/R_a)_{t-12}$	0.017067	0.0096515	1.768
$d\ln(R_b/R_a)_{t-14}$	0.026683	0.0092931	2.871
$d\ln(R_b/R_a)_{t-15}$	0.016035	0.0094348	1.700
$d\ln(B)_{t-1}$	0.50900	0.045887	11.093
$d\ln(M4)$	0.42312	0.074714	5.663

plus 8 significant monthly dummies

$R^2 = 0.779288$ $F(18, 231) = 45.312$ [0.0000]
$\sigma = 0.00623193$ DW = 2.08

Variance instability test: 0.6197*[a]
Joint instability test: 4.97487*

AR 1-7F(7, 224) = 0.83771 [0.5570]
ARCH 7 F(7, 217) = 0.82098 [0.5708]
Normality $Chi^2(2)$ = 2.5605 [0.2780]
Xi^2 F(28, 202) = 1.0057 [0.4634]
Xi*Xj F(150, 80) = 0.98781 [0.5328]
RESET F(1, 230) = 1.2309 [0.2684]

Data definitions:
B: Permanent building society deposits, end of month ($*m*)
*M*4: Volume of money, definition M4, end of month ($*m*)
R_b: Interest rate, deposits with P. B'lding Soc.s ($*m*), % per annum
R_a: Interest rate, major trading banks fixed deposits, % per annum

[a] The * following both instability tests indicate that the null hypothesis of constancy was rejected at the 5% level of significance.

ordinary least squares, nonlinear least squares and maximum likelihood. The last two methods yielded estimated coefficients which were almost identical to those generated by OLS.[20] Consequently, we focus on the OLS results in Table 1.

We estimated eq. (1) over a sample period culminating in 1988(8), the month before the Statutory Reserve Deposit Ratio, imposed on Australian banks, was abolished, inducing a structural discontinuity in the deposit share of non-converting building societies (see Fig. 1). This was followed by

[20] Tests for cointegration between the percentage change in building society deposits [$\ln B_t - \ln B_{t-1}$] and the logistic term $(B/M4)_{t-1}$ were conducted over the period 1967(11)–1985(5). The residuals were found to be I(0) by both the Dicky Fuller (DF) and Augmented Dicky Fuller (ADF) tests in Pc-Give 8. Moreover, the residuals from the regression in Table 1 were also found to be I(0). Thus, spurious regression is not present (these results are available from the authors by request).

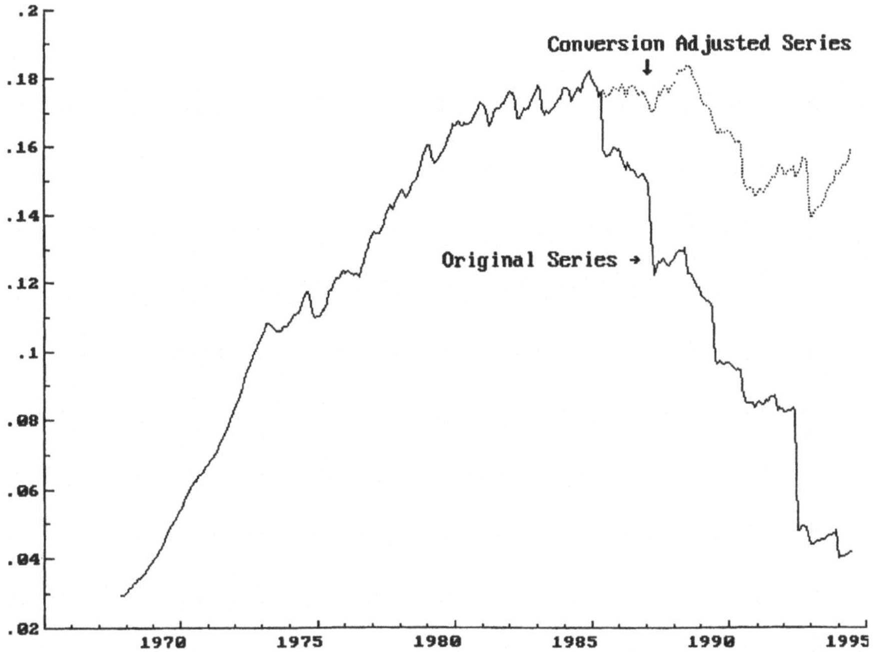

Fig. 1. The share of Australian building society deposits in M4 (1967(11)–1994(8))

a period of intense competitive pressure and loss of market share which culminated in the collapse of the third largest institution in the sector (the Pyramid Building Society) in 1990. To allow estimation over the 1985(6)–1988(8) period, the ABSD series was adjusted to remove the effect of conversions of building societies to banks which occurred after the first phase of bank deregulation in 1984.[21] This eliminated the discrete declines associated with each conversion but did not affect the growth rate in other months.

The results are very similar to those obtained using quarterly data. The derived estimate of k is close at 0.189 and the pattern of interest differential effects is also similar. The lagged dependent variable plays a stronger role, because of the shorter observation interval. An examination of the diagnostic tests indicate that the overall fit is very good (see Fig. 2 for actual to predicted plots). There is no indication of error autocorrelation, ARCH, heteroscedasticity, or normality problems using the standard tests provided in Pc-Give. Thus, there is little indication that the residuals indicate any serious misspecification problems in the parametric model estimated. However, it is worth noting that the forecasting performance of the equation is inferior to that of the quarterly version, using a five-year forecasting

[21] This was undertaken by working out the proportion that each converting building society contributed to the actual building society sector the month before it converted, and then adjusting upwards the series by this (constant) factor for all future time periods in the sample, inclusive of the converting month. Details of these conversions are available from the authors.

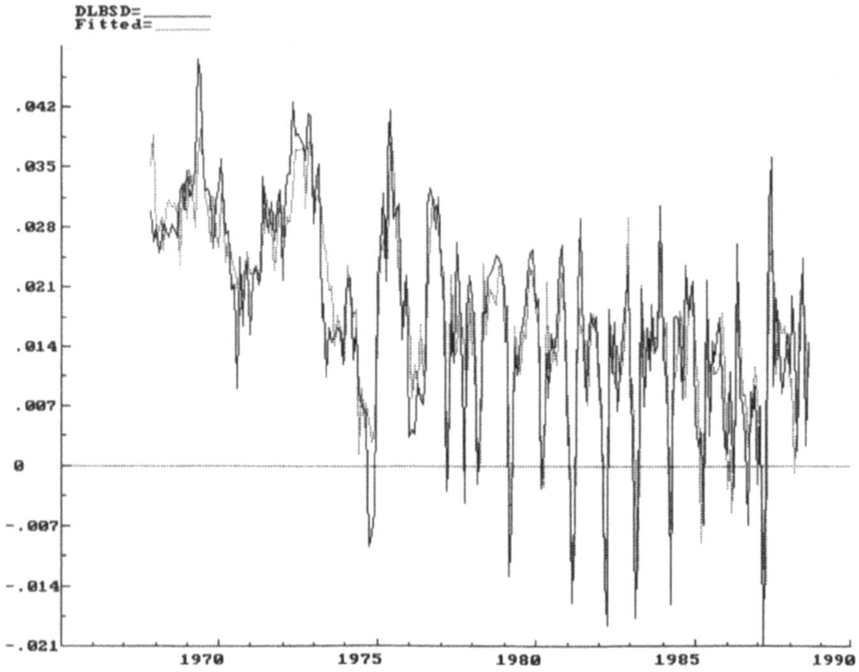

Fig. 2. Actual to predicted plots for eq. (9) in Table 1 (1967(11)–1988(8))

period, as in Foster and Wild (1998). The Chow test is passed, but the Chi-sq test fails.[22] However, examination of the actual to predicted plots reveals no prediction bias and significant prediction error is recorded in only four months. These results are likely to be due to the fact that there are seasonal dummies in the specification, which are well known to affect parameter stability testing, particularly if they pick up outliers due to series breaks, etc.[23] The variance instability and joint parameter stability tests reject at the 5% level, indicating emerging model fragility in the saturation phase.[24]

[22] For a forecasting horizon of 1980(1)–1985(5), the test results are: Chow F(65,126) = 1.1923 [0.1998] and Forecast $\text{Chi}^2(65)$ = 108.91 [0.0005]** (** denotes rejection at both the 5% and 1% levels of significance).

[23] Tests for cointegration between the percentage change in building society deposits $[\ln B_t - \ln B_{t-1}]$ and the logistic term $(B/M4)_{t-1}$ were conducted over the period 1967(11)–1988(8). The residuals were found to be I(0) by both the Dicky Fuller (DF) and Augmented Dicky Fuller (ADF) tests in Pc-Give 8. The residuals from the regression in Table 2 were also tested and found to be I(0). Thus, spurious regression is not present (these results are available from the authors by request).

[24] It should be noted that these stability tests are passed over the sample period 1967(11)–1985(5) for the specification Table 1. Therefore, this indicates that it is over the period 1985(6)–1988(8) that instability considerations become more prevalent. This time period corresponds to the period completely characterised by saturation.

4 The application of moving window spectral methods

We will now report the results obtained from subjecting the standardised (scaled) residuals drawn from our estimated ABSD model to moving window spectral techniques. A computer program, coded in FORTRAN, was employed to generate the time-varying spectra, with the Parzen lag window being employed in all empirical investigations. The time path of the scaled residuals associated with the results documented in Table 1 are depicted in Fig. 3. Plots of the power spectrum for the first and last (non-overlapping) data partitions of one hundred observations are depicted in Figs. 4 and 5. Two outcomes are evident. First, the observed spectral decompositions are within associated 95% confidence intervals. Second, homogeneity tests, devised in Wild (1996), undertaken on an individual, aggregate and induced basis, establish clearly that the spectral decomposition (shape) between the first and last data partitions for each set of residuals differ significantly, thus indicating that the residual structure of the process displays the properties of weak non-stationarity, time-irreversibility and structural change.[25]

It is evident that, for the first data partition (Fig. 4), that most of the power of the process is concentrated around low frequency components, as anticipated, in the early growth intensive stage of a logistic diffusion process which is characterised by self-organisational change.[26] This contrasts with the last partition (Fig. 5) where power is concentrated around high frequency components. This confirms that the saturation phase of the logistic diffusion process is characterised by the type of rapid oscillatory behaviour which is associated with the emergence of structural discontinuity and increasing uncertainty with regard to the longer term future of the process in question.[27]

These properties were further investigated by spectral decomposition as a function of time. This analysis was activated by employing the methodology discussed in Section 2, enabling us to observe the temporal pattern of non-stationarity. Thus, it can be established whether observed changes in the spectral decomposition occur smoothly or not. Furthermore, some indication of when changes in spectral decomposition occurred can be obtained. The time plot is reported in Fig. 6, for an underlying partition size of 100 observations.[28]

---

[25] See Wild (1996) for details of these new tests and illustrative results using the residuals derived from Table 1 in this paper.

[26] The frequency values highlighted in the power spectrum plots range from a sixteen year cycle, which is indistinguishable from a trend, at a 0 frequency to a 2 monthly cycle at a frequency of 10.

[27] Spectra corresponding to partition sizes of 70, 50 and 40 observations were also examined but are not reported here. In general, the results indicate that a partition size of 70 should probably be regarded as a lower bound for the effective estimation of the power spectrum in the first phase of the diffusion process under investigation. Moreover, a partition size of 50 might be the most useful partition size to investigate the critical behaviour in the saturation phase, given the prominence of high frequency components.

[28] These surface diagrams were computed using the software package MATLAB (published by the Math Works Inc).

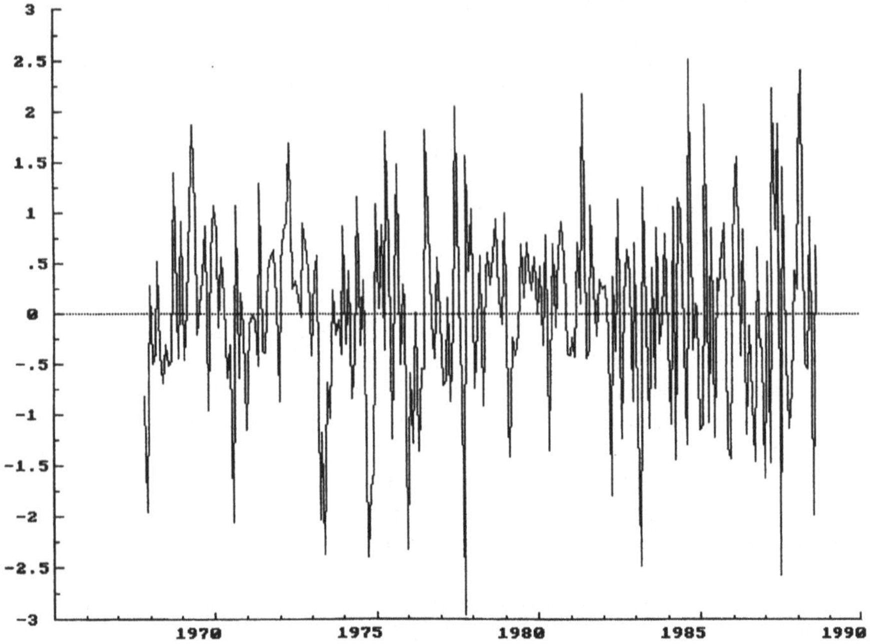

Fig. 3. Standardised residuals for eq. (9) in Table 1 (1967(11)–1988(8))

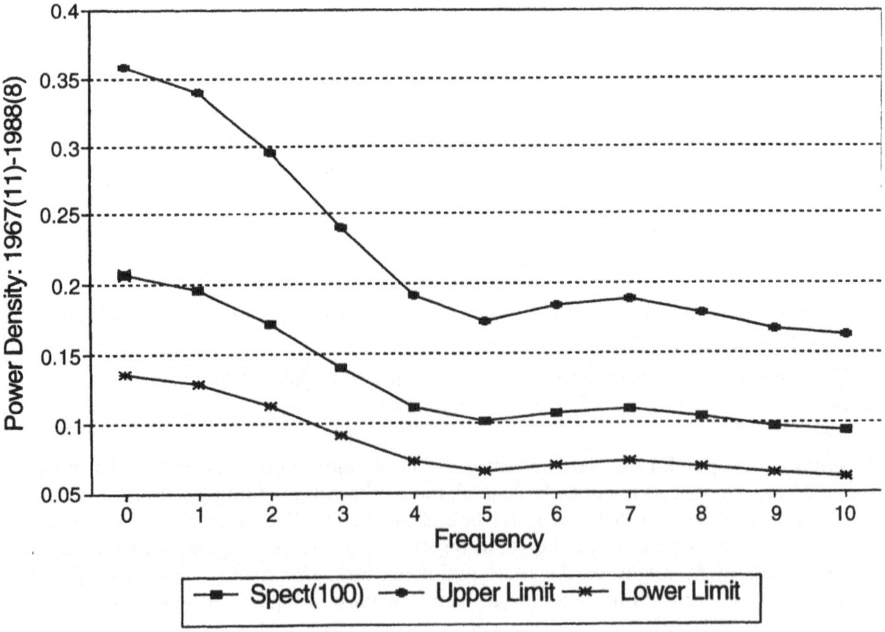

Fig. 4. Plot of power spectrum first partition (size = 100)

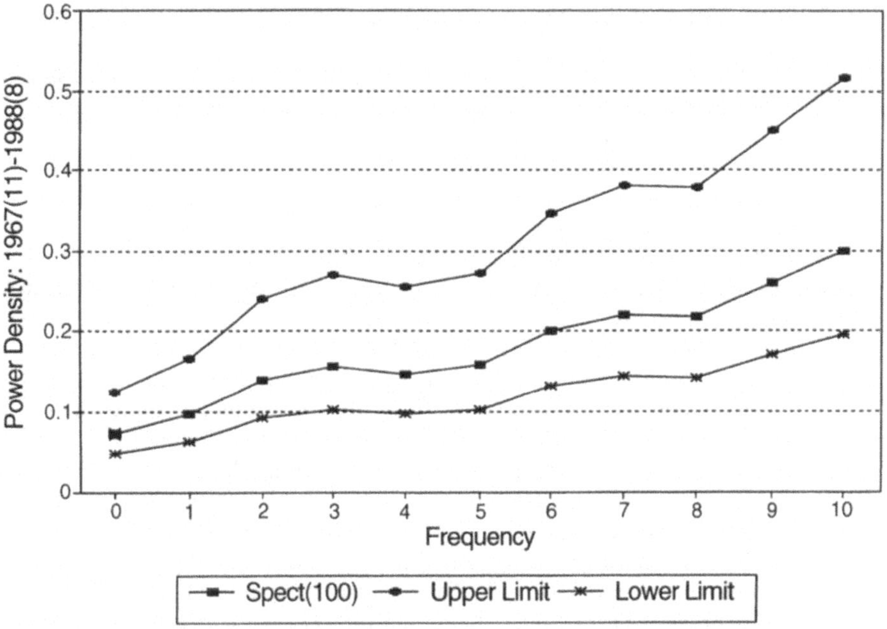

Fig. 5. Plot of power spectrum last partition (size = 100)

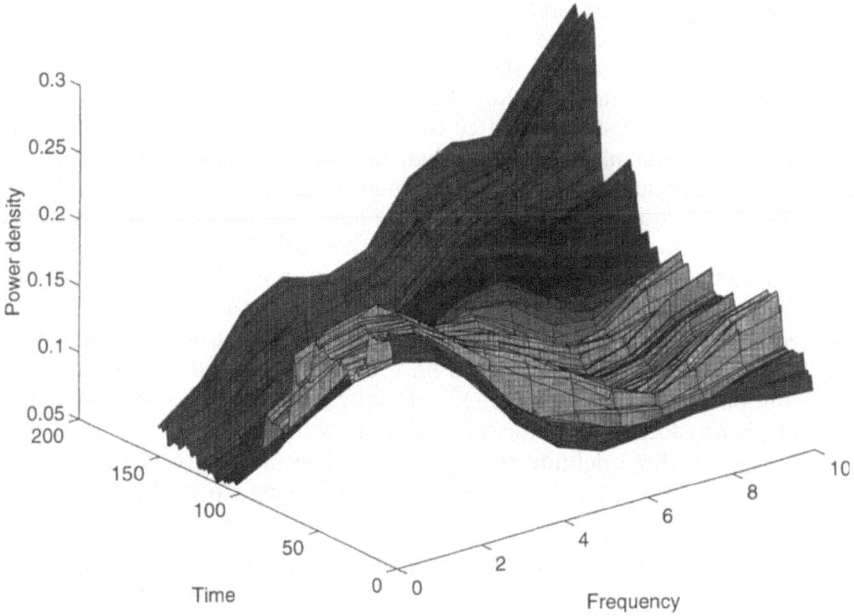

Fig. 6. Spectrogram plot (1967(11)–1988(8))

It is evident that the process is time-irreversible with low frequency components being prominent early on, with a gradual shift in prominence towards middle frequency components being observed as time progresses, at least up to partition 87.[29] There is an increase in the relative importance of middle and higher frequency components, discernible by the ridge that can be seen towards the back of the chart, corresponding to frequency components 5–10. This ridge emerges after increasing evidence of instability, beginning in partitions 88–91, which are centred upon April 1979 to August 1979.[30] This is followed by another distinct episode over partitions 92 to 99, which are centred about September 1979 to March 1980. The pronounced fall in the power of low frequency components is indicative of increasing structural instability. Moreover, there is also evidence of emerging power associated with middle and high frequency components which can be associated with the pronounced 'bunching' of the scaled residuals after 1980 which can be discerned from Fig. 3. The final form of the ridge emerges abruptly in partition 100, which is centred upon April 1980 with increasingly prominent higher frequency components (i.e., frequency components 8–10) emerging over the last 20 frames. Overall, these observations suggest that structural instability began to increase over the period 1977–79. The spectrogram plot suggests that the onset of saturation commenced from about 1977–78 onwards, with evidence that the self-organisational process had clearly entered this stage by 1980–81.

Having established that the spectrogram evidence supports the view that evolutionary change is present, is it the case that the behaviour of the residual variance over time also supports this view? The regression diagnostics in Table 1 indicate that the residual variance is 'well-behaved'. However, in the context of short-time spectral analysis implemented, the variance of the process is permitted to vary – being computed for each data partition. The time paths of the residual variance, corresponding to the two sets of standardised residuals for an underlying partition size of 100 observations, is reported in Fig. 7. It is evident that the process is not homoscedastic. Specifically, certain distinctive trends emerge. First, the residual variance increases over the first 25 partitions followed by a plateau for the next 40 partitions. This is then followed by a (slight) monotonic decreasing path for partitions 35 to 89, followed by a slight monotonic decreasing path for partitions 65–100, followed by a slight monotonic increasing path for partitions 101–121. Finally, the path for partitions 122–151 display a steep monotonic increasing trend.[31]

In general, three definite trends emerge. The first corresponds to that identified previously, namely, a monotonic increasing path. This is what we

[29] 'Composite time period' 87 encompasses a 100 observation data partition (window) based on the period January 1975 to April 1983, with March 1979 being the approximate mid-point.

[30] This data encompasses partitions incorporating time periods within the 'envelope' February 1975 to September 1983.

[31] The sharp upward trend in the residual variance in Chart 7 is consistent with the outcome of the reported Pc-Give variance instability test indicating non-constancy.

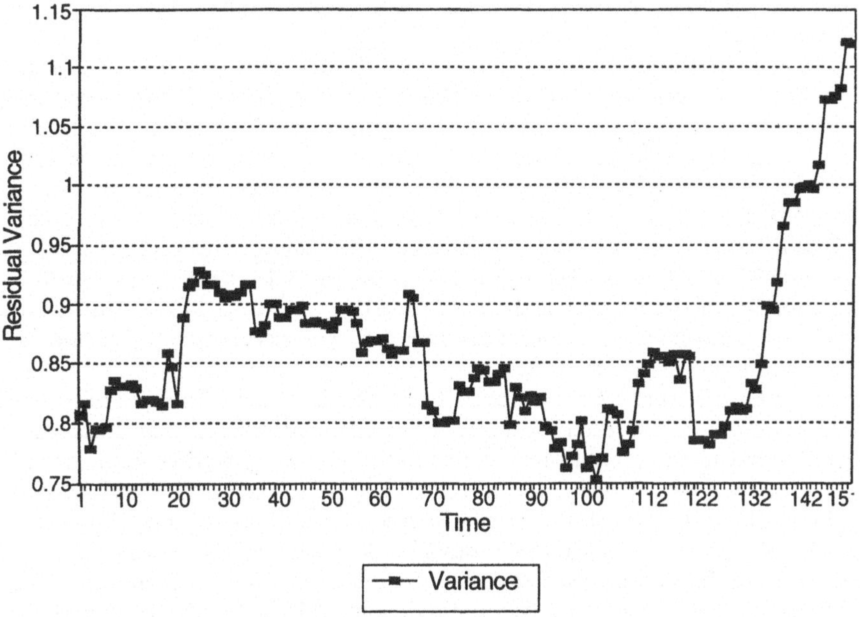

Fig. 7. Time path residual variance (partition size = 100) (1967(11)–1988(8))

would expect in the emergent stage of a process of self-organisational change: faster growth is associated with a widening basin of attraction, reflecting increased flexibility. The second trend is also observed, namely, of a monotonic decreasing path. Again, this is what we would expect as saturation is approached and the basin of attraction narrows, as inflexibility and inertia begin to dominate behaviour. Finally, the third trend of a concluding steep monotonic increasing path is observed in Chart 7. This last trend is in line with the emergence of critical behaviour, as shocks cause the narrowed basin of attraction to be exceeded, causing structural damage to the system. In particular, not only does the residual variance increase significantly, but the underlying oscillatory tendencies begin to exhibit considerable variation across relatively short time scales – as suggested by the very dominant high frequency components in the spectrogram plot in Chart 6.

Therefore, the evidence from the time plots of residual variance also provides support to the hypothesis that the observed logistic diffusion process is associated with self-organisational change. Furthermore, the observation of three separate and distinctive trends in residual variance calls into question whether it is legitimate to talk about a homoscedastic process, given the general and definitive nature of the observed trends. We would argue that the property of constant variance, which is supported by conventional diagnostic tests for the entire sample in Table 1, is not satisfied in the above plots. This, in turn, calls into question the ability of conventional econometric tests of heteroscedasticity to really establish if the residual variance is time invariant, a condition required for covariance stationarity.[32]

In general, the above findings relating to the qualitative shifts in both the spectral decomposition and magnitude of the residual variance, together with the confirmation of the statistical significance of these shifts, confirm the presence of weak non-stationarity in the residual structure of the process. In econometric terms, it is this fundamental non-stationarity which confirms the true self-organisational character of the process. Specifically, we cannot use fixed parameter techniques to whiten the residuals – there is too much variation in structure between the growth intensive and saturation phases of the process to be able to derive an approximately invariant variance/covariance structure required for the successful application of conventional estimation approaches.

Techniques were also employed to establish whether the second-order non-stationarity observed in the spectrogram and residual variance plots was related to the conditional or unconditional second-order moments of the process. Our *a priori* expectation is that, if the process is self-organisational, then the non-stationarity which has been observed should hold for the *unconditional* second order moments. As such, the oscillatory patterns observed in the standardised residuals documented in Chart 3 should *not* be eliminated (i.e. 'whitened') by employing an ARCH/GARCH modelling framework.[33] Evidence supporting this hypothesis was found in the Engle ARCH test results automated in Pc-Give 8, which were obtained for the specification in Table 1. The null hypothesis of no ARCH structure could not be rejected for a wide assortment of lag lengths.

A GARCH(1,1) framework was also employed to model the residuals generated by the two specifications documented in Table 1.[34] The GARCH coefficients were all found to be very small in magnitude, and together with the significance tests, call into question the ability of a GARCH(1,1) specification to model the residuals. The 'conditional' standard error (deviation) was computed and the 'conditional' standardised residuals were computed and overlaid on those depicted in Fig. 3. It was found that the GARCH residuals had the same qualitative patterns evident in the residual plot in Fig. 3. As such, GARCH modelling did not 'whiten' the residuals or remove the oscillatory patterns which were previously observed our spectral decomposition. There were only slight differences in the tips of residuals.[35]

Attempts to fit higher order GARCH models generated line search problems in the numeric optimisation procedures employed in the estimation procedure. This is not unexpected given that the sum of the GARCH

---

[32] These tests centre around regressing the residual sum of squares on a constant, squares of regressor variables, and possibly on its own lag structure.

[33] See Engle (1982) and Bollerslev (1986).

[34] The algebra code used for the GARCH(1,1) modelling using Pc-Give 8 for the two models is available on request.

[35] The plot of the overlaid OLS and GARCH scaled residuals, as well as the spectrogram and residual variance plots associated with the GARCH residuals are available from the authors on request.

coefficients including the MA and AR parts are very small. Under such circumstances, numeric convergence problems are likely to arise. Attempts to fit a GARCH(1,1) model to residuals generated by the specification in Table 1 also ran into line search problems when applied over the full sample. However, a convergent GARCH(1,1) solution was obtained using appropriately modified algebraic code.[36] Once again, very small coefficient values were recorded, confirming again that the patterns observed in the scaled residuals, in Charts 4 and 5, do not appear to be generated by ARCH or GARCH processes.

5 Conclusions

Our objective has been to discover a method of detecting self-organisational change in time series data, which can be modelled using a logistic diffusion approach. It has been shown that examination of the time-varying properties of residual structure can enable us to detect the presence of the three properties of self-organisational change, namely, time irreversibility, structural change and true uncertainty. The results obtained in our chosen case study provide strong support to the hypothesis that all three properties are present. Specifically, the three phases of the identified logistic diffusion process were found to have different spectral decompositions. First, power is concentrated on low frequency components in the growth intensive stage. Second, in the middle phase – around the point of inflection – power is concentrated on middle frequency components. Third, and importantly, the saturation phase exhibits dominant high frequency components, indicating the presence of instability and uncertainty concerning the 'long run' structural integrity of the system. These findings confirm strongly that time-irreversibility is present and the manner in which the spectral decomposition changes over time supports the hypothesis that structural change of a self-organisational type is also present.

Evidence concerning the time path of residual variance provided further support to the hypothesis that self-organisational change is present. In particular, the combination of falling residual variance and rising power of high frequency components in early saturation provides a very distinctive pattern. Furthermore, the rise in residual variance late in the saturation phase is consistent with the emergence of a critical stage in which some structural disintegration is occurring.

An endogenous process, such as self-organisation, whereby a dissipative structure enters a developmental niche, cannot be expressed in terms of movement from one stable equilibrium to another. Endogenous processes are non-equilibrium in nature and, as such, tend towards boundary limits which, when approached, lead to instability, rather than stability. Only exogenously-driven processes can be considered, in a strict sense, in terms of stable equilibria and intervening disequilibrium mechanisms. The modelling strategy which we have adopted, does allow, however, for exogenous impacts on the endogenous growth path. Furthermore, we have depicted a

[36] The algebraic code and the GARCH results are available on request.

self-organisational process as a moving, temporary equilibrium one with a narrowing basin of attraction. As such, disequilibrium deviations and offsetting homoeostatic corrections still operate. We have stressed that applying a logistic diffusion model can capture the smooth, self-organisational features of evolutionary development, but it is in the patterns of the residuals that the non-deterministic features of evolutionary change can be detected.

To what extent are other economic variables measured by time series data also of this type? An answer to this question is important because the methods of dealing with non-stationary time series in conventional econometric methodology are dedicated to the isolation of exogenous models with equilibrium/disequilibrium characteristics, yet the time series data involved may not be compatible with such an interpretation. Specifically, transformations are usually undertaken to ensure that no non-stationarity associated with low frequency variation is evident. This type of non-stationarity has been associated with the existence of explosive roots which generate trend in mean and possibly variance. However, in our study, even when these transformations are undertaken and diagnostic tests passed, the accompanying spectral properties show time variation, reflecting fundamental non-stationarity and time-irreversibility in the residual structure of the underlying process. This is clear in the shifting spectral decomposition, which implies change in both the underlying oscillatory properties of the process and in the role that permanent and short-time forces play in explaining the evolution of the process under consideration.

Furthermore, evidence was obtained which suggests that distinctive trends in the residual variance, when plotted as a function of time, exist even when conventional tests suggest that these should not be present. This suggests that one cannot necessarily assume that a process is stationary, even if trend in mean and variance are rejected in standard residual tests. Clearly, additional tests, of the type introduced in this paper, are necessary to ensure that the variance/covariance structure of the process is truly independent of time.

Our evidence also suggests that structural change might primarily reflect a confluence of factors, which have the basic characteristic of a short-time scale of variation. Moreover, our ability to predict the approach of discontinuous structural transition may be associated with such short run behaviour. This contrasts with large sample tests, such as the Chow test, which can identify structural change only after it has occurred, but cannot provide any basis for predicting its likelihood or enable analysts to come to some type of judgement about its likelihood, before it actually arises. From the perspective of economic forecasting, the presence of hidden non-stationarity, of the type we have identified through shifting spectral decomposition, causes problems for naive model extrapolation using estimated parameters. The onset of structural discontinuity will often induce large forecasting errors, which have been all too common in the past.

Our approach enables a researcher to establish whether the process under consideration is self-organisational or disequilibrium in character. If it is the former, then the viability of extrapolative forecasting depends on which phase of the diffusion process self-organisational change is in. In the initial phase, extrapolative forecasting is viable. In the saturation phase, structural uncertainty precludes such extrapolation. Instead, the spectral evidence can provide an early warning of structural discontinuity, which could prove invaluable to policy-makers, allowing time for regulatory changes to avert system collapse and to promote a new phase of evolutionary development.

Although we believe that we are the first to offer a coherent methodology to detect self-organisational change in time series data, what we have achieved in this paper must be regarded as exploratory. Further development of the methodology is necessary before it can become a versatile approach to economic modelling and forecasting. In particular, we have focussed upon non-stationary aspects of self-organisational processes and ignored nonlinear aspects which are likely to be responsible for the actual occurrence of structural discontinuity, once advanced saturation has been attained. It is clear that the residuals we have investigated are likely to contain a mixture of both aspects. The spectral methods we have employed cannot detect non-linearity and, therefore, remain something of a 'blunt instrument' in pin-pointing the precise timing of discontinuity and its aftermath, ranging from system death through to a smooth structural transition to a new developmental path. Further research, applying cross-spectral, bi-spectral and poly-spectral methods would appear to be worthwhile in order to discover whether the non-stationary and non-linear features of the residuals of an evolutionary model can be disentangled in meaningful ways.

References

Alchian AA (1950) Uncertainty, evolution and economic theory. Journal of Political Economy 58: 211–222

Allen JB, Rabiner LR (1977) A unified approach to short-time Fourier analysis and synthesis. Proceedings of the IEEE 65(11): 1558–1564

Andersen ES (1994) Evolutionary economics: Post-Schumpeterian contributions. Pinter Press, London

Ashley RA, Patterson DM, Hinich MJ (1986) A diagnostic test for nonlinear serial dependence in time series fitting errors. Journal Of Time Series Analysis 7(3): 165–178

Bollerslev T (1986) Generalised autoregressive conditional heteroscedasticity. Journal of Econometrics 31: 307–327

Boulding KE (1980) Evolutionary economics. Sage, Beverly Hills, CA

Brock WA, Hsieh DA, Lebaron, B (1991) Nonlinear dynamics, chaos, and instability: Statistical theory and economic evidence. MIT Press, Cambridge, MA

Cohen L (1989) Time–frequency distributions – A review. Proceedings of the IEEE 77(7): 941–981

Dixon R (1994) The logistic family of discrete dynamic models. In: Creedy J, Martin V (eds) Chaos and non-linear models in economics. Edward Elgar, Aldershot

Doornik JA, Hendry, DF (1994) PC GIVE 8.0. An interactive econometric modelling system. Thomson, London

Engle RF (1982) Autoregressive conditional heteroscedasticity, with estimates of the variations in United Kingdom inflations. Econometrica 50: 987–1007

Engle RF, Granger CWJ (1987) Co-integration and error correction; Representation, estimation, and testing. Econometrica 55(2): 251–276

Flanagan JL (1972) Speech analysis synthesis and perception, 2nd edn. Springer, New York
Foster J (1992) The determination of Sterling M3, 1963–88: an evolutionary macroeconomic approach. The Economic Journal 102: 481–496
Foster J (1993) Economics and the self-organisation approach: Alfred Marshall revisited? The Economic Journal 103: 975–991
Foster J (1994) The self-organisation approach in economics. In: Burley P, Foster J (eds) Economics and thermodynamics: New perspectives on economic analysis. Kluwer, Boston
Foster J, Wild P (1995) The application of time varying spectra to detect evolutionary change in economic processes. Department of Economics, University of Queensland, Discussion Paper No 182 (September)
Foster J, Wild P (1996) Economics and the science of synergetics. Journal of Evolutionary Economics 6: 239–260
Foster J, Wild P (1998) Econometric modelling in the presence of evolutionary change. Cambridge Journal of Economics 21: forthcoming
Granger CWJ, Hatanaka M (1964) Spectral analysis of economic time series. Princeton University Press, New Jersey
Granger CWJ (1993) Strategies for modelling nonlinear time-series relationships. Economic Record 69: 233–238
Granger CWJ (1966) The typical spectral shape of an economic variable. Econometrica 34: 150–161
Granger CWJ, Engle R (1983) Applications of spectral analysis in econometrics. In: Brillinger DR, Krishnaiah PR (eds) Handbook of statistics, Vol 3, pp 93–109. North-Holland, Amsterdam
Griliches Z (1957) Hybrid corn and the economics of innovation. Econometrica 25: 510–522
Hammond JK, Harrison RF, Tsao YH, Lee JS (1993) The prediction of time-frequency spectra using covariance-equivalent models. In: Subba Rao T (ed) Developments in time series analysis. In honour of Maurice B. Priestley, pp 355–373. Chapman & Hall, London
Hodgson J (1993) Economics and evolution. Polity Press, Cambridge
Jenkins GM, Watts DG (1968) Spectral analysis and its applications. Holden-Day, San Francisco
Kay SM (1988) Modern spectral estimation. Prentice-Hall, Englewood
Koopmans LH (1983) A spectral analysis primer. In: Brillinger DR, Krishnaiah PR (eds) Handbook of statistics, Vol 3, pp 169–183. North-Holland, Amsterdam
Lovell BC (1991) Techniques for non-stationary spectral analysis. Unpublished Ph D Thesis, Electrical Engineering Department, University of Queensland
Loynes RM (1968) On the concept of spectrum for non-stationary processes. Journal of the Royal Statistical Society, Ser. B, 30: 1–30
Nelson R (1995) Recent evolutionary theorising about economic change. Journal of Economic Literature 33: 48–90
Nelson R, Winter S (1982) An evolutionary theory of economic change. Belknap Press, Cambridge
Nerlove M (1964) Spectral analysis of seasonal adjustment procedures. Econometrica 32: 241–285
Portnoff MR (1980) Time-frequency representation of digital signals and systems based on short-time Fourier analysis. IEEE Transactions on Acoustics, Speech, and Signal Processing 28: 55–69
Priestley MB (1965) Evolutionary spectra and non-stationary processes. Journal of the Royal Statistical Society, Ser. B, 27: 204–237
Priestley MB (1966) Design relations for non-stationary processes. Journal of the Royal Statistical Society, Ser. B, 28: 228–240
Priestley MB (1981) Spectral analysis and time series. Academic Press, London

Priestley MB (1988) Non-linear and non-stationary time series analysis. Academic Press, London
Rabiner LR, Schafer RW (1978) Digital processing of speech signals. Prentice-Hall, New Jersey
Rao AG, Shapiro A (1970) Adaptive smoothing using evolutionary spectra. Management Science 17(3): 208–218
Schafer RW, Rabiner LR (1973) Design and simulation of a speech analysis-synthesis system based on short-time Fourier analysis. IEEE Transactions on Audio and Electroacoustics 21: 165–174
Stokes HH (1991) Specifying and diagnostically testing econometric models. Quorum Books, New York
Subba Rao T, Gabr MM (1984) An introduction to bispectral analysis and bilinear time series models. Springer, Berlin Heidelberg New York
Vromen J (1995) Evolutionary economics. Routledge, London
Wild P (1996) Distribution theory for evolutionary spectra homogeneity test. School of Economic Studies Discussion Paper Series, University of Manchester, No. 9629

Modelling growth in economic systems as the outcome of a process of self-organisational change: a fuzzy regression approach

Bryan Morgan[1] **and John Foster**[1]

[1]Department of Economics, The University of Queensland, Brisbane QLD 4072, Australia

Abstract: Modelling evolutionary economic processes presents a challenge to traditional econometric methods. One of the authors has proposed an augmented logistic diffusion model to represent growth through a period of self-organisational structural change. In this paper the use of one type of fuzzy regression is explored by applying the technique to a combination of an augmented logistic diffusion model and data that have elsewhere been extensively investigated using spectral methods. In the fuzzy regression approach, the parameters of the logistic diffusion model are estimated as fuzzy numbers. Local parameter corrections are produced for each parameter as part of the estimation procedure. The local parameter corrections are plotted graphically and interpreted, in the light of self-organisation theory, as showing the change in variability of model parameters through time. The results of the fuzzy regression support the conclusion that the data are produced by a self-organising process.

Key Words: Fuzzy Regression, Logistic Diffusion Model, Self-Organisation.

JEL classification: C49, G21

1 Introduction

In the economy and its sectors and sub-sectors growth fluctuates. Sometimes growth follows sigmoid paths, culminating in periods of rapid or slow decline, but we also see growth cycles, where growth makes a transition from one sigmoid path to another. Evolutionary economists generally view such nonlinearities in growth paths as the outcome of ongoing structural change in the economic system under consideration. Thus, the difficulties that conventional economic modellers encounter, using linear econometrics, are no surprise to evolutionary economists. However, when structural change is dominated by diffusion processes, such methods can perform quite well in tracking growth – it is the phases of discontinuous structural change, when old systems become obsolete and novelty emerges to provide the basis of new diffusion processes, that spectacular breakdowns in conventional models occur. It follows that it is not necessary to eliminate the use of econometric models, but rather to make them specific to historical periods, corresponding to phases of diffusion. However, it is also necessary to construct econometric models from a theoretical perspective which is explicitly evolutionary, focussing on processes rather than outcomes. From an evolutionary perspective, model breakdown becomes the normal expectation and, indeed, something that a researcher should be able to elucidate upon, on the basis of result diagnostics.

In Foster and Wild (1995) , an econometric approach to modelling growth in the presence of structural change, which is viewed as self-organisational in character, is proposed. This approach is built upon the logistic growth equation. It is widely accepted that a process self organisational development, where there are cumulative increases in complexity and organisation, will yield a growth trajectory of this type. It is noted that economic self-organisation differs from physio-chemical and biological self organisation in several respects and an augmented logistic diffusion modelling (ALDM) approach was developed to allow for this. Using the case of the growth of the market share of a particular class of deposit accepting institution, which entered a niche, provided by a particular regulatory regime, it was shown that such an approach can be used successfully in the presence of ongoing structural change. However, it was conceded that evidence of a logistic trajectory is necessary but not sufficient for accepting a self-organisational interpretation of growth, in preference to one which envisages such a path as a disequilibrium one between two equilibrium steady states.

In Foster and Wild (1998), it is argued that it is possible to establish whether a self-organisational process exists by examining the unexplained residuals generated by an ALDM using spectral methods. The estimated ALDM is viewed as reflecting the deterministic component of the growth process, with the non-deterministic component being picked up in the residuals. By applying moving window spectral methods it is possible to see if there is a tendency for a movement towards a stable equilibrium, as would be suggested by the disequilibrium interpretation of the logistic equation, or towards a state of structural instability, as would be suggested by self-organisation theory. The evidence from the chosen deposit institution case study provided strong support for the self-organisation interpretation.

Encouraging though this evidence is, it seems somewhat arbitrary to envisage a non-equilibrium process as one of fixed parameter determinism combined with non-deterministic elements. The combination of positive and negative feedback is well expressed in the logistic equation but one would expect that the parameters themselves in the ALDM should have emergent properties. The ALDM does not allow for parameter variation and, thus, any such variation must also be consigned to the residuals. Unpublished exploratory research by the authors, using varying parameter estimation based upon Kalman filter methods, did confirm that the limit to which a system tends does itself evolve. However, because the evolution of the limit is also subject to a logistic trajectory, it was found that the fixed parameter logistic could still capture nonequilibrium 'meta parameters' which are informative and meaningful. From a non-equilibrium perspective, it is difficult to separate the evolution of the limit from the evolution of the system itself. They clearly must co-evolve if we are to retain the idea of a nonequilibrium trajectory.

The key issue is whether the basin of attraction around the moving *local* equilibrium changes. Such movement relates to the manner in which the system under investigation can cope with external shocks. This, in turn, relates to the flexibility of the system. Thus, the residuals we examined using spectral methods should contain parametric variation. The parameters of an estimated logistic equation should have a 'fuzzy' quality, which should reduce as structural development occurs. We can interpret the presence of such a quality as reflecting nonlinearities in the system which cannot be captured in a linear regression equation. When a self-organising system reaches the saturation phase of its development, we should expect to observe rises in parameter variation, associated with breakdown in the system, culminating in structural discontinuity, when the basic logistic equation itself should break down.

Viewing residual error as affected by varying states of parameter fuzziness, as well as the effect of external shocks, requires a different perspective on modelling. In the remainder of this paper we shall explain how such a perspective can be operationalised and then we shall apply it to our case study.

2 Fuzzy Set Theory: A Brief Introduction

Fuzzy set theory is a system of multivalued logic introduced by Lotfi Zadeh in 1965 [1] as a way of dealing with the imprecision and uncertainty found in many 'real world' problems, particularly those involving lin-

[1] A number of attempts at producing systems of multivalued logic preceded Zadeh (1965). See McNeil and Frieburger (1993) for an account of these developments.

guistic variables. Although not free from criticism [2], fuzzy set theory has been successfully applied in a number of disciplines, the most conspicuous being control theory in engineering and expert systems in computer science. As well as these applied fields, there is a large body of literature that develops fuzzy mathematics corresponding to many of the areas of standard mathematics. Fortunately, all that is required to proceed to fuzzy regression is an understanding of the basic concepts of fuzzy set theory. These concepts are presented in this section following a very brief review of some ideas from classical set theory.

Classical set theory is one of the foundation stones of modern mathematics. It utilises a system of bivalent logic that has been predominant in Western thought for more than two millennia and is based on two axioms which Aristotle (384-322 BC) proposed in his *Metaphysics*. The first is the Law of Contradictions which forbids a statement being both true and not true at the same time. The second is the Law of the Excluded Middle which disallows anything other than these mutually exclusive truth values (McNeil and Frieburger, 1993)[3]. In classical set theory an element either belongs to a set or it does not i.e. for a collection of elements $x \in X$, each element can either belong or not belong to a set A, $A \subseteq X$. The statement "x belongs to A" is either true or it is not.

As an example, consider a set whose elements consist of tall men. Using classical set theory we must choose some (arbitrary) height, say 180cm, as a cut-off point above which men are tall and below which men are not tall. Fuzzy set theory abandons Aristotle's axioms and allows an element to *partially* belong to a set, consequently it can also partially belong to a complementary set. In our example of a set of tall men, we may decide that all men above 185cm are definitely tall and we assign them 100% membership of the set; men who are less than 165cm are definitely not tall and have a degree membership equal to zero; and men whose height lies between 165cm and 185cm have a degree of membership that lies between zero and 100%. The men in the intermediate range belong to both the set "tall" and its compliment "not tall". Figure 1 shows representations of the classical and fuzzy sets of tall men.

---

[2] For example, see Laviolette (1995).

[3] The Law of Contradictions: The same thing cannot at the same time both belong and not belong to the same object and in the same respect.

The Law of the Excluded Middle: Of any subject, one thing must be either asserted or denied. (quoted in McNeill and Frieberger, 1993, p53)

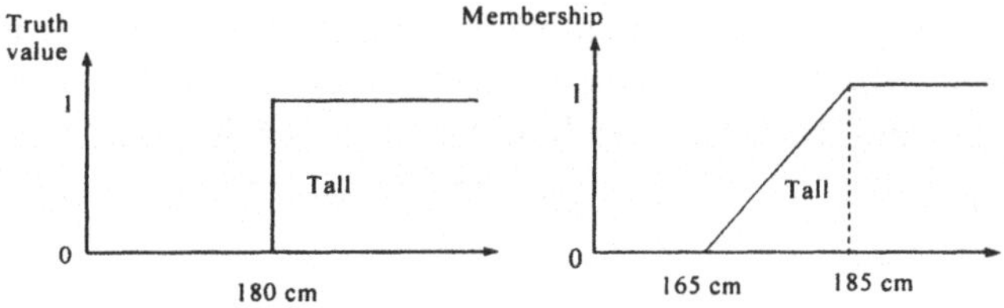

Classical set Fuzzy set **Fig. 1.**

A fuzzy set, then, is made up of ordered pairs where the first component of a pair is the element of the set and the second is that element's grade of membership of the fuzzy set[4]. For some element x of fuzzy set $\widetilde{A}$, the membership function $\mu_{\widetilde{A}}(x)$ is generally normalised so it takes values from zero to one. The shape of the membership function is ad hoc, but triangular membership functions are often used for tractability.

The question that naturally arises is how can the concept of a fuzzy set be used in economic analysis. One method is in the representation of empirical relationships. In orthodox econometrics the imprecise nature of observed economic relationships is represented by assuming that variables have a stochastic component. An alternative approach is to define the parameters as fuzzy numbers. For example, a parameter may described as being equal to "about 4". This value can be represented by the fuzzy number $\widetilde{4}$ with a triangular membership function centred on the crisp number 4 (Figure 2).

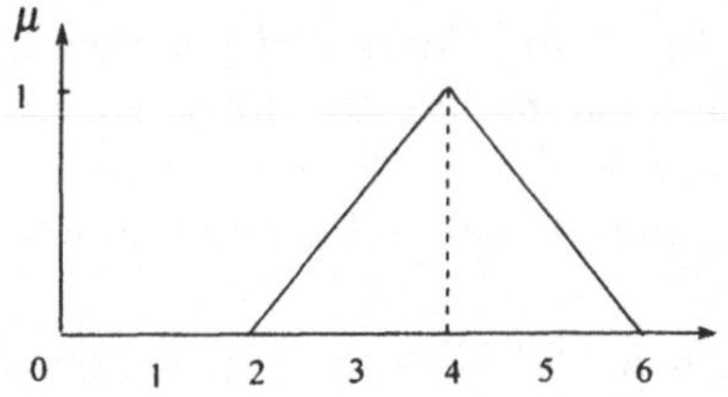

Fig. 2.

[4] Zimmerman (1991, p 11) formally defines a fuzzy set as follows:

> If X is a collection of objects denoted generally by x then a fuzzy set $\widetilde{A}$ in X is a set of ordered pairs
>
> $$\widetilde{A} = \{x, \mu_{\widetilde{A}}(x) | x \in X\}$$
>
> where $\mu_{\widetilde{A}}(x)$ is the membership function or grade of membership of x in $\widetilde{A}$ which maps X to the membership space M. The range of the membership function is a subset of non negative numbers whose supremum is finite.

The benefit of using a triangular membership function can be seen from this example as the fuzzy set can be completely specified in terms of the *apex* of the triangle and the *spread* i.e. half the length of the base. For some element t of the fuzzy set $\widetilde{T}$, with apex T and spread s, the membership function is given by

$$\mu_t(t) = 1 - \min\{1, |t - T|/s\} \tag{2.1}$$

The values for which the fuzzy set has non zero grades of membership are called the *support* of the fuzzy set and the upper and lower limits are the *support boundaries*.

In the next section the concept of a fuzzy number is extended to that of a fuzzy equation and the fuzzy regression problem is introduced. A more detailed introduction to fuzzy mathematics and its applications can be found in Klir and Yuan (1995) or Zimmerman (1991). An introduction to fuzzy set theory can also be found in Mansur (1995) who applies fuzzy mathematics to problems of economic theory, in particular the analysis of oligopolistic competition.

3 Fuzzy Regression and Fuzzy Equations

There are a number of approaches to fuzzy regression. As with probabilistic regression estimation procedures such as maximum likelihood, least squares and linear programming can be used. Three types of fuzzy regression model can also be identified. One approach assumes the data are crisp (precise) and the model parameters are fuzzy numbers. Alternatively, the data can be treated as being fuzzy and the model parameters crisp. In the third model both the data and parameters are fuzzy. Kacprzyk and Fedrizzi (1992) contains a comprehensive collection of papers covering these categories of fuzzy regression model and estimation procedures.

In this paper a linear fuzzy regression model with fuzzy parameters and crisp data is examined and the estimation method used is a least squares procedure developed by Aivars Celminš (1987b). This relatively simple model is a useful starting point to the investigation of fuzzy regression as it is analogous to probabilistic ordinary least squares used widely in econometrics. It is also useful as the basic concepts outlined here can be extended to more complex estimation problems. Celminš (1987a,b, 1991, 1992) has developed least squares estimation procedures for all three categories of fuzzy regression model with model functions that are multidimensional and nonlinear in the parameters. Celminš (1992, p. 153) states in relation to other types of fuzzy regression: 'Our approach differs from these in that our models and data structures are more general and that we are not striving for exact solutions but are content with approximate estimates of the fuzziness of the solution.' Celminš uses his method to analyse cross sectional data in ballistics research but in this paper we apply it to time series data. In this context the accuracy of the fuzziness of the solution is not a major issue and, as is shown below, the point estimates of the model parameters are comparable to OLS estimates. The primary feature of interest of Celminš method is that it appears to provide a way of estimating and interpreting parameter variation through time.

Before considering Celminš' regression algorithm in the next section, some of the features of the fuzzy function that represents the imprecise economic relationship are considered.

The model equation for the fuzzy regression with crisp data and fuzzy parameters is:

$$y = \boldsymbol{X}\widetilde{\boldsymbol{T}}$$

or $y = \tilde{t}_1 + \tilde{t}_2 x_2 + \tilde{t}_3 x_3 + \ldots + \tilde{t}_p x_p$

where $\widetilde{\boldsymbol{T}}$ is the p-dimensional vector of fuzzy parameters.

Being a fuzzy set, the parameter vector $\widetilde{\boldsymbol{T}}$ is represented by a set of ordered pairs:

$$\widetilde{\boldsymbol{T}} = \left\{ \boldsymbol{t}, \mu_{T}(\boldsymbol{t}) \middle| \boldsymbol{t} \in \boldsymbol{R}_p \right\}$$

where $\boldsymbol{t}$ is an arbitrary crisp element of the fuzzy set and $\mu_{T}(\boldsymbol{t})$ is that element's grade of membership of $\widetilde{\boldsymbol{T}}$.

Celminš' method assumes the function is twice differentiable with respect to the relevant components and the membership function is given by a p-dimensional conical function. [5] Figure 3 illustrates the case where $\widetilde{\boldsymbol{T}}$ is a 2 dimensional fuzzy vector i.e. where $\widetilde{\boldsymbol{T}}$ has two fuzzy components $(\tilde{t}_1, \tilde{t}_2)$.

The triangular membership functions of the components, $\tilde{t}_1$ and $\tilde{t}_2$, are obtained by projecting from the vector's conical membership function to the corresponding coordinate axis. The area within the elliptical base is the *support* of $\widetilde{\boldsymbol{T}}$ and the ellipse is the *support boundary* of $\widetilde{\boldsymbol{T}}$. Note also

[5] Celminš (1987b, p. 669) states that 'The restriction to model parameter vectors with conical membership functions is probably of minor importance because of the general uncertainty of the particulars of the fuzziness of the fitting function.'

that the principal axes of the support ellipsoid are not necessarily parallel to the coordinate axes.

Just as the 1-dimensional fuzzy number with a triangular membership function can be described by the apex and spread of the membership function (Equation 2.1), a fuzzy vector with a conical membership function can be fully specified by the crisp *apex*, $\boldsymbol{T}$, and the *panderance matrix* $\boldsymbol{P}_T$ of the fuzzy vector.

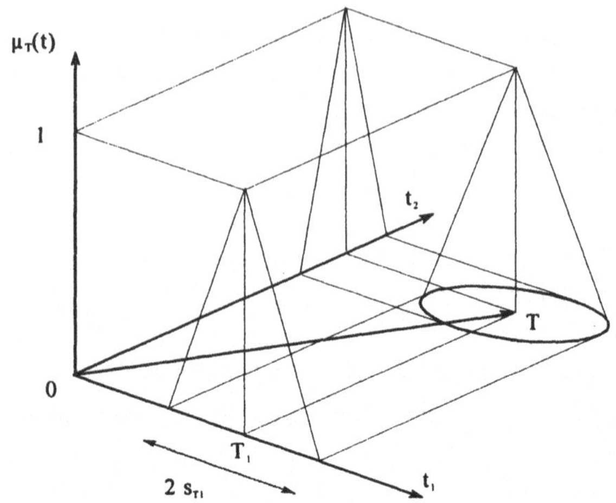

Fig. 3. (From Celminš, 1991)

The panderance matrix warrants a brief discussion as it plays an important role in the Celminš fuzzy regression procedure. The panderance matrix is a positive definite matrix, the diagonal elements of which are the square of the spreads of the corresponding components of $\tilde{\boldsymbol{T}}$. The off diagonal elements, e.g. p_{ij}, show the interaction between components $\tilde{t}_i$ and $\tilde{t}_j$. It defines the membership function as follows. The distance between an arbitrary element $\boldsymbol{t}$ of $\tilde{\boldsymbol{T}}$ and the apex $\boldsymbol{T}$ is given by the elliptic norm

$$\|\boldsymbol{t}-\boldsymbol{T}\| = \left[(\boldsymbol{t}-\boldsymbol{T})^T \boldsymbol{P}_T^{-1}(\boldsymbol{t}-\boldsymbol{T})\right]^{1/2}$$

and the membership function for element $\boldsymbol{t}$ is

$$\mu_T(\boldsymbol{t}) = 1 - \min\{1, \|\boldsymbol{t}-\boldsymbol{T}\|\}$$

The elliptical boundaries of the support of the membership function are given by the equation

$$(\boldsymbol{t}-\boldsymbol{T})\boldsymbol{P}_T(\boldsymbol{t}-\boldsymbol{T})=1.$$

The solution to the fuzzy regression model is a fuzzy equation and some of its characteristics are now considered. Since $\widetilde{\boldsymbol{T}}$ is a fuzzy parameter vector, the fuzzy equation

$$y=\tilde{f}(\boldsymbol{X})=f(\boldsymbol{X},\widetilde{\boldsymbol{T}})$$

is made up of a set of crisp equations $y=f(\boldsymbol{X},\boldsymbol{t})$ with crisp parameter vectors, $\boldsymbol{t}$. In other words, a fuzzy equation is a fuzzy set of equations. Any fixed $\boldsymbol{t}$ of $\widetilde{\boldsymbol{T}}$ defines a particular crisp equation of the fuzzy set of equations and therefore defines a crisp relationship between components of $\boldsymbol{X}$. The crisp equations $y=f(\boldsymbol{X},\boldsymbol{t})$, which are elements of the fuzzy equation $y=f(\boldsymbol{X},\widetilde{\boldsymbol{T}})$, are assigned the same membership value that $\boldsymbol{t}$ has of $\widetilde{\boldsymbol{T}}$ i.e.

$$\mu_f(f(\boldsymbol{X},\boldsymbol{t}))=\mu_T(\boldsymbol{t}).$$

The membership function of $f(\boldsymbol{X},\widetilde{\boldsymbol{T}})$ is specified in terms of the distance between the crisp "apex" function $f(\boldsymbol{X},\boldsymbol{T})$ and an arbitrary crisp element $f(\boldsymbol{X},\boldsymbol{t})$ so that

$$\|f(\boldsymbol{X},\boldsymbol{t})-f(\boldsymbol{X},\boldsymbol{T})\|_{fT}=\|\boldsymbol{t}-\boldsymbol{T}\|_T=\left[(\boldsymbol{t}-\boldsymbol{T})^T\boldsymbol{P}_T^{-1}(\boldsymbol{t}-\boldsymbol{T})\right]^{1/2}$$

The solution $\boldsymbol{X}_f(\boldsymbol{t})$ of the crisp equation $y=f(\boldsymbol{X},\boldsymbol{t})$ is a hypersurface which is the set of all points $\boldsymbol{X}$ that satisfy the equation. The fuzzy solution $\widetilde{\boldsymbol{X}}_f$ contains all points $\boldsymbol{X}$ which satisfy $y=f(\boldsymbol{X},\widetilde{\boldsymbol{T}})$ for some $\boldsymbol{t}\in\widetilde{\boldsymbol{T}}$ and any point $\boldsymbol{X}$ has a set (possibly empty) of parameters, $\boldsymbol{t}$, having a membership value $\mu_t(\boldsymbol{t})$ which satisfy the fuzzy equation. $\boldsymbol{X}$, the crisp element of the fuzzy solution $\widetilde{\boldsymbol{X}}_f$, is assigned the highest membership value of that set of parameters

$$\mu_f(\boldsymbol{X})=\max_{t:f(\boldsymbol{X},\boldsymbol{t})=0}\mu_t(\boldsymbol{t})$$

If X does not solve $y = f(X, \widetilde{T})$ for any $t \in \widetilde{T}$, i.e. $X \notin \widetilde{X}_f$, then X has a zero membership grade.

Thus the concept of a fuzzy number described here provides a method of representing imprecise relationships between variables that is fundamentally different to the probabilistic representation found in orthodox econometrics. Using Celminš approach the regression problem becomes one of estimating the apex value of the fuzzy number and its spread. The next section provides an overview of the least squares algorithm that yields a solution for the fuzzy regression problem.

4 Celminš Least Squares Algorithm for a Fuzzy Model

In the previous section we saw that an imprecise relationship can be represented by a fuzzy equation $y = f(X, \widetilde{T})$. This fuzzy equation is a set of crisp equations $y = f(X, t)$ where t is an element of the fuzzy set $\widetilde{T}$ with a degree of membership given by

$$\mu_T(t) = 1 - \min\{1, \|t - T\|\} \tag{4.1}$$

The regression problem is one of finding an estimate of the fuzzy parameters, i.e. finding an estimate of the crisp apex vector T and the panderance matrix P_T where spread of the elements of the T are equal to square roots of the diagonal elements of P_T. For a given set of observation vectors $(y_i, X_i) \in R_{p+1}$ $i = 1, \ldots s$, we require that the model equation is satisfied at the observed points for parameter values t_i that have a high grade of membership of $\widetilde{T}$. In other words, the crisp equation $y_i = f(X_i, t_i)$ passing through observation point i, should have a high membership value, $\mu_T(t)$, of the fuzzy equation $y = f(X, \widetilde{T})$. It follows that an observation vector $X_i = (1, x_{2,i}, \ldots, x_{p,i})$ will then also have a high grade of membership of the fuzzy solution $\widetilde{X}_f$.

The problem can be reformulated by letting c_i, the *local parameter corrections*, represent the difference between T and t_i i.e. $T + c_i = t_i$. Now we want to satisfy the equation

$$y_i = f(X_i, T + c_i) \quad i = 1, \ldots, s \tag{4.2}$$

for small values of c_i.

It is the local parameter corrections that are of particular interest in time series analysis as they can be interpreted as the temporal parameter variation about the apex parameter values. Given the appropriate model, they may have a meaningful interpretation. This is one of the features of this form of fuzzy regression which differentiates it from probabilistic regression. The interpretation of the local parameter corrections is discussed further in the following section.

Celminš (1987b) shows that a solution to the regression problem can be found in terms of the following least squares minimisation problem.[6]

Minimis $$W = \sum_{i=1}^{s} \boldsymbol{c}_i \boldsymbol{P}_T^{-1} \boldsymbol{c}_i \tag{4.3}$$

subject to $$f(\boldsymbol{X}_i, \boldsymbol{T} + \boldsymbol{c}_i) = y_i \quad i = 1,\ldots,s \tag{4.4}$$

and $$\mu_T(\boldsymbol{T} + \boldsymbol{c}_i) > \gamma^* \quad i = 1,\ldots,s \tag{4.5}$$

The second constraint (4.5) specifies the minimum membership value which the crisp parameter solution $\boldsymbol{t}_i$ has of $\widetilde{\boldsymbol{T}}$. This value may vary depending on the problem. The simplest approach and the one that will be adopted here is to require all elements $\boldsymbol{t}_i$ of $\widetilde{\boldsymbol{T}}$ to have a membership grade greater than zero.

The constrained minimisation problem has been stated in terms of three crisp unknowns $\boldsymbol{T}$, $\boldsymbol{c}_i$ and $\boldsymbol{P}_T$ with observation vector (y_i, $\boldsymbol{X}_i$) and the form of the function given. The problem is formulated in terms of a Lagrangian function and solutions found for the normal equations to give explicit linear equations for $\boldsymbol{T}$ and $\boldsymbol{c}_i$:

$$\boldsymbol{T} = \boldsymbol{P}^E \sum_{i=1}^{s} g_i y_i (1, x_{2,i}, \cdots, x_{p,,i})^T \tag{4.6}$$

$$\boldsymbol{c}_i = -g_i(\boldsymbol{X}_i \boldsymbol{T} - y_i)\boldsymbol{P}^E (1, x_{2,i}, \cdots, x_{p,i})^T \tag{4.7}$$

where g_i is the weight of the i-th observation and $\boldsymbol{P}^E$ is the estimate of the panderance matrix. The weights, g_i, are calculated according to

$$g_i = 1 \Big/ \left[(1, x_{1,i} \cdots x_{p,i}) \boldsymbol{P}^E (1, x_{1,i} \cdots x_{p,i})^T \right] \tag{4.8}$$

The minimisation problem as it is formulated above in Equations (4.3), (4.4) and (4.5) assumes that the panderance matrix, $\boldsymbol{P}_T$, is known.

---

[6] See Celminš (1987b) or Morgan (1996) for a more detailed exposition of the estimation procedure.

However it is not known and in Equations (4.6) to (4.8) an estimate of the panderance matrix is used. It can be shown that the estimated panderance matrix can be calculated using Equation (4.9).

$$\boldsymbol{P}^{E} = \left[\sum_{i=1}^{s} g_i \boldsymbol{f}_{\theta i}^{T} \boldsymbol{f}_{\theta i}\right]^{-1} \tag{4.9}$$

where $f_{\theta i}$ is the differential of the function with respect to the parameter vector, i.e. the vector $\boldsymbol{X}_i = (1, x_{2,i}, \ldots, x_{p,i})$.

The problem is not solved at this stage as there is a circular relationship between $\boldsymbol{P}^{E}$ and g_i in Equations (4.8) and (4.9). Celminš (1987b) proposes an iterative estimation procedure to solve for $\boldsymbol{T}$ and $\boldsymbol{P}_T$ concurrently. This procedure utilises the fact that the degree of fuzziness of the estimated equation is, in one sense, arbitrary. For example, consider the two dimensional vector in Figure 3. The elliptical boundary of the membership support can be increased or decreased, that is the vector made more or less fuzzy, by scaling the panderance matrix up or down. The scaling affects the magnitude of the spreads of the elements but not the relationship between the spreads. The membership values of the elements of the fuzzy set are adjusted appropriately. Similarly the panderance matrix of the fuzzy regression equation can be scaled up or down. Once estimates of $\boldsymbol{T}$ and $\boldsymbol{P}_T$ are made, the panderance matrix can be scaled so that the observation furthermost from the fuzzy solution will lie just on the support boundary. This means that constraint (4.5) is met for $\gamma^* = 0$. The distance measure between a crisp observation, $\boldsymbol{X}_i$, and the fuzzy solution $\widetilde{\boldsymbol{X}}_f$ is given by the *discord* (Celminš 1987b)

$$D_i = \left|\boldsymbol{X}_i\boldsymbol{T} - y_i\right|\left(\boldsymbol{f}_{\theta i}\boldsymbol{P}_T\boldsymbol{f}_{\theta i}^{T}\right)^{-1/2}$$

where $\left(\boldsymbol{f}_{\theta i}\boldsymbol{P}_T\boldsymbol{f}_{\theta i}^{T}\right)^{1/2}$ is the spread of the function.

The iteration procedure is as follows. An initial approximation is made of $\boldsymbol{P}_T$ using Equation (4.9) with $g_i = 1$ and Equation (4.6) is solved. This provides an initial estimate of the apex $\boldsymbol{T}$. The panderance matrix is then scaled so that the observation with the greatest discord lies on the support boundary and has a membership value of zero. The scaling factor is the value of the discord for this observation. All other observations have a membership value greater than zero. New weights, g_i, are calculated using Equation (4.8) and the scaled estimate of the panderance matrix. These weights are used in Equation (4.9) to calculate a revised estimate of the panderance matrix. Equation (4.6) is solved again and the procedure repeated. Each iteration provides a better estimate of $\boldsymbol{T}$ and $\boldsymbol{P}_T$

and the process is continued until a suitable convergence criterion is satisfied. Once convergence has been achieved the local parameter corrections are calculated using Equation (4.7).

In summary, the algorithm produces estimates of the fuzzy parameter vector $\tilde{\boldsymbol{T}}$, i.e. $\boldsymbol{T}$ and $\boldsymbol{P}_T$, and the local parameter corrections $\boldsymbol{c}_i$. The parameter apex vector $\boldsymbol{T}$ provides an estimate of the central tendency of the function. The spreads, i.e. the degree of fuzziness, of the elements of $\boldsymbol{T}$ are obtained by taking the square root of the diagonal elements of the panderance matrix $\boldsymbol{P}_T$. The off diagonal elements capture the interactions between the components of $\tilde{\boldsymbol{T}}$. The local parameter corrections, $\boldsymbol{c}_i$, are here interpreted as capturing the temporal parameter variation in a time series model. In the following section the results of a fuzzy regression are compared to the results of an OLS regression and the use of the local parameter corrections is demonstrated.

5 The Case of Australian Building Society Deposits

In Foster and Wild (1995) an augmented logistic diffusion modelling (ALDM) approach was developed to apply in periods of growth which could be associated with structural development of a self-organisational type. The growth of the market share of deposits in Australian Building Societies in the postwar era of bank regulation was selected as a good example, involving obvious increases in complexity and organisation, both in the range of services offered and the organisational innovations introduced within Societies. In all aspects of the retail deposit market, they represented the leading edge of change. Strong evidence was discovered that a logistic diffusion trajectory was present. In Foster and Wild (1998) it is established, using moving window spectral methods, that there is support for the view that such a trajectory was indeed of a self-organisational type. In this paper, we use the same example for comparative purposes. Using monthly data, the following ALDM was estimated:

$$\begin{aligned}\ln(B)_t-\ln(B)_{t-1} &= b_1[1-(B/M4_{t-1}/k)] - b_1 a[\ln(R_b/R_a)_t..\ln(R_b/R_a)_{t-n}]\\ &+b_2[\{\ln(R_b/R_a)_t-\ln(R_b/R_a)_{t-1}\}\ldots\{\ln(R_b/R_a)_{t-n}-\ln(R_b/R_a)_{t-n1}\}]\\ &+ c[\ln(B)_t-ln(B)_{t-1}]_{t-1} + m[\ln(M4)_t-\ln(M4)_{t-1}] + e_t \qquad (5.1)\end{aligned}$$

where:
- B: building society deposits
- M4: bank plus building society deposits
- R_b: average rate of interest on building society deposits
- R_a: average rate of interest on bank deposits

Table 1. OLS estimates of eq.(5.1) for 1967(11) to 1988 (8) [a]

Variable	Coefficient	Std.Error	t-value
Constant	0.016534	0.0020292	8.148
$B/M4_{t-1}$	-0.087599	0.0112870	-7.761
$d\ln(R_b/R_a)_t$	0.023656	0.0093019	2.543
$d\ln(R_b/R_a)_{t-3}$	0.017400	0.0092186	1.888
$d\ln(R_b/R_a)_{t-7}$	0.016857	0.0095484	1.765
$d\ln(R_b/R_a)_{t-9}$	0.021391	0.0093088	2.298
$d\ln(R_b/R_a)_{t-12}$	0.017067	0.0096515	1.768
$d\ln(R_b/R_a)_{t-14}$	0.026683	0.0092931	2.871
$d\ln(R_b/R_a)_{t-15}$	0.016035	0.0094348	1.700
$d\ln(B)_{t-1}$	0.509000	0.0458870	11.093
$d\ln(M4)$	0.423120	0.0747140	5.663
plus 8 significant monthly impulse dummies			
R^2Adj.	=0.779288 F(18, 231)=45.312 [0.0000]		
σ	=0.00623193 DW= 2.08		
Variance Instability Test:	0.6197* [b]		
Joint Instability Test:	4.97487*		
AR 1- 7F(7,224) =	0.83771 [0.5570]		
ARCH 7 F(7,217) =	0.82098 [0.5708]		
Normality Chi²(2) =	2.5605 [0.2780]		
Xi² F(28,202) =	1.0057 [0.4634]		
Xi*Xj F(150, 80) =	0.98781 [0.5328]		
RESET F(1,230) =	1.2309 [0.2684]		

[a] '*d*' denotes the first difference of a variable.
[b] The * following both instability tests indicate that the null hypothesis of constancy was rejected at the 5% level of significance.

It is important in applying the fuzzy regression approach that we know that we are dealing with a relationship between variables which is robust. We can establish this by, first of all, applying OLS estimation to obtain a parsimonious representation of the growth process under consideration. In Table 1 below, the OLS results obtained from estimating an ALDM of the growth of Australian Building Societies are reproduced from Foster and Wild (1998). Table 2 contains the results from estimating the same model using the fuzzy regression method explained in Section 4.

Table 2. Fuzzy estimates of eq.(5.1) for 1967(11) to 1988 (8)

Variable	Coefficient Apex	Coefficient Spread
Constant	0.0118	0.03064
$B/M4_{t-1}$	-0.0931	0.1280
$d\ln(R_b/R_a)_t$	0.0224	0.1630
$d\ln(R_b/R_a)_{t-3}$	0.0067	0.1639
$d\ln(R_b/R_a)_{t-7}$	0.0152	0.1649
$d\ln(R_b/R_a)_{t-9}$	0.0219	0.1747
$d\ln(R_b/R_a)_{t-12}$	-0.0060	0.1814
$d\ln(R_b/R_a)_{t-14}$	0.0057	0.1682
$d\ln(R_b/R_a)_{t-15}$	-0.0016	0.1827
$d\ln(B)_{t-1}$	0.4452	0.5680
$d\ln(M4)$	0.6893	0.9710

The results reported in Tables 1 and 2 indicate that there is broad similarity between the apex values of the fuzzy regression and the OLS parameter estimates. The Appendix provides a graphical representation of the local parameter corrections for the parameters in the model. Instead of residual errors for the function, we have a set of local parameter variations for every month of our sample. Such a decomposition enables us to examine the process of structural development from a different perspective. The local parameter corrections are normalised by dividing by the respective parameter spreads. Normalisation is carried out as it is the oscillation of the corrections that is of interest. Dividing by the spreads makes the results dimensionless and comparable among the parameters. [7]

These results are striking. Prior to 1981 there is evidence of noticeable parameter fuzziness: this is most marked in the 1967-71 period for the constant term and the $B/M4_{(t-1)}$ term. This is in line with what we might expect from self-organisation theory – the early phase of structural development will be characterised by a turmoil of opportunity-taking and accelerating macroscopic growth. However, the most striking finding is that, by the early saturation phase (1981-1984), parameter fuzziness has diminished greatly. Once again, self-organisation theory suggests that, by

[7] Only the local parameter corrections for the first four interest rate differential terms are shown. The results for the remaining lags are similar and it is the other variables that provide the more interesting results.

the onset of saturation, the structure of the system becomes relatively rigid and inflexible. After 1985, following bank deregulation in 1984, we can see the impact of emerging structural 'micro-breakdowns'. In this period, across all three key parameters, fuzziness reaches its highest level. However, the fuzziness is more oscillatory in character than in the early phase of the logistic, echoing our findings using the evolutionary spectra approach.

On examining the local parameter corrections (lpcs) over the 1985-1988 period it is clear that the basic diffusion rate, captured by the constant term, has become increasingly unstable, but in an unbiased way around the crisp parameter. The lpcs on the logistic term behave differently: after the enactment of bank deregulation in 1984, there is a pronounced downward bias in the lpcs which implies a fall in the k limit. This is followed by an upward trend in the lpcs until early 1988, suggesting a recovery of k, as building societies attempted to adapt to the new regulatory regime in order to protect their market share. This trend was reversed in 1988 when a second phase of bank deregulation began to be enacted. The lpcs on the lagged dependent variable show the most oscillation. In the ALDM approach the inclusion of such a variable is justified because of the presence of homoeostatic 'cushioning' of shocks. Increased oscillation is indicative of the fact that micro-breakdowns in the system render such cushioning less effective. This is, again, what self-organisation theory predicts in the saturation phase.

The lpcs for the first differences of the interest rate differentials do not show such clear patterns – implying that depositors reactions to them did not change significantly along the logistic. However, close inspection does indicate that there is a general increase in fluctuation after about 1980. This may be associated with the changing phases of the logistic or it may be because of the emergence of a more complex range of deposit products and associated financial services. Our model is extremely simple, including only average interest rates on 'basic' deposits, so it is not possible to interpret these lpcs on any meaningful way.

In order to provide something other than visual analysis of the local parameter corrections, the sample period is broken up into three subsamples based on our interpretation of the underlying process, namely the periods from November 1967 to May 1981, June 1981 to May 1985, and June 1985 to the end of the sample in August 1988. These periods correspond to the pre-saturation phase, early saturation and late saturation, respectively. The variances of the lpcs were calculated for each variables across the different phases of the logistic and compared using the F-test for sample variances.[8] The results are recorded in Table 3. The null hypothesis that there is no statistically significant differences in the variances across phases is rejected for all the non-interest rate differential variables. As there are no discernible patterns in the lpcs of the interest rate differentials, the results for these variables are not recorded.

Table 3. F tests on parameter variances

	Nov-67 to May-81 vs Jun-81 to May-85	Jun-81 to May-85 vs Jun-85 to Aug-88	Nov-67 to May-81 vs Jun-85 to Aug-88
Variable	p value	p value	p value
Constant	1.75E-08	1.44E-12	0.001063
$B/M4_{t-1}$	2.04E-07	7.27E-10	0.016319
$d\ln(B)_{t-1}$	0.003327	8.34E-08	3.83E-05
$d\ln(M4)$	0.000785	1.45E-05	0.039159

It is apparent from these results that the fuzzy regression approach enables us to identify oscillatory patterns which can provide support for the hypothesis that the observation of a logistic diffusion trajectory is indicative of the presence of self-organisational development. An advantage over moving window spectral methods, applied to residual errors, is that we obtain information concerning specific parametric connections. However, the fuzzy regression approach we have adopted views all variation from a fixed parametric 'crisp' relationship as the sum of parametric variation. In practice, it makes sense to use both moving window spectral methods on OLS residuals and fuzzy regression techniques to discover if both offer compatible findings. Furthermore, when data limitations prevent the use of the former, it is always possible to adopt the latter approach.

[8] For two populations with a common characteristic that is normally distributed and has equal variances, the ratio of the sample variances, $F = \frac{s_1^2}{s_2^2}$, will follow an F distribution. The null hypothesis for the test is that the samples come from populations of equal variance.

6 Conclusions

In this paper we have introduced the fuzzy regression technique as a method suitable for identifying the presence of self-organisational change in circumstances where it can be shown that a growth path follows a logistic trajectory. The latter is viewed as reflecting the deterministic component of the process and the identification of local parameter corrections provides a way of decomposing the non-deterministic component of the process. We have shown that a logistic growth path, which has already exhibited self-organisational features, using moving window spectral methods, also exhibits such features using the fuzzy regression technique. Morgan (1996) has shown that, in an example where it can be argued that little in the way of structural change of a self-organisational type is likely to be present, the fuzzy regression technique provides confirmation that this is, indeed, the case. Thus, the fuzzy regression approach can provide a versatile estimation and diagnostic technique to apply, in addition to conventional econometric approaches. Furthermore, it offers a new perspective upon the presence of heteroskedasticity in econometric models. What is viewed as a 'problem' in conventional econometric modelling may provide a useful indication that self-organisational change underlies the time series data under consideration. The application of fuzzy regression methods can help to clarify whether this is the case. Naturally the interpretation offered here is dependent on the regression model being well specified. An omitted significant variable, for example, will have an impact on the local parameter corrections, just as it does on OLS residuals. In this example confidence in the specification of the model is based on the very extensive diagnostic testing carried out by Foster and Wild (1995, 1998).

However, what is offered in this paper remains exploratory and preliminary. More general fuzzy regression techniques can be used, for example, accounting for variable fuzziness, and they can be integrated into other varying parameter approaches, such as the Kalman Filter and its derivatives. Already, the results we have generated show that useful information can be provided to regulators and policy makers. These more complex approaches are likely to permit us to cope with greater degrees of nonlinearity than are present in a logistic equation, and, thus, help to establish more concrete links between the emerging 'science of complexity' and economic modelling using time series data.

References

Celminš, A. (1987a), 'Least Squares Model Fitting To Fuzzy Vector Data', *Fuzzy Sets and Systems*, 22, pp. 245-269.

Celminš, A. (1987b), 'Multidimensional Least-Squares Fitting Of Fuzzy Models', *Mathematical Modelling*, 9 (9), pp. 669-690.

Celminš, A. (1991), 'A Practical Approach To Nonlinear Fuzzy Regression', *SIAM Journal of Scientific and Statistical Computing*, 12 (3), pp. 521-546.

Celminš, A. (1992), Nonlinear Least-Squares Regression In Fuzzy Vector Spaces', in *Fuzzy Regression Analysis* ed. by J. Kacprzyk and M. Fedrizzi.

Celminš, A. (1994), 'Fitting A Fuzzy Function To Crisp Data', unpublished mimeo.

Celminš, A. (1996), 'Spread Of A Fuzzy Function', unpublished mimeo.

Foster, J. and Wild, P. (1995) 'The logistic diffusion approach to econometric moddeing in the presence of evolutionary change' UQ Department of Economics Discussion Paper No. 181.

Foster, J. and Wild, P. (1998) 'Detecting self-organisational change in economic processes exhibiting logistic growth' *Journal of Evolutionary Economics*, 8 (forthcoming).

Kacprzyk, J. and Fedrizzi, M. (1992), *Fuzzy Regression Analysis*, Warsaw: Omnitech.

Klir, G.J. and Yuan, B. (1995), *Fuzzy Sets And Fuzzy Logic: Theory and Applications*, Upper Saddle River: Prentice Hall PTR.

Laviolette, M. (1995), 'Fuzzy Logic: Great Hope or Grating Hype?', *Chance*, 8 (4), pp. 15-19.

Mansur, Y. M. (1995), Fuzzy Sets and Economics: Applications of fuzzy mathematics to non-cooperative oligopoly, Aldershot: Edward Elgar.

McNeill, D. and Frieburger, P. (1993), Fuzzy Logic: The Discovery of a Revolutionary Computer Technology - and How It Is Changing our World, New York: Simon and Schuster.

Morgan, B. (1996), 'Empirical Analysis in an Evolutionary Setting: A Fuzzy Approach', *European Association for Evolutionary Political Economy 1996 Conference Papers.*

Zadeh, L.A. (1965), 'Fuzzy Sets', *Information and Control*, 8, pp. 338-353.

Zimmermann, H. J. (1991), *Fuzzy Set Theory - and Its Applications*, Boston: Kluwer Academic Publishers.

Appendix: Graphical Representations of the Local Parameter Corrections

Constant

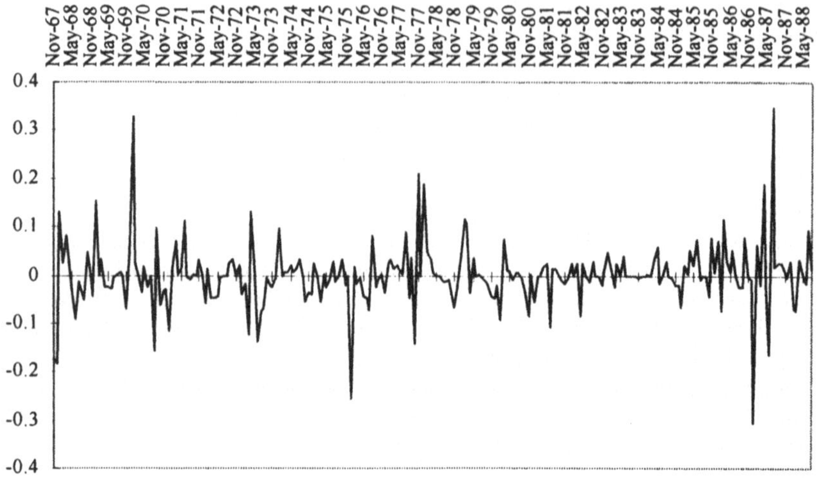

Local parameter corrections for the constant term

B/M4(t-1)

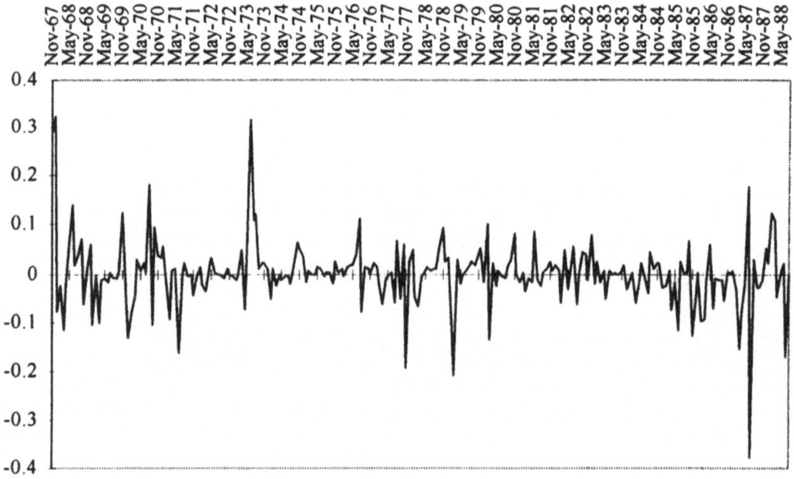

Local parameter corrections for the logistic term

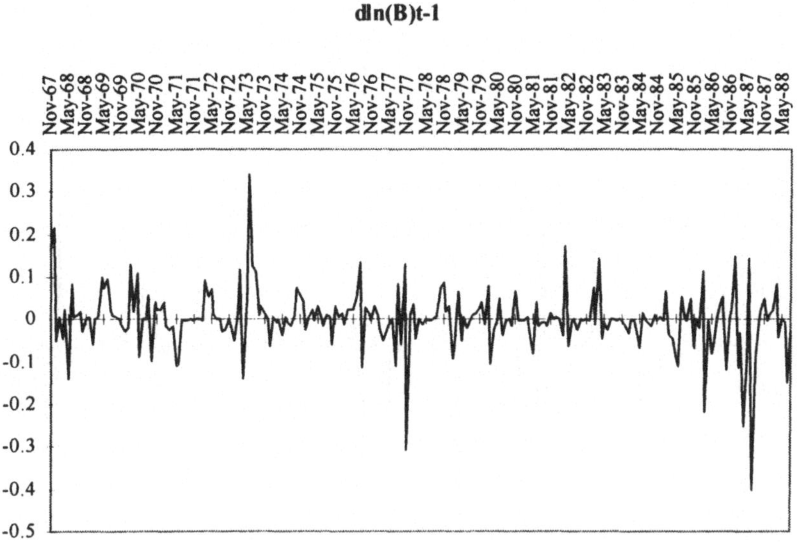

Local parameter corrections for the lagged dependent variable.

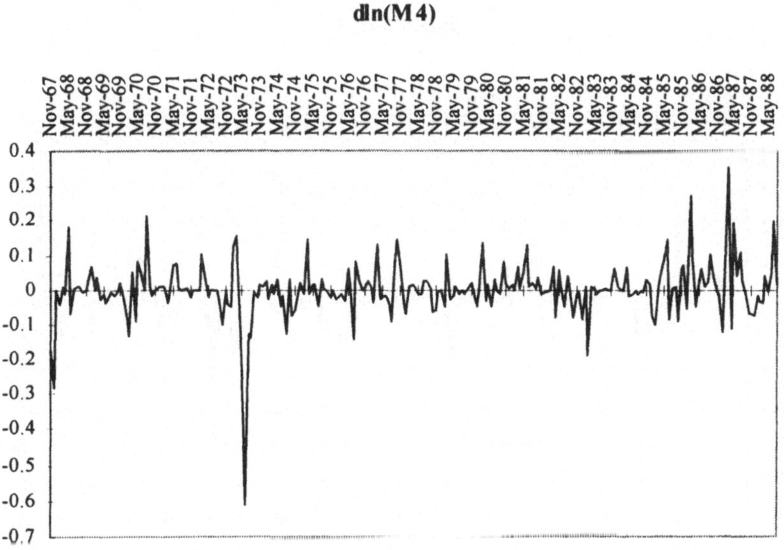

Local parameter corrections for the 'capacity growth' term.

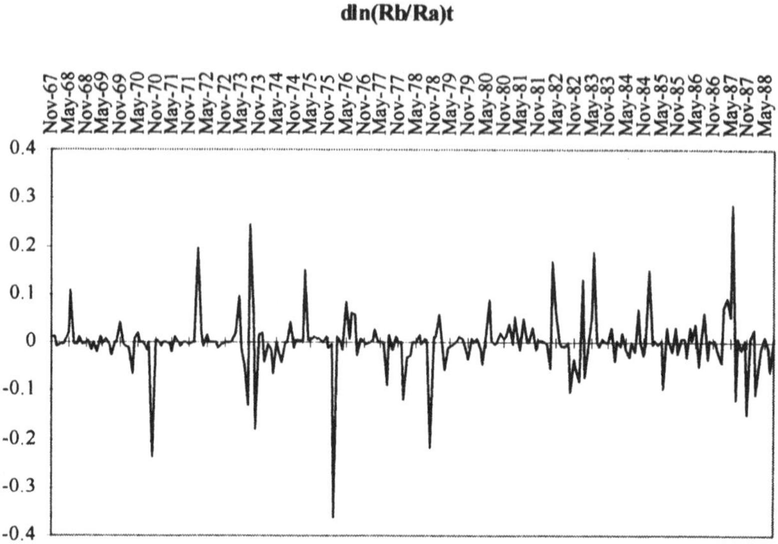

Local parameter corrections for the interest differential term.

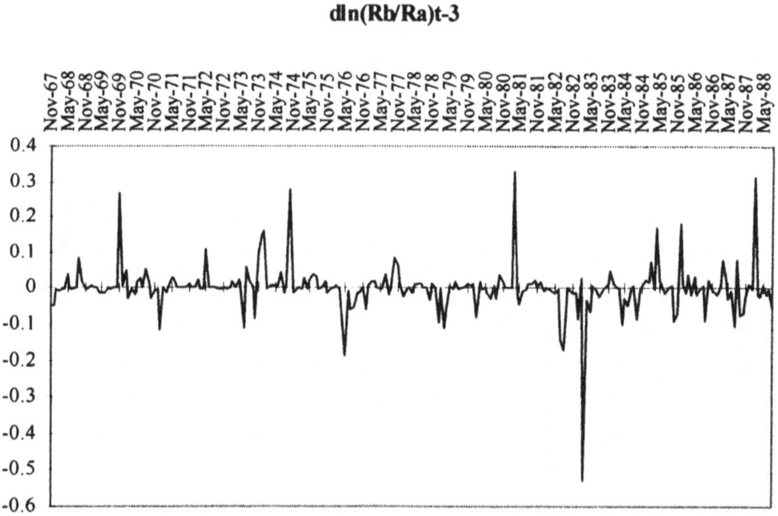

Local parameter corrections for the interest differential term lagged three periods.

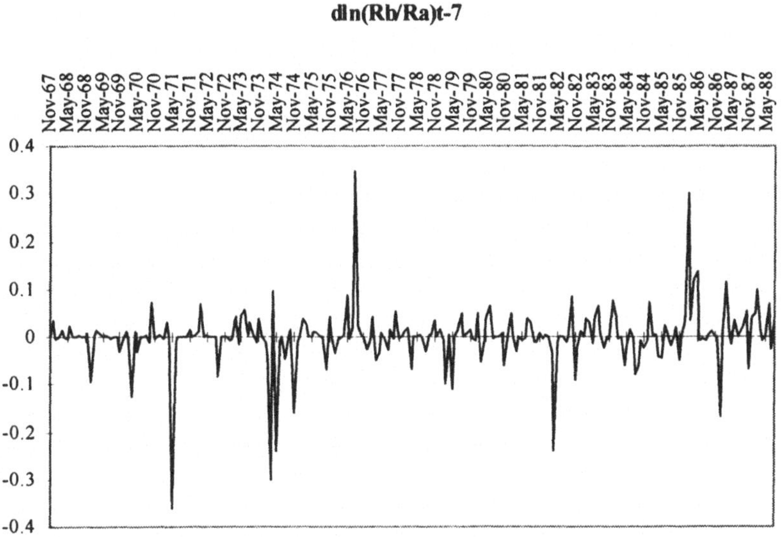

Local parameter corrections for the interest differential term lagged seven periods.

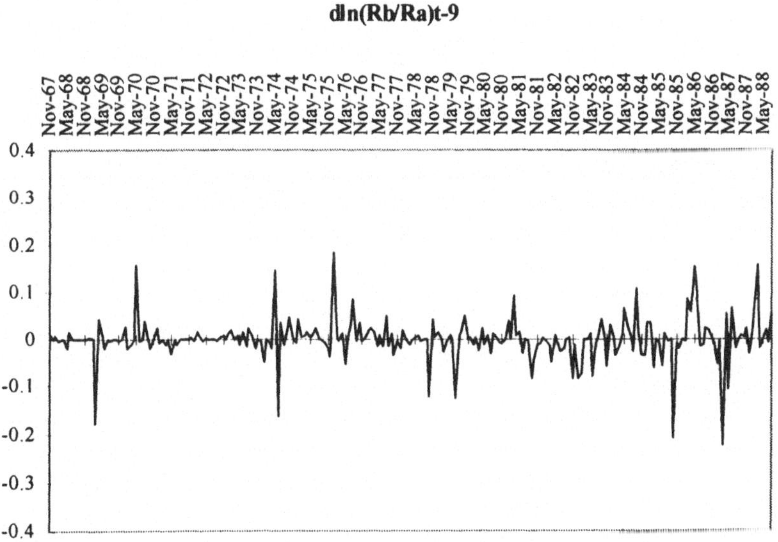

Local parameter corrections for the interest differential term lagged nine periods.

Variety and economic development: conceptual issues and measurement problems*

Koen Frenken[1], Pier Paolo Saviotti[2], Michel Trommetter[2]

[1]Centre for Science and Policy, University of Utrecht
P.O.Box 80083, 3508 TB Utrecht, The Netherlands,
e-mail: k.frenken@geog.uu.nl

[2]Institut National de la Recherche Agronomique (INRA), Unit Sociologie et Economie de la Recherche & Développement (SERD), Université Pierre Mendès-France, Boite Postale 47, 38040 Grenoble cedex 9, France,
e-mail: saviotti@grenoble.inra.fr, michel@grenoble.inra.fr

Abstract: For any evolutionary theory of economic development, the understanding of the determinants of variety and its effects on economic systems is of central importance. On the one hand, increasing returns tend to standardize technologies thus reducing product variety. On the other hand, the resulting efficiency gains generate resources that allow for the development of new products that contribute to long-term growth. The net variety effect on economic systems remains an empirical question. We propose two variety measures, the entropy measure and Weitzman's maximum likelihood procedure. It is argued that the two measures are complementary since entropy indicates the variety in a frequency distribution, while Weitzman's measure is based on a distance measure. We apply both measures to data on product characteristics of aircraft (1913-1984) and helicopters (1940-1983). Aircraft variety has been increasing rapidly after the emergence of a dominant design in the thirties. The rising variety of aircraft is related to the increase of the span of performance, which is analogous to the size of the habitat of a biological species. The larger the habitat, the larger the number of niches which is expected to occur. A dominant design is established in each niche. Helicopter variety has been decreasing after a dominant design emerged as innovations hardly in-

* Koen Frenken gratefully acknowledges the financial support received from the European Commission under TMR-grant ERB4001GT961736. We are grateful to Stéphane Lemarié for his efforts put in the programming of the Weitzman measure. We thank Steven Klepper, Stéphane Lemarié, Alban Richard and two anonymous referees for their comments.

creased the span of performance. The presence of aircraft technology in the higher end of the helicopter market limited the commercial potential of technological improvements in helicopters.

Key Words: technological evolution, variety, niche theory, dominant design, product life-cycle, market differentiation, entropy, Weitzman

JEL-classification: L15 – L93 – O3

1 Introduction

The underlying motivation of this paper is the role of qualitative change in economic development. Modern economies contain a large number of entities (products, services, methods of production, competencies, individual and organisational actors, institutions), which are qualitatively novel and different with respect to those existing in previous economic systems. The observation that there has been a very great deal of qualitative change in economic development would probably not be denied by any economist. Where, however, there would be differences is about the role of qualitative change. In order to facilitate the discussion two extreme hypotheses can be introduced: first, qualitative change is an accidental by-product of economic development; second, qualitative change is an essential component of economic development. The first hypothesis is the one implicitly present in most economic growth models, where qualitative change is not denied, but it can only be accepted *ex post*. The second hypothesis is central to a Schumpeterian approach, in which radical innovations change the nature of the economic system and promote the long-term continuation of economic development.

In some previous papers by one of the authors, it is argued that the concept of variety is crucial in order to overcome the gap between modelling without qualitative change and more descriptive approaches which can encompass this phenomenon (Saviotti, 1991, 1994, 1996; Saviotti, Mani, 1995). Qualitative change has important implications for several aspects of economics. For example, one of the basic conditions of perfect competition, that all firms produce homogeneous and identical products, does not hold anymore. Several types of competition exist, ranging from perfect to monopolistic to Schumpeterian competition. Once qualitative change is taken into account, a unique framework encompassing all these types of competition can be developed. Furthermore, especially for radically new goods and services, users and producers cannot be aware of all their properties before they are created. Wants and preferences are created gradually by means of a learning process involving both producers and consumers. These considerations have implications for a truly dynamic demand theory.

The evolution of product variety can take many different shapes depending upon the rate of technical progress, the industrial dynamics, the market environment and the presence of dynamic increasing returns. The relative importance of the determinants of variety can be expected to be rather specific to technologies. For example, technologies that are used as components in final products may well show different dynamics than technologies used in final products. Furthermore, mass produced goods can be expected to depend more heavily on process innovation and dynamic increasing returns than specialised products. For this reason, it might be helpful to study the evolution of a substantial number of technologies in a systematic empirical way, as to find out which dynamics are rather general, and which dynamics are specific to particular technologies. This requires the development of a common methodology which is the central concern of the present study.

A particularly important application of the measurements of variety that we describe in this paper, is to test theories of industrial and technological evolution. Students of technological change have introduced concepts such as dominant design and product life-cycle (Utterback, Abernathy, 1975; Abernathy, Utterback, 1978), technological regime (Nelson, Winter, 1977), and technological paradigm (Dosi, 1982; Constant, 1980). The dominant design model holds that the number of competing designs increases initially but later falls as a set of standardized technological principles emerges. This standardization process is usually associated with a "lock-in" into a dominant design as a result of increasing returns to adoption (Arthur, 1989). Similarly, technological regimes and technological paradigms describe prolonged periods of incremental innovation within standardized technological frameworks.

Recently, these concepts have been incorporated into theories of industrial evolution. Such theories attempt to correlate the rates of entry and exit in an industry, the net number of firms at each time, and the product and process innovations that occur during the lifetime of the technology. Such theories can be considered modern versions of the product lifecycle hypothesis. Utterback and Suarez (1993) propose a theory of industrial 'shakeout' based on the emergence of a dominant design. After a convergence on a dominant design entry slows down and exit occurs. Similarly, Jovanovic and MacDonald (1994) assume that an exogenous technological innovation creates an industry and that a subsequent refinement of the initial innovation gives rise to further entry. Firms lacking behind in implementing this refinement are then forced to leave the market leading to a shakeout. Klepper (1996) developed a model in which increasing returns to R&D lead to an advantage to size that contributes to a shakeout (see also, Klepper, Simons, 1997). Without entering into the details of these models we can observe that they all rely heavily on concepts and measurements of technological change. For example, the concept of dominant design lacks an operational definition that allows us to establish its presence in a given industry at a given time. Furthermore, counts of product and process innovations are crucial to detect a dominant design and to link its presence to patterns of industrial organization.

The measures of product variety that we propose in this paper can be of great help in clarifying and testing the previous concepts and theories. Though this paper is not primarily aimed at detecting dominant designs, it can give us important insights about their emergence and implications. Dominant designs imply a convergence of technologies on a set of common characteristics. In this way, the variety of designs may fall, although this is not always the outcome, as it will be explained later. In other words, there is a relationship between variety and the emergence of a dominant design, even if this relationship is not simply an inverse proportionality. Furthermore, as it will be discussed at greater length later in this paper, variety can grow by means of the emergence of new niches, that later become fully fledged technological populations. Thus, during technological evolution, a given technology becomes more and more heterogeneous in the range of services it supplies. Whether a given dominant design can be dominant in all the niches into which a technology separates is thus an open question that we will discuss later.

The paper is organised as follows. In the second section, we summarise some theoretical considerations about the role of variety in economic growth and industrial evolution. In the third section, we compare two variety measures: the entropy measure and Weitzman's diversity measure. The properties of both measures are discussed for discrete and continuous data. It is argued that the two measures can be considered as being complementary, since they highlight different aspects of variety. In the fourth section, we apply both measures to product characteristics of 731 aircraft models (*1913-1984*) and 144 helicopter models (*1940-1983*). Both variety measures show an increase in aircraft variety and a decrease in helicopter variety. Our explanation of the observed differences is elaborated on the basis of niche theory. Summary and conclusions are listed in the final section.

2 The role of variety in economic development

Qualitative change creates new entities, which are different and distinguishable from the pre-existing ones. The composition of the economic system changes because new entities emerge and some pre-existing ones disappear. In order to understand the relationship between qualitative change and economic development, we need to be able to represent analytically and to measure the composition of an economy. Variety is the variable chosen here to represent and to measure the composition of the economic system. We can in principle think of defining and measuring variety as the net number of the distinguishable entities created by economic development. To be slightly more accurate, if we think of economic processes as the transformation of inputs into outputs, we can define variety as 'the number of actors, activities and objects necessary to characterise an economic system'. The concept of variety used here is similar to what biologists call diversity, by which they mean the number of species living in a given habitat (May, 1973; Pielou, 1977).

2.1 Variety and growth

Our concept of variety is intended to be applied to the development of large economic systems over long periods of time. It differs somewhat from the traditional use of the economic concept of variety in analyses on competition and of optimal product variety in a given state of technology and preferences (e.g., Lancaster, 1975). Here, we are interested in the evolution of technologies and of the user environments in which they operate. In earlier work, one of the authors discussed more explicitly the role of variety in economic development, and proposed two hypotheses (Saviotti, 1996):

- Hypothesis 1: The growth in variety is a necessary requirement for long-term economic development.
- Hypothesis 2: Variety growth, leading to new sectors, and productivity growth in pre-existing sectors, are complementary and not independent aspects of economic development.

There is both empirical evidence and theoretical support for these two hypotheses. Empirically, the variety of several technologies has been observed to grow, in some cases enormously, during the last two hundred years. Although this phenomenon is not reflected in some economic statistics (e.g. output), the evidence for variety growth is considerable. The absence of variety from economic statistics is rather a proof that measurements are not blindly empirical, but that they reflect pre-theoretical categories. No one who is unaware or uninterested in variety will try to measure it.

The theoretical support for the two hypotheses comes from Pasinetti's models (1981, 1993) of economic development and structural change. These models contain a variable number of sectors, that is, they take into account the composition of the economic system and its relationship to economic development, a problem that is almost excluded *ex ante* from traditional and new growth models. According to Pasinetti, an economy with a constant composition, constant productivity growth and saturation of demand in particular goods and services, would not be stable. Such an economy would generate under-utilisation of resources, including unemployment. However, while technological change leading to productivity growth would be partly responsible for this imbalance, it could also provide a form of compensation. Technological change creates new goods and services, and therefore new sectors, which can 're-employ' the resources made redundant by the imbalance arising in the pre-existing sectors.[1] For this reason, one expects variety to grow at least at the supra-sectoral level. Thus, the above hypotheses can be expected to hold only at relatively high levels of aggregation (e.g. that of a national economy) and over long periods of time.

Even if Pasinetti is exceptional in taking into account explicitly the composition of the economic system, some other growth models include aspects of the changing composition of the economic system. For example, Romer's models (1987, 1990) include the growth in the number of capital goods amongst the consequences of innovation. More recently, Weitzman (1998) proposed to extend the neo-classical growth model with a production function for new knowledge which is generated by means of recombining existing knowledge. The underlying combinatorial logic in the growth in 'ideas' can be expected to lead to a growing variety. These models provide some support for the hypothesis of variety growth.

2.2 Variety and industry evolution

The attempts to measure variety in the following part of this paper are limited to the industry level. The two previous hypotheses were expected to hold only at a sufficiently high level of aggregation, yet this level of aggregation was not defined, even if a national economy was given as an example. Our data here are at the industry level but cover the most important producing countries. Thus the level of aggregation chosen is both higher and lower than the one we had given as an example. Even more fundamentally, we do not exactly know what is the minimum level of aggregation. The basic economic mechanisms leading to variety growth may well apply to individual sectors too, provided that they make up a large part of the total economy. Assuming demand saturation at some point in time, process innovations free resources for radical product inno-

[1] In this sense the complementarity between variety growth and productivity growth in pre-existing sectors bears a considerable similarity to that between productivity growth in agriculture and investment in the new industries during the process of industrialisation (see, Kuznets, 1965).

vations. When these resources are used for product developments which aim at creating new niches in the same sector, product variety is expected to rise in the course of time. The analysis in this paper can help us to understand better what is the minimum level of aggregation required to study these phenomena.

In absence of a condition requiring a minimum level of aggregation, the hypothesis that variety grows in the course of economic development seems somewhat contradictory with respect to the product life-cycle models in industrial organization, and in particular to the dominant design model (Utterback, Abernathy, 1975; Abernathy, Utterback, 1978). This apparent contradiction can in principle be explained by means of the existence of a minimum level of aggregation and by the complementarity between productivity growth and variety growth (Hypothesis 2). The convergence of a technology on a dominant design, which allows the technology to become more efficient by adopting standard equipment and procedures, reduces the internal variety of the technology. Its growing efficiency generates the resources required to create other new technologies, thus leading to a growth in variety at the highest possible level of aggregation. Thus, the reduction in internal variety following from the emergence of a dominant design can be seen as one of the possible mechanisms of productivity growth, that by means of hypothesis 2 contribute to raise the overall variety of the system. For example, there is evidence that variety in agricultural tractors first decreased following the emergence of a dominant design, but subsequently increased due to product differentiation (Saviotti, 1996). A same phenomenon seems to have happened in the history of motor cars: after the emergence of the T-Ford the number of product families has risen over time (standard, sports, family, city, etc.). In fact, the standardization made possible by the dominant design may allow a greater and more differentiated range of product models to be produced. Thus, in principle there is no contradiction between variety growth and the existence of dominant designs.

Empirical evidence suggests that the emergence of dominant designs is a rather general phenomenon in many different industries.[2] However, the results have been based on a loose definition of the concept of dominant design. Furthermore, the effects of a dominant design on product and process innovation are analysed by means of the counting of product and process innovations. These data on innovations are rather subjective and difficult to compare. Alternatively, we propose in this study to measure innovations as changes in the characteristics of the products. Such an

[2] For empirical evidence, see Gort and Klepper (1982), Tushman and Anderson (1986), Anderson and Tushman (1990), Utterback and Suarez (1993). In a recent empirical study, Klepper and Simons (1997) questioned the dominant design concept.

approach eliminates a large part of the difficulties of counting product innovations.

3 Measurements

3.1 Product characteristics

The representation of variety used here follows from a representation of product technology based on a set of product characteristics (Saviotti, Metcalfe, 1984; Sahal, 1985; Saviotti, 1996). Adopting a characteristics representation, each product model corresponds to a point in a space with a number of dimensions equal to the number of characteristics describing the product. The models of different producers are similar but not identical and they occupy neighbouring positions in characteristics space. Thus the set of product models described by the same characteristics and occupying a self-contained and distinguishable region of characteristics space constitutes a technological or product population. Product populations can undergo several types of changes in the course of time. For example, their position and their density can change (*figure 1*) and they can separate into different populations (*figure 2*).

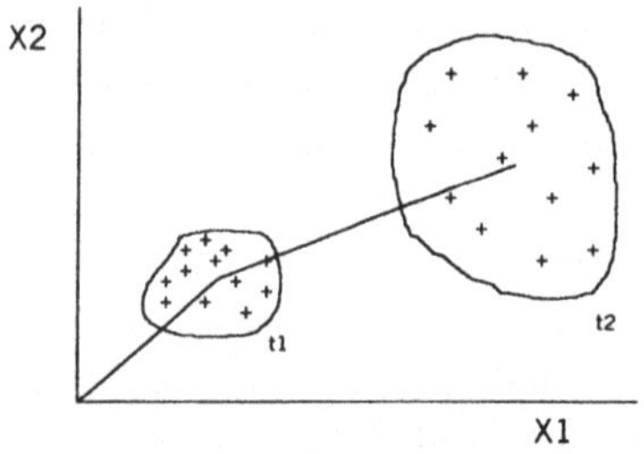

Fig. 1. Between times t_1 and t_2 the position and density of the technological population change. The centre of the technological population describes a trajectory. X_1 and X_2 are the characteristics representing the product technology considered

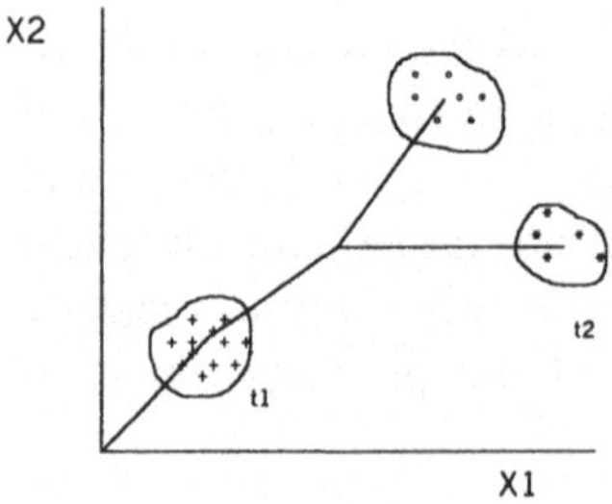

Fig. 2. During the evolution of the technological population specialisation takes place, giving rise to a bifurcation in the trajectory. X_1 and X_2 are the characteristics representing the product technology considered

The characteristics representation of product technology provides an adequate representation of product competition (Hotelling 1929). When outputs are differentiated the products of different competitors give rise to a product population of competing products. The distance between product models within a population is a measure of their degree of dissimilarity: the more different products are, the further away they will be in characteristics space. In turn, a higher population density implies a lower average distance between models and thus a greater similarity. In general, competition is proportional to the density in a product population.

The characteristics approach to product technology enables us to give a definition of innovation that can be the basis for a more accurate and objective measurement of innovation. We have already discussed counting of product and process innovations as a way to test the implications of a dominant design. Counting product innovations depends on a subjective and usually implicit definition of innovation. Furthermore, the weights of different innovations are not known and very difficult to evaluate. We can define an innovation as anything that either changes the values of the existing characteristics of a technology or introduces new characteristics. A measure of the size of the innovation will then be given by the distance between a technical artifact that contains it and one that does not. If we measure distances over a long period of time, the importance of the characteristics that are in greater demand will increase, thus providing a form of implicit weight.

In the rest of the paper we develop measures of product diversity/variety based on the characteristics representation. The advantage of these measures to test the dominant design hypothesis is that there can be growing product variety even when there is no registered product innovation. For example, in a relatively mature technology, such as motor cars or agricultural tractors, variety can grow by means of an increase in the number of families of models. This increase in variety may be the result of the growth in process efficiency afforded by the emergence of a dominant design. Thus we can see that product and process technology are not independent and that the simple counting of product innovations may turn out to be misleading. Furthermore, we can observe, and this will be confirmed by our results in this paper, that growing variety is not incompatible with the existence of a dominant design. In fact, as the variety of a given product grows, the number of possible niches grows and a dominant design is established in each niche.

In order to measure the variety of a product population, we discuss two methodologies that have been proposed by biologists to study evolutionary processes. The first methodology concerns the entropy methodology which applies to the frequency distribution of product characteristics. The second methodology is taken from Weitzman (1992), and is essentially a maximum likelihood procedure measuring the most probable structure of differentiation using any distance measure between two products in characteristics space.

3.2 Entropy

The entropy value of a distribution measures the degree of dividedness or uncertainty in a distribution (Theil 1967, 1972). The entropy measure is given by:

$$H(X) = c \sum_{i=1}^{A} p_i \log(1/p_i) \qquad (i=1,\ldots,A) \qquad (1)$$

where p_i stands for the frequency of members of class i in a technological population consisting of a total of A classes. By convention, the constant c is usually set to 1. The logarithmic can be 2 for variety in bits or the natural logarithm for "nits". The measure applies to data that are classified in classes along a dimension in which each observation is exclusively assigned to one of the classes. For example, a technological population can be described by its distribution among engine types (diesel, gas, petrol).

Entropy measures the degree of uncertainty in a probability/frequency distribution. Its minimum value equals zero when all observations lie in one and the same class, i.e., there is one class i for which holds $p_i = 1$, so we have $H_{min} = \log 1 = 0$. In this case, one technological variant totally dominates the market, and the product population is characterised by minimum variety. Entropy takes on the maximum value when the chance of finding an entity of a particular class is equally distributed. Then, all classes have the same relative frequency equal to $p_i = 1/A$, so we have $H_{max} = \log A$. In that case, all technological variants have an equal share, and the population is characterised by maximum variety. For example, if we would characterise cars by their engine type (diesel, gas, petrol), maximum entropy would be the case when an equal number of car models has a diesel engine, a gas engine, and a petrol engine. Note that the maximum possible entropy is dependent upon the number of classes A which equals three in the example. The larger the number of classes, the larger the possible maximum entropy. This property of the entropy measure takes into account that the possible technological variety does not only depend upon the distribution of products, but also upon the number of distinguishable types of products. The introduction of a new class along a dimension (e.g., electric engine) increases the maximum possible variety.

The entropy measure for multivariate frequency distributions along dimensions X_1, X_2, etc., is given by:

$$H(X_1, X_2, \ldots) = \sum_{i=1}^{A} \sum_{j=1}^{B} \ldots \, p_{ij\ldots} \log(1/p_{ij\ldots}) \; (i=1,\ldots,A; j=1,\ldots,B;\ldots) \quad (2)^3$$

The multivariate entropy value measures the combined variety along several dimensions at the same time. It is easily verified that the maximum entropy in the multivariate case equals the logarithm of the product of the number of classes along each dimension (*log AB*...).[4]

Example

The entropy formula can be applied to distributions of discrete product characteristics in a straightforward manner. Consider the following observations on two characteristics of four aircraft models:

Table 1. Data example of discrete product characteristics

	X_1: Engine type	X_2: Wing type
Product 1	jet	delta
Product 2	jet	swept
Product 3	turboprop	swept
Product 4	turboprop	swept

Let X_1=1 stand for a jet aircraft, X_1=2 for a turboprop aircraft, X_2=1 for an aircraft with delta wing, and X_2=2 for an aircraft with swept wing. Four possible *technological variants* can be distinguished (jet/delta-wing, jet/swept-wing, turboprop/delta-wing, and turboprop/swept-wing). Their bivariate frequencies are: p_{11}=.25, p_{12}=.25, p_{21}=.00 and p_{22}=.50, and the univariate frequencies become $p_{1.}$=.50, $p_{2.}$=.50, $p_{.1}$=.25 and $p_{.2}$=.75. The matrix containing the univariate and bivariate probabilities is given in *Table 2*.

[3] For $x = 0$, $x \cdot \log_2 x \equiv 0$.

[4] The entropy measure has a number of other analytical properties (Theil, 1967, 1972; Leydesdorff, 1995), which can be used in the analysis of technological evolution based on product characteristics. In particular, the difference between the bivariate entropy and the sum of the univariate entropies is known as the *expected mutual information*, and serves as a measure of dependence between two dimensions. See also, Frenken (forthcoming).

Table 2. Frequency-matrix of technological variants

	$X_1 = 1$	$X_1 = 2$	
$X_2 = 1$	$p_{11}=.25$	$p_{21}=.00$	$p_{.1}=.25$
$X_2 = 2$	$p_{12}=.25$	$p_{22}=.50$	$p_{.2}=.75$
	$p_{1.}=.50$	$p_{2.}=.50$	

The univariate entropy values are:

$$H(X_1) = 0.5 \cdot {}^2\log 2 \; + \; 0.5 \cdot {}^2\log 2 \; = \; 1.00$$

$$H(X_2) = 0.25 \cdot {}^2\log 4 \; + \; 0.75 \cdot {}^2\log 1.33 \; = \; 0.81$$

And, the multivariate entropy equals:

$$H(X_1, X_2) = 0.25 \cdot {}^2\log 4 \; + \; 0.25 \cdot {}^2\log 4 \; + \; 0.5 \cdot {}^2\log 2 \; = \; 1.50$$

The bivariate entropy is smaller than its maximum entropy which equals ${}^2\log AB = {}^2\log 4 = 2$, indicating that the observations are not equally distributed. The frequency of aircraft incorporating a turboprop engine and a swept wing is higher than the other aircraft types.

The entropy measure allows one to take into account the effects of qualitative change on product variety. Each time a firm introduces a new class of a characteristic, such as a new engine type or a new type of material, this leads to a new product variant (a new cell in the matrix). The entropy of the product population then rises, *ceteris paribus*. More generally, as an indicator of technological change, entropy measures the net effect of the basic evolutionary mechanisms of innovation which increases entropy/variety and market selection which decreases entropy/variety. The entropy of a product distribution rises when, *ceteris paribus*, a firm introduces in new design feature. Following the example in *table 1*, a new product variant is created when a firm introduces the first turboprop delta-wing aircraft which renders the value of p_{21} positive. The entropy of a product distribution falls when, *ceteris paribus*, one or a limited number of product variants starts dominating the market. Following the example, this could happen when the frequency of turboprops with swept-wings rises relative to the other product variants. Then, p_{22} rises and consequently, the entropy H falls. When one product variant completely dominates the whole industry (i.e., has unit probability), then the entropy value falls to zero indicate complete product standardisation.

3.3 Weitzman's measure of diversity

Weitzman's (1992) measure of diversity is based on a maximum likelihood grouping procedure using some distance measure ''d'' (difference or degree of dissimilarity). The grouping procedure generates the *structure of differentiation* between entities (here, products) following some distance definition. Therefore, the choice of distance measures bears a direct influence on the diversity value of a set of products. We will discuss two distance measures below.

In any case, the distance measure between two products d(x, y) needs to satisfy the following conditions:[5]

$$d(x,y) \geq 0 \tag{3}$$

$$d(x, x) = 0 \tag{4}$$

$$d(x, y) = d(y, x) \tag{5}$$

If we suppose that there exist a not empty set S, the diversity of the set S called V(S) is the solution of the recursion:

$$V(S) = \max_{y \in S} (V(S \backslash y) + d(S \backslash y, y)) \tag{6}$$

where S\y stands for a set S except product y, and d(S\y,y) for the smallest distance between S\y and product y. Weitzman (1992) showed that the solution of this recursion is unique once the initial conditions, $V(x) \equiv d_0$, $\forall$ x, are specified for any value of d_0 (in the following, we take $d_0 = 0$). The formula holds that the diversity of a population is the maximum, over all members in the population, of the distance of a member from its closest neighbour, plus the diversity of the population without that member. Note that the equation can only be solved recursively. Since the number of recursions increases exponentially with the number of observations in the set, the measure is computationally practicable only for sets smaller than around 20 to 25 observations on a standard computer.[6]

Weitzman (1992) argued that his measure has the properties that are usually associated with diversity, thus proving to be a useful measure from a pragmatic point of view. These properties are fivefold:

---

[5] Here, we use a notation where *x* and *y* stand for different products. The notation *x* should not be confused with X_1 and X_2 which stand for different product characteristics as in formula (2) in *section 3.2*.

[6] For a 20x20 matrix, one needs around one minute. For each observation added, computing time doubles.

I. *Monotonicity in elements*: if we add a new element y to a set S that does not already contain y, then the diversity value increases at least by d(S, y).
II. *Twin property*: if we add an element y that is identical to some element x belonging to S, that does not modify the diversity.
III. *Link property*: there exist at least one element y in S that verify : $V(S) = V(S \backslash y) + d(S, y)$.
IV. *Continuity in distances*: let $|S| = |S'|$ such that S can be mapped one-to-one onto S', then it can be shown that for $\forall \varepsilon > 0$, it holds that $|V(S) - V(S')| < \varepsilon$.
V. *Monotonicity in distances*: if all distances between elements of S increase, V(S) increases.

Thus, Weitzman's diversity measure contains all the minimal properties that have been associated with diversity (mainly with respect to biological systems). By contrast, the entropy measure shares only the first property of monotonicity: for each possible set *S*, it holds that if a new element is added to the set, the entropy value always rises as the number of classes *A* increases. The second property of Weitzman's measure, the twin property, is not a property of the entropy measure. If one uses the entropy measure, it is never the case that the twin property is satisfied for any set *S*. The addition of an element of an already existing class always changes the frequency distribution $(p_1,\ldots,p_A)$, and the entropy of the distribution changes accordingly. As explained above, the change in the entropy as a result of an element added can be either positive or negative. The entropy increases if the element added is a member of a relative scarce species, while the value will fall if the element added is a member of a relative abundant species. With regard to the third, fourth and fifth properties of the Weitzman measure, a comparison with the entropy measure cannot be made since the entropy measure is not based on a distance measure. The essential difference between the entropy measure and the Weitzman measure thus holds that the former takes into account the relative frequency of elements while the latter takes into account the distance among them.

A crucial aspect in the application of Weitzman's measure is the choice of the distance measure. In general, different distance measures will generate different diversity values for the same set of observations. Below, we discuss two different distance measures which can be applied to discrete and continuous data, and we give numerical examples of both distance measures.

Example of discrete data

In the case of discrete variables a straightforward measure is given by the Hamming distance between a pair of products. This distance measure is simply the number of discrete characteristics in which two products differ, and is thus analogous to the number genes in which two organisms differ (cf. Weitzman, 1993: 165).

Following our data example of discrete product characteristics listed in *Table 1*, the matrix of pair-wise Hamming distances is given in *Table 3*. Note that product 3 and product 4 are grouped together, since their mutual Hamming distance equals zero (d(3,4)=d(4,3)=0).

Table 3. Matrix of Hamming distances (following data example in Table 1)

	Product 1	Product 2	Product 3 (and 4)
Product 1	d(1,1)=0		
Product 2	d(2,1)=1	d(2,2)=0	
Product 3 (and 4)	d(3,1)=2	d(3,2)=1	d(3,3)=0

The maximum likelihood recursion adds up to:

$$V(S) = 2 + 1 = 3$$

In this particular case, we have two possible evolutionary trees with equal (maximum) variety value (V=3). The evolutionary tree which maps the structure of product differentiation becomes:

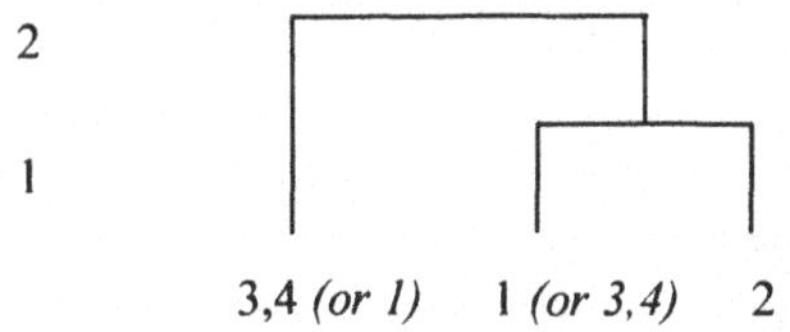

Example of continuous data

In the case of continuous variables, the distance among two observations can be measured in Euclidean space. If products are described by multiple characteristics, one can use Pythagoras' formula. However, distances in a multi-dimensional Euclidean space are dependent upon the unit of measurement (km/h, miles/h, etc.). For this reason, one can normalise the univariate distance using the mean value (Saviotti, 1988). Then, the distance between two products in continuous characteristics space is given by:

$$D(x,y)=\sqrt{\left(\frac{X_{1_x}-X_{1_y}}{\sum X_1/N}\right)^2+\left(\frac{X_{2_x}-X_{2_y}}{\sum X_2/N}\right)^2+\dots} \qquad (7)$$

for sets containing N observations.

Consider then, the data example of continuous product characteristics given in *Table 4*.

Table 4. Data example of continuous product characteristics

	X_1 : Engine power (kWatt)	X_2 : Speed (km/h)
Product 1	1000	60
Product 2	1500	200
Product 3	1200	220
Product 4	5000	400

The matrix of the normalised Euclidean distances between each pair of products is given by *Table 5*.

Table 5. Matrix of normalised Euclidean distances

	Product 1	Product 2	Product 3	Product 4
Product 1	0			
Product 2	0.677	0		
Product 3	0.733	0.165	0	
Product 4	2.402	1.848	1.929	0

The maximum likelihood recursion adds up to:

$$V(S) = 0.165 + 0.733 + 2.402 = 3.300$$

The corresponding evolutionary tree which maps the structure of product differentiation, becomes:

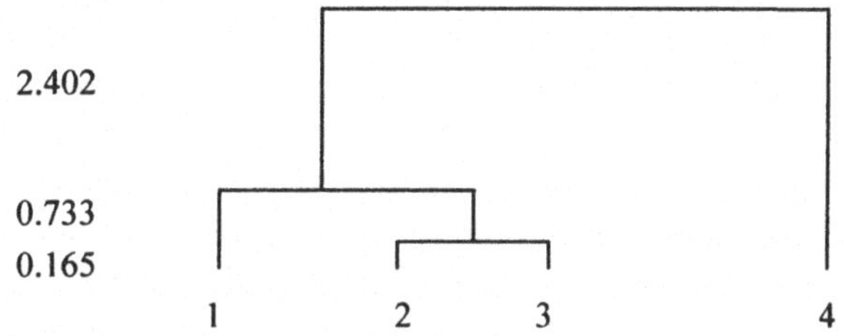

3.4 Summary

Weitzman's variety measure is calculated by means of a reconstruction of the most likely hierarchical tree of a population, based on the characteristics of the population members. The maximum likelihood recursion has five minimal properties that a variety measure based on distances has to meet. However, Weitzman's measure does not take into account the frequency distribution of the different species. For this reason, entropy can be considered as a complementary measure of variety since it takes the number of species and their respective frequencies into account.

The two variety measures relate to two central topics in evolutionary theory of technological change. The entropy measure is especially indicative of the emergence of a dominant design since the domination of a product population by a single type of technology renders the frequency distribution very skewed. Consequently, the entropy of the population is expected to fall indicating a decrease in technological variety in the population. Weitzman's diversity measure is based on technological distances between products, and is especially useful to measure the emergence of distinct market niches in characteristics space through product differentiation.

Using both measures, one can relate changes in the degree of technological standardisation as indicated by the entropy measure to changes in product differentiation as indicated by Weitzman's measure. Importantly, these changes do not necessarily point to the same direction. Weitzman's measure of a product population may be high when the entropy value is low. This is the case when a single design dominates the population, but alternative designs survive in regions in characteristics space far from the dominant design. These alternative designs may concern very specialised products for which little demand exists. Weitzman's measure may also be low when the entropy is high. This is the case when many different product designs co-exist and have more or less equal shares in the population, but which are very close to another in characteristics space. In this case, many product varieties exist which are only slightly different from each other.

An important drawback of the application of the entropy measure on product characteristics is that it cannot be applied in a straightforward manner to continuous product characteristics. The entropy measure can only be applied to data that are classified in classes of observation. Along continuous dimensions the choice of the number of classes and their width involves decisions that remain to some extent arbitrary.[7] We apply the methodologies to data on product characteristics of aircraft and helicopters. Details concerning the data and measurements are given in *section 4.1*. In *section 4.2*, we discuss the results on three variety measures: *(i)* the entropy of discrete characteristics, *(ii)* the Weitzman measure of discrete characteristics, and *(iii)* the Weitzman measure of continuous characteristics. By doing so, we can make two comparisons. First, we compare the entropy and the Weitzman measure on the basis of the results on discrete characteristics (*section 4.3*). Second, we compare the variety dynamics of discrete characteristics and continuous characteristics on the basis of the two results on the Weitzman measure (*section 4.4*). We analyse the evolutionary trees as generated by the Weitzman measure of the first and last period of aircraft history to give an idea of the development in product differentiation (*section 4.5*). Finally, we develop an evolutionary explanation of the different paths of technological development in aircraft technology and helicopter technology (*section 4.6*).

4 Application

4.1 Data description

We apply the entropy measure and Weitzman's diversity measure to two databases containing discrete and continuous product characteristics. The data concern 731 aircraft models (*1913-1984*), and 144 helicopter models (*1940-1983*) taken from *Jane's Encyclopedia of Aviation* (Jane's, 1978, 1989). The description of the data including their sources are listed in *Appendix 1*. Each product model is described by the same set of characteristics. This implies that our analysis does not deal with qualitative change resulting from the creation of new characteristics. However, as explained above, qualitative change does not only concern the emergence of new characteristics, but also the emergence of new classes of a existing characteristic. For example, the first aircraft incorporating a jet engine is

[7] Theil and Fiebig (1984) developed a methodology to measure the entropy of a continuous distribution by taking the distance between observations as the basis of a probability assignment.

qualitatively different from aircraft models incorporating a different engine type (e.g., piston propeller), and thus adds to the variety in the population of products. The latter type of qualitative change is central to in our empirical analysis below.

We have defined a product population as the set of products present in a market at a particular point in time. As explained, the variety of a product population is based on the degree of dissimilarity between product models in characteristics space. Thus, the data analysis does not concern the market shares of particular products, but the characteristics of distinct product models. In other words, the analysis focuses on the *technological* evolution of products (as in the examples of *figure 1* and *figure 2*), and not the *industrial* evolution of market shares of products. Each product is assigned a date corresponding to its year of introduction. Information on the year of its removal is lacking, so we don't know how long a particular product model has been on the market. Therefore, we measure the technological variety of a particular period on the basis of the *new* products which are introduced during a period. Thus, for each new product it holds that its contribution to the variety is only measured at the time of its introduction on the market.[8]

In the databases, the number of new products introduced per year differ to a large extent. Since the variety measures are sensitive to the number of observations, we need to re-label the data in a chronological order of periods with the same number of observations. In this way, we can measure the change in variety which is due to the shifts in the *composition* of a population of constant size, and obtain normalised variety measures.[9] This poses a problem since the constitution of chronological peri-

[8] We can distinguish between two types of product variety analysis. If only the date of introduction of a new product is available, one can measure the variety of *new* product offerings at given moments in time, as we do in the remainder of the paper. If data on the life-span are also available, i.e. the number of years that a product is offered on the market, then one can measure the variety of *existing* product offerings at given moments in time. The values of the two variety measures are different only if the life-span of products in different product families is systematically different. For example, it may be the case that new, specialized designs which are usually offered only rarely, tend to have a long life-span (e.g. Boeing 747), while new, standard designs tend to have a short life-span (e.g. Cessna aircraft). This would imply that first variety measure which is applied here, can be expected to underestimate to some extent the variety as defined by the second measure. We are intending to collect data on the life-span for a subset of our data, and to correlate life-span with some product characteristic. If we find a strong correlation for the products in the subset, we can estimate the life-span for other products from their value of this particular product characteristic.

[9] Put another way, we measure periods in event time instead of real time. Note that simulation models share the perspective that technological systems are 'updated' by events rather than in real time (cf. Arthur 1989).

ods of N cases per periods requires that we assign data within a single year to different periods. Suppose we have 12 new products introduced in year 1901 and 8 new products in year 1902, and we want to constitute two periods containing an equal number of observations ($N=10$). In that case, we need to assign 10 observations from 1901 to the first period, and 2 observations from 1901 to the second period together with the 8 observations from 1902. This is done by random assignment and several times. The results below are the mean values of five runs for aircraft and three for helicopters. Since the computing time needed to calculate Weitzman's measure grows exponentially with the number of observations, we are forced to work with relatively small numbers of observations per period. We have chosen $N=17$ for aircraft thus yielding 43 periods, and $N=12$ for helicopters thus yielding 12 periods. In the graphs, we plot the variety values per period and not per year. The years that corresponds to each period are given in *Appendix 2*.

4.2 Results

The multivariate entropy values for the six discrete characteristics of aircraft are given in *figure 3(a)*, and the values for the Weitzman measures for discrete and continuous characteristics of aircraft are given in *figure 3(b)* and *figure 3(c)*. In the same order, the result for helicopters are given in *figure 4(a-c)*. For both technologies, we find clear long-run trends. The values for aircraft variety are rising while the values for helicopter variety are falling. These trends thus suggest that aircraft variety has been steadily increasing over time, while helicopter variety has been steadily decreasing over time. Importantly, both the entropy measurement and the two Weitzman measurements show the same upward trend for aircraft and downward trend for helicopters.

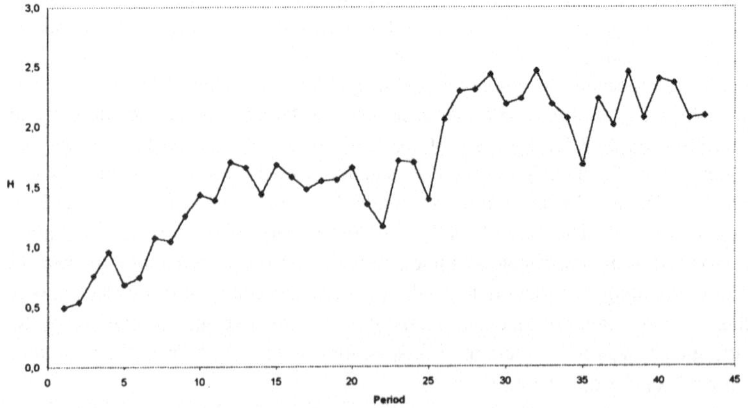

Fig. 3(a). Entropy value on discrete variables of aircraft

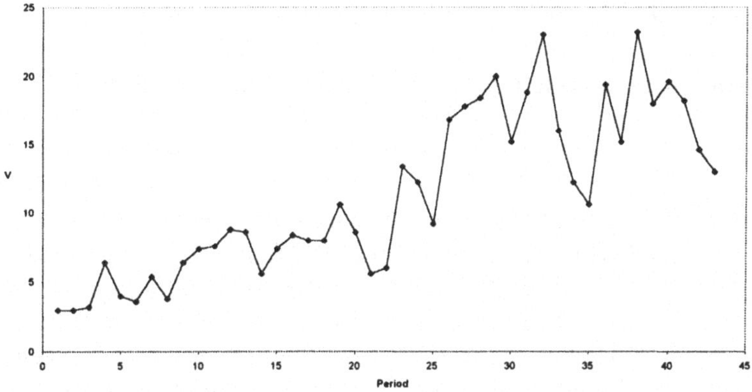

Fig. 3(b). Weitzman's measure on discrete variables of aircraft

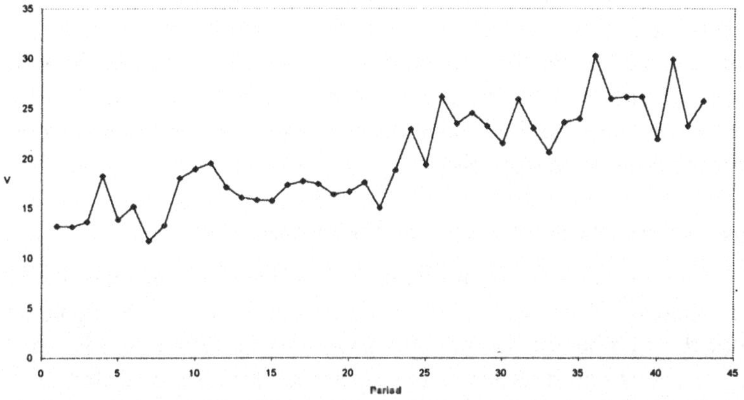

Fig. 3(c). Weitzman's diversity measure on continuous variables of aircraft

To what extent are the results compatible with general historical accounts? In aircraft studies, the 1936-Douglas DC3 is commonly considered as the dominant design constituted by a two-engine, all-metal monoplane with cantilever wings, piston engines and propellers (Miller, Sawers, 1968; Constant, 1980). The subsequent design trajectory DC3-DC7 has also been the prime example of Nelson's and Winter's (1977) concept of a technological regime, which resembles the dominant design concept. Inspection of the results for aircraft in *figures 3(a-c)* teaches us that for all three variety measures, on average, the values slightly drop around periods 12-22 which corresponds to the years 1933-1942. This temporary decline in variety may well reflect the effects of standardisation of the dominant design Douglas DC3 on the specifications of other aircraft. However, the rapid increase of variety after period 22 clearly shows that the dominant design in aircraft did not prevent the long term variety to grow. The aircraft population progressively differentiated through a series of subsequent innovations to meet a large range of different demands.

The helicopter industry has witnessed a different evolution. The results in *figure 4(a-c)* indicate the highest variety around periods 2 and 3 which correspond to years 1954-1959. Hereafter, helicopter variety tends to decrease according to all three variety measures. The variety peak in the fifties coincided with the introduction of the first twin turboshaft design by Kaman in 1954. This design became the dominant design in the following thirty years and can be understood as constitutive of a technological regime in helicopter design (Bilstein, 1996; cf., Saviotti, Trickett, 1992). Contrary to aircraft technology, the helicopter variety continued to decrease after a dominant design emerged, which suggests a typical example of a product life-cycle with a drop in product innovation and in product variety after the emergence of a dominant design.

Before turning to possible explanations of these different development paths in aircraft and helicopters in *section 4.6*, we first discuss the empirical results in further detail by means of comparisons between the results of the entropy and the Weitzman measure and between the results on discrete and continuous characteristics.

4.3 Comparison between entropy and Weitzman measure

As explained above, the entropy measure and Weitzman's measure focus on different aspects of the variety of a product population. Entropy takes into account the number of technological variants and their relative frequencies. The Weitzman measure is based on the structure of differentiation between products in Hamming (discrete) or Euclidean (continuous) space. Both measures are complementary, and they allow us to distinguish between different variety dynamics at different stages of development.

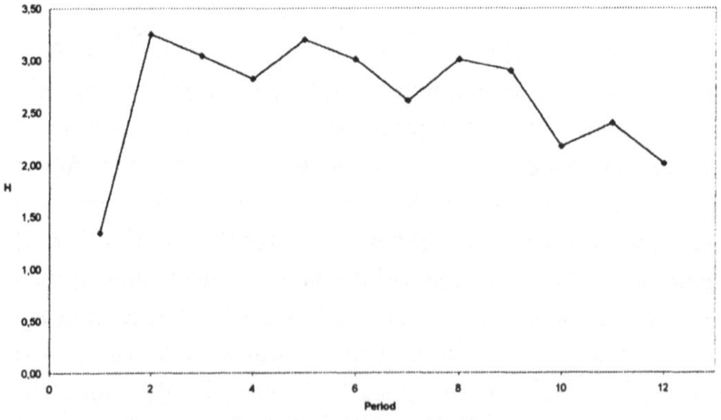

Fig. 4(a). Entropy on discrete variables of helicopters

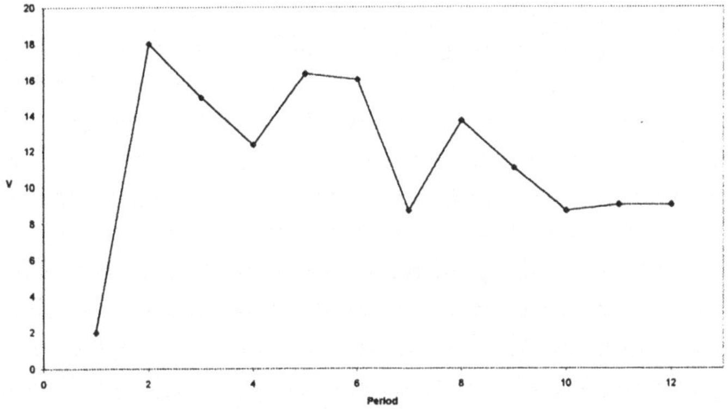

Fig. 4(b). Weitzman's measure on discrete variables of helicopters

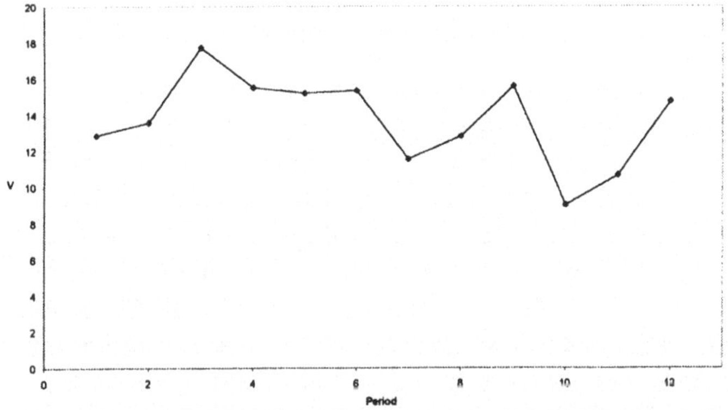

Fig. 4(c). Weitzman's measure on continuous variables of helicopters

The results on aircraft and helicopters show that the long-run trends in entropy and Weitzman measurements are very similar. However, during some periods, the direction and rapidity of change is different for the entropy and the Weitzman measure (since entropy is only applied to discrete characteristics, the comparison between entropy and the Weitzman measure is solely based on the results on the discrete characteristics). It is clear that when we compare *figure 3(a)* and *figure 3(b)* on discrete characteristics of aircraft, the entropy is rising more rapidly during the first half of the history, while the Weitzman measure increases most rapidly during the second half of the history. This result is interesting since it shows that during the first half of aircraft history, many different product designs have been developed through the development of new design features such as three-, four-, six- and twelve-engine lay-outs, various wing designs, monoplane, biplane and triplanes, one- and two-tail designs, and one, two or three fins. This rise in the number of technological variants is reflected in the rapidly rising entropy value. However, these new variants did not immediately differentiate since the Weitzman value based on Hamming distances is still rather low during the first half of the aircraft history. Only during the second half, Weitzman values 'catch up' with entropy values indicating that the variety of product designs took on a more differentiated form rendering the Hamming distance between product higher.

In the case of helicopters, the main trend during the whole history is similar in *figure 4(a)* and *figure 4(b)*. For smaller periods of time, we did not find clear differences as we did for aircraft. The two variety measures change in very similar ways during most periods, which suggests that the different aspects of variety followed the same dynamic. Changes in frequency distribution as measured by entropy and changes in mutual distances on which Weitzman's measure is based, kept the same pace.

4.4 Comparison between discrete and continuous characteristics

The discrete and continuous product characteristics do not only require a different treatment, but they also differ in terms of their meaning in the context of technological change. Discrete characteristics concern *qualitative* descriptions of a product. Products which differ in terms of discrete characteristics thus constitute different technological variants within a population. For example, turbopropeller aircraft is qualitatively distinct from jet aircraft. The set of discrete characteristics make up the design code of a product, analogous to the genotype of an organism in biology. A change in one of the design features of a product through innovation can thus be considered analogous to mutation in an organism.[10]

Continuous characteristics are quantitative variables: products differ along these dimensions only to a certain degree (bigger, faster, etc.). It is along these dimensions that products can be compared and thus directly compete in terms of costs and services. For example, higher engine power usually implies higher costs of production and operation. A large wingspan is important to generate lift for transport services, but at the same time it decreases manoeuvrability which is essential in fighter operations. And, the speed level is obviously important in fighters' operations as well as in airline operations. Thus, the market environment selects primarily on the continuous characteristics, in a way analogous to natural selection

[10] Using the same representation of a product as a string of design features, Birchenhall (1995) and Windrum and Birchenhall (1998) modeled the technological evolution of product populations using genetic algorithms. See also Kauffman (1993) and Frenken *et al.* (1998) on the analogy between genetic code and design code using Kauffman's the NK-model.

on phenotypic traits of organisms. Continuous characteristics therefore, are considered as the phenotypic characteristics of a product.[11] This classification of characteristics is similar to Herbert Simon's (1969) distinction between the description of the internal structure of a system and the interface of a system which regulates the interaction with the environment.[12]

The results on the changes in variety of discrete and of continuous variables can then be appreciated as indicating the development of the internal structure of products and of their environment, respectively. Since we only applied the Weitzman measure to both discrete and continuous characteristics, the comparison is made solely on the basis of the graphs on the Weitzman measure (*figure 3(b,c)* for aircraft, and *figure 4(b,c)* for helicopters. The results on the Weitzman measure show that both for aircraft and helicopters, the *change* in variety has been larger in discrete characteristics than in continuous characteristics. However, since the two Weitzman measures are based on different distance measures, this result is misleading. Comparisons between the graphs can only be made by comparing the trends. With regard to the trends, we find that the graphs for discrete characteristics show more fluctuations that the graphs for continuous characteristics. This difference between discrete and continuous characteristics is especially clear for aircraft, and to a lesser extent for helicopters. The larger fluctuations in the variety of discrete, 'genotypic' characteristics are expected since these characteristics are the qualitative design features on which the environment selects. Changes in genotypic characteristics are introduced when it is expected that the new design will lead to an improvement in phenotypic performance as represented by continuous characteristics. As the results indicate, it is rarely the case that the introduction of a new design immediately leads to a sharp increase in performance and/or the creation of a new niche. New designs are tried, compete with one another, and eventually either survive or become extinct. Thus we can expect to notice greater discontinuities when calculating the variety of a technological system based on its discrete than on its continuous product characteristics.

4.5 Evolutionary trees

As shown in *section 3*, Weitzman's maximum likelihood recursion generates evolutionary trees which reconstruct the most likely lines of descent

[11] Note that the product characteristics such as the number of engines and the number of wings are not continuous but discrete characteristics since firms can only choose among integers along these dimensions.

[12] The distinction between qualitative, genotypic characteristics and quantitative, phenotypic characteristics relates to the distinction between technical and service characteristics but does not necessarily coincide with it (Saviotti, Metcalfe, 1984).

of product groups. To illustrate the evolution of niches as measured by product distance in continuous, 'phenotypic' space, we listed the tree for the very early aircraft history (*figure 5*, period 1: 1913-1916) and for the very aircraft recent history (*figure 6*, period 43: 1979-1984). The trees follow from the Weitzman calculation for continuous product characteristics (using the first run). Thus, the length of the branches correspond to the Euclidean distance among the members of the population. For each observation, we listed the values of the continuous characteristics.

On the basis of the two evolutionary trees of the first and last period, two observations can be made. These observations are tentative since we did not systematically check the differentiation structure using the trees for the in-between periods. First, the number of niches in aircraft technology is smaller in the early history than in the recent history, which is consistent with the result of rising variety in continuous characteristics in *figure 4(c)*. In the first period 1913-1916 we distinguish three niches, while in the last period 1979-1984 we find up to six niches. Interestingly, the niches in the first period depend mostly on differences in the values of engine power and maximum take-off weight. In contrast, the niches in the last period depend each on different subsets of product characteristics including length, take-off weight, speed and range. This suggests that the rise in the number of niches relates to the rising number of characteristics on which firms compete.

Second, the grouping of product *within* niches has become more differentiated over time. In the first period, most products are grouped in classes with a narrow range of values of product characteristics as is indicated by the small distances between products in a class. In the last period, products are grouped in smaller classes which cover a larger range of values of product characteristics as indicated by the large distance between products within a group. The two results suggest that the increase in variety is both a result of increased differentiation between niches and within niches. This implies a typical *nested structure of differentiation* of niches containing sub-niches.

firm	Lake	Piper	Harbin	BAe Jetstream 31	FMA	Aermacchi	Gulfstream Am.	Rockwell	BAe	Dornier	Shorts	Embraer	BAe	General Dyn.	Dassault-Br.	Boeing	Boeing
model	LA-4-200	PA-28	Y-121	(communter)	1A-63	MB-339K	Gulfstream III	Sabreliner 65	146-200	128-2	360	120	Jetstream 31	F-16XL	S. Mirage 4000	757-200	767-200
design code	AACAAA	AACAAA	BBCAAA	BBCAAA	DACAAA	CACAAA	DBCAAA	DBAAAA	BBCAAA	ABCAAA	BBCAAA	BBCAAA	DDAAAA	DABAAA	DBBAAA	DBAAAA	DBAAAA
niches	→ *small-sized, light business aircraft*				→ *subsonic fighters*		→ *long-range business*		→ *medium-sized, short-range passenger*					→ *supersonic fighters*		→ *large passenger*	
engine power	149	149	746	1342	1400	1780	9120	2960	3580	566	1750	2237	11152	10000	17108	32000	38320
wing span	11,58	10,67	17,23	15,85	9,69	11,05	23,72	15,37	30,63	15,55	22,81	19,78	26,34	10,43	12	37,95	47,57
length	7,6	7,62	14,86	14,37	10,93	10,79	25,27	14,3	26,06	11,41	21,59	20	28,545	16,51	18,7	47,32	48,51
max. take-off weight	1220	1247	5500	6600	4650	6150	30935	10886	22090	3842	11793	9600	40597	21772	16100	104325	136080
max. speed	241	282	282	488	740	907	916	916	474	325	393	500	778	2156	2500	863	863
range	1327	1334	1280	1167	1500	1222	7495	5106	1545	642	1697	2907	2473	4630	3700	4800	5749

Fig. 5. Evolutionary tree of period 1, 1913 -1916. Diversity value V(S) = 13,2 (based on the first run)

firm	Sikorsky	Voisin	Ago	Bristol	Junkers	Airco	R.A.F.	Utva	Albatros	Avro	Albatros	LFG	LVG	Albatros	A. Whitw.	Bristol	Airco
model	Le Grand	X	c.1	F.2	J.1	DH.6	B.E.2.C.	F.B.5	B.II	504K	D.II	C.II	C.II	C.I	FK.8	Scout	DH.5
design code	ADCBAA	AACBAA	AACBAA	AACBAA	AACAAA	AACBAA	AACBAA	AACBAA	AACBAA	AACBAA	AACBAA	AACBAA	AACBAA	AACBAA	AACBAA	AACBAA	AACBAA
niches	→*large passenger*	→*medium bombers and fighters*				→*small bombers and fighters*											
engine power	298	223.6	164	205	89,4	67	67	74,5	82	82	119	119	119	119	119	74,5	82
wing span	28	17,9	14,5	12	16	11	11,28	11,13	12,8	11	8,5	10,3	12,85	12,9	13,3	7,5	7,8
length	20	10,35	9,8	7,9	9,1	8,3	8,31	8.28	7.6	9	7,4	7,7	8,1	7,9	9,6	6.3	6,7
max. take off weight	4080	2200	1946	1292	2175	920	972	930	1070	830	888	1310	1400	1190	1275	653	676
max. speed	96	135	138	201	155	106	116	113	105	145	175	165	130	140	157	177	175
range	150	500	500	600	300	300	300	402	400	402	250	600	500	400	450	350	525

Fig. 6. Evolutionary tree of period 43, 1979-1984. Diversity value V(S) = 25.7 (based on the first run)

For each product we also listed the 'genotypic' design code based on the discrete product characteristics. The design code is expressed in letters (A,B, etc.), and their meaning corresponds to the classification given in *Appendix 1*. In this way, we are able to check whether branches that are neighbours in Euclidean, phenotypic space are also close in Hamming, genotypic space. The results for *figure 5* indicate that in the first period the products that are more distant in Euclidean space are also more distant in Hamming space. Thus, the two product representations coincide. However, the results for the last period in *figure 6* show that while for most branches the distances in Euclidean 'phenotypic' space and in Hamming, 'genotypic' space coincide, some cases deviate. For example, in Euclidean space, BAe Jetstream 31 is part of the niche that we labelled 'medium-sized, short-range passenger aircraft' together with BAe 146, Dornier 126, Shorts 360 and Embraer 120. However, when we compare the design code of the BAe Jetstream 31 with the other products in the population, we observe that in Hamming space, the BAe Jetstream 31 is closest to Rockwell Sabreliner and the two Boeings.

The distances in terms of discrete variables thus do not map one-to-one onto distances in continuous variables. This result points to complex relationships between qualitative variables and quantitative variables. In this context, complex system models such as genetic algorithms and the *NK*-model prove relevant for modelling non-linear relationships between qualitative design features of a population of products (Kauffman, 1993; Frenken *et al.*, 1998, 1999). One of the outcomes of these models holds that larger genotypic distances do not necessarily imply larger functional differences since complex relations among design features may render distant genotypes more or less equally fit (i.e. the 'fitness landscape' contains local optima).

4.6 Why aircraft and helicopter evolution differ?

The application to aircraft and helicopters allows for an interesting comparison since the two technologies have the same prime function (transport through air). The main result holds that aircraft variety has been increasing and helicopter variety has been decreasing. In order to understand this difference between aircraft and helicopters in a more precise manner, we need to consider the specific development and impact of various innovations. In the case of aircraft, the discontinuity noticed after period 22 corresponds to the beginning of the diffusion of the jet engine just after the second world war. Bearing this in mind, we can interpret the evolution of aircraft technology up to period 22 as the initial creation of a multiplicity of designs followed by the establishment of a relatively dominant design in piston propeller in the thirties, in particular the 1936-Douglas DC3 with a monoplane, two-engine, one-fin lay-out. The growth in variety following period 22 can be attributed to the increased performance afforded by the jet engine. The introduction of the jet engine allowed aircraft to be bigger, to fly faster and further, and to carry more weight. Through this revolutionary technology, the span of aircraft technology increased rapidly and in several dimensions.

Following an interpretation proposed by one of us (Saviotti, 1996), the range of performance of a technology can be compared to the habitat of a biological species. Niche theory predicts that the number of niches that can be created in a given habitat is proportional to the size of the habitat (May, 1973). The greater the span of this habitat, the greater the number of niches that can be created within it. An increase in the range of its performance allows a technology to become more specialised and differentiated, thus leading to an increase in variety. In the particular case of the jet engine in aircraft technology, its introduction led eventually to the development of the turbofan, while it induced as new type of propeller type being the turbopropeller engine. Each of these technologies specialized in distinct niches in which it had a comparative advantage. If we further bear in mind that the piston propeller engine survived in a niche, though a shrinking one, we can conclude that the evolution of aircraft technology after the introduction of the turbojet engine consisted of a progressive specialisation and differentiation of the technology itself and the services it provides.

Descriptive statistics teach us that the general pattern of differentiation in discrete and continuous characteristics that occurred during the post-war aircraft history, has been:

1. Small-sized, short-range, low-payload, low-speed aircraft (predominantly, one-engine piston propellers with straight wings)
2. Medium-sized, short-range, low-payload, low-speed aircraft (predominantly, two-engine turboprops with straight wings)
3. Large-sized, long-range, large-payload, high-speed aircraft (predominantly, two-/four-engine turbofans with swept wings)
4. Small-sized, medium-range, low-payload, supersonic aircraft (predominantly, one-/two-engine jets with delta wings)

The first niche corresponds largely to business, trainer and agricultural aircraft, the second niche to small passenger, cargo and STOL-aircraft, the third niche to large bomber, passenger and cargo aircraft, and the fourth niche to fighters. Thus, in each of the different niches a different dominant design has become established.

Contrary to aircraft, the span of performance of helicopters is very limited and did not increase substantially during its evolution. Upper bounds of speed are around 350 km/h and upper bounds of range around

1000 km. In a sense, helicopter technology is in itself a niche in the air transport market and it is used only for very specific purposes (ambulance mission, troop transport, off shore). R&D investments aiming at increasing the span of performance of helicopters, for example increasing its speed and range, have an uncertain pay-off since these high-performance helicopters would then compete with aircraft technology which is already present in this segment. In other words, attempts to enlarge the niche for helicopters would encounter inter-technological competition with aircraft technology. This provides an explanation why helicopter variety did not grow. As the span of performance could not expand, progressive differentiation in helicopter technology could not occur. The comparison between aircraft and helicopters thus underscores the importance of inter-technological competition between technologies in addition to intra-technological competition within a single technology (Saviotti, 1996).

Product variety in the helicopter population even decreased to a certain extent as one design became dominant from the sixties onwards. But even for helicopter technology, it must be noted that the dominant design (two turboshaft engines + one rotor) is dominant only in a statistical sense. A subset of helicopters has a different design based on two rotors, which are used for heavy military transport. However, since only a limited number of this helicopter type has been developed, its contribution to the variety is small.

5 Summary and conclusions

In this paper we first discussed the importance of variety as an indicator to monitor the composition of the economic system. We described two different but complementary methodologies to measure variety and we reported the results of their application to aircraft and helicopters. What we are finding here is that while we can expect variety to grow above a sufficiently high level of aggregation, below such a level the behaviour of variety can change depending on the technology considered. The results obtained in this paper allow us to start hypothesising some of the determinants of variety below the critical level of aggregation. For example, the width of the range of services provided by the technology is such a determinant. A wide span provides the analogue of a biological habitat into which a large number of niches can be created, thus raising the variety of the system. When innovation is directed towards expanding the span of services, technological variety is expected to grow. When innovations are competing for a given (small) span of services, variety may well decrease as increasing returns tend to favour a limited number of designs. We observed the first dynamic in the history of aircraft and the second dynamic in the history of helicopters.

Our results have also important implications for the concept of dominant design. As we pointed out in *section 3* our measures of variety represent a better way of testing the existence of a dominant design than counts of innovations. The results give us a version of the dominant design somewhat different from that of the initial model. In the technologies we studied dominant designs appear, but they are not as dominant as implied by the initial version of the concept. After the emergence of a dominant design, product variety may increase as the technology splits into several niches, and a different design becomes dominant in each niche. For example, in aircraft several designs coexist, one in each of the niches into which the technology can be subdivided. This can be considered a technological division of labour, which originated historically as each design established itself in a niche in which it had a comparative advantage. Moreover, even in a technology without a clear differentiation pattern, as in the case of helicopters, several designs may coexist, with one of them being only statistically dominant. Thus our representation of product technology coupled with the two types of measurements proposed allow us to detect the presence of competing designs, where each design is identified by a set of characteristics, and to detect the niche(s) in which a design can eventually become dominant. For what concerns product innovation, our measurements of variety constitute a more objective and comparable measure than counts of innovation.

We conclude our paper by mentioning three directions in which our results encourage us to pursue further research. First, confirmation of the determinants of variety discussed in this paper is required. This involves further empirical analysis of other technologies. Second, the factors determining the growth of variety discussed here can be incorporated in models of technological evolution, industrial dynamics and firm behaviour (Saviotti, 1998). For example, they could be integrated into the models on product life-cycles and industry shakeout as discussed above. Third, the measures of variety we have started developing here can be used to study the relationships between variety growth on the one hand and output growth, employment growth and trade growth on the other hand.

References

Abernathy W, Utterback J (1978) Patterns of industrial innovation. Technology Review 50: 41-47

Anderson P, Tushman ML (1990) Technological discontinuities and dominant designs: a cyclical model of technological change. Administrative Science Quarterly 35: 604-633

Arthur WB (1989) Competing technologies, increasing returns, and lock-in by historical events. Economic Journal 99: 116-131

Bilstein RE (1996) The American Aerospace Industry. Twayne Publishers/ Prentice Hall International, New York

Birchenhall C (1995) Modular technical change and genetic algorithms. Computational Economics 8: 233-53

Constant EW (1980) The Origins of the Turbojet Revolution. Jon Hopkins University Press, Baltimore London

Dosi G (1982) Technological paradigms and technological trajectories. A suggested interpretation of the determinants and directions of technical change. Research Policy 11: 147-162

Frenken K (forthcoming) A complexity approach to innovation networks, Research Policy

Frenken K, Marengo L, Valente M (1998) Modelling decomposition strategies in complex fitness landscapes. Implications for the economics of technological change. Paper presented at the Seventh Conference of the International Schumpeter Society, Vienna, Austria, 13-16 June

Frenken K, Marengo L, Valente M (1999) Interdependencies, nearly-decomposability and adaptation. In: Brenner T (ed) Computational Techniques to Modelling Learning in Economics. Kluwer, Boston etc

Gort M, Klepper S (1982) Time-paths in the diffusion of product innovations. Economic Journal 92: 630-653

Hotelling H (1929) Stability in competition. Economic Journal 39: 41-57

Jane's (1978) Jane's Encyclopedia of Aviation. Jane's Publishing Company Ltd, London

Jane's (1989) Jane's Encyclopedia of Aviation. Studio Editions, London

Jovanovic B, MacDonald GM (1994) The life cycle of a competitive industry, Journal of Political Economy 102: 322-347

Kauffman SA (1993) The Origins of Order. Self-Organization and Selection in Evolution. Oxford University Press, New York Oxford

Klepper S (1996) Entry, exit, growth and innovation in the product life cycle, American Economic Review 86: 562-583

Klepper S, Simons KL (1997) Technological extinctions of industrial firms; an inquiry into their nature and causes, Industrial and Corporate Change 6: 379-460

Kuznets S (1965) Economic Growth and Structure. Norton, New York

Lancaster, KJ (1975) Socially optimal product differentiation. American Economic Review 65: 567-585

Leydesdorff, L (1995) The Challenge of Scientometrics. The Development, Measurement, and Self-Organization of Scientific Communications. DSWO Press Leiden University, Leiden

May, RM (1973) Stability and Complexity in Model Ecosystems. Princeton University Press, Princeton

Miller R, Sawers D (1968) The Technical Development of Modern Aviation. Routledge & Kegan Paul, London

Nelson RR, Winter SG (1977) In search of useful theory of innovation. Research Policy 6: 36-76
Pasinetti LL (1981) Structural Change and Economic Growth. Cambridge University Press, Cambridge
Pasinetti LL (1993) Structural Economic Dynamics. Cambridge University Press, Cambridge
Pielou EC (1977) Mathematical Ecology. John Wiley, New York
Romer P (1987) Growth based on increasing returns due to specialization. American Economic Review 77: 56-62
Romer P (1990) Endogenous technical progress. Journal of Political Economy 98: 71-102
Sahal D (1985) Technological guideposts and innovation avenues. Research Policy 14: 61-82
Saviotti PP (1988) The measurement of changes in technological output. In: Van Raan AFJ (ed) Handbook of Quantitative Studies of Science and Technology. North-Holland, Amsterdam
Saviotti PP (1991) The role of variety in economic and technological development. In: Saviotti PP, Metcalfe, JS (eds) Evolutionary Theories of Economic and Technological Change. Harwood Academic Publishers, Chur Philadelphia
Saviotti PP (1994) Variety, economic and technological development. In: Shionoya Y, Perlman M (eds) Technology, Industries and Institutions : Studies in Schumpeterian Perspectives. University of Michigan Press, Ann Arbor
Saviotti PP (1996) Technological Evolution, Variety and the Economy. Edward Elgar, Cheltenham Brookfield
Saviotti PP (1998) Technological evolution and firm behavior. In: Lesourne J, Orléan A (eds) Advances in Self-Organization and Evolutionary Economics. Economica, London Paris Genève
Saviotti PP, Mani G (1995) Competition, variety and technological evolution : a replicator dynamics model. Journal of Evolutionary Economics 5: 369-392
Saviotti PP, Metcalfe JS (1984) A theoretical approach to the construction of technological output indicators. Research Policy 13: 141-151
Saviotti PP, Trickett A (1992) The evolution of helicopter technology, 1940-1986. Economics of Innovation and New Technology 2: 111-130
Simon HA (1969) The Sciences of the Artificial. MIT Press, Cambridge MA London
Theil H (1967) Economics and Information Theory. North-Holland, Amsterdam
Theil H (1972) Statistical Decomposition Analysis. North-Holland, Amsterdam London
Theil H, Fiebig DG (1984) Exploiting Continuity. Maximum Entropy Estimation of Continuous Distributions. Ballinger, Cambridge MA
Tushman ML, Anderson P (1986) Technological discontinuities and organizational environments. Administrative Science Quarterly 31: 439-465
Utterback JM, Abernathy WJ (1975) A dynamic model of product and process innovation, Omega 3: 639-656
Utterback JM, Suarez FF (1993) Innovation, competition and industry structure, Research Policy 22: 1-21
Weitzman ML (1992) On diversity. Quarterly Journal of Economics 107: 363-406
Weitzman ML (1993) What to preserve ? An application of diversity theory to crane conservation. Quarterly Journal of Economics 108: 157-183
Weitzman ML (1998) Recombinant growth. Quarterly Journal of Economics 113: 331-360
Windrum P, Birchenhall C (1998) Is product life-cycle theory a special case? Dominant designs and the emergence of market niches through coevolutionary learning. Structural Change and Economic Dynamics 9: 109-134

Appendix 1: Description of the data

Aircraft

Number of observations: 731
Time span: 1913-1984

Discrete characteristics (classes + design code in brackets):

Engine type	piston-propeller(A), turboprop(B), jet(C), turbofan(D), rocket(E)
Number of engines	one(A), two(B), three(C), four(D), six(E), eight(F), twelve(G)
Wing type	swept(A), delta(B), straight(C), variable swept(D)
Number of wings	monoplane(A), biplane(B), triplane(C)
Number of booms	one(A), two(B)
Number of fins	one(A), two(B), three(C)

Continuous characteristics (unit of measurement in brackets):

Engine power (in kilowatts)
Wingspan (in meters)
Length (in meters)
Maximum take-off weight (in kilogram)
Maximum speed (in kilometers per hour)
Range (in kilometers)

Helicopters

Number of observations: 144
Time span: 1940-1983

Discrete characteristics (classes in brackets):

Engine type	piston, piston turbo, ramjet, gas generator, turboshaft
Number of engines	one, two, three
Number of blades	two, three, four, five, six, seven, eight
Number of shafts	one, two
Number of rotors per shaft	one, two

Continuous characteristics (unit of measurement in brackets):

Engine power (in kilowatts)
Rotor diameter (in meters)
Length (in meters)
Maximum take-off weight (in kilogram)
Maximum speed (in kilometers per hour)
Range (in kilometers)

Appendix 2: Years for each period

Aircraft

(731 observations; 43 periods of 17 observations)

1. 1913-1916	2. 1916-1917	3. 1917	4. 1917-1919
5. 1919-1923	6. 1923-1926	7. 1926-1928	8. 1928-1929
9. 1929-1931	10. 1931-1932	11. 1932-1933	12. 1933-1934
13. 1934-1935	14. 1935	15. 1935-1937	16. 1937
17. 1937-1938	18. 1938-1939	19. 1939	20. 1939-1940
21. 1940-1941	22. 1941-1942	23. 1942-1943	24. 1943-1944
25. 1944-1945	26. 1945-1948	27. 1948-1950	28. 1950-1953
29. 1953-1954	30. 1954-1956	31. 1956-1958	32. 1958-1959
33. 1959-1962	34. 1962-1963	35. 1963-1965	36. 1965-1967
37. 1967-1968	38. 1968-1970	39. 1970-1971	40. 1971-1974
41. 1974-1976	42. 1976-1978	43. 1978-1984	

Helicopters

(144 observations; 12 periods of 12 observations)

1. 1940-1954	2. 1954-1957	3. 1957-1959	4. 1959-1961
5. 1961-1963	6. 1963-1966	7. 1966-1967	8. 1967-1971
9. 1971-1974	10. 1974-1978	11. 1978-1981	12. 1981-1983

Reassessing the empirical validity of the human-capital augmented neoclassical growth model*

Elias Dinopoulos[1], Peter Thompson[2]

[1]Department of Economics, University of Florida, Gainesville, FL 32611, USA
(e-mail: dinopoe@dale.cba.ufl.edu)
[2]Department of Economics, University of Houston, Houston, TX 77204, USA
(e-mail: pthompso@bayou.uh.edu)

Abstract. We reassess Mankiw, Romer and Weil's [MRW] version of the Solow model using, as did MRW, cross-sectional data to estimate the steady-state equation governing income per capita levels. The model fails in two critical areas. First, plausible factor shares obtained by MRW are not robust to the substitution of two measures of human capital that are more precise than the secondary school enrollment rates used by MRW. Second, the null hypothesis of an exogenous and identical level of technology in all countries is rejected. We also explain why the Solow model performed well despite the above shortcomings.

Key words: Economic growth – Solow model – Technology – Human capital

JEL-classification: O2, O3

1 Introduction

This paper is concerned with a paradox in the modern study of comparative economic growth. Consider first the remarkable empirical performance of the neoclassical model of growth, reported by Mankiw, Romer and Weil (1992 – hereafter MRW) in a paper that has attracted much attention in recent years. Using samples of up to 98 countries with data covering the period 1960–85, they estimated a structural equation from the Solow (1956) growth model, augmented to include human capital as an input in the

* We appreciate helpful comments from Wolfgang Keller, Sam Kortum, Steven Klepper and participants in seminars at Florida, Houston, and Augsburg.

production process. The human-capital augmented model relates the level of income per capita to the expected level of technology, the rate of population growth, and the shares of GDP devoted to physical and human capital investment. The augmented equation accounts for over three-quarters of the international variation in incomes per capita; cross-sectional regressions yield plausible estimates of factor income shares that are consistent with prior information; and measured rates of convergence, when appropriately conditioned on country-specific parameters, are consistent with the predictions of the model. In the words of MRW (p. 421),

> adding human capital to the Solow model improves its performance. Allowing for human capital eliminates the worrisome anomalies – the high coefficients on investment and on population growth in our . . . regressions – that arise when the textbook Solow model is confronted with the data. The parameter estimates seem reasonable. And . . . we are able to dispose of a fairly large part of the model's residual variance.

MRW obtained these results under the assumptions that technological progress is assumed to grow exogenously at a constant rate, and that every country has access to exactly the same expected level of technology.

Consider next a decade of theoretical developments that have resulted in numerous Schumpeterian (R&D-based) models of endogenous technological change, and that have focused the attention of many researchers on the influence that country-specific variables exert over rates of technological progress[1]. There is now an enormous empirical literature linking growth rates to a wide array of choice variables[2]. Hall and Jones (1997) have shown that international differences in total factor productivity are large, and that these differences can be predicted by country-specific variables. And, finally, a recent line of research estimating structural Schumpeterian models has had considerable success estimating the parameters of these models[3]. Together, these developments lend strong support for the endogeneity of technological progress, and for the relevance of the Schumpeterian view to comparative economic growth[4].

In view of these developments in the field of Schumpeterian growth, the empirical performance of the neoclassical model documented by MRW is

---

[1] The seminal papers are Aghion and Howitt (1992), Grosssman and Helpman (1991), Romer (1990), Segerstrom, Anant and Dinopoulos (1990). Segerstrom, Anant and Dinopoulos called their models *Schumpeterian*, while Aghion and Howitt called theirs a model of *creative destruction*.

[2] Numerous examples of the sort of work that has been done in this area can be found in Barro and Sala-i-Martin (1995). Levine and Renelt (1992) have an interesting critical review of this literature.

[3] Arroyo and Dinopoulos (1996), Caballero and Jaffe (1993), Dinopoulos and Thompson (1996, 1997), and Thompson (1996) have estimated structural models of Schumpeterian growth.

[4] While it is true that some models generate exogenous long-run technological change (see, for example, Jones, 1995; Kortum, 1997; Segerstrom, 1998), *all* Schumpeterian models link growth rates to country-specific parameters, and levels of technology to a wide array of choice variables.

paradoxical, and needs explaining. If a country's level of technology is endogenous to choice variables that clearly vary across countries, how can a model which assumes otherwise perform so well? Our intention in this paper is to persuade the reader that the solution to this paradox is, in fact, straightforward. Simply put, we will argue that the human-capital augmented neoclassical model does *not* perform well.

Our line of investigation focuses on MRW's choice of proxy for human capital saving rates: secondary school enrollment rates (SCHOOL). MRW point out that if saving rates are proportional to SCHOOL, their estimation procedure will yield unbiased estimates of factor income shares. However, we will argue that SCHOOL is proportional neither to human capital saving rates, nor even to human capital levels. On the contrary, data on secondary school enrollment rates systematically overestimate international variations in human capital, and this has important consequences for the empirical performance of the neoclassical growth model.

We therefore reassess the performance of the MRW version of the neoclassical growth model by substituting two alternative measures of human capital for SCHOOL. The first measure is, like MRW's, an *input-based* measure constructed primarily from schooling data. The second is an *output-based* measure constructed by Hanusheck and Kim (1996) that attempts to measure directly the quality of a country's labor force from performances in six internationally-comparable mathematics and science test scores[5]. We then assess whether, to use MRW's words, "the parameter estimates seem reasonable". Adopting MRW's criteria for reasonableness, we ask whether the implied income shares of physical and human capital are consistent with prior information, whether they sum to less than one, and whether the model's restrictions can be rejected.

Our answers to these questions are as follows. First, we show that the new indices generate highly implausible factor income shares. Human capital's share of income is estimated to be 1.62 when we use our input-based human capital index, and 0.73 when the output-based index is used; physical capital's share is about 0.45, significantly greater than the customary one third; and in both cases returns to scale in capital are greater than one. Restrictions designed to hold the income shares to plausible levels are easily rejected. We show that these anomalous results can be explained by disposing of MRW's identifying assumption that the expected technology level is the same in all countries. We show instead that the expected technology level in each country is strongly and positively related to its human capital level, a result consistent with a broad class of Schumpeterian models of endogenous technology. Finally, we explain how MRW's choice of SCHOOL induced a systematic bias that led to their favorable assessment of the neoclassical growth model.

Our analysis extends a small literature that has been critical of MRW's model. Arcand and Dagenais' (1994) have argued that the model performs

---

[5] We have shown elsewhere that both of these human-capital measures outperform the MRW measure in cross-country growth regressions that estimate parameters of an augmented version of Romer's (1990) model of endogenous technological change. See Dinopoulos and Thompson (1997).

poorly when estimated in an errors-in-variable framework. Grossman and Helpman (1994) and Howitt (1997) have pointed out the implications of imposing a constant rate of technological change on all countries, an assumption that not only fails our test, but that is also rejected in Keller's (1997) estimation of the neoclassical growth model for regions of East and West Germany. Lichtenberg (1992) has shown that the inclusion of R&D capital in the neoclassical production function alters the implied shares of physical capital. And, finally, Benhabib and Spiegel (1994) have shown that an alternative index of human capital stocks, constructed by Kyriacou (1991), fails to enter significantly in regressions of a standard neoclassical production function.

The layout of the remainder of the paper is as follows. The next section presents a short exposition of the MRW version of the neoclassical growth model. Section 3 introduces the new measures of human capital and examines their implications for the MRW analysis. Section 4 presents a Schumpeterian version of the neoclassical model with country-specific technology levels that explains the source of the anomalies in the revised MRW estimations. Section 5 offers an explanation for why the MRW appears to perform well when secondary school enrollment data are used as a proxy for human capital saving rates. Section 6 concludes.

2 The human-capital augmented neoclassical growth model

We summarize here MRW's version of the human-capital augmented neoclassical growth model. The aggregate production of final output, $Y(t)$, takes the Cobb-Douglas form,

$$Y(t) = K(t)^{\alpha} H(t)^{\beta} (A(t)L(t))^{1-\alpha-\beta} \ , \tag{1}$$

where $K(t)$ and $H(t)$ are physical and human capital endowments, $L(t)$ is labor, and $A(t)$ indexes the level of technology. Let s_k and s_h be the constant fractions of output invested in physical capital and human capital respectively, with $s_k + s_h < 1$. The capital stocks are assumed to evolve according to the following equations,

$$\dot{k}(t) = s_k y(t) - (n + \gamma + \delta)\ k(t) \ , \tag{2}$$

$$\dot{h}(t) = s_h y(t) - (n + \gamma + \delta)\ h(t) \ , \tag{3}$$

where $y(t) = Y(t)/A(t)L(t)$, $k(t) = K(t)/A(t)L(t)$ and $h(t) = H(t)/A(t)L(t)$ denote quantities per effective unit of labor, n is the exogenous rate of population growth, δ is the common rate of physical and human capital depreciation, and $\gamma = \dot{A}(t)/A(t)$ denotes the exogenous rate of technological change. Equation (2) reflects the standard assumptions that one must forego exactly one unit of final good to obtain one additional unit of physical capital, that physical capital depreciates at a constant rate, and that physical capital per effective labor unit also declines in the face of population growth and technological progress.

Equation (3) imposes exactly the same assumptions on human capital, assumptions which in this case should not be taken too literally. First, we know very little about how resource expenditure generates human capital. Hanusheck and Kim (1996), for example, fail to find a relationship between educational expenditure per pupil and performance on mathematics and science tests. Second, it is difficult to explain why human capital should depreciate independently of the rate at which educated workers retire from the labor force. The purpose of these assumptions is simply to allow MRW to treat human and physical capital symmetrically.

Given (2) and (3), diminishing returns to scale in physical and human capital (i.e., $\alpha + \beta < 1$) ensure that this economy converges to a steady state defined in quantities per unit of effective labor by

$$k^* = \left(\frac{s_k^{1-\beta} s_h^{\beta}}{n+\gamma+\delta}\right)^{1/(1-\alpha-\beta)}, \tag{4}$$

and

$$h^* = \left(\frac{s_k^{\alpha} s_h^{1-\alpha}}{n+\gamma+\delta}\right)^{1/(1-\alpha-\beta)}. \tag{5}$$

Equations (4) and (5) are obtained by setting $\dot{k} = \dot{h} = 0$ in (2) and (3), and solving the resulting two equations simultaneously.

There are two approaches one can take to estimate the steady-state of this model. First, one can substitute (4) and (5) into (1) and take logarithms, yielding an equation relating steady-state per capita GDP to the two saving rates and to population growth:

$$\ln\left(\frac{Y(t)}{L(t)}\right) = \ln(A(t)) + \frac{\alpha}{1-\alpha-\beta}\ln(s_k) + \frac{\beta}{1-\alpha-\beta}\ln(s_h) - \frac{\alpha+\beta}{1-\alpha-\beta}\ln(n+\gamma+\delta). \tag{6}$$

In the second approach, one takes the steady-state level of human capital per effective worker, h^*, as a datum. Substituting (2) into (1) after setting $\dot{k} = 0$, one obtains an equation relating per capita GDP to the physical capital saving rate, the human capital level, and population growth:

$$\ln\left(\frac{Y(t)}{L(t)}\right) = \ln(A(t)) + \frac{\alpha}{1-\alpha}\ln(s_k) + \frac{\beta}{1-\alpha}\ln(h^*) - \frac{\alpha}{1-\alpha}\ln(n+\gamma+\delta). \tag{7}$$

Of course, the two approaches are theoretically equivalent, and substituting (5) into (7) will generate (6). However, there is an important practical difference between them. Equation (7) does not require that we use the rather artificial equation governing the evolution of productive human capital, as long as we have access to data on human capital levels. Equation (6), in contrast, requires data on human capital investment rates rather than human capital levels, but it does require that we use the implausible assumptions on human capital embedded in (3).

MRW choose to estimate the parameters in equation (6) for three samples: a sample of 98 non-oil exporting economies; a sample of 75 intermediate economies comprised of all countries in the larger sample except those whose data received a grade of "D" from Summers and

Table 1. Estimates of the steady-state equations with secondary school enrollment rates as proxy for human capital investment

	Dependent variable: $\ln(Y/L)$ in 1985	
	I Equation (6)	II Equation (7)
Observations	98	98
Unrestricted regression:		
$\ln(s_k)$	0.69 (.13)	0.46 (.15)
$\ln(s_h)$	0.66 (.07)	–
$\ln(h^*)$	–	0.37 (.04)
$\ln(n + \gamma + \delta)$	−1.73 (.41)	−0.91 (.44)
R^2	0.78	0.78
Restricted regression:		
Implied α	0.31 (.04)	0.34 (.06)
Implied β	0.28 (.03)	0.27 (.05)
Test of restriction p-value	0.41	0.33

Standard errors in parentheses. $\gamma + \delta$ assumed to be 0.05 for all countries. Constant term not reported here. Column I is from MRW, Table 2; Column II are authors' calculations.

Heston (1988)[6]; and the 22 OECD countries with populations in excess of one million. Data on population growth, GDP and investment in physical capital are taken from Summers and Heston (1988). The rate of investment in human capital is proxied by the percentage of the working-age population enrolled in secondary school. MRW assume that countries deviate randomly from their steady-state at time t, so that $A_i(t) = a(t) + \varepsilon_i$ where $a(t)$ is common to all countries and ε_i is a country-specific disturbance assumed to be uncorrelated with the regressors.

Column I of Table 1 reports the results from MRW's OLS regressions of (6) for their largest sample[7], along with the implied values of α and β obtained by imposing the restriction that the sum of the slope coefficients equals zero. Although MRW did not do so, we can also estimate (7) from their data. Using *a priori* reasonable values of $\alpha = \beta = 0.3$, equation (5) allows us to construct an index of human capital levels from their data on saving rates and population growth. The resulting OLS regressions on equation (7), and the implied values of α and β obtained after imposing the

[6] A grade of "D" is given to countries for which the data are, to use Griliches' (1992) memorable phrase, "the figment of someone's imagination".

[7] MRW's model finds most support with the largest sample. As our analysis is critical, we shall restrict attention to this sample.

restriction that the sum of the coefficients on $\ln(s_k)$ and $\ln(n + \gamma + \delta)$ equals zero, are reported in column II.

The results for the two approaches are the same. First, the implied factor income shares are about one-third for each type of capital. MRW argue that these shares are plausible. Physical capital's implied share is consistent with observations from national accounts, while human capital's implied share is consistent with MRW's interpretation of U.S. wage differentials.[8] Second, the single overidentifying restriction in each equation is not rejected. Third, the regressions account for over three-quarters of the variation in incomes per capita.

A further implication of the results in Table 1 is that the returns to reproducible factors of production, $\alpha + \beta$, are in each case significantly less than one[9], leading MRW (p. 409) to conclude that

> Overall, the findings reported in this paper cast doubt on the recent trend among economists to dismiss the Solow growth model in favor of endogenous-growth models that assume constant or increasing returns to scale in capital. One can explain much of the cross-country variation in income while maintaining the assumption of decreasing returns.

In the remainder of this paper we assess the reliability of MRW's conclusions.

3 Measuring human capital

Questions concerning the measurement of human capital are central to our assessment of these results. As MRW (pp. 418–19) note,

> Measurement of human capital presents great practical difficulties. . . .[N]ot all spending on human capital is intended to yield productive human capital: philosophy, religion, and literature, for example, although serving in part to train the mind, might also be a form of consumption. We use a proxy for the rate of human capital accumulation, s_h, that measures approximately the percentage of the working-age population that is in secondary school. . . . This variable, which we call SCHOOL, is clearly imperfect . . . [y]et if SCHOOL is proportional to s_b then we can use it to estimate. . . ; the factor of proportionality will affect only the constant term.

We argue that SCHOOL is proportional neither to human capital saving rates, nor to human capital levels. On the contrary, we will show that data on secondary school enrollment rates systematically overestimate human capital levels in rich countries and underestimate them in poor countries.

---

[8] MRW calculate the plausible human capital share as follows. The U.S. minimum wage is about 50% of the average wage, suggesting that 50% of total labor income represents the return to human capital. As labor's share of GDP is about 0.7, this implies that β is about 0.35. Presumably because physical capital's share is roughly constant across countries, MRW assume that this calculation also applies to other countries.

[9] As MRW point out, their model becomes an endogenous-growth model (of the simple AK type) if $\alpha + \beta = 1$.

3.1 Secondary school enrollment rates and human capital

We see several problems with using secondary school enrollment rates as a proxy for the human capital saving rate. First, enrollment rates seem to us more appropriately viewed as a measure of human capital levels. Assume that a constant fraction of the labor force is of an age that makes it eligible for secondary education. Then, secondary school enrollment rates are proportional in steady-state to the fraction of the population that is educated, and they are also proportional to average years of schooling in the labor force. Both of these have traditionally been viewed as indicators for labor-augmented human capital levels[10].

Second, these school enrollment rates ignore pre- and post-secondary education, yet there is ample evidence to suggest that significant gains to productive human capital are also secured at these other levels of education[11]. Third, ignoring the correlation between ability and education generates misleading inferences about the effects of increasing enrollment rates (Becker, 1964, pp. 171–81). Fourth, human capital can also be accumulated outside the formal education system. It may arise from on-the-job training, from learning by doing, and from myriad social interactions that do not lend themselves to measurement. In MRW's framework, a country with no secondary schools produces nothing.

Finally, the marginal product of formal education is likely to be diminishing, as expanding enrollment rates are typically associated with increased emphasis on the acquisition of knowledge that is not directly productive, and with the provision of education to individuals less able to exploit it. Mulligan and Sala-i-Martin (1995) have recently provided some evidence on this score. Using census wage and education data for the United States, they constructed six Divisia indices of human capital over the period 1940–1990. From these indices, they calculated average annual growth rates of 0.29, 0.36, 0.37, 0.41, 0.42 and 0.49 percent. The average of their six measures, 0.4 percent, compares with a growth rate for average years of schooling of 0.8 percent. Mulligan and Sala-i-Martin concluded that growth in school enrollment rates in the United States have overestimated the growth rate of productive human capital by as much as 100 percent[12].

In summary, we believe that more precise measures of human capital are required. New measures should allow for different levels of education and ability, and they should allow for human capital levels to be positive even without secondary school education. Moreover, given the difficulty in interpreting equation (3), one would be well served by focusing on the

---

[10] The empirical section of Becker's (1964) classic study of human capital clearly takes this position.

[11] See, for example, John, Murphy and Pierce's (1993) study of the returns to post-secondary education in the United States.

[12] One way to think about Mulligan and Sala-i-Martin's results in the context of the neoclassical model is to interpret $(H^{\beta/1-\alpha-\beta}L)$ as measuring labor supply in efficiency units. Then, for $\alpha = \beta = 1/3$, a one percent increase in H should generate a one percent increase in the relative wage of skilled and unskilled workers, double the increase found by Sala-i-Martin.

measurement of human capital levels rather than human capital saving rates. Naturally, one would like to construct a new index of human capital using the methodology developed by Mulligan and Sala-i-Martin. Unfortunately, such an index requires detailed census data that are just not available. In the next section, we describe two feasible alternatives to secondary school enrollment rates that we will then use to assess the performance of the neoclassical growth model.

3.2 Alternative measures of human capital

We assess the performance of the MRW version of the neoclassical growth model using two very different data sets. The first, developed formally in the Appendix, is an index of human capital levels which, while consistent with the analysis of Mulligan and Sala-i-Martin, requires only data that are readily available for a large international sample. The index is an extension of an efficiency-based measure suggested by Dinopoulos and Segerstrom (1998). It allows ability to vary among a population, and households to decide optimally the amount of education their members receive. The index provides for significant levels of human capital even when school enrollment rates are low; it exhibits diminishing returns to formal education; and human capital depreciates as the result of educated workers exiting the labor force. The data required to calculate the index – demographic data, and enrollment rates at primary, secondary and tertiary levels – were readily available for all 98 countries in MRW's sample except Chad and Sudan. We take our observations from 1965, to minimize the possibility of feedback effects from 1985 income to enrollment rates.

In order to avoid any concerns about the effect that simple changes in the scale of the human capital index might have on the performance of the neoclassical model, we scale the index in a manner as favorable as possible to MRW's results. Using values of $\alpha = \beta = 0.3$, we construct implied steady-state saving rates from equation (5). We then proportionally adjust our raw human capital levels so that the sample mean saving rate recovered from (5) has a mean of 0.055, the same as SCHOOL. We shall refer to the resulting scaled index as the DST index of human capital levels.

While DST attempts to resolve many of the difficulties that arise with SCHOOL, it is nonetheless an input-based index that relies heavily on school enrollment rates. Our second index, constructed by Hanusheck and Kim (1996), is the result of attempts to measure directly the quality of the labor force from performances on six internationally-comparable mathematics and science test scores. The tests were taken at different points in time and each test had a different number of participating countries. While each test was designed to facilitate international comparisons, the tests are not directly comparable across time. Thus, Hanusheck and Kim adjust for drift over time using data from the U.S. National Assessment of Educational Progress, standardized tests that are designed for intertemporal comparisons. The index, which we shall denote by HK, is also scaled so that saving rates giving rise to HK in steady-state would have the same mean as SCHOOL. HK includes measured and projected data, but their data cover only a subset of 71 countries from MRW's sample.

Table 2. Least squares estimation of equation (7)

	Dependent variable: $\ln(Y/L)$ in 1985		
	I. SS	II. DST	III. HK
Observations	98	96	71
Unrestricted regression:			
$\ln(s_k)$	0.73	0.80	0.88
	(.13)	(.13)	(.20)
$\ln(h^*)$	0.67	2.92	1.38
	(.08)	(.36)	(.26)
$\ln(n + \gamma + \delta)$	−1.76	−0.63	−1.07
	(.42)	(.47)	(.53)
R^2	0.77	0.76	0.68
Restricted regression:			
$\ln(s_k)$	0.86	0.79	0.91
	(.12)	(.13)	(.18)
$\ln(h^*)$	0.65	2.90	1.30
	(.08)	(.35)	(.26)
$\ln(n + \gamma + \delta)$	−0.86	−0.79	−0.91
	(.12)	(.13)	(.18)
R^2	0.77	0.76	0.68
Implied α	0.34	0.44	0.48
	(.06)	(.04)	(.05)
Implied β	0.25	1.62	0.73
	(.05)	(.28)	(.19)
Test of restrictions			
p-value	.03	0.73	0.76

Standard errors in parentheses. $\gamma + \delta$ assumed to be 0.05 for all countries. Constant term not reported.

We shall postpone until Section 5 a comparison of the cross-country distribution of the three human capital measures. We turn, instead, to an evaluation of the neoclassical growth model when it is presented with three different measures of human capital: SCHOOL, interpreted now as a measure of human capital *levels* (which we shall denote by SS), the alternative input-based measure, DST, and the output-based measure, HK.

3.3 Estimation

Table 2 summarizes the results of estimating equation (7) with the three alternative measures of human capital.[13] Consider first the results in column I, in which SS was used. The implied shares of physical and human capital

[13] In an earlier version of this paper we also estimated equation (6), treating the new human capital indices as proxies for the saving rate, s_h. The outcome of that exercise was a rejection of the identifying restrictions of the model at high levels of significance. We do not report those results here, because they are as likely to stem from an inappropriate use of the human capital indices as they are from shortcomings of the model.

obtained from the restricted estimation of (7) are 0.34 and 0.25 respectively, and about 80 percent of the international variation in incomes per capita is explained by the model. These are, of course, essentially the same as MRW's results in Table 1. However, in contrast to the earlier results, the single overidentifying restriction implied by (7) is rejected. That is, we cannot use the restricted regression to construct estimates of α and β. Instead, we must use the *unrestricted* regressions, which generates two pairs of mutually inconsistent parameter values. Using the unrestricted OLS coefficients on $\ln(s_k)$ and $\ln(h^*)$, we obtain implied parameter values of $\{\alpha = 0.42, \beta = 0.39\}$, while the coefficients on $\ln(n + \gamma + \delta)$ and $\ln(h^*)$ yield implied values of $\{\alpha = 0.64, \beta = 0.24\}$. Using secondary school enrollment rates as a proxy for human capital levels thus leads to a rejection of the model. Moreover, attempts to infer the values of factor income shares from a regression that does not impose the restriction generate implied shares for physical capital that are too high.

Columns II and III of Table 2 report the regression results for our preferred indices of human capital. Although the bases of these two indices are very different, they generate remarkably similar results. First, the explanatory power of the regression remains high. Second, the implied income share of physical capital is 0.44 when DST is used, 0.48 with HK, both of which are a little high (the two standard error intervals exclude values less than 0.36). Third, for both indices, the estimate of human capital's share is now much too large. For DST, it is 1.62, while for HK it is 0.73.

The sum of the implied factor shares are, with DST and HK, greater than one. This implies that a necessary condition for the existence of a steady state in the neoclassical model is not satisfied. Moreover, as the overidentifying restriction is not rejected, these parameter estimates are very similar to those obtained from the unrestricted OLS coefficients. Thus, our preferred human capital indices tell a very different story about MRW's version of the neoclassical growth model. Either we reject the overidentifying restriction of the model (and thus obtain mutually inconsistent pairs of parameter estimates); or we fail to reject the restriction but obtain instead implied factor income shares well in excess of one (and in excess of 2 for one measure). Either case demands that we reject the neoclassical growth model.

Our rejection of MRW's model raises two important questions. First, why does the model perform poorly when our preferred human capital indices are used? Second, what is it about MRW's human capital proxy that makes the model perform well when SCHOOL is used as a proxy for the saving rate? The remainder of the paper addresses these two questions. In Section 4 we provide evidence that the key failing of the model lies in its assumption of an exogenous and identical expected technology level in all countries. In Section 5 a comparison of our human capital indices with SCHOOL sheds some light on the second question.

4 On technology levels

MRW's estimation of the neoclassical model imposes a common expected technology on all countries. One can, in principle, test the assumption of common technology using cross-sectional data, and in this section we test it against a plausible Schumpeterian alternative. Our alternative assumes that the rate of advance of the technological frontier is exogenous at the rate γ (or, more precisely, is unexplained), but that a country's relative technology level, A_R, depends on its endowment of human capital per effective worker:

$$A_R = \phi h^{\psi} \ . \tag{8}$$

The evolution of technology captured by our alternative can be viewed as a reduced form for a number of Schumpeterian growth models incorporating international technology diffusion (e.g., Eaton and Kortum, 1995; Howitt, 1997). In the presence of diffusion, the rate of technological progress increases with human capital levels, but declines as a country advances relative to the rest of the world. Eventually the two effects cancel, leading to a steady state in which permanent technology differences are sustained by differences in human capital levels, but in which all countries grow at the same rate.

Testing the neoclassical model with (8) as the alternative is a straightforward task. Substituting (8) into (6), and using (5) to remove h^* yields,

$$\ln\left(\frac{Y}{L}\right) = \ln(\phi) + \frac{\alpha(1+\psi)}{1-\alpha-\beta}\ln(s_k) + \frac{\beta+(1-\alpha)\psi}{1-\alpha-\beta}\ln(s_h) - \frac{\alpha+\beta+\psi}{1-\alpha-\beta}\ln(n+\gamma+\delta) \ , \tag{9}$$

which is the appropriate equation to estimate when human capital saving rates are available.

When our data measure human capital levels, substituting (8) into (7) yields an implementable equation that does not involve s_h:

$$\ln\left(\frac{Y}{L}\right) = \ln(\phi) + \frac{\alpha}{1-\alpha}\ln(s_k) + \frac{\beta+(1-\alpha)\psi}{1-\alpha}\ln(h^*) - \frac{\alpha}{1-\alpha}\ln(n+\gamma+\delta) \, . \tag{10}$$

In both cases, setting $\psi = 0$ recovers the corresponding equation of the neoclassical model. The only difficulty (it is, of course, a considerable one) is that the three parameters of interest, α, β and ψ, are not separately identified. Equation (9) maintains the restriction from (6) that the sum of the slope coefficients is zero, and equation (10) maintains the restriction from (7) that the sum of the coefficients on $\ln(s_k)$ and $\ln(n+\gamma+\delta)$ is zero. Both equations therefore have only two independent slope coefficients, from which we would like to estimate three parameters. We will therefore conduct the test under the identifying restriction that $\alpha+\beta = 0.6$, a restriction that MRW have suggested is plausible.

Table 3 reports the results from nonlinear least squares estimation of (9) and (10). Equation (9) was estimated using SCHOOL, while equation (10) was estimated with DST and HK. The unrestricted OLS regressions are, of course, identical to those already reported in Tables 1 and 2. Tests of the restrictions on the slope coefficients were also reported in column I of Table 1,

Table 3. NLLS estimation of equations (9) and (10)

	Dependent variable: ln(*Y*/*L*) in 1985		
	I SCHOOL	II DST	III HK
Observations	98	96	71
ψ	−0.02	2.61	1.16
	(.04)	(.32)	(.23)
α	0.31	0.43	0.48
	(.04)	(.04)	(.05)
β	0.29	0.17	0.12
	(.04)	(.04)	(.05)
$\ln(\phi)$	7.8	7.2	6.68
	(.14)	(.10)	(.16)
R^2	0.78	0.76	0.68

Standard errors in parentheses. $\gamma + \delta$ assumed to be 0.05 for all countries. Column I estimates parameters in equation (9). Columns II and III estimate parameters in equation (10).

and columns II and III of Table 2. We do not estimate (10) with SS because the restriction was rejected in this case (see column I of Table 2).

The key observation is that in columns II and III the null hypothesis $\psi = 0$ is easily rejected, while it is not rejected in column I. We conclude that when DST or HK are used, there is strong evidence that technology levels are positively related to human capital levels. That is, when we restrict factor income shares to a level that MRW not only claim is plausible, but that they cite in their positive evaluation of the neoclassical model, we find that the assumption of equal expected technology levels in all countries is not supported by the data.

There is, of course, nothing startling about the mechanism behind these results. In equation (10), β and ψ are negatively related for any given coefficient on $\ln(h^*)$. Holding ψ at zero, as we did in Table 2, we find that β is too large. In Table 3 we constrain β to a smaller value, and this forces ψ to increase. Contrast this with the results in column I of Table 3. The plausible restriction on $\alpha + \beta$ is very similar to the value that was obtained when ψ was held to zero in column I of Table 1. Thus, in Table 3 we obtain an implied value of ψ that is not significantly different from zero[14].

5 Why do MRW's results look so good?

Why should MRW's analysis with secondary school enrollment data generate such favorable results for the neoclassical growth model even though SCHOOL is a poor measure of human capital saving rates, and technology differences among countries are systematically related to human capital levels? There are two aspects to this question. First, we must explain the

[14] The regressions in Table 3 cannot yield higher coefficients of determination than were obtained previously, before equations (9) and (10) contain exactly the same regressors as equations (6) and (7).

high explanatory power of MRW's regressions. Second, we must explain the plausible factor income shares.

The reason for the high explanatory power of the regressions is straightforward: even though secondary school enrollment rates may not be a good proxy for productive human capital, they are an excellent proxy for income. That is, SCHOOL is correlated with per capita income, not only because education promotes higher income, but also because education is a normal consumption good. Moreover, MRW construct SCHOOL from average enrollment rates over the entire period 1960–85, and the possibility that the correlation between income and SCHOOL[15] is dominated by causality going from the former to the latter cannot be ignored.

Our explanation of the plausible factor income shares obtained by MRW is this: *sheer luck*. A simple thought experiment will illustrate. Consider the following production technology:

$$\ln\left(\frac{Y}{L}\right) = a_0 + \alpha \ln(k) + \beta \ln(h) \ , \tag{11}$$

in which a_0 indexes technology. Assume further that, in the Schumpeterian tradition, the level of technology is $a_0 = \phi + \psi \ln(h)$, where ϕ can be thought of as a component of technology that is common to all countries, and ψ is the elasticity of technology with respect to each country's human capital per effective worker. Thus, the true model is

$$\ln\left(\frac{Y}{L}\right) = \phi + \alpha \ln(k) + (\psi + \beta) \ln(h) \ , \tag{12}$$

and if h is measured correctly, one can expect an econometrician to recover an unbiased estimated of $(\psi + \beta)$.

But now assume that the econometrician observes $h' = \mu h^{v}$ and, further, that he believes the true model is (12). The econometrician will obtain an unbiased estimate of $(\psi + \beta)/(1 + v)$, but will interpret it as an estimate of β. So if the econometrician has a correct prior belief that β is one third he will find his results plausible as long as $v \approx 3\,\psi$.

From column II of Table 3, we obtained with DST an estimate of $\hat{\psi} = 2.6$, which implies that a value of v close to 9 would lead to a plausible value of β, even though an incorrect measure, h', of human capital is being used in place of h. Figure 1 plots the relationship between DST and the h' obtained on using SCHOOL as a proxy for the human capital saving rate[16]. Clearly, v is significantly greater than one. In fact, a regression of $\ln(h')$ on a constant and $v \ln(h)$ yields $\hat{v} = 8.5$ ($\sigma_{\hat{v}} = 0.4$, $R^2 = 0.81$), which is equal to $3.2\hat{\psi}$. Consequently, secondary school enrollment rates yield a plausible estimate of human capital's share of income when expected technology is held constant across countries, and the neoclassical model appears to be

[15] After controlling for variations in population growth and investment rates, school 'explains' almost half of the residual variance in income levels.

[16] The data for h′ were obtained by substituting the observed values of n and s_k and $\alpha = \beta = 0.3$ into equation (5).

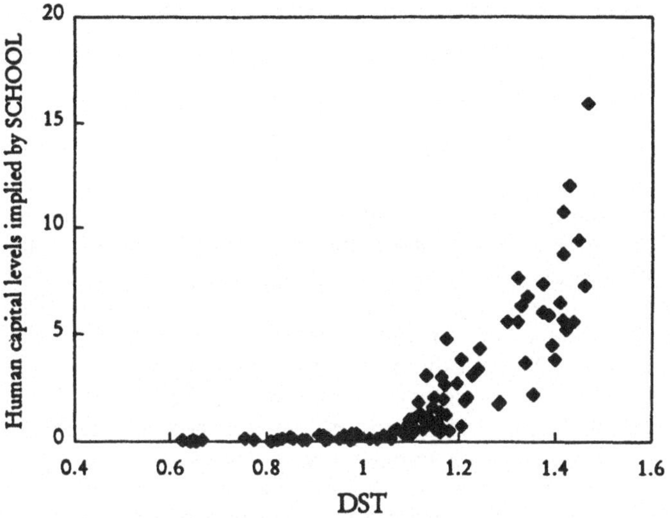

Fig. 1. DST and SCHOOL human capital levels

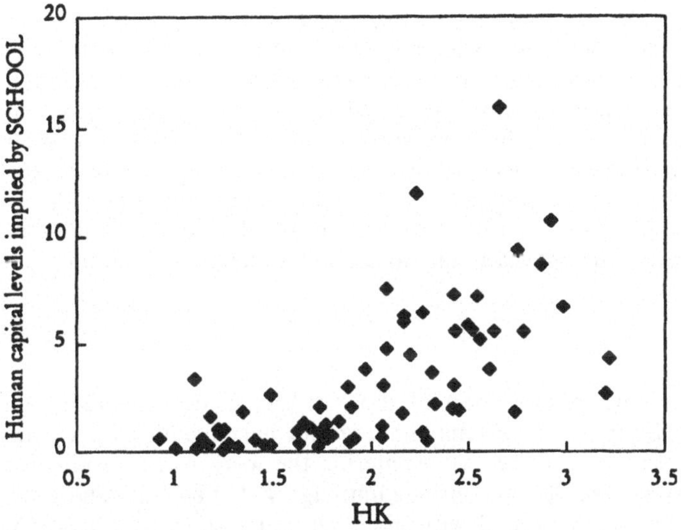

Fig. 2. HK and SCHOOL human capital levels

well behaved. A similar analysis follows from the alternative index HK, which is plotted against the h' implied by SCHOOL in Fig. 2.

In summary, MRW's results look so good for two reasons. First, their proxy for human capital is highly correlated with income because education is a consumption good. Second, they obtain plausible factor income shares because their index imposes too much cross-country variability in human capital levels, a feature of the data that biases the estimate of β downwards.

The extent of the bias is just sufficient to generate a plausible value for β when the expected level of technology is incorrectly assumed to be identical in all countries.

6 Conclusions

Our reassessment of the human-capital augmented neoclassical model focused on MRW's use of secondary school enrollment rates as a proxy for human capital saving rates. We argued that this measure vastly overstates international variations in (productive) human capital, and we re-estimated MRW's model using two very different indices that in our view are superior along several dimensions. When estimated with secondary school enrollment rates, the neoclassical model yields plausible estimates of factor shares, and international variations in technology are not detectable. In contrast, the new indices generate implied factor shares that are highly implausible, and there is strong evidence that international variations in the level of technology are large. In conclusion, the performance of the neoclassical model depends critically on which measure of human capital is the more plausible. Given a preponderance of supporting evidence, we believe the case for the new indices is clear.

Our results, obtained from modern cross-sectional data, should also be interpreted in light of what is has already been learned from long-run time series evidence. Taken together, the evidence clearly supports the notion that technological change is endogenous. Moreover, we do not think that international variations in technology are "small" in the sense that models that ignore them can nonetheless perform adequately in empirical work. On the contrary, the evidence supports the Schumpeterian contention that a technological explanation must lie at the very heart of an understanding of the large and persistent international variations in income per capita.

Appendix

We describe here our construction of the DST human capital index. An individual with ability $\theta \in [\theta_0, \theta^0]$ may undergo formal education for s years prior to joining the work force. After entering the work force, productive employment can be expected to continue until age T. Let $\omega(\theta, s)$ denote the constant wage for an individual with ability θ and s years of education; $\omega(\theta, s)$ is differentiable, increasing and strictly concave in both arguments. Schooling is chosen to satisfy

$$s^*(\theta) = \arg\max_s \left\{ \int_{t+s}^{t+T} e^{-\rho(v-t)} \omega(\theta, s)\, dv; \quad s \geq 0 \right\} . \tag{A1}$$

We make the following assumption about the returns to education:

$$\frac{\partial\omega(\theta,s)/\partial s}{\omega(\theta,s)} \text{ is increasing in } \theta \ .$$

That is, more able individuals gain more from education.[17] It is then easy to show that more able individuals choose more schooling. The first-order condition is

$$\frac{\partial\omega(\theta,s)/\partial s}{\omega(\theta,s)}=\frac{\rho}{1-e^{-\rho(T-s)}} \quad . \tag{A2}$$

As the left hand side of (A2) increases with θ, $s^*(\theta)$ is increasing with θ. Conversely, let $\theta_{\min}(s')$ denote the minimum ability for which $s^*(\theta) > s'$; by the implicit function theorem, $\theta_{\min}(s')$ is increasing in s'.

We assume that human capital, measured in efficiency units, can be indexed by

$$H(t)=\Phi A(t)N(t)\int_{\theta_0}^{\theta^0}\theta(1+s(\theta))^{\phi}\,dF(\theta) \ , \tag{A3}$$

where F is the distribution function of θ.

In order to construct an empirical index, we need to provide some structure to the model. First, we assume that agents can only choose from a countable set of education levels, $s\in\{s_0,s_1,s_2,\ldots\}$, where $\theta_{\min}(s_i) > \theta_{\min}(s_j)$ for any $i > j$. We will specifically assume that individuals may choose among only four options: $s_0 = 0$ (no formal education); $s_1 = 6$ (primary education); $s_2 = 11$ (secondary education); and $s_3 = 15$ (tertiary education). These options correspond to educational levels for which international data are available.

Second, each household is modeled as a dynastic family whose size grows at the rate $n = \beta - \delta$, where β is the birth rate and δ is the death rate. All members of a household are assumed to have the same ability. Individuals live for an interval D, implying that $\delta N(t+D) = \beta N(t)$. Thus, $\delta = n/(e^{nD} - 1)$ and $\beta = ne^{nD}/(e^{nD} - 1)$. Consider, then, the subset of the population that chooses schooling level s_j. In this subset, the skilled workers are the older workers (who have completed school):

$$\int_{\theta_{\min}(s_j)}^{\theta_{\min}(s_{j+1})}\int_{t-D}^{t-s_j}\beta N(v)\,dv\,dF(\theta)=\int_{\theta_{\min}(s_j)}^{\theta_{\min}(s_{j+1})}\Gamma_j N(t)\,dF(\theta) \ , \tag{A4}$$

where $\Gamma_j = [e^{n(D-s_j)} - 1]/[e^{nD} - 1] < 1$.

Third, we assume that $F(\theta)$ is uniform on the unit interval. Let $(1-\theta_j)$ denote the fraction of the work force that chooses at least education level s_j. Then, the average ability of households choosing exactly education level s_j is $(\theta_{j+1} + \theta_j)/2$, where $\theta_4 = 1$ and $\theta_0 = 0$. Thus, steady-state human capital per effective worker is given by

[17] One should, in this context, interpret ability broadly. It not only reflects intellectual or physical ability to engage in productive activity, but also the social and economic constraints that affect an individual's ability to exploit his or her personal aptitude for work.

Table A1. DST index of human capital

Algeria	1.097	Bangladesh	0.985	Argentina	1.284
Angola	0.873	Hong Kong	1.194	Bolivia	1.134
Benin	0.855	India	1.153	Brazil	1.155
Botswana	1.065	Indonesia	1.125	Chile	1.242
Burkina Faso	0.653	Israel	1.134	Colombia	1.123
Burundi	0.808	Japan	1.417	Ecuador	1.149
Cameroon	1.160	Jordan	1.166	Paraguay	1.166
Central Afr. Rep.	1.031	South Korea	1.207	Peru	1.161
Congo	1.087	Malaysia	1.168	Uruguay	1.357
Congo-Brazaville	1.139	Myanmar	1.131	Venezuela	1.093
Egypt	1.146	Nepal	0.756		
Ethiopia	0.645	Pakistan	0.917		
Ghana	1.097	Philippines	1.172	Austria	1.418
Ivory Coast	0.980	Singapore	1.244	Belgium	1.461
Kenya	0.961	Sri Lanka	1.219	Denmark	1.449
Liberia	0.907	Syria	1.115	Finland	1.467
Madagascar	1.059	Thailand	1.106	France	1.388
Malawi	0.920			West Germany	1.374
Mali	0.774			Greece	1.411
Mauritania	0.666	Canada	1.324	Ireland	1.430
Mauritius	1.211	Costa Rica	1.135	Italy	1.395
Morocco	1.043	Dominican Rep.	1.133	Netherlands	1.374
Mozambique	0.884	El Salvador	1.099	Norway	1.412
Niger	0.642	Guatemala	0.976	Portugal	1.400
Nigeria	0.849	Haiti	1.013	Spain	1.339
Rwanda	0.960	Honduras	1.102	Sweden	1.422
Senegal	0.928	Jamaica	1.331	Switzerland	1.284
Sierra Leone	0.833	Mexico	1.121	Turkey	1.175
Somalia	0.624	Nicaragua	1.103	United Kingdom	1.439
South Africa	1.181	Panama	1.173		
Tanzania	0.824	Trinidad & Tobago	1.230	Australia	1.303
Togo	0.990	USA	1.324	New Zealand	1.344
Tunisia	1.207			Papua New Guinea	0.950
Uganda	0.973				
Zambia	0.977				
Zimbabwe	1.072				

$$h(t) = \frac{H(t)}{A(t)N(t)} = \Phi \sum_{j=0}^{3} \frac{(\theta_{j+1} - \theta_j)}{2} (\theta_{j+1} - \theta_j)(1 + s_j)^{\phi} \Gamma_j \ . \tag{A5}$$

Fourth, we need to select values for ϕ, which measures the elasticity of productive human capital with respect to schooling, and for the proportionality factor, Φ. For the former, we turn to Mulligan and Sala-i-Martin's [1995] labor-based measures of human capital in the United States discussed earlier, that suggest a value for ϕ of about 0.5.

It turns out that the choice of Φ has no bearing on the results that follow[18], but to avoid concerns that may linger over the question of scale, we calibrate the index for consistency with SCHOOL under the assumption

[18] The choice of Φ only affects estimates of the intercept, which is of no direct interest.

that MRW's model is correct. Given h^*, we can construct from equation (5) an implied saving rate that in steady state would generate h^*. We do so using the observed physical capital investment rates and population growth rates, and a common value of 0.3 for α and β. We then choose Φ so that the sample mean of the implied saving rates is equal to the mean of SCHOOL.

Data for the construction of the index are obtained from the *United Nations World Development Report*. We used 1965 primary, secondary, and tertiary enrollment rates as our estimates for $(1 - \theta_1)$, $(1 - \theta_2)$, and $(1 - \theta_3)$.[19] We used the lesser of life expectancy or 65 years for D. The resulting index is provided in Table A1.

References

Aghion P, Howitt P (1992) A model of growth through creative destruction. Econometrica 60: 323–351

Arcand JL, Dagenais M (1994) Economic growth in a cross section of countries: Do errors in variables really not matter? Mimeo, University of Montreal

Arroyo C, Dinopoulos E (1996) Schumpeterian growth in expanding economies: Time-series evidence from the US. Mimeo, University of Florida

Barro RJ, Sala-i-Martin X (1995) Economic growth. McGraw-Hill, New York

Becker GS (1964) Human capital. A theoretical and empirical analysis with special reference to education, 3rd edn. University of Chicago Press, Chicago

Benhabib J, Spiegel MM (1994) The role of human capital in economic development: Evidence from aggregate cross-country data. Journal of Monetary Economics 34: 143–174

Caballero R, Jaffe AB (1993) How high are the giants' shoulders? An empirical assessment of knowledge spillovers and creative destruction in a model of growth. NBER Macroeconomics Annual 1994

Dinopoulos E, Segerstrom PS (1998) A Schumpeterian model of protection and relative wages. American Economic Review (forthcoming)

Dinopoulos E, Thompson P (1996) A contribution to the empirics of endogenous growth. Eastern Economic Journal 22: 389–400

Dinopoulos E, Thompson P (1997) R&D-based long-run growth in a cross section of countries. Mimeo, University of Florida

Eaton J, Kortum SS (1995) International patenting and technology diffusion. NBER working paper no. 5207

Griliches Z (1992) Discussion of F. Lichtenberg, R&D investment and international productivity differences. In: Siebert H (ed) Economic growth in the world economy, pp 110–112. Mohr, Tübingen

Grossman GM, Helpman E (1991) Innovation and growth in the global economy. MIT Press, Cambridge, MA

Grossman GM, Helpman E (1994) Endogenous innovation in the theory of growth. Journal of Economic Perspectives 8: 23–44

Hall RE, Jones CI (1997) Fundamental determinants of output per worker. Mimeo, Stanford University

Hanushek EA, Kim D (1996) Schooling, labor force quality, and the growth of nations. Mimeo, University of Rochester

[19] Enrollments rates are measured as the numbers of pupils divided by the number of children within a specified age group. On the occasions when enrollment rates at primary school exceeded 1 (because of variations in the definitions of each level of education), we set the rate equal to 1.

Howitt P (1997) Steady endogenous growth with population and R&D inputs growing. Mimeo, Ohio State University

Jones CI (1995) R&D-based models of economic growth. Journal of Political Economy 103: 759–784

Juhn C, Murphy KM, Pierce B (1993) Wage inequality and the rise in returns to skill. Journal of Political Economy 101: 410–441

Keller W (1997) From socialist showcase to mezzogiorno? Lessons on the role of technical change from East Germany's post-world war II growth performance. NBER working paper no. 6079

Kortum SS (1997) Research, patenting, and technological change. Econometrica 65: 1389–1420

Kyriacou G (1991) Level and growth effects of human capital. Working paper 91–26, CV Starr Center, New York University

Levine R, Renelt D (1992) A sensitivity analysis of cross-country growth regressions. American Economic Review 82: 942–963

Lichtenberg FR (1992) R&D investment and international productivity differences. In: Siebert H (ed) Economic growth in the world economy, pp 89–110. Mohr, Tübingen

Mankiw NG, Romer D, Weil DN (1992) A contribution to the empirics of economic growth. Quarterly Journal of Economics 107: 407–437

Mulligan CB, Sala-i-Martin X (1995) Measuring aggregate human capital. NBER working paper no. 5016

Romer PM (1990) Endogenous technological change. Journal of Political Economy 98: S71–S102

Segerstrom PS (1998) Endogenous growth without scale effects. American Economic Review (forthcoming)

Segerstrom, PS, Anant TCA, Dinopoulos E (1990) A Schumpeterian model of the product life cycle. American Economic Review 80(5): 1077–1091

Solow RM (1956) A contribution to the theory of economic growth. Quarterly Journal of Economics 70: 65–94

Summers R, Heston A (1988) A new set of international comparisons of real product and price levels estimates for 130 countries, 1950–1985. Review of Income and Wealth 34: 1–26

Thompson P (1996) Technological opportunity and the growth of knowledge: A Schumpeterian approach to measurement. Journal of Evolutionary Economics 6: 77–97

Institutions, entrepreneurship, economic flexibility and growth - experiments on an evolutionary micro-to-macro model

Gunnar Eliasson[1] and Erol Taymaz[2]

[1]KTH, The Royal Institute of Technology, Dept. Of Industrial Economics, 100 44 Stockholm, Sweden
[2]METU, Middle East Technical University, Ankara

Abstract. The capacity of an economic system to grow through competitive entry and flexible adjustment is investigated on a firm based evolutionary simulation model of the Swedish economy. Entry, speed of exit and of labor market reallocation define *flexibility*. Entry is determined by observed profit opportunities in markets and growth, among other things, through dynamic competition by way of entry. Both entry and growth ultimately depend on the existence of property rights institutions that reduce the uncertainty surrounding private access at any time to the expected present value of future profits from investment commitments today.

We find that in a predictable market regime (stable, relative foreign prices) long run growth benefits from slow market adjustments. Fast reallocation creates price instability, erroneous expectations and (easily) cost overshooting. Rapid new entry, however, is always growth promoting in the long run.

The positive scenario for slow market adjustment is completely reversed under an unstable (unpredictable) external market regime, when flexibility in the production system is needed to reallocate resources smoothly and without cost escalation.

Different methods of econometrically representing and estimating the magnitudes involved in non-linear evolutionary models are presented.

1 An Evolutionary Theory of Economic Growth

Endogenizing economic growth is a new ambition among growth economists, provided the model stays within the neoclassical, exogenous equilibrium, price-taking framework. This is where we find the so-called "new growth theory" of Romer (1986) and Lucas (1988) and others. However, already Marshall (1890, 1919), attempting to deal with the increasing returns - growth problem in the Walrasian model, and supported by Young (1928), concluded that such a theoretical framework provides no more than economic growth hinged onto an exogenous growth trend (Eliasson 1992a). Evolutionary (growth) theory to warrant the name, takes you outside the WAD framework. Then endogenous growth can be modeled. The critical assumption has to do with the state space within which the model world operates; we call it the investment opportunity set (Eliasson 1990a, 1991, 1992a).

In Eliasson (1996a,1998b) a three stage model of economic growth was suggested. Under the assumptions of the *Knowledge Based Information Economy* (Eliasson 1990b) the immensity of the investment opportunity set (the state space of the model) is clarified. This opportunity set determines the basic axiomatic foundation of the *Experimentally Organized Economy* (EOE, Eliasson 1987, 1991a, 1996a, Ch. 2) in which growth is endogenously moved[1] through experimental selection by way of the four investment growth mechanisms *entry*, *reorganization*, *rationalization* and *exit* of Table 1.

Table 1. The four fundamental Investment Mechanisms

1. Entry
2. Reorganization
3. Rationalization
4. Exit

Source: Eliasson 1996a, p. 45 .

The Experimentally Organized Market Economy

In the EOE

(1) free competitive entry (item 1 in Table 1) into the investment opportunity set defines access and keeps firms in the market under a con-

[1] In the true sense, and not by exogenous assumption as in Romer's (1986) or Lucas's (1988) so called new growth theory.

stant threat of being competed down along a Salter (1960) performance curve, or out of business (item 4). Incumbent firms respond by reorganizing and/or rationalizing (items 2 and 3), and in the process individual firms grow or contract.

(2) the economics of the assumed state space means that choice of market and technology determines the outcome, but that such choice often fails, defining competitive exit (item 4) as a normal cost for economic development.

With competitive selection through business experiments (being the main vehicle for economic growth) the main function of markets, and the main concern of policy makers will be how institutions are organized such that all competent decision makers needed are in place to minimize the incidence of two types of errors, namely; (1) to keep losers for too long and (2) to terminate winners prematurely. This organization of selection is formulated in terms of a *competence bloc theory* (Eliasson - Eliasson 1996, Eliasson 1999) in which the minimum necessary actors with competence are identified. The organization of the competence bloc determines the *efficiency of selection.*

Completeness is one criterion for efficient selection through experimental choice. The completeness of the competence bloc defines the incentives for innovative and entrepreneurial activity through new entry in particular. New entry in turn initiates competition. This *dynamics of selection* is what keeps the economy in motion. For incentives to be credible institutions that reduce the uncertainty surrounding the (property) rights to the expected present value of investment commitments today have to be in place (Eliasson 1998a).

The existence of such required institutions are assumed in the analysis to follow. The evolutionary firm based macro model MOSES that we use approximates the EOE. The interpretation of simulation results, however, will be done as if simulations have been run in the context of the knowledge based information economy with selection taking place in a competence bloc setting, only partially explicit in the model.

Two problems will be addressed, namely the importance of (1) entry and (2) production flexibility for long run economic growth.

2 An Evolutionary Model of the Experimentally Organized Economy - a brief presentation

The evolutionary model used to demonstrate the magnitudes involved going from entrepreneurial entry at the firm level to macroeconomic growth specifies the institutions of the economy and the competence bloc in a crude, albeit appropriate way. The main actor in the model is the business firm. Aggregation is explicit through dynamic markets up to the national economy. The model can be seen as a generalized Salter curve analysis (Eliasson 1991a), that approximates the experimentally organized economy. It is mainly deterministic and highly non-linear, exhibiting typical chaotic characteristics.

Specification - overview

The Swedish micro-to-macro (M-M) model MOSES[2] features individual firms competing in dynamic markets and determining their own environment and economic growth in the process. The method of analysis is simulation. The model is fully implemented and calibrated on data for the Swedish economy, notably a special business firm survey defined on the format of the MOSES firm model and carried out annually by the Federation of Swedish Industries since 1975 (see Eliasson 1977, Albrecht 1992).

The model was originally designed to study the micro foundations of economic growth and the transmission of inflationary impulses through markets (Eliasson 1977, 1978). Over the years the model has been used to study and quantify the macroeconomic effects of various microeconomic phenomena, like technological change in firms, the organization of markets, notably the labor market and the capital market, workers' training in firms, industrial subsidies, entry and exit, and more recently the formation of technological systems and competence blocs (see for instance Ballot - Taymaz 1998, Carlsson 1991, Carlsson - Taymaz 1995, Carlsson - Eliasson - Taymaz 1997, Eliasson 1982, 1995a,b).

The Swedish M-M model is a Leontief-Keynesian 11-sector model where the manufacturing sector has been replaced by four product markets in which firms operate in competition with one another in the product, labor and financial markets. MOSES actors face convex production (manufacturing, research and learning) and utility sets that are, however, constantly shifted outward as a result of ongoing learning, investment and competition. No differentiability or market clearing assumptions are imposed. Hence, "multiple equilibria" are possible even though it is principally wrong to discuss the model in those terms. The firm production model represented in four markets is tied to an eleven (4+7) sector Keynesian-Leontief structure that is closed with a non-linear consumption expenditure and a financial feed back system. Growth is endogenized under an upper technology constraint associated with new investment in best-practice technology, endogenously determined in individual firms, and individual firm R&D spending. Case studies have been used to tailor individual firm specification, for instance to structure the observation and

[2] For *M*odel *O*f the *S*wedish *E*conomic *S*ystem.

measurement of the introduction of information and communications technologies in the firm, and how the performance of the firm as a whole is affected. The model runs on a database of more than 150 real Swedish firms and divisions of large firms that is updated annually. There are about 75 additional "synthetic" firms, introduced the initial year, to make up for the difference between the national accounts macro levels and the sum of real firms. Hence, the model is defined and estimated (and calibrated) at the Swedish national accounts level. Case studies have been carried out on several of these firms or divisions. The model and its application has been documented in several books and in international scientific journals (see, for instance, Ballot - Taymaz 1998, Eliasson 1977, 1978, 1985, 1991a and Albrecht, 1989, Albrecht et al., 1992, Taymaz, 1991a).

The MOSES model is comprehensive in the sense that all relevant feed backs are at work; income generation and demand feed backs, changing quantities in one market generate multimarket feed back of prices and quantities and ditto for a price change. We have recently devoted considerable effort to attempts to represent the allocation mechanisms in the financial system and how they have been influenced by information and communications technology (see Eliasson 1995a, Eliasson - Taymaz 1999).

This means that (roughly speaking) the model features simultaneous, but constantly inconsistent ("disequilibrium") price and quantity settings in markets that are only incompletely cleared through price and quantity adjustments to these inconsistencies. This feature is important for the dynamics of resource allocation over markets. One could say that the micro-to-macro model is a generalized Salter curve analysis (Salter 1960, Eliasson 1991a), where the Salter curves are placed in an endogenized market price system and constantly updated as the model economy progresses.

For the purpose of the empirical presentation to follow, it is important to understand that economic growth in this model occurs through the four investment mechanisms of Table 1. One can also say that *growth* in the model occurs *through competitive selection* (Eliasson 1996b). Hence, it is necessary to explain how competition is created through the incentives to commercialize technology and the requisite competence accumulation and made possible through the absence of institutions and other obstacles that restrict free competitive entry in markets. The first aspect is studied through the model of what we call a *competence bloc*. The second aspect requires a more thorough institutional analysis which we only touch upon in this paper.

The competitive success of firms in this process is studied through cases and measurement. The competitive growth process of Table 1 is endogenized in the model. Entry and exit are particularly important for the long-run behavior of the economy.

The competitive entry and exit process will be elaborated further below.

The MOSES model is fundamentally deterministic. Four mechanisms are, however, partly stochastic. Even though we plan a more elaborate deterministic specification at some later time these mechanisms, we believe, include processes that are inherently stochastic. They are:

(1) Direction of search for jobs in the labor market, or rather, the direction of flows of information from firms to job searchers.
(2) The degree of success of R&D outcomes, thus allocating winners and losers on individual firms.[3]
(3) Given incentives, the probability that entry will occur *this* period, or more precisely, the number of new firms, is determined stocastically.
(4) New firm characteristics (see further below).

A particularly important variable is expected excess profits over the current long-term interest rate[4]. This profit variable influences investment that upgrades the production structure in firms and the rate of entry in markets.[5] Labor and capital productivity characteristics of new investment are upgraded by an exogenously determined rate. Individual firm R&D investment raises the probability that the individual firm will score a winning investment with productivity characteristics far above the average[6] (item 2 in the list above). The new investment then integrates with existing capital equipment which takes on the new productivity characteristics in proportion to the relative size of the new investment (see Eliasson 1991a, pp. 165 ff). Productivity characteristics of new entrants are a drawing from a similar distribution (item 4 above) only that the spread is much wider. For practical measurement reasons the MOSES model runs on well defined observation units (firms or divisions) that either enter or exit or grow or shrink through the investment process. Reorganization (item 2 in Table 1), hence, is restricted to internal firm reorganization. Practical measurement problems and sheer lack of knowledge prevent us from generalizing the model of reorganization to the

[3] For practical reasons this option has been turned off in the simulation experiments to be reported on in this paper.

[4] called $\dot{\varepsilon}$, see (3a) in Eliasson (1991a).

[5] Potential new entrants observe the $\dot{\varepsilon}$ recorded in the market.

[6] In this R&D module, which has not been used in this paper, "labor and capital productivity characteristics of new investment" are endogenous. They depend on the success of R&D which, in turn, depends on R&D investments and general human capital stock of the firm. Hence, it is not constant for all firms. This endogenous technical change is a novel feature of the model. See further Ballot - Taymaz (1998) and Eliasson (1985, pp. 280 ff.).

internal economy of the firm, for instance making the trade off between internal and external reorganization through the M&A market explicit (see further discussion in Eliasson 1996a).

Firms in the model learn about their external market environment through adaptive smoothing formula, where projections are corrected using past mistakes and adjusted for risk aversion, using squared prediction errors from the past (see Eliasson 1991a, pp. 161 f). The entire economy "learns" through competitive selection by way of the four investment mechanisms of Table 1 (see Eliasson 1992b, pp. 24 f).

The entry, the (stochastic) search in the labor market and expectations learning mechanisms play particular roles in the analysis to follow.

This evolutionary model is used to demonstrate the magnitudes involved going from entrepreneurial entry and competitive exit at the micro firm level and labor allocation between firms to macroeconomic growth.

Calibration

Whenever possible econometric techniques have been used to estimate firm and macro parameters. To estimate the parameters of the production system a special survey (designed to fit the MOSES firm model) carried out every year by the Federation of Swedish Industries is used (see Albrecht 1992). It should be emphasized that detailed data base measurement to a large extent relieves us of many estimation problems that have to be solved in more aggregate models, for instance, the use of many very detailed measurements capturing the internal characteristics of individual firms.[7]

A number of parameters still cannot be estimated using conventional econometric techniques. With all measurement and estimation done and exogenous data collected for a historic period a specially developed calibration program (Taymaz 1991b) is used to fit the model to a selection of critical macroeconomic variables through repeated simulations.

The principle of the calibration program is to determine a set of parameter values that minimizes the "difference" between simulation results and the pre-selected control variables. Since the model is specified at the firm level for the manufacturing industry, we use the data on aggregate manufacturing industry (manufacturing output, manufacturing employment, manufacturing prices, etc.) as control variables for the calibration.

---

[7] For instance, Salter curves are measured by ranking and reranking individual firms initially (data base measurement) and as the simulation process goes on. There is far more information in such measured Salter curves than in Salter curves represented by the estimated parameters of multidimensional bellshaped curves. Similarly the labor market process is represented by individual confrontations, comparisons and decisions by firms and labor, rather than by estimated macro reaction coefficients.

The calibration program uses directed random search algorithms to minimize a distance criterion. There are three distance criteria that can be used for calibration: squared distance (the weighted average of the sum of squared differences between simulated variables and real variables), absolute distance (the weighted average of the sum of absolute differences between simulated variables and real variables), and maximum distance (the weighted average of the maximum differences between simulated variables and real variables). The weights assigned to each variables are determined by the user. The directed random search algorithms of the calibration program has been shown to be quite powerful and converges quickly to a local optimum. The calibration program performs a pure random search to determine a confidence interval for the global optimum that is used to assess the goodness of fit of the local optimum found by the program. All experiments summarized in this paper use the parameter set calibrated against historic control variables for the period 1982-1990.

3 Flexibility

Flexibility of an economy is supported by *heterogeneity* and *redundancy,* notably in the human capital characteristics (competence, labor market, etc.) of the competence bloc. Flexibility has two dimensions; *internal* within the firm and *external* between firms. Internal flexibility all the way down to the shop floors of production is represented by the reorganization item in Table 1. External flexibility is represented by the entry and exit items in Table 1 and through the corresponding ability of the labor market to reallocate people. Hence, the concept of flexibility is more broadly defined than is conventional in economic analysis. Above all we focus on the scope for reallocation of resources within the opportunity set (of Marschak - Nelson 1962) which necessarily takes us outside traditional neoclassical theory (Carlsson 1989).

Flexibility makes it possible to reorganize production to exploit new business opportunities that arise in the market and to counter often unexpected negative developments (vulnerability). At a higher level of aggregation flexibility is engineered through (a) the entry and exit process in the market (items 1 and 4 in Table 1) , (b) the capacity of incumbent firms (as represented in the model) to adjust through items 2 and 3 and (c) the ability of markets to reallocate factors of production between firms, notably over the labor market. Flexibility enhancing mechanisms should, hence, be seen as being supported by incentives and moved by competition, both in turn being supported by the appropriate (albeit unspecified) institutions. In the model analysis to follow flexibility occurs in these three dimensions; unused capacity, new investment, and turnover of labor and firms.

Unused capacity

Redundancy in the form of unused capacity is always present, and the extent of it explains how much firms can expand existing production without creating inflation in the labor market and without having to hire more labor or to invest. Both redundant labor and redundant machine capacity are explicit at the firm level in the model and data on the same categories have been collected through the special firm survey (see Albrecht 1992). In the short term a firm can also expand capacity through hiring more people in the labor market. Such hiring, however, tends to raise the level of wages in the labor market and affect other firms' propensity to invest and grow (see below).

New investment, expanding existing capacity and making production more competitive

In the long run, furthermore, production expansion can be further enhanced through new investment. New investment normally means both more cost efficient production on the existing production lines and the possibility of shifting production capacity in new directions. This flexibility is partly achieved through new investment in the same type of production as before, or through reorienting production, in both ways making the firm more competitive.

These are the cyclical and the investment aspects of flexibility.

Flexibility through firm turnover

The most important dimension of long-run flexibility, however, is to be able to reallocate production to radically new markets, for instance in response to a relative price change. The MOSES model is only capable of achieving such reallocation at a level of aggregation above the base unit (a firm, a division). This practical restriction corresponds well with empirical facts. Firms have rarely managed to achieve radical reorganization within the existing hierarchy and when it has been possible it has been through dramatic destruction of the existing hierarchy, decomposing the firm into several new firms, or adding new firms through acquisitions (cf. the recent history of IBM and AT&T). Flexibility of the relative type is achieved in the MOSES model through the entry and exit process (see Table 1) combined with changes in the rates of expansion and contraction of incumbent firms enforced through the new competition. The dual side of entry and exit is important. If bad performers are not forced out of business, releasing labor, the entry process may become inflationary and the growth effects will be smaller (see Eliasson - Lindberg 1981).

Flexibility through labor turnover

Flexibility at the firm level has to be supported by mobility of factors of production, notably the reallocation of labor and flexibility in the markets for mergers and acquisition (M&A). Both market characteristics are represented in the model through varying arbitrage speeds .

While the M&A markets are not represented explicitly in the experiments to be reported on here (see Eliasson - Taymaz 1999) the labor market is fairly explicitly represented and the allocation medium has been improved in recent years by the explicit modeling of on-the-job competence development and genetic learning algorithms (Ballot - Taymaz 1998). Particularly important for our flexibility experiments is the capacity of labor markets to reallocate people, either by inducing them to leave current employers or moving people on when they have lost their jobs (see further below).

4 Competitive Entry as an Endogenous Growth Agent

Experimental selection is the moving force of the EOE. In the evolutionary model MOSES that we use in our analysis it occurs by way of the four investment growth mechanisms in Table 1. Competitive pressure in markets is defined by the ex ante slope of the Salter performance curves, including not yet realized entry. Incumbent firms along the Salter curve are challenged in factor and product markets by superior firms and have to respond to that challenge. But "superior" firms are in turn challenged by those responses to competition. This keeps the competitive selection process of Table 1 constantly challenging all incumbent firms, and it means that we have to understand the innovative entry process to understand economic growth (see Eliasson 1991b). Innovative entry has to do with the incentives embodied in the competence bloc, that are in turn supported by institutions, notably those supporting property rights. In our particular case we are concerned with the property rights that guarantee the ownership of future expected profits from investment commitments today, i.e. the property rights that reduce the uncertainties associated with the right to manage, and access the returns from the assets and to trade in the same assets (Eliasson 1998a). Without these institutions the incentives that move entry has no economic meaning. Hence institutions, notably property rights institutions ultimately support incentives and, hence innovative competitive entry and thus economic growth.

The entry specification of the MOSES model has two dimensions; (1) incentives to enter and (2) the characteristics of the entering firms. Once a firm has entered the market it behaves as an incumbent firm, the only difference being that it normally begins operating at full capacity. However, a new firm has to hire workers in the market, and might not be able to recruit all workers it need at its maximum offering wage.

New firms enter in response to observed excess rents[8] in the market, indicating profit opportunities. The characteristics of the entering firm (size, performance etc.) have been tailored to studies made on entering firms and actual entry is a drawing from a distribution of such firm characteristics. The average performance of an entering firm is somewhat below the average for incumbents in the same market, but the spread is very much larger (see Eliasson 1991b). This means that the failure (exit) rate for entering firms is much above that for incumbents, partly because a large part of the entering firms turn out to be low performers and partly because the entering firms are smaller than incumbents and rapidly run out of resources. This is the case both for the MOSES firms and for real firms. On the other hand, surviving high performance new entrants will subject the existing firms to competition and force them to improve performance or exit, a property we have had in the model from the very beginning (Eliasson 1978, p. 52 ff.) that should also be a property of real firm life.

Our proposition is that incumbent firms have only limited possibilities of reorganizing production in the very long run compared to the range of flexibility achieved through new entry. If industrial structures abroad are upgraded faster than in Sweden, price competition will force down wages and/or profitability among Swedish producers, reducing investment and growth. Eventually, without entry the economy will start contracting. This means that viable new entry is necessary in the long run to sustain growth along an exponential (constant) growth trajectory. Hence, the net effect recorded for entry over the very long run may be faster than exponential, because in the alternative case, without entry, the industry will eventually start contracting (negative growth; see Eliasson 1995c).

5 Results from Entry and Flexibility Experiments

We have designed a set of comparable entry experiments to demonstrate the role of economic systems flexibility under different market institutions and circumstances, and to illustrate the quantities involved. The lack of flexibility is expressed in terms of lost ("less") output.

---

[8] ε , see Eliasson (1991a, p. 158).

Market conditions are defined in two scenarios;

1. stable relative foreign prices
2. fluctuating relative foreign prices.

Foreign prices are exogenous.

Design of experiments

Fluctuating relative prices means that some markets are subjected to sudden negative and positive price shocks occasioned by exogenous relative foreign price shocks of long duration around the assumed trends in relative foreign prices that define the stable price scenario. In the long run (on the horizon) relative prices are the same as in the stable price scenario. Along the way, on the other hand, some firms have suffered from negative experiences that they have had to cope with. The experiments have been designed, however, such that negative and positive relative price shocks should cancel over the experiment.[9]

Under these two market scenarios (stable and unstable foreign relative prices) we study the individual and combined effects on long term (100 years, by quarter) growth in manufacturing production of going from;

a. normal to fast labor market reallocation
b. normal to fast exit of inferior firms
c. no entry to entry of new firms

Labor market arbitrage is governed by many parameters in the model influencing the propensity of firms to offer high wage increases to attract labor, to raise its own wage level in order not to lose people, or the rate at which people leave a firm when they have accepted the new wage offer, etc. Such wage offers will contribute to a better allocation of labor, but they may also disrupt the allocation process if based on erroneous expectations. In this experiment we only vary one labor market parameter, namely the reservation wage of labor, telling how much above the current wage the wage offer has to be to induce change of job. The calibrated "gamma" coefficient is 30 percent In the fast labor market scenario it has been lowered to 10% percent. We have also performed a regression

[9] The design, however, means that a market could suffer from a low relative price compared to the stable price scenario for many years, only to see the price return suddenly to the trend and stay there. Such asymmetries, of course, reflect a negative experience for the firms in the market. It should also be noted that firms will permanently disappear (exit) during a negative price shock compared to the stable case, and vice versa, enter during a positive price experience, thus causing permanent (irreversible) change in the structure of the model economy.

analysis to ascertain the sensitivity of macro output to that particular parameter (see below).

In the normal scenario firms *exit* when they run out of equity.[10] But they can also be made to exit faster after a grace period during which they have not been able to reverse a deteriorating profit development. It is also possible to speed up the exit rate from serious liquidity problems. In the fast exit scenario resources, notably labor, are released faster than in the normal case and made available to other, growing firms.

Entry in response to profit opportunities in the market is specified by a parameter (called "entry") controlling the number of drawings (the number of entrants) from the multidimensional distribution of potential entrants mentioned above, for each given incentive level, i.e. for the level of observed excess profits in the market at each particular time.

In the MOSES model no price fluctuations mean approximate "plannable" circumstances for the firm in the sense that it will soon learn that long term relative product price development will not change and that it can make reasonably reliable price predictions.

With little disturbing competitive dynamics from the ongoing world economy more flexibility of production will not help much. Adding new entry increases long term output somewhat. Speeding up the exit rate (fast exit) only lowers output somewhat. This negative effect is, however, very strong if the labor market is speeded up, everything else the same. This is the situation for firms in a generous and predictable external world.

Experiments are identified by Evxyz (see Table 2).

v takes the value 1 if exit rate is high, 0 otherwise;
x takes the value 1 if labor market adjustment is fast, 0 otherwise;
y takes the value 1 if entry occurs, 0 otherwise;
z takes the value 1 if growth of foreign prices fluctuates, 0 otherwise.

Results from simulation analysis

Two sets of experiments were performed:

1. Different combinations of (entry; no entry), (slow, fast labor market), (low, fast exit) and constant and fluctuating foreign prices were run. See Table 2. For each of these experiments 50 Monte Carlo experiments were carried out on the stochastic specifications (see above) to test for robustness in the long term outcome (see the "fans" in Figure 1), i.e. to test the effects of each specification on growth. Each simulation covered 100 years by quarter. Table 2 shows the outcome in

[10] To be precise, when they have experienced negative net worth in six quarters in a row.

GNP on the 100 year horizon; average, maximum and minimum values for 50 experiments.
2. Complete grid search over the entry (ENTRY) and labor market parameters (GAMMA) to perform a regression analysis. The log of manufacturing output was regressed on the entry and gamma (reservation wages) parameters in a large number of experiments corresponding to 441 (21*21) sets of parameter values.

Table 2. Simulation results

Experiment	Average	Min.	Max.	Max./Min.
E0000	33142	28205	38416	1.4
E0001	25394	23 040	28049	1.2
E0010	34110	29777	37904	1.3
E0011	35021	30611	37767	1.2
E0100	22365	18699	25318	1.4
E0101	13708	10061	16111	1.6
E0110	27359	18194	36448	2.0
E0111	25480	20204	32361	1.6
E1000	29533	26035	35486	1.4
E1001	27268	24991	29432	1.2
E1010	30535	27419	33152	1.2
E1011	32001	28881	35810	1.2
E1100	23536	20179	29667	1.5
E1101	23240	21413	24699	1.2
E1110	26744	17928	30531	1.8
E1111	31515	26478	37439	1.4

Specification of experiments

v= 0	means normal exit rate;	= 1 means	fast exit
x =0	normal labor market;	= 1	fast labor market
y =0	no entry;	= 1	entry
z =0	stable (predictable) foreign prices;	= 1	unstable foreign prices

As can be seen from Table 2 there is a large spread in average outcomes for the different experiments, and if the lowest and highest outcomes are compared the differences are on the order of magnitude of almost one to four. By varying the four parameters entry, exit rate, labor market speed and stability of markets we have been able to generate long term (100 year) differences in the rate of growth of GNP on the order of magnitude of one percentage point per annum. And the difference is only marginally smaller, or one to 3.8 if we vary only entry, exit and labor market adjustment in the unstable price scenario (cf. MAX E0011 with MIN E0101 in Table 2). The four factors clearly matter in the very long run and the explanations are not all the time as expected. Above all, the reason such very large long-run differences as those recorded in Table 2 from variations in institutionally based market process determining parameters is the enormous state space or investment opportunity set of the model. The more efficient this state space [11] is searched out by individual actors the better the macro outcome. This is the idea of the competence bloc. Obviously, this market allocation of information and competence can only be reasonably represented in a micro based model.

If we start from a no entry, slow labor market, slow exit and stable (predictable) relative prices scenario (E0000) and then introduce unstable foreign relative prices (going to E0001) a significant reduction in long term output is recorded, to 76 percent of the outcome in the E0000 experiment. Speeding up the labor market (going from E0000 to E0100) will only create domestic price instability and reduce output. Remember that with stable (read predictable) foreign prices a very flexible labor market is not needed. The economy is, so to speak, fairly predictable and almost plannable. And if we introduce, in addition (going from E0100 to E0101) unstable and unpredictable prices output is further reduced. Apparently flexible labor market adjustment is not sufficient to cope with unpredictable foreign price disturbances. We also have to increase exits and "release" labor (going from E0101 to E1101) to prevent erratic, unpredictable disturbances in the wage setting of the labor market from killing growth, or instead to add entry (going from E0101 to E0111) to restore output. Also note that in this scenario it matters more to increase the exit rate than to increase entry, because it is sufficient, and always less costly in terms of wage inflation, to release labor from the bad firms to be reallocated to the best incumbent firms under non-inflationary conditions

[11] This state space, furthermore, is not exogenously determined. We call it the *Särimner* effect. The pig *Särimner* of the Viking sagas returned the next morning alive, after having been eaten for supper the day before. In the positive sum game of the MOSES economy state apace even grows as part of economic learning in the market (Eliasson 1987, p. 29, 1996a, pp. 27 f). To search and learn, however, requires local receiver competence and there are rapidly diminishing short-term returns to learning (Eliasson 1992a). This introduces the convexity of the production set that keeps the operating range of the MOSES economy bounded from above.

than to force high performing entrants to outbid incumbents for labor [12] Hence, if we combine new entry with fast releases of people from the bad firms (fast exit) and a fast labor market (low reservation wages) under long run unstable foreign prices (when flexibility is needed , going to E1111) the long run positive output effect is very large (E1111>E0111>E0101).

Apparently, however, the largest effect on long-term output is achieved if the flexibility can be organized without costly wage escalation. Hence, strong entry in combination with unstable foreign prices (E0011) generate the highest long-term (average) output. It is also of interest to note that a stable market environment (stable foreign prices) helps in the long run if cost inflation can be contained. Full predictability with new entry (E0010) gives strong long-term growth performance, even better than what is achieved with fast exit (E1010). Apparently fast exit means that firms with good long-term profits exit accidentally even in the stable price scenario.

The interesting thing is that long term performance is even (somewhat) better if we change into an unstable foreign market regime with entry only (going from E0010 to E0011). There may be two explanations. One is technical in the sense that the difference is small and may change sign after another decade of simulations. There is also an interesting economic explanation. With optimally balanced flexibility in the production system an unstable market environment may in fact raise the opportunities in the economy compared to the predictable environment, if the actors (firms) are capable of exploiting them, and they are if the production system at large is sufficiently flexible. This exploitation predominantly takes place through new entry. This observation is consistent with Antonov - Trofimov (1993) who find, in experiments on the same model that long-term performance increases (under an unstable market regime) when decisions are taken by actors individually, not being constrained by centrally imposed guidelines, in their case guidelines based on either Keynesian or neoclassical econometric model predictions. Centrally imposed guidelines represent a reduced understanding of the economy, or a misunderstanding of the economy compared to a completely decentralized and unregulated decision process where each actor bases its decision on its individual experience and individually conceived future. The optimal collective decision of society is then achieved through decentralized, individual and often inconsistent ("experimental") decisions in the market, each being rational on the basis of its own particular information sets and logic.

[12] But notice that the growth rate is higher in E0111 (entry) than in E1101 (exit).

Graphic illustrations

Figure 1 compares two widely diverging simulations (E0001 and E0011). Each "fan" represents one set of 50 simulations with the seed variations listed above. "Max entry", "Average entry" and "Min entry" lines show the maximum, average and minimum values of 50 runs of the E0011 experiment, and "Max no-entry", "Ave no-entry" and "Min no-entry" lines the corresponding values for the no-entry (E0001) experiment. The "butterfly" effect of non-linear systems theory ("chaos") is clearly visible. Each seed variation generates a widely diverging outcome, but with a very long delay. The partial problem now is whether the institutional change represented by going from no entry to entry significantly increases economic growth performance. The average outcome is always superior in the positive entry case. Apparently, however, uncontrolled for circumstances represented by the particular seed setting can generate better individual outcomes in the no entry case, and vice versa. The policymaker who wants to promote growth through increasing structural flexibility through promoting entry, obviously is not in full control, but has to take a risk. Our question is if the average outcome in the entry case is significantly larger than in the no entry experiment.[13]

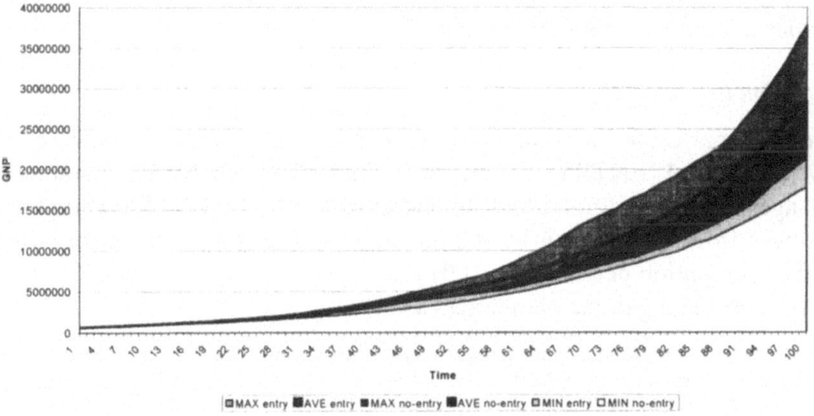

Fig. 1. Monte Carlo simulation results, entry (E0010) and no-entry (E0001) experiments

[13] From a policy decision point of view this is, however, by no means a sufficient question to ask. While the individual firm owner risks his own capital, the policy maker can mess up the whole economy, partly by not understanding (using for instance a Keynesian macro model instead of our model) but also because of uncontrolled for stochastic variations like those above. See also Eliasson - Taymaz (1992).

As shown in Figure 1, a change in the initial seed number may lead to a rather different outcome in the long run. The effect of random events is magnified in the long run by the non-linear structure of the model because the variance of outcomes grows exponentionally over time . This poses a special problem in the comparison of different sets of experiments, each representing a specific institutional arrangement. Statistical and econometric tools can be used to test if a certain institutional change has a significant effect on macroeconomic growth in the sense of producing a significantly higher average outcome. The two sets of experiments in Figure 1 are significantly different. For example, if we would like to test if entry matters in an unstable environment, we can compare mean values of E001 and E0011 experiments by using standard test statistics. It is also possible to test the effects of a parameter (like the entry rate) by running a large number of simulations by incrementally changing the parameter value. A simple regression model then can be used to test the significance of the parameter value. However, as explained before, it becomes difficult to find a statistically significant difference between two scenarios because the variances of each set of experiments increase rapidly over time. We can also use a weaker criterion, stochastic dominance, to compare two sets of experiments. A set of experiments dominates stochastically over another set if its cumulative outcome distribution lays above the latter's cumulative distribution. We use all these three techniques to compare simulation results.

Econometric analysis

We have performed a complete grid search over a predetermined set of GAMMA and ENTRY parameter values. The GAMMA parameter changes from zero to one by 0.05 increments and the ENTRY parameter changes from zero to four by 0.2 increments. The (log) GNP level at the end of simulation period (year 100) was regressed on a quadratic function of the entry and gamma parameters as follows:

$$\underset{}{LGNP} = \underset{(374.32)}{16.63} \underset{(1.91)}{+0.254} GAMMA - \underset{(-1.39)}{0.164}\, GAMMA^2 + \underset{(4.88)}{0.162}\, ENTRY - \underset{(-2{,}54)}{0.019}\, ENTRY^2 - \underset{(-0.63)}{0.017}\, GAMMA * ENTRY$$

n = 439 (2 outliers are omitted)
Adj R2 = 20.24

Apparently all coefficients except the interaction variable are highly significant telling the story that Entry and Gamma independently influence growth positively in the long run.

The Gamma influence is non-linear. For small values of gamma (very fast labor market) the influence is negative. It then increases (positive) to an optimum level, to be reduced again at a higher level of rigidity when the negative effect of the squared variable begins to dominate. The entry parameter also has a non-linear effect on macroeconomic performance.

The interaction variable was not significant. It seems that there is a complex interaction between the Gamma and Entry parameters in generating higher growth rates. When a non-linear interaction term, $GAMMA^{ENTRY}$, instead of GAMMA*ENTRY, is added to the model, it has a statistically significant positive coefficient (t=2.75). In other words, entry will generate the largest effect on output at high Gamma values, i.e. for a slow, or at least not too fast labor market. Figure 2 plots the GNP level at the end of a simulation against ENTRY and GAMMA parameter values. A complete grid search is performed, i.e. there are 441 points. The vertical axis is GNP, horizontal axes are ENTRY and GAMMA values. The "optimum" GAMMA and ENTRY parameter values are 0.8 and 4.9, respectively. But we can see from the figure that the target surface is rather flat and that there are many other entry and gamma combinations with lower gamma values that produce almost as high GNP outcomes.

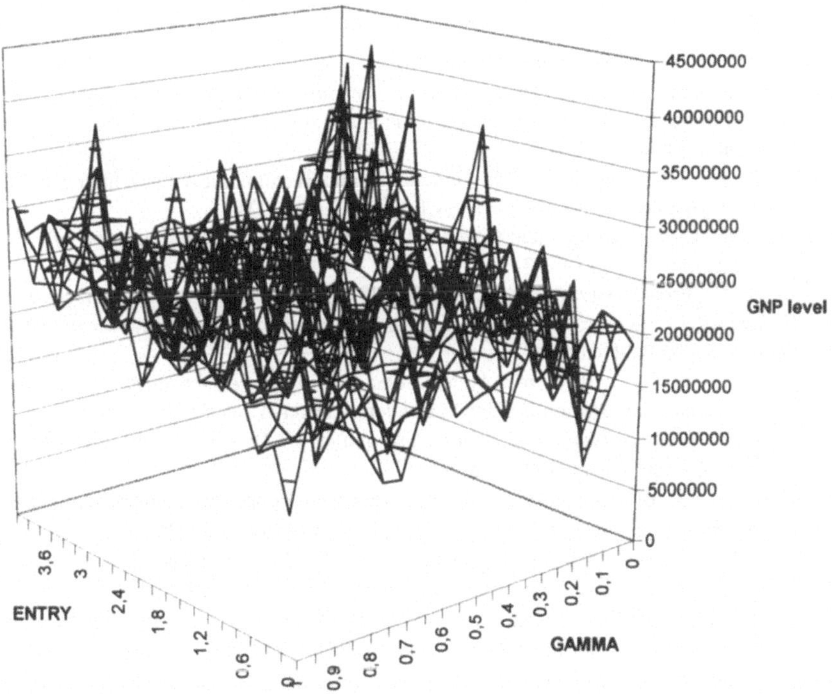

Fig. 2. Grid Search over Entry and Gamma Parameters

Conclusions

The simulation experiments demonstrate that (under reasonable assumptions) very large, long-run macroeconomic effects can occur as the result of differences in the institutions influencing entry and exit behavior of firms and the mobility of labor. These three circumstances are all related to the flexibility of production, and appear to be most important when the economy is subjected to external, unpredictable change in foreign (exogenous) prices, i.e. as should be expected, when flexibility is needed.

Under stable external prices firms soon learn to predict their market environment rather reliably. The economy, to them is, so to speak more plannable. Under such a scenario higher flexibility in terms of fast reactions can cause disturbances that are negative for growth.

References

Albrecht, James W., 1989. *MOSES Code*. Stockholm: IUI.

Albrecht, J., 1992. Documentation of the Planning Survey Data: Cross Sector and Panel; in Albrecht, J. et al. (1992).

-------- et al., 1992. *MOSES Database*. Stockholm: IUI.

Antonow, Mikhail - Georgi Trofimov, 1993. Learning through Short-Run Macroeconomic Forecasts in a Micro-to-Macro Model, *Journal of Economic Behavior & Organization*, 21, No. 2 (June).

Ballot, Gérard - Erol Taymaz, 1998. Human Capital, Technological Lock-in and Evolutionary Dynamics; in G. Eliasson and Ch. Green, eds. (1998).

Carlsson, Bo, 1989. Flexibility and the Theory of the Firm, *International Journal of Industrial Organization*, 7, 179-203.

--------, 1991. Productivity Analysis: A Micro-to-Macro Perspective; in E. Deiaco, E. Hörnell and G. Vickery (eds.), *Technology and Investment. Crucial Issues for the 1990s*. London: Pinter Publishers.

--------, (ed.), 1995. *Technological Systems and Economic Performance: The Case of Factor Automation*. Boston/Dordrecht/London: Kluwer Academic Publishers.

--------, (ed.), 1997. *Technological Systems and Industrial Dynamics*. Boston/Dordrecht/London: Kluwer Academic Publishers.

Carlsson, Bo - Erol Taymaz, 1995. The Importance of Economic Competence in Economic Growth: A Micro-to-Macro Analysis; in Bo Carlsson (ed.) (1995).

Carlsson, Bo - Gunnar Eliasson - Erol Taymaz, 1997. The Macroeconomic Effects of Technological Systems; Micro-macro simulation; in Bo Carlsson, ed. (1997).

Eliasson, Gunnar 1977. Competition and Market Processes in a Simulation Model of the Swedish Economy, *American Economic Review*, 67 (1), 277-281.

--------, 1978. *A Micro-to-Macro Model of the Swedish Economy*. Conference Reports 1978:1. Stockholm: Industriens Utredningsinstitut (IUI).

--------, 1982. Electronics, Economic Growth and Employment -- Revolution or Evolution; in H. Giersch (ed.), *Emerging Technologies: Consequences for economic growth, structural change and employment*. Kiel.

--------, 1985. *The Firm and Financial Markets in the Swedish Micro-to-Macro Model -- Theory, Model and Verification*. Stockholm: Industriens Utredningsinstitut (IUI).
--------, 1987. *Technological Competition and Trade in the Experimentally Organized Economy*, Research Report No. 32. IUI, Stockholm.
--------, 1990a. The Firm as a Competent Team, *Journal of Economic Behavior and Organization*, 13 (3), June.
--------, 1990b. The Knowledge-Based Information Economy; Chapter 1 in G. Eliasson, S. Fölster et al. (1990).
--------, 1991a. Modeling the Experimentally Organized Economy - Complex Dynamics in an Empirical Micro-Macro Model of Endogenous Economic Growth, *Journal of Economic Behavior and Organization*, 16 (1-2), 153-182.
--------, 1991b. Deregulation, Innovative Entry and Structural Diversity as a Source of Stable and Rapid Economic Growth, *Journal of Evolutionary Economics*, (1), 49-63.
--------, 1992a Business Competence, Organizational Learning, and Economic Growth: Establishing the Smith-Schumpeter-Wicksell (SSW) Connection; in F.M. Scherer - M. Perlman, eds. (1992).
--------, 1992b. The MOSES Model - Database and Applications; Chapter I in Albrecht et al. (1992).
--------, 1995a. The Macroeconomic Effects of New Information Technology – with Special Emphasis on Telecommunications; in D. Lamberton (ed.), *Beyond Competition*. Amsterdam: Elsevier Science Publishers B.
--------, 1995b, The Economics of Technical Change -- The macroeconomic consequences of business competence in an experimentally organized economy, *Revue d'Économie Industrielle, Numero Exceptionnel*.
--------, 1995c, *Economic Growth through Competitive Selection - on the very strong cumulative selection forces working in an historic perspective;* paper presented at the EARIE 22nd Annual Conference, 3-6 September 1995, Juan Les Pins.
--------, 1996a. *Firm Objectives, Controls and Organization – the use of information and the transfer of knowledge within the firm*. Boston/Dordrecht/London: Kluwer Academic Publishers 1996.
--------, 1996b. Endogenous Economic Growth through Selection; in A. Harding, (ed.), *Microsimulation and Public Policy*. Amsterdam: North-Holland.
--------, 1998a. From Plan to Market, *Journal of Economic Behavior and Organization*, 34 (1), 49-68.
--------, 1998b. Svensk Datorindustri - en kompetensblocksanalys av dess framväxt och försvinnande; i Heum, P. (ed.), *Kompetense og verdiskaping*, SNFs Årsbok 1998. Fagboksförlaget, 1998.
--------, 1999. *Industrial Policy, Competence Blocs and the Role of Science in Economic Development;* Revised version of paper presented to the International Conference of the Joseph A. Schumpeter Society in Vienna 1998. To be published in *the Journal of Evolutionary Economics*, Vol. 10, 1-2, 2000.
Eliasson, Gunnar - Åsa Eliasson, 1996. The Biotechnological Competence Bloc, *Revue d'Economie Industrielle*, 78-4^0, Trimestre.
Eliasson, Gunnar, Stefan Fölster et al., 1990. *The Knowledge Based Information Economy*. Stockholm: IUI.
Eliasson, Gunnar - Christopher Green (eds), 1998. *The Microeconomic Foundations of Economic Growth*, The University of Michigan Press, Ann Arbor, 1998. Stockholm: City University Press.

Eliasson, Gunnar - Thomas Lindberg, 1981. Allocation and Growth Effects of Corporate Income Taxes; in G. Eliasson and J. Södersten (eds.), 1981, *Business Taxation, Finance and Firm Behavior*, Conference Reports 1981:1. Stockholm: IUI.

Eliasson, Gunnar - Erol Taymaz, 1992. The Limits of Policy Making; an analysis of the consequences of boundedly rational Government using the Swedish micro-to-macro model (MOSES). Working Paper No. 333, IUI, Stockholm.

Eliasson, Gunnar - Erol Taymaz, 1999. Modeling Derivatives in MOSES - the integration of computing communications and financial services. Mimeo, KTH, Stockholm (March).

Lucas, R.E., Jr., 1988. On the Mechanics of Economic Development, *Journal of Monetary Economics*, 22 (1), 3-42.

Marschak, T. and R.R. Nelson, 1962. Flexibility, Uncertainty, and Economic Theory, *Metroeconomica*, XIV, 42-58.

Marshall, Alfred, 1890. *Principles of Economics*. London.

--------, 1919. *Industry and Trade*. London.

Romer, P.M., 1986. Increasing Returns and Long-Run Growth, *Journal of Political Economy*, 94 (5), Oct., 1002-1037.

Salter, W.E.G., 1960. *Productivity and Technical Change*. Cambridge University Press, Cambridge, MA.

Scherer, F.M. - M. Perlman, eds., 1992. *Entrepreneurship, Technological Innovation, and Economic Growth. Studies in the Schumpeterian Tradition*, The University of Michigan Press, Ann Arbor 1992.

Taymaz, Erol, 1990. *A Micro-Simulation Analysis of Manufacturing Firms' Demand for Telecommunications Services*; Chapter V in G. Eliasson et al. (1990).

--------, 1991a. *MOSES on PC: Manual, initialization, and calibration*. Stockholm: IUI.

--------, 1991b. Calibration, Chapter III in Taymaz (1991a).

--------, 1992a. Initial State Dependency - Sensitivity Analyses on MOSES; in Albrecht, J. et al. (1992).

Young, P.C., 1928. Increasing Returns and Economic Progress, *Economic Journal*, XXXVIII, (152), 527-542.

Interaction between public policies and technological competition under environmental risks

Gilbert Laffond[1], Jacques Lesourne[1] and François Moreau[1]

[1]Laboratoire d'Econométrie, Conservatoire National des Arts et Métiers, 2 rue Conté, 75003 Paris, France

Abstract. This paper examines the interaction between two random processes: (1) a process of technological competition among several mature polluting technologies and a new technology which is environmentally friendly, but the cost of which depends on the adoption rate; (2) a random process of learning about the environmental impact of technologies by the public policy maker who may decide, according to the results, on taxation or prohibition of certain technologies. The ability of the public authorities to ensure the survival of the most environmentally friendly technology is analyzed. The role of various parameters is discussed, especially the interaction between the choice of risk thresholds which determine the intervention of public authorities (i.e. the implementation of the precaution principle) and the policy maker's learning rate for environmental risks (i.e. the speed with which beliefs in risks regarding the most recent research results are adjusted). Some paradoxical effects arising from the implementation of the precaution principle on the survival of the most environmentally friendly technology are pointed out. The model illustrates problems encountered in practice like the choice of the European Union policy in the face of NO_x emissions from cars.

Key words: Technological competition - precaution principle - government policy - learning

JEL-classification: O33; O38; Q38

1 Introduction

A technology policy is traditionally legitimated by market failures (imperfect information, imperfect competition, externalities) which can generate a suboptimal diffusion path (the diffusion of a technology can be too fast or too slow) (Stoneman, Diederen, 1994). However, the intrinsic dynamic character of an innovation uncomfortably fits with the lifeless nature of an equilibrium framework (Metcalfe, 1994). Therefore, according to the evolutionary theory of economic change, a technology policy should not focus on the sole control of the scope and direction of R&D but should rather take an interest in the whole Schumpeterian trilogy "invention - innovation - diffusion"[1]. The goal of a Pareto-optimal diffusion path is thus replaced by objectives based on system variety and satisfying technology selection processes. Arthur (1988, 1989) and David (1985, 1993) have highlighted the path-dependent and irreversible phenomena which characterize technology diffusion processes subjected to the hypothesis of increasing returns. Competition among substitute technologies leads more often than not to the standardization of one of the competing technologies. This standardization can constitute a suboptimal equilibrium because in such a process the choice of one individual in one period depends on the behavior of all the individuals in the previous periods and the entrance of individuals into the market generally occurs in a random manner. The more a technology was chosen in the past, the more it will be adopted in the future. The advantage of the standardization process is that it generates a greater economic efficiency (transaction cost economies, network externalities...). Nevertheless, the possible emergence of a suboptimal standard forces the policy maker to assess this advantage by considering the available information on the merits of each of the technologies. Cowan (1991) has pointed out that, under the imperfect information hypothesis, the aim of a technology policy should be to preserve technology diversity until enough information on the merits of the competing technologies has been accumulated.

In the field of competition among environmentally risky technologies, the role of the policy maker appears to be much less trivial[2]. In this case, the efficiency of a policy in preserving technological diversity is often questioned. To maintain several possibly risky technologies in competition does not only lead to economic inefficiency, but also increases the likelihood of an ecological and/or human catastrophe. The experience of such catastrophic events and the dread of endangering the welfare of future generations form the basis for concepts on sustainable development and the precaution principle. According to the latter, taking regulatory measures (prohibiting a technology for instance) in order to prevent possible catastrophic risks may be legitimate even when strong scientific evidence on causal relationships or the extent of potential damage is

---

[1] This is the approach used in the works on National Innovation Systems (Nelson, 1993).

[2] This contribution does not deal strictly with technology policy but with the effect of the environmental policy alone on technological competition.

lacking. In the environmental field, the technological competition process has to be analyzed together with the policy maker's learning process on the risks generated by competing technologies. This article deals with the interaction between these two random processes of technological competition and the policy maker learning about environmental risks, and the consequences of this interaction in terms of its capacity to promote the most environmentally friendly technologies.

The modeling of the interaction between these two random processes cannot be solved analytically and thus, following the tradition of many works in this field - including of course that of Nelson and Winter (1982) - we rely on simulation. Moreover this contributes to the richness of our results. This article demonstrates the need to call into question the principle of maintaining technological diversity in the context of a sustainable development policy and analyzes the ability of the public authorities to ensure the survival of the most environmentally friendly technology. This ability depends on (1) random research results concerning the dangers of the various technologies and the speed with which the public authorities correct their beliefs in the risks according to the latest research results; (2) the history (the date on which the authorities' decision comes into effect is an essential parameter for its efficiency) and (3) the quality of the simultaneous management of the different control variables (environmental taxation, the resolve in applying the precaution principle). Consequently, this model allows us to highlight possible paradoxical effects arising from the implementation of the precaution principle.

This paper will unfold as follows: after the presentation of the model (section 2), we will analyze in more detail the technological competition process (section 3) followed by the interaction between the two processes (section 4). To conclude, we will illustrate the results of the model by an example inspired by a real case.

2 The model

In this paper, three technologies are in competition ($k = 1, 2, 3$). These three technologies may be adopted freely and are associated with different environmental risks. In this section we will study in succession the complex public decision-making process on environmental risks which is twofold (a specific learning process on the risks associated with the different technologies, and a specific decision process), and the technological competition process. This model considers the competition between three technologies rather than a dual competition as in the standard models. On the one hand, such a configuration is more realistic in the field of environmentally risky technologies where three types of technology coexist (polluting technologies, technologies incorporating a depollution module and intrinsically clean technologies). On the other hand, the possibility of an exogenous elimination of technologies (by means of public intervention) requires, if we are to consider the conditions under which the best technology for the environment might not survive, that we extend the competition to three technologies in order to ensure a fruitful discussion.

2.1 The public learning process on technological risks

Each of the three technologies carries a specific and *a priori* unknown environmental risk. In order to improve their knowledge of the respective risks of the different technologies, the public authorities implement certain research programs. The environmental risk induced by the use of a specific technology, or, more generally, by any industrial system may be modeled using a Cumulative Complementary Distribution Function (CCDF)[3]. A point on such a curve represents the probability of an event with consequences (a number of deaths for example) above a given level. In this paper, Y^k stands for the specific risk level of a given technology k, where $Y^k \in \{0, 1, ..., 10\}$ and is the highest level indicated by this technology's CCDF. In the example depicted in figure 1, technology A carries a risk level as high as 6 (because of a rather high probability in generating events with minor consequences) whereas the risk level of technology B would be 8 (because of the significant probability of events with major consequences).

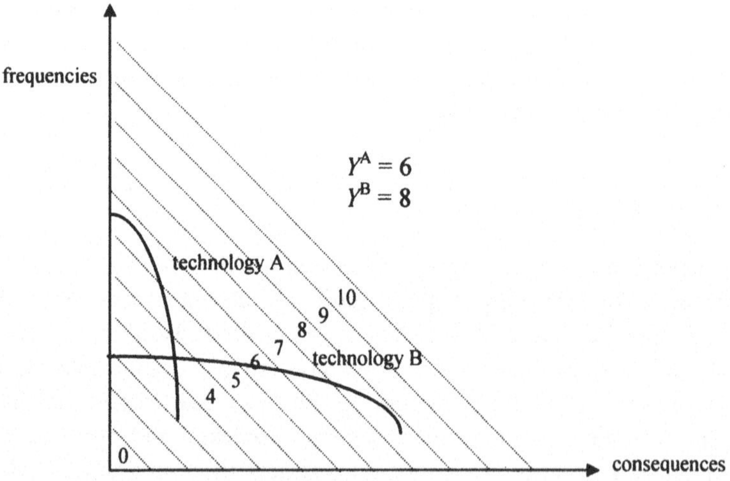

Fig. 1. Assessment of Y^k using a CCDF

[3] For more details on the method of Quantitative Risk Analysis applied to catastrophic risks see, for example, Allen *et al.* (1992).

To account for imperfect information, the risk level Y^k of each technology k remains unknown. In order to discover these levels, certain research programs are developed from one period to the next and we shall denote by Y_t^k the estimated risk level of technology k during period t. During period t, the result of the research on the risk level of technology k is a random variable X_t^k. We shall assume that all the X_t^k are independent variables with the same expected value Y^k and the same variance σ_k^2. In fact, as pointed out by Foray and Grübler (1996), the discovery of environmental problems is often the result of a process of "research by accident". The discovery of the hazards of DDT or of the Antarctic "ozone hole" are well known examples of such random processes.

As a matter of fact, the estimated risk level will not depend just on the most recent discoveries. Some inertia is embedded in the process, and the previous estimated levels are taken into account by the public authorities. We assume that Y_t^k, the estimated risk level during period t, is given by:

$$Y_t^k = (1-\beta)\, Y_{t-1}^k + \beta\, X_t^k \tag{1}$$

β, a parameter chosen by the policy maker, represents the adjustment speed of the estimated risk level (this could be described as the belief in risk levels) for each technology. β appears to be a learning rate for the real technological risk level. During the same "history" the value of parameter β cannot obviously be changed. At time t, the policy maker can use an estimated risk level for technology k, Y_t^k, given by:

$$Y_t^k = \sum_{\tau=0}^{t} \beta(1-\beta)^{\tau} X_{t-\tau}^k \tag{2}$$

With:

$$E(Y_t^k) = Y^k - (1-\beta)^{t+1} Y^k \tag{3}$$

$$V(Y_t^k) = \sigma_k^2 \beta^2 \left[\frac{1-(1-\beta)^{2t+2}}{1-(1-\beta)^2} \right] \tag{4}$$

A small value of β induces a slow adjustment in the beliefs: this can delay the awareness of the high risk levels associated with a polluting technology when the first results from the research process indicated low risk levels. On the contrary, a high β coefficient accelerates the convergence of the mathematical expectation of the estimated risk level with the real level (Y^k). To sum up, from expression (3) it turns out that the speed of convergence of the expected Y_t^k with Y^k is all the faster if β is high. On the other hand, it might appear surprising that the variance of the risk estimations increases with time (expression (4)). This is due to the fact that at each date t the public authorities' belief in the risks induced by a technology is a biased estimator of the real risk (see expression (3)). In any case, this result does not lessen the relevance of the model: when implementing the precaution principle, any confidence in the evaluation of risks has to, by definition, be rejected. Nevertheless, it is possible to demonstrate that if a non-biased estimator is used (even though the public authorities have no reason whatsoever to imagine that their assessment of the level of risks might be biased), then the variance in the estimations decreases with time[4].

In this paper, the research and estimation processes are applied independently to the three technologies. During period t the public policy maker has to make a decision concerning the environmental risk of technology k. This decision will be taken on the basis of Y_t^k: the public authorities will define two intervention levels $n \leq m$ so that if:

- $Y_t^k < n$ the estimated risk level of technology k is low enough: no action is taken;
- $n \leq Y_t^k \leq m$ the government decides to fix a taxation rate λ imposed on technology k. This tax is irreversible and the price of access to technology k will remain forever increased by a tax even if the risk level associated with this technology becomes lower than n in the future;
- $m < Y_t^k$ the public authorities implement the precaution principle and forbid the use of technology k. This ban is also irreversible.

In this model, the n and m risk levels, that determine public authority decisions, are kept constant with time. It is clear that this hypothesis implies that relying on the estimated risk level does not matter. This fact is compatible with the precaution principle: according to this principle, it is not acceptable to delay intervention and wait for entirely reliable information.

To analyze the interaction between the parameter describing the sensitivity of the public authorities to progress in research (coefficient β) and

---

[4] $\hat{Y}_t^k = \left(\dfrac{1}{1-(1-\beta)^{t+1}}\right) Y_t^k$ is such an estimator without bias. We then verify that $E(\hat{Y}_t^k) = Y^k$ and that $V(\hat{Y}_t^k) = \dfrac{\sigma_k^2 \beta^2}{1-(1-\beta)^2}\left[\dfrac{1+(1-\beta)^{t+1}}{1-(1-\beta)^{t+1}}\right]$ decreases with time.

the thresholds for public intervention (n and m) we will specify, without loss of generality, a distribution of the X_t^k variables (table 1) which has the required characteristics in terms of the relative risks for the environment. Here, technology 1 is the most friendly to the environment and technology 3 the most polluting. The distribution proposed in table 1 is such that $Y^1 < Y^2 < Y^3$.

Table 1. Distribution of the research results on risks

X_t^k	0	1	2	3	4	5	6	7	8	9	10
Prob (X_t^1)	0.05	0.20	0.50	0.10	0.05	0.04	0.02	0.01	0.01	0.01	0.01
Prob (X_t^2)	0.01	0.02	0.05	0.12	0.50	0.15	0.10	0.02	0.01	0.01	0.01
Prob (X_t^3)	0.01	0.01	0.02	0.02	0.02	0.04	0.13	0.23	0.40	0.08	0.04

Given the irreversible nature of the environmental policy's consequences on the technologies, an increase in the adjustment speed of the beliefs in risks can also lead to an overestimation of the risk of the least polluting technologies (remember that the variability of the estimated risk levels increases with β). Figures 2 and 3 illustrate this phenomenon of overestimation of the risks and show the rise in taxation or prohibition frequency for increasing values of β. For each value included between 0.1 and 0.9, the frequencies express the number of simulations (over one hundred) where the different technologies have been respectively taxed or forbidden, with the number of periods T set to 100 and intervention thresholds n set to 5 and m set to 8. Figure 3 shows that, with a high value of β ($\beta > 0.5$), a "research accident" leading to the wrong conclusion that technology 1 is a risky one can be sufficient to generate the prohibition of this technology[5].

Thus, it is clear that as a result of the learning process, expressed here by the sensitivity to the most recent research results, the public authorities acquire a better knowledge of the relative risks of the various technologies and are therefore able to set-up a suitable environmental policy and can in this way improve the effectiveness of their intervention. However, a too brisk learning process may lead to false conclusions on the dangers caused by the most environmentally friendly technologies.

---

[5] In this model the evolution of Y_t^n appear as a random walk. The intervention thresholds constitute absorbing barriers and the date on which these barriers are reached is clearly a stopping time. We are not aware of any analytical tools which are capable of comparing stopping time distributions for such processes. This is one of the main reasons for resorting to simulation in this model.

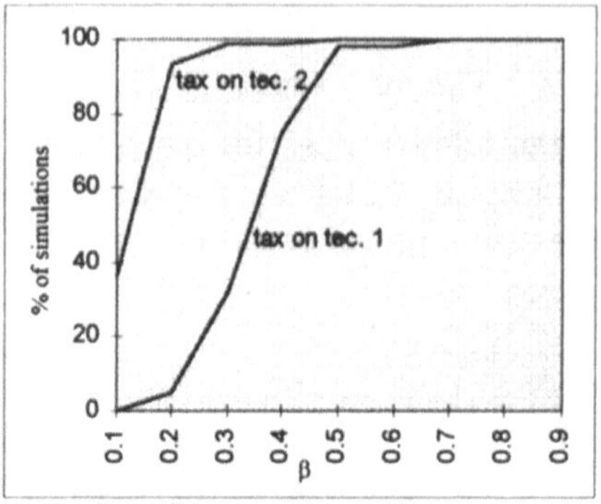

(technology 3 is always taxed)

Fig. 2. Impact of β on the frequency of taxation

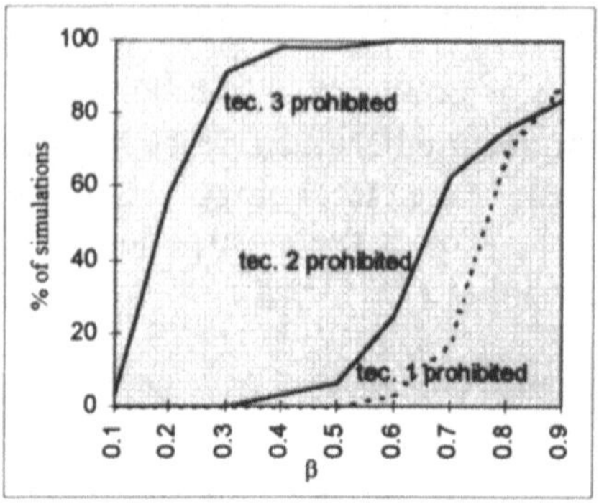

Fig. 3. Impact of β on the frequency of prohibition

2.2 Supply side of the technological competition process: the dynamics of relative costs

The dynamics of the supply side of the technological competition, is clearly related to the evolution in the relative costs of the three technologies. As said previously, the lowest environmental risks are obtained with technology 1. This technology is, at the beginning of the process, not fully developed, and its operating costs are higher than those of the other two. However, a significant adoption rate for this technology could lead to a decrease in its cost and price (through diminishing returns due to scale and learning) and thus to a reinforcement of the adoption rate and of the development of this technology. The cost of the other two technologies decreases slowly and at the same pace, while we should recall that we assumed the one with the highest costs (namely technology 2) bears the lowest environmental risks.

Within each period t, production is made under constant returns and we shall denote the operational unit cost to propose technology k to the users as $c_k(t)$. To simplify the presentation, we shall only study the evolution of $c_1(t)$, which we consider as the relative cost of technology 1 with respect to technologies 2 and 3. The evolution rate of $c_1(t)$ will rely on two components γ_1 and γ_2. With respect to c_2 and c_3, the first component represents the relative decrease of c_1 when the adoption level of technology 1 is not sufficient and the second one represents the relative increase of c_1 associated with higher adoption levels. If the learning effect and the economies of scale during period t are neglected, c_1 is naturally increased by $(1 + g)$:

$$\gamma_1(t+1) = (1+g)c_1(t) \tag{5}$$

On the contrary, when learning and economies of scale do matter, the cost of technology 1, relative to a limit value c_1^*, is reduced by (1 - h):

$$\gamma_2(t+1) - c_1^* = (1 - h)\,(c_1(t) - c_1^*) \qquad (6)$$

The cost $c_1(t+1)$ is a weighted combination of these two extreme values. The weights given to these two extreme costs will depend on $P_1(t)$, i.e. the market share of technology 1 in period t. In fact, the propensity of the company using technology 1 to reduce costs and the importance of its efforts in this direction are increasing functions of $P_1(t)$. We shall only assume that:

$$c_1(t+1) = (1 - P_1(t))\,\gamma_1(t+1) + P_1(t)\,\gamma_2(t+1) \qquad (7)$$

Using the notation $\theta = g/(g+h)$, (7) becomes:

$$c_1(t+1) = c_1(t) + (g+h)\,c_1(t)\left[\theta - P_1(t) + (1-\theta)\frac{c_1^*}{c_1(t)}P_1(t)\right] \qquad (8)$$

Condition (8) illustrates that the relative cost of the technology cannot decrease if the market share of this technology is insufficient (the economies of scale and learning effect are not greater enough to ensure a reduction in costs at least equal to the other two technologies). A simple calculation in fact shows that the condition $c_1(t+1) < c_1(t)$ implies that expression (9) is verified:

$$P_1(t) > \frac{\theta}{1-(1-\theta)\dfrac{c_1^*}{c_1(t)}} \qquad (9)$$

We denote the right hand side of this inequality by $R_1(t)$. $R_1(t)$ clearly represents the minimal market share of technology 1 required for its cost to decrease from period t to period $t+1$. Intuition suggests that the relative cost of technology 1 decreases all the more easily if the economies of scale and learning for technology 1 are more important than those which characterize technologies 2 and 3 (g reduced in comparison to h, or in other words, reduced θ). This decrease in $c_1(t)$ will also be all the greater if the potential to improve costs is important (this is the case when $c_1(t) / c_1^*$ is low). Actually, the more $c_1(t)$ approaches c_1^*, the greater is the required market share to reduce costs further.

To sum up, in the study of the dynamics of $c_1(t)$, θ and c_1^* appear to be the decisive parameters. However, their respective roles are different: θ is related to the evolution rate of technology 1, and the gap $(c_1(t) - c_1^*)$ represents the possible size of this improvement. We shall observe a decrease in the cost $c_1(t)$ during period t if the market share $P_1(t)$ of technology 1 is large enough ($P_1(t) \geq R_1(t)$). This, as we shall see in the next section devoted to the study of demand, will strengthen the attraction of technology 1 in the following period. We discover here the main features of models analyzing competing technologies with positive feed-back and increasing returns: the probability for technology 1 to be chosen in period t is all the higher if its market share was important in the preceding period. The decrease of the relative cost of technology 1 appears to be simultaneously an outcome and a cause of the increase in the market share of this technology. The development process and the diffusion process for technology 1 strengthen one another. We observe the joint phenomena known as "diffusion through learning" and "learning through diffusion".

2.3 Demand for technologies

During period t, N individuals enter the market and each individual i chooses a technology k which provides him with a utility U_k^i given by:

$$U_k^i = \omega_k^i f_k(c_k) \qquad (10)$$

ω_i^k is a "personal preference parameter" which is typical of individual i and $f_k(c_k)$ is a decreasing function of the cost c_k of technology k which determines directly the price of acquiring this technology by the individuals. $f_k(c_k)$ represents the way individuals assess the cost associated with technology k and, possibly, other features of this technology. For example, if $f_k(c_k) = 1/c_k$, as we will assume in the following, only cost matters: for the same cost, different technologies are "global" substitutes[6]. During each period t a random set of N individuals is taken from a set of potential buyers, with uniform probability. The preference parameters for a given technology are randomly distributed in the set of potential buyers according to a uniform distribution over [0,1]. Between technologies, the distributions of the preference parameters are independent.

Each individual chooses to adopt the technology that gives him the largest utility level. During period t, $N_1(t)$ represents the number of adopters of technology 1. $N_1(t)$ is a random variable which is distributed according to Bernoulli's law $B(N, \Pi_1)$ where $\Pi_1 = \Pi_1(t)$ is the expected market share of technology 1 during period t. The random nature of the market share is due to the heterogeneity of the agents and may be related, for example, to the fact that from one period to another, individuals who enter the market (a random subset of the whole population of individuals) may have different attitudes towards ecological aspects. These individu-

[6] One could also assume that $f_k(c_k) = \alpha_k / c_k$, where α_k may be interpreted as the result of a marketing policy. All the individuals are induced by this policy to take into account "globally" the specific features of each technology k.

als may weight differently the costs of the different technologies according to their "environmentally friendly" aspects.

The expected market share of technology 1 during period t, $\Pi_1(t)$, is a function of f_1, f_2 and f_3. It is easy to show that:

$$\text{if } f_1 \leq f_2 \leq f_3 : \qquad \Pi_1 = \frac{f_1^{\,2}}{3 f_2 f_3} \tag{11}$$

$$\text{if } f_2 \leq f_1 \leq f_3 : \qquad \Pi_1 = \frac{f_1}{2 f_3} - \frac{f_2^{\,2}}{6 f_1 f_3} \tag{12}$$

$$\text{if } f_2 \leq f_3 \leq f_1 : \qquad \Pi_1 = 1 - \frac{f_3}{2 f_1} - \frac{f_2^{\,2}}{6 f_1 f_3} \tag{13}$$

$P_1(t)$, the market share of technology 1 during period t is a random variable, with expected value $\Pi_1(t)$ and variance $\Pi_1(t)\,(1 - \Pi_1(t))\,/\,N$.

To sum up, the evolution in the demand for each technology is therefore characterized by the occurrence of increasing returns on adoption (as the more a technology is selected the more its cost and therefore its price tend to decrease). But the impact of these increasing returns on adoption may be thwarted by personal preferences (environmental awareness for example) in the set of individuals appearing on a given date in the market. These preferences may cause the individuals to be more or less sensitive to the price of each technology and therefore leads to a random variable in the demand.

3 Analysis of the technological competition process

This section is devoted to a separate analysis of the competition process between technologies. Its purpose is to lay emphasis on the impact of a change in the relative costs on the dynamics of the process. In order to simplify the presentation, we shall assume, in this section, that, during any period t, the number N of acting individuals is infinite. This will allow us to consider demand as not being random. This simplifying assumption will be suppressed in the next section. We will then have $P_1(t) = \Pi_1(t)$ and we shall assume that $f_k(c_k) = 1/c_k$.

One can compute, from (11) to (13), the market share of technology 1 during period t, as a function of $c_1(t)$, c_2 and c_3 (assuming, without loss of generality, that $c_3 \leq c_2$).

$c_1(t) < c_3 < c_2$ $$P_1(t) = 1 - c_1(t)\left(\frac{1}{2c_3} + \frac{c_3}{6c_2^{\,2}}\right) \tag{14}$$

$c_3 < c_1(t) < c_2$ $$P_1(t) = \frac{c_3}{2c_1(t)} - \frac{c_3 c_1(t)}{6c_2^{\,2}} \tag{15}$$

$c_3 < c_2 < c_1(t)$ $$P_1(t) = \frac{c_2 c_3}{3c_1(t)^2} \tag{16}$$

The dynamics of the process is closely related to $P_1(t)$, the market share of technology 1. If $P_1(t)$ is high enough, the relative cost of technology 1 will decrease with respect to the operating costs of the two other technologies. If this is not the case, it will increase: the choice of technology 1 by individuals will be less probable in the sequel, and its survival will be compromised. Assume that c_2, c_3, c_1^* and θ are fixed, figures 4 and 5 can then help us to analyze the dynamics of $c_1(t)$. This analysis shows that one of the two following cases may occur.

Figure 4 illustrates the first case. The curves $P_1(t)$ and $R_1(t)$ do not intersect. Without the intervention of public authorities, technology 1 would disappear, since its operating costs will grow to infinity (let us remember that in this section the process is a deterministic one, since we suppressed any kind of random feature in the demand). The second case (as illustrated by figure 5) is more interesting. The curves $P_1(t)$ and $R_1(t)$ intersect twice, and we shall denote a and b ($a \leq b$) as the abscissae of these two intersection points. During a given period t, if $c_1(t) > b$, then $P_1(t) < R_1(t)$, the relative cost of technology 1 will grow indefinitely during the following periods and this technology will disappear. If $a < c_1(t) < b$, then $P_1(t) > R_1(t)$ and the cost of technology 1 will decrease towards a or a value smaller than a, but greater than c_1^*. Finally, if the relative cost of technology 1 is such that $c_1(t) < a$, then $P_1(t) < R_1(t)$ and the cost of technology 1 will increase towards a. Two special cases occur when $c_1 = a$ or $c_1 = b$ and represent equilibrium states in the process. The first case is a stable equilibrium, and the second one is unstable. Of course, these deterministic conclusions will be somewhat perturbed by the introduction of a random demand.

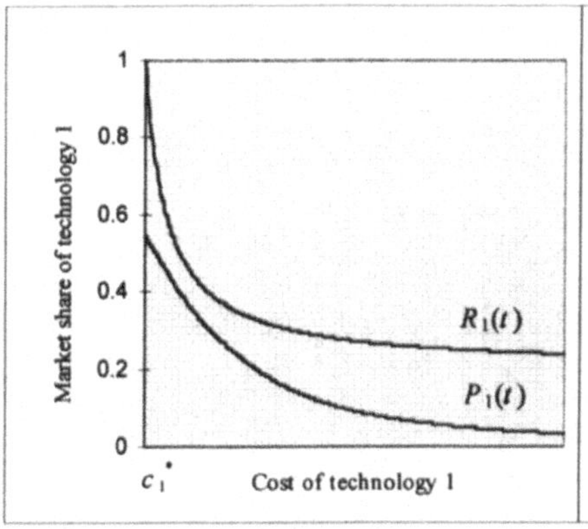

Fig. 4. First case of the dynamics of the relative cost of technology 1

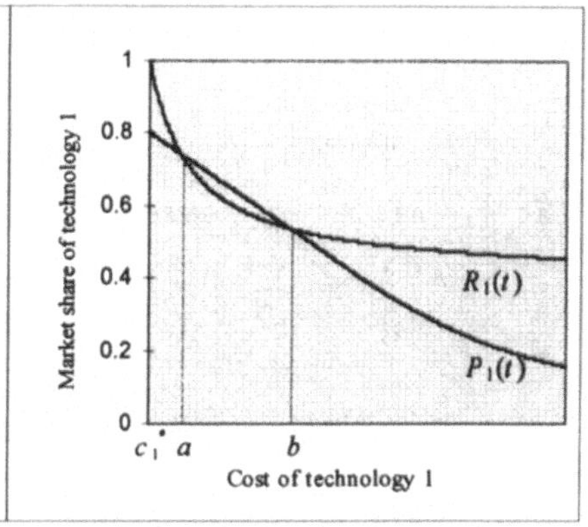

Fig. 5. Second case of the dynamics of the relative cost of technology 1

In order to simplify the analysis of the role of different parameters such as the relative costs of technologies, c_1^* (the potential limit value for the cost of technology 1) and θ which is related to the decreasing rate of technology 1's relative cost (the smaller θ is the greater this rate is), we shall stick to the case of two competing technologies (1 and 2). Assume that θ is fixed, it will be convenient to define $Y = c_2/c_1^*$ and $X = c_1/c_1^*$. The two curves $P_1(t)$ and $R_1(t)$ will not intersect if Y is smaller than $Y(\theta)$, they will have a tangential intersection with an abscissa of $X(\theta)$ if $Y = Y(\theta)$, and, finally, will have two intersection points with abscissae $a < X(\theta) < b$ if Y is greater than $Y(\theta)$. The functions $X(\theta)$ and $Y(\theta)$ are as follows:

$$\theta \leq 0.25; \qquad Y(\theta) = 8\theta(1-\theta); \qquad X(\theta) = 2(1-\theta) \tag{17}$$

$$\theta > 0.25; \qquad Y(\theta) = \frac{\left(1+\sqrt{\theta}\right)^2}{2(1-\theta)}; \qquad X(\theta) = 1 + \sqrt{\theta} \tag{18}$$

The curves $X(\theta)$ and $Y(\theta)$ are depicted in figure 6. A necessary condition for the perenniality of technology 1 is that the two curves $P_1(t)$ and $R_1(t)$ intersect, i.e. $Y \geq Y(\theta)$. The analysis shows that if θ is very small, technology 1 can survive even if $c_2 < c_1^*$; if $\theta < 0.25$, then technology 1 can survive in situations where $c_1(t) > c_2$. But when $\theta > 0.25$, the survival of technology 1 after period t requires $c_1(t) < c_2$.

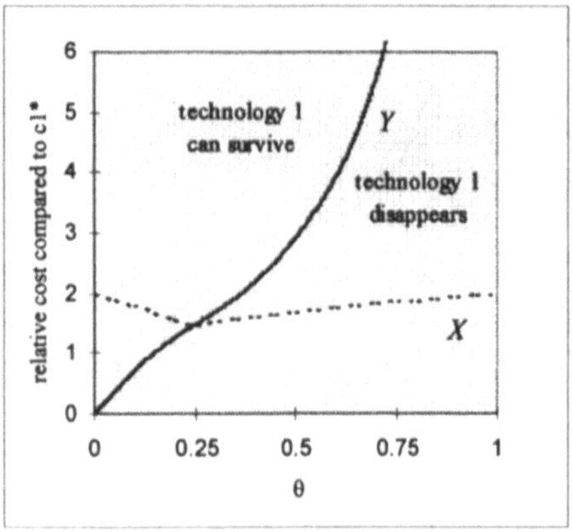

Fig. 6. Survival conditions for technology 1 as far as θ, c_2/c_1^* et c_1/c_1^* are concerned

The perenniality of technology 1 depends on the respective values of θ, X and Y. The analysis shows that three cases must be distinguished according to the value of θ:

- if $\theta < 0.25$, then technology 1 can survive if (figure 7):

$$(X < 2(1-\theta) \quad \text{and} \quad Y \geq 8\theta(1-\theta) \tag{19}$$

$$X > 2(1-\theta) \quad \text{and} \quad Y \geq \frac{2\theta X^2}{X-(1-\theta)} \tag{20}$$

As we have seen above, technology 1 cannot survive if $Y < Y(\theta)$. This minimum level of Y applies if the cost of technology 1 remains low ($X \leq X(\theta)$). When the cost of technology 1 increases above this limit value, then c_2 must also increase. We notice that, in this first case, the cost c_2 of technology 2, sufficient to promote the survival of technology 1, remains smaller than the cost of technology 1.

- If $0.25 < \theta < 0.5$, the conditions are as follows (figure 8):

$$X < 1+\sqrt{\theta} \quad \text{and} \quad Y \geq \frac{\left(1+\sqrt{\theta}\right)^2}{2(1-\theta)} \tag{21}$$

$$1+\sqrt{\theta} < X < \frac{(1-\theta)}{(1-2\theta)} \quad \text{and} \quad Y \geq \frac{X(X-1+\theta)}{2(1-\theta)(X-1)} \tag{22}$$

$$X > \frac{(1-\theta)}{(1-2\theta)} \quad \text{and} \quad Y \geq \frac{2\theta X^2}{X-(1-\theta)} \tag{23}$$

The analysis is similar to the previous one. When X is small (21), a minimum value $Y(\theta)$ is sufficient. When X increases above $X(\theta)$, as in (22) and (23), a larger Y value is necessary: in the case of (22) the condition implies that $c_1(t) < c_2$ while in the case of (23) this restriction is not necessary. In fact, the survival of technology 1 depends simultaneously on θ (related to the cost adjustment speed) and on the size of the gap between the actual value $c_1(t)$ and the potential minimum value c_1^*: this last factor is relatively high for the condition in (23).

- If $\theta > 0.5$, the conditions are as follows (figure 9):

$$X < 1+\sqrt{\theta} \quad \text{and} \quad Y \geq \frac{\left(1+\sqrt{\theta}\right)^2}{2(1-\theta)} \tag{24}$$

$$X > 1+\sqrt{\theta} \quad \text{and} \quad Y \geq \frac{X(X-1+\theta)}{2(1-\theta)(X-1)} \tag{25}$$

In this last case we just notice that the survival condition implies that c_2 is always greater than $c_1(t)$.

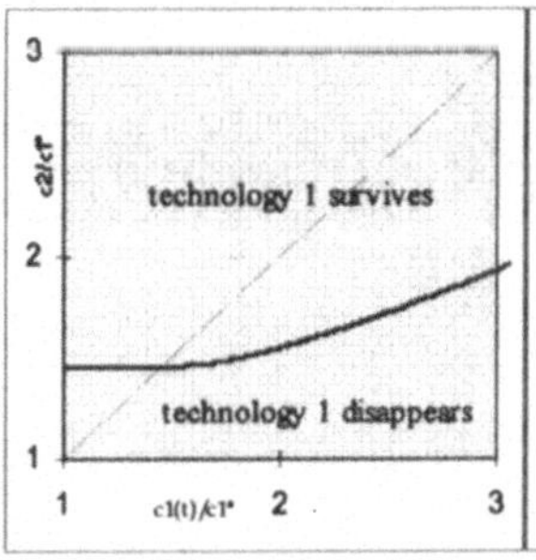

Fig. 7. Survival conditions for technology 1 with $\theta < 0.25$

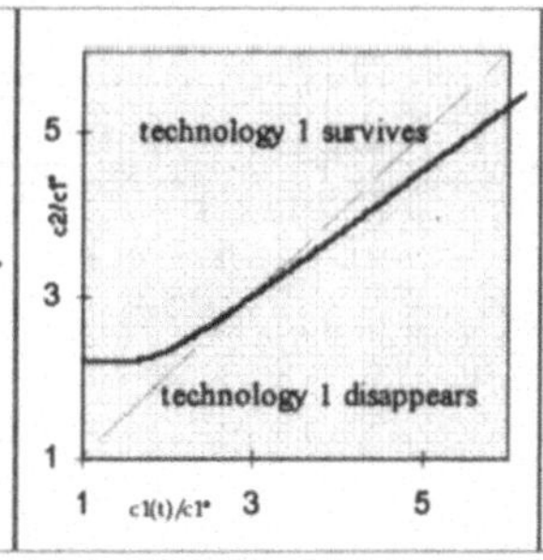

Fig. 8. Survival conditions for technology 1 with $0.25 < \theta < 0.5$

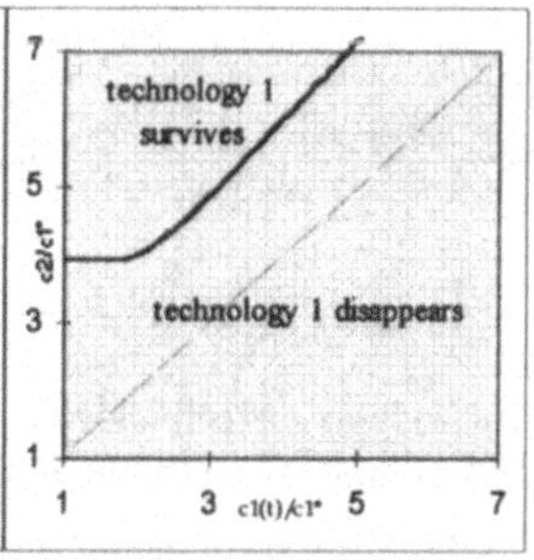

Fig. 9. Survival conditions for technology 1 with $\theta > 0.5$

Public authorities can interfere in the technological competition process by means of a change in the relative costs of the technologies c_2 and $c_1(t)$. In fact, by imposing a taxation rate λ on technology 2, public authorities can transform a terminal state for technology 1 into a state where technology 1 can survive. The two following remarks are of interest:

(1) Starting with a given terminal state for technology 1, the burden of taxation imposed on technology 2 could be alleviated (if $P_1(t)$ and $R_1(t)$ do not intersect) or suppressed (if the two curves do intersect) some periods later. An example of such a case is illustrated by figure 10. At time $t = 0$, let $c_1(0) = b$. Without taxation, technology 1 will disappear. After taxing technology 2, the new market share of technology 1 will be high enough to induce a decrease of the costs of this technology towards a. But, the survival of technology 1 without taxes is ensured as soon as $c_1(t) < c$. Therefore as soon as $c_1(t) < c$, it will become possible to suppress the taxation of technology 2 and ensure the survival of technology 1.

(2) The later taxation takes place, the higher the tax level must be in order to ensure technology 1 can survive. In fact, under terminal conditions, the cost of technology 1 increases with time.

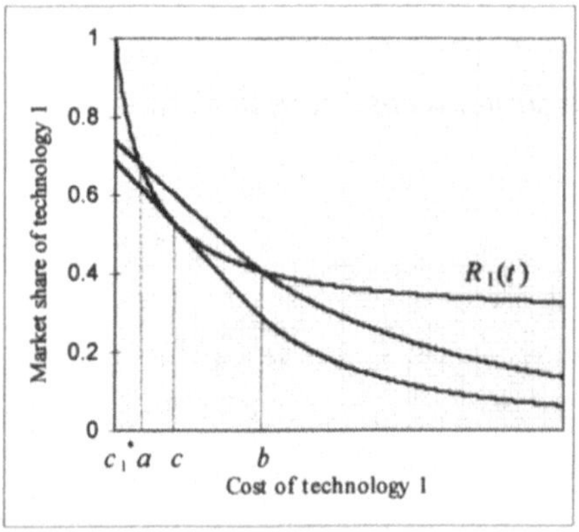

$P_1(t)$ with tax on technology 2
$P_1(t)$ without tax on technology

Fig. 10. The case of temporary tax

4 The interaction of the two processes

In this section we will analyze to what extent the interaction between the public's learning process on the risks and the technological competition is likely to affect the ability of the public authorities to ensure the promotion of the most environmentally friendly technology.

>From a situation of standardization or of technological domination, six factors could help the emergence of an innovative technology or, to put it in other words, the escape from lock-in (Cowan, Hulten, 1996): (1) a crisis in the existing technology, (2) regulation, (3) a technological breakthrough producing a significant decrease in the costs of the innovative technology, (4) changes in consumers' taste, (5) the existence of niche markets which allow the development of the emerging technology, (6) scientific results which point to the limits of the existing technology or the advantages of the emerging one. In the field of technological competition subjected to environmental risks, these six factors can simultaneously promote the emergence of an environmentally friendly technology instead of a polluting one. Most often the following process occurs: a scientific result (6) warns public opinion and is likely to induce a change in the preferences and the behaviors of the individuals (4). However, such an effect is often insufficient to push on its own the system towards another equilibrium. A regulatory change (2), possibly under the pressure of public opinion, appears as essential to promote environmentally friendly technology.

The public authority's intervention in a technological competition process, whose aim is to promote a given technology, is often biased (David, 1987). First of all, an early intervention in the process is generally speaking more cost efficient (the Narrow Policy Windows Paradox). Secondly, this ensures that the number of firms affected by this intervention is kept to a minimum. Those who initially adopted a technology which was then forbidden by the policy maker for instance (Angry Orphans). But the main drawback of an early intervention is that the available information on the real merits of the technologies when in competition remains restricted (the Blind Giant's Quandary). A late intervention presents of course the opposite advantages and drawbacks. In the environmental field, public intervention in a competition process presents an additional problem: the dilemma between short-term and long-term environmental objectives. The development of truly innovative green technologies needs a long-term perspective, while incremental improvements (through end-of-pipe technologies) are also necessary. End-of-pipe technologies offer clear advantages to firms because of their greater short-term adaptability in comparison to more radical (cleaner) process innovations. The system can be locked in a counterinnovative solution because of the lack of long-term research incentives (Foray, Grübler, 1996).

In our model, we can consider that at time $t = 0$, two technologies (2 and 3) are present on the market and that a third one (technology 1) tries to enter it. Three reasons could make the entry, and the survival of technology 1, possible even if its cost is higher at the beginning of the process: (1) technologies 2 and 3 are more risky from an environmental point of view and this environmental risk is becoming a criterion in the technology assessment for the policy maker (when $t = 0$, the three risks are supposed to be equal to zero, i.e. the public authorities have no a priori belief in the risks posed by the various technologies and these beliefs will be formed in an endogenous way by the research process); (2) the cost of technology 1 will decrease if this one is adopted sufficiently by individuals; (3) demand is random because the criterion for an individuals' decision is not limited to the cost. In our model, the short-term / long-term dilemma is expressed by the fact that technology 1 (the innovative one) can disappear to the advantage of technology 2 (the end-of-pipe one) after the taxation or the prohibition of technology 3. After having discussed the role of the various parameters in the interaction of the two processes, we shall analyze the implications as regards public policy.

4.1 Discussion of the parameters

In order to study the interaction between the two processes we will of course consider the technological competition process as random[7]. The study of the coupling between the two processes leads us to analyze survival conditions for environmentally friendly technologies. Several simulations have been carried out. For each set of parameters, one hundred histories, with a number of periods (T) equal to one hundred, have been generated. Because of the random process, the death of technology 1 is not necessary synonymous with a zero market share at the end of the T periods. Thus, an end of game convention is required to decide on the survival or the death of technology 1. This convention will be as follows: technology 1 can be considered as alive in the competition process if at time $T : P_1(T) > R_1(T)$[8].

The survival of technology 1 will depend on (1) its specific potential (expressed by θ and by the relative value of the costs $c_1(0)$, c_2, c_3 et c_1^*), (2) the real risks generated by each of the three technologies and (3) the policy of risk management which will be implemented by the policy maker (the parameters for this policy are β, λ, n et m). The individual role of some of the parameters is quite intuitive: the survival rate of technology 1 decreases with θ, $c_1(0)$ and c_1^* and increases with c_2 and c_3[9]. Other

[7] In the following simulations, the number of individuals, N, has been fixed at 500.

[8] When $T = 100$, technology 1 can subsist in a marginal state, as a niche, because of the random nature of demand (some confirmed ecologists may exist). The existence of technological niches has been pointed out by Arthur (1988) when increasing returns are bounded or when we consider local externalities (see, for example, David, 1993 or Dalle, 1995).

[9] In all the simulations that we have carried out, the following values have been used (unless stated otherwise): $c_1(0) = 1.5$, $c_2 = 1.3$, $c_3 = 1$, $c_1^* = 1.1$. The probability distribution for the risk levels deduced from the research is that described in table 1.

things being equal, the rate of survival of technology 1 is all the greater if Y^1 is low and Y^2 and Y^3 are high. The role of the parameters which are under the control of the policy maker is, on the other hand, much less evident and justifies a more thorough discussion.

The role of the speed of adjustment to the beliefs in risks (coefficient β)

The survival of technology 1 increases with β. Indeed, the higher β is, the greater is the probability of fixing the beliefs of the policy maker on the risks generated by technologies 2 and 3 at a higher level. And any taxation or prohibition of these technologies is favorable to technology 1. Two remarks must however be made:

- if the public authorities correct too quickly their beliefs in the risks (high value of β), technology 1 will be penalized because of the increasing probability of this technology being taxed or prohibited (see figure 11). So long as $\beta < 0.7$, the chances that technology 1 is still in competition after 100 periods are all the greater since the public authorities adjust quickly their beliefs in the risks. But when this adjustment is too quick, the probability that technology 1 is itself forbidden, due to a "research accident", is no longer negligible (see figure 3).

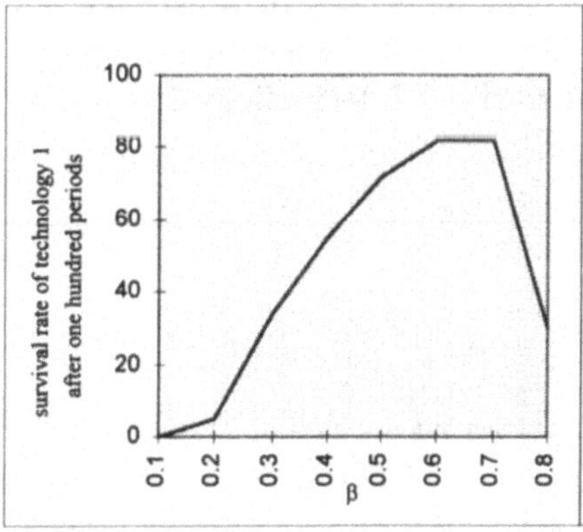

$\theta = 0.11$, $\lambda = 1.2$, $n = 5$, $m = 8$

Fig. 11. Dependency of the survival rate of technology 1 on β

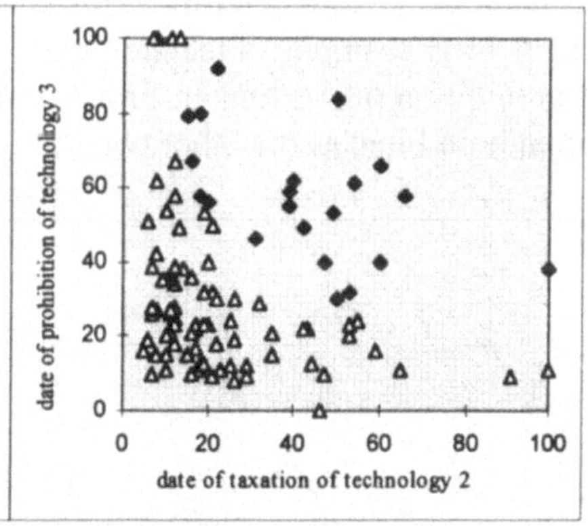

$\theta = 0.1$, $\beta = 0.3$, $\lambda = 1.4$, $n = 5$, $m = 8$
Δ = techn. 1 survives, ♦ = techn. 1 disappears

Fig. 12. Impact of the date of public interventionon the survival rate of technology 1

- the survival of technology 1 does not only depend on the fact that technologies 1 and 3 are taxed or banned at any moment in the process. History does matter: the date the policy maker intervenes appears as an essential parameter. A delayed intervention may irremediably condemn technology 1. This is the Narrow Policy Windows Paradox. Figure 12 demonstrates that two criteria prevail when the survival of technology 1 is analyzed: an early taxation of technology 2 and/or an early prohibition of technology 3 (the white triangles in figure 12). The survival of technology 1 can thus depend on historical accidents, that is to say on the random results of the research on risks.

The role of tax level

It might be evident that a tax fixed at a high level is favorable to the survival of technology 1 as the probability that this one is taxed is less than that for technologies 2 and 3. Oddly enough, the impact of λ is not so obvious. When β is low, the survival rate of technology 1 increases with λ. As β rises, the random character of taxation becomes prejudicial to technology 1 and penalizes this one relatively more than technologies 2 and 3 which are anyway quickly taxed (see figure 13). The explanation for the bi-modal feature in the survival rate of technology 1 when $\lambda = 2.0$ is the following: when β rises from 0.1 to 0.3, technology 1 does not support any tax but the taxation frequency of technology 2 and the prohibition frequency of technology 3 increases (see figures 2 and 3). As β increases further to 0.5, the positions of the two polluting technologies are changing just in a marginal manner, whereas the taxation frequency of technology 1 is perceptibly increasing. For the values of β between 0.5 and 0.7 the positions of technologies 1 and 3 are stable but the technology 2 prohibition rate is higher. Finally, when $\beta > 0.7$, technology 1 is just as often prohibited as the other two.

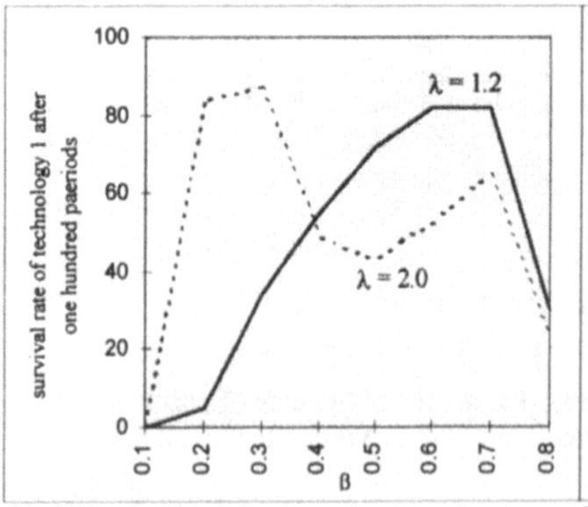

$\theta = 0.11, n = 5, m = 8$

Fig. 13. Impact of the interaction of β and λ on the survival of technology 1

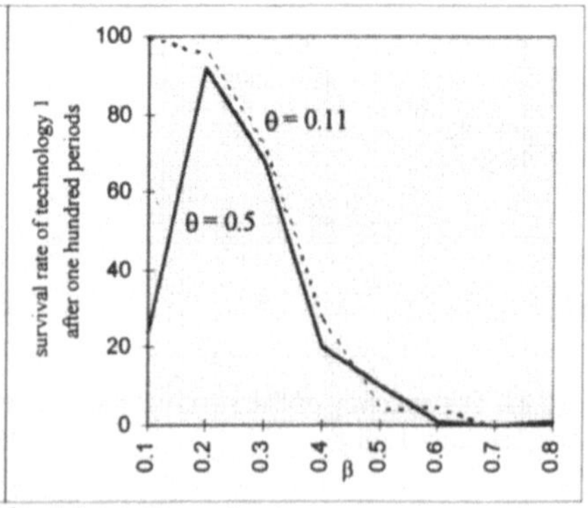

$\lambda = 1.2, n = 3, m = 5$

Fig. 14. Impact of θ on the survival of technology 1

Thus, simultaneously resorting to a restrictive taxation (λ high) and to a policy of adjusting quickly the perception of technological risks on the basis of the most recent research results appears to be unfavorable to supporting technology 1 in an effective manner. These two control levers seem to be antinomic.

The role of the regulatory taxation and prohibition thresholds

The role of the regulatory taxation and prohibition thresholds is quite prevalent in this model. If the policy maker sets n and m to a low level, it means that the implementation of taxation or the prohibition of technologies will occur rapidly and frequently. In this configuration, the lower β is, the more often technology 1 survives. But, if β increases, the probability of technology 1 also being affected by the environmental policy is greater and the survival rate decreases. It must be mentioned that when θ is low, taxation of technologies 2 and 3 is not necessary to ensure the survival of an environmentally friendly technology. On the contrary, a taxation of technology 1 endangers its survival (see figure 14)[10].

When n and m are fixed at a higher level, the survival rate of technology 1 increases continuously with β (except for the highest value of β). Thus, it turns out that the policy maker cannot use simultaneously both control levers presented by the risk management policy (n, m) and the belief adjustment rate to promote the survival of technology 1 (see figure 15). It must be stated, however, that setting (n, m) and β to low values appears as the best configuration for technology 1. All things being equal, this configuration ensures the highest survival rate for the environmentally friendly technology.

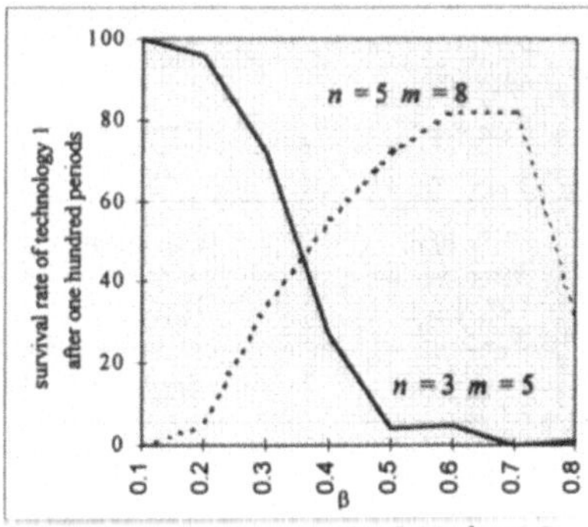

$\theta = 0.11, \lambda = 1.2$

Fig. 15. Impact of the interaction of (n, m) and β on the survival of technology 1

[10] This is, even if the reasons are quite different, a classical dilemma in environmental policies: the fact that regulation is often more demanding on emerging technologies than on existing ones may have a negative effect on innovation.

4.2 Paradoxes due to the implementation of the precaution principle

Under major environmental risks, two ways of implementing the precaution principle can be distinguished: the first one, which we will call the "unlocking form", involves restricting the choice of adoption by the taxation or prohibition of certain technologies. The second one, termed "locking form", does not leave any choice and imposes the adoption of a specified technology, usually the one which is considered as the least damaging to the environment, given the available imperfect information at the date of intervention.

The "unlocking" form of the precaution principle

In the model proposed here, only this way of implementing the precaution principle has been considered. The parameters which control the intensity of this implementation are the intervention thresholds. We will qualify the precaution principle as "strict" when the implementation methodology is characterized by the policy maker interfering in the technological competition process as soon as his beliefs in the risks reach a low level. On the contrary, with a "weak" precaution principle, the public authorities only intervene if beliefs attain a high level. Paradoxically, the "strict" precaution principle does not guarantee the highest survival rate for technology 1. Indeed, managing the learning policy on the risks and the choice of the tax levels turn out to be essential control variables.

In our model, the "strict" precaution principle corresponds to low values of n and m and the "weak" principle to high values of these parameters. Table 2 sums up the discussion on the sets of values of the parameters which ensure the highest survival rate for technology 1.

Table 2. Conditions for the highest survival rate of technology 1

	(n, m)	β	λ
"strict" precaution principle	low	low	low or high
"weak" precaution principle	high	high	low
		low	high

The different variables that the policy maker can control appear as alternatives and cannot be activated simultaneously. To guarantee the highest survival rate for technology 1 with the "strict" precaution principle, it is necessary for β to be kept at a low level. Otherwise, technology 1 will often be prohibited because of "research accidents". As we said previously (figure 15) such a policy - (n, m) low, β low - leads to the highest survival rate for technology 1 (even if the use of the more polluting technologies can then be continued for a relatively long time). Despite this, the implementation of such a policy by public authorities seems at the very least unlikely. Indeed, how is it possible to justify that the policy maker does not take into account recent research issues which reveal alarming risks for the environment or public health (Y_{t+1}^k closer to Y_t^k whereas X_{t+1}^k is high)? Thus, the policy maker is often prone to adopt a higher learning rate which is incompatible with the implementation of the "strict" precaution principle.

A "weak" precaution principle is compatible with both high and low values of β. Under these conditions, the tax level becomes a main variable. If the policy maker corrects his beliefs in risks quickly (under the pressure of a public opinion sensitive to ecological arguments or traumatized by a recent catastrophe) and sets simultaneously a high tax level (possibly for the same reasons), this is clearly unfavorable to the emergence or the survival of the most environmentally friendly technology. In the case of a high learning rate, technology 1 can be prematurely taxed owing to the random nature of the research on risks. With a high tax level, the market share of technology 1 will then collapse under the fatal threshold. In other words, if the learning rate on risks is high, the hazardous nature of technologies 2 and 3 for the environment will be known and, thus, it turns out to be pointless to tax these alternatives too severely. On the contrary, when β is low, the probability of discovering early on that technologies 2 and 3 must be forbidden is lower. It is thus advisable to resort to a greater tax level in order to favor the survival of technology 1 which, on the other hand, is unlikely to be subject to such a taxation. In other words we can make the following proposal:

> *when the environmental awareness of the public is high (encouraging the public authorities to correct promptly their beliefs in the risks), the industrial lobbying for a well thought-out use of the other levers used to control environmental policy (risk levels triggering intervention, tax levels) may appear as reasonable.*

"Locking" precaution principle

Another problem brought up by the implementation of the precaution principle lies in the fact that, under the pressure of public opinion, the policy maker is often compelled to make a clear-cut decision as soon as the estimated level of risk exceeds the acceptability threshold (m in the model). However, the prohibition of a polluting technology is not always sufficient to be considered as a clear-cut decision. In some cases the use of one of several competing technologies is required by the policy maker. Thus, let us suppose in our model that at time t technology 3 is prohibited. If the public authorities, through regulations, create a lock-in by imposing the adoption of the technology with the minimum costs, it is likely that technology 2 will emerge as a standard. Even so technology 1 is more environmentally friendly and might also offer the minimum costs in the future (if $c_1^* < c_2$). This perverse effect due to the implementation of the precaution principle belongs to the more general notion of a bias in public policies known as the Blind Giant's Quandary (David, 1987). In other words:

> *the implementation of the precaution principle can, through a regulatory lock-in, appear as unfavorable to the environment. An irreversible choice is made based on imperfect information and the competition process will not necessarily be locked-on to the most environmentally friendly technology.*

5 Conclusion

The use of the model presented in this paper to analyze some examples of competition between green technologies (innovative ones or end-of-pipe ones) and polluting technologies encounters a major limitation: the lack of strategic and opportunist behaviors. Nevertheless, the results of this model are not inconsiderable. One of these is to underline the strategic nature for the companies of an intervention in a technological competition process which could be fatal to them. A brief outlook on the history of the catalytic exhaust system as the standard solution against acid rains provides us with a suitable illustration of this phenomenon[11].

From an environmental point of view, three gasoline engine technologies could be considered as being in competition ten years ago: the "classical" engine, the engine which used unleaded gasoline with a catalytic exhaust system (end-of-pipe solution), and the lean-burn engine (the innovative one). At the beginning of the eighties, some scientific discoveries (a X_t^k series) pointed, especially in Germany, to the responsibility of automotive pollution (among others) in the phenomena of acid rain and "waldsterben". Given this information on the hazard posed by the usual technology, our model shows that, after taxation or prohibition of a polluting technology, the probability of the innovative technology emerging

[11] Concerning this issue see, for instance, Roqueplo (1988), Hourcade *et al.* (1992) or Godard (1996).

as a standard or, at least, taking some market share was significant. But the reality has been very different. In June 1985, automotive pollution norms were adopted in a EEC directive imposing the adoption of catalytic exhaust systems and unleaded gasoline (because the performances of the lean-burn engine were insufficient at the time to comply with these norms). The explanation of this lock-in does not lie in the random process of research on environmental risks. Strategic behaviors of different actors mattered much more. The companies which were developing the two alternative technologies could be clearly distinguished: French companies had more of an advantage with the lean-burn engine and German ones with the catalytic exhaust system technology. The European Union, under the joint pressure of public opinion and industrialists, attached great importance to the latest results from the research on acid rain (which in our model corresponds to the use of a high value for β), whereas these results were, and still are, the subject of a large scientific controversy among the different European countries. Moreover the European Union decided to implement the "locking" form of the precaution principle (by imposing some very restrictive norms and a short delay for compliance). The competition process was interrupted before the merits of all the competing technologies could clearly be identified.

Thus, our model undeniably seems to contribute to emphasizing the complex nature of the interaction between the technological competition process and the public decision-making process under environmental risks. There are several possible ways of improving this model including the introduction of strategic behaviors and the diverse tools available to the public authorities (not only modifications to market mechanisms, but also the exogenous creation of niches for innovative technologies by public purchases or contributions to improve the cost efficiency of certain technologies by research grants).

References

Allen FR, Garlick AR, Hayns MR, Taig AR (1992) The Management of risk to society from potential accidents. Elsevier Science, London

Arthur B (1988) Competing technologies: an overview. In: Dosi G *et al.* (eds) Technological change and economic theory. Pinter, London

Arthur B (1989) Competing technologies, increasing returns and lock-in by historical events. Economic Journal 99: 116-131.

Cowan R (1991) Rendements croissants d'adoption et politique technologique. In: De Bandt J, Foray D (eds) L'□valuation □conomique de la recherche et du changement technique. Editions du CNRS, Paris

Cowan R, Hulten S (1996) Escaping lock-in: the case of electric vehicle. Technological Forecasting and Social Change 53: 61-79.

Dalle JM (1995) Dynamiques d'adoption, coordination et diversité. La diffusion des standards technologiques. Revue Economique 46: 1081-1098.
David P (1985) Clio and the economics of QWERTY. American Economic Review 75: 332-337.
David P (1987) Some new standards for the economics of standardization in the information age. In: Dasgupta P, Stoneman P (eds) Economic policy and technological performance. Cambridge University Press, Cambridge
David P (1993) Path-dependence and predictability in dynamic systems with local network externalities: a paradigm for historical economics. In: Freeman C, Foray D (eds) Technology and the wealth of nations. Pinter, London
Foray D, Grübler A (1996) Technology and environment: an overview. Technological Forecasting and Social Change 53: 3-13
Godard O (1996) Social decision-making under conditions of scientific controversy, expertise and the precautionary principle. In: Joerges C, Ladeur KH, Vos E (eds) Integrating scientific expertise into regulatory decision-making. National experiences and European innovations. Nomos Verlag, Baden-Baden
Hourcade JC, Salles JM, Théry D (1992) Ecological economics and scientific controversies. Lessons from some recent policy making in the EEC. Ecological Economics 6: 211-233.
Metcalfe JS (1994) Evolutionary economics and technology policy. Economic Journal 104: 918-930
Nelson RR, Winter S (1982) An evolutionary theory of economic change. Belknap Press, Cambridge.
Nelson RR (1993) National innovation systems. Oxford University Press, Oxford
Roqueplo P (1988) Pluies acides : menaces pour l'Europe. Economica, Paris
Stoneman P, Diederen P (1994) Technology diffusion and public policy. Economic Journal 104: 931- 944.

The manufacturer's authorised representative in the EU is Springer Nature Customer Service Centre GmbH, Europaplatz 3, 69115 Heidelberg, Germany. If you have any concerns regarding our products, please contact ProductSafety@springernature.com

Printed and bound by CPI Group (UK) Ltd, Croydon, CR0 4YY
01/10/2026
02225951-0015